NE

MARX, MARGINALISM AND

Also by Simon Clarke

THE DEVELOPMENT OF CAPITALISM
FINANCIAL ASPECTS OF ECONOMIC SANCTIONS ON SOUTH
  AFRICA
THE FOUNDATIONS OF STRUCTURALISM
KEYNESIANISM, MONETARISM AND THE CRISIS OF THE STATE
ONE-DIMENSIONAL MARXISM (*with Terry Lovell, Kevin McDonnell,
  Kevin Robins, Victor Seidler*)
PROBLEMS OF GROWTH IN THE THIRD WORLD
*THE STATE DEBATE

*Also published by Macmillan

Marx, Marginalism and Modern Sociology
From Adam Smith to Max Weber

Simon Clarke
Senior Lecturer in Sociology
University of Warwick

Second Edition

© Simon Clarke 1982, 1991

All rights reserved. No reproduction, copy or transmission of
this publication may be made without written permission.

No paragraph of this publication may be reproduced, copied or
transmitted save with written permission or in accordance with
the provisions of the Copyright, Designs and Patents Act 1988
or under the terms of any licence permitting limited copying
issued by the Copyright Licensing Agency, 33–4 Alfred Place,
London WC1E 7DP.

Any person who does any unauthorised act in relation to this
publication may be liable to criminal prosecution and civil
claims for damages.

First edition 1982
Reprinted 1983
Second edition 1991

Published by
MACMILLAN ACADEMIC AND PROFESSIONAL LTD
Houndmills, Basingstoke, Hampshire RG21 2XS
and London
Companies and representatives
throughout the world

Printed in Hong Kong

Typeset under L^{A}T$_E$X at the University of London
Computer Centre

ISBN 0–333–54829–9 (hardcover)
ISBN 0–333–54830–2 (paperback)

A catalogue record for this book is available
from the British Library.

Contents

1	**The Origins of Modern Sociology**	**1**
	Talcott Parsons and the voluntaristic theory of action	1
	The problem of order and the theory of action	3
	Marx's critique of political economy	6
	From social reform to modern sociology	8
2	**Classical Political Economy**	**12**
	A theory of society	12
	The materialist conception of society	13
	The physiocratic theory of society	18
	Smith's Theory of Moral Sentiments	21
	The Wealth of Nations	24
	Smith's contribution to social theory	30
	The limits of Enlightenment	35
	Ricardo's completion of the system	39
	Conservatism, radicalism and socialism	43
3	**Alienated Labour and the Critique of Political Economy**	**49**
	The critique of Hegel's theory of the state	52
	From political philosophy to the critique of private property	56
	Proudhon, Engels and the critique of political economy	59
	Alienated labour and the critique of capitalism	62
	Alienated labour and the critique of private property	66
	Alienated labour and the critique of money	70
	Hegel and the critique of political economy	78
	Marx's early critique of political economy	81
	The limits of the early critique	86
4	**Value, Class and the Theory of Society**	**92**
	Marxism and the critique of political economy	92

The critique of political economy and the labour theory of value	96
The magnitude of value and the form of value	100
Money as a social relation	104
The theory of value and the theory of society	108
Capital as a social relation	113
The capitalist labour-process	118
The capitalist process of exchange	121
The 'trinity formula' and the theory of class	126
The capital relation and its forms	128
The Ricardian contradiction	132
Formal and determinate abstraction	140
5 Political Economy and its Sociological Critics	**144**
Classical political economy and the labour theory of value	144
The classical economic laws	148
Classical political economy and the birth of sociology	153
The Positivist critique of political economy	156
Classical political economy and the German Historical School	161
Herbert Spencer's liberal Sociology	166
The decline and fall of political economy	170
Social reform and the limits of Sociology	174
6 The Marginalist Revolution in Economics	**182**
The marginalist revolution	183
The problem of prices and the problem of reform	185
The marginalist theory of price	189
The marginalist theory of society	194
Facts and values in economic science	202
7 The Irrationality of Marginalist Economics	**207**
The irrationality of exchange and the problem of money	210
The irrationality of exchange and the problem of competition	213
The irrationality of exchange and the division of labour	219
The irrationality of capitalism: the marginalist theory of profit	221
The contradictory social form of capitalist production	228

8 From Marginalism to Modern Sociology — **235**
Economic theory, social economics and the tasks of sociology — 235
The theory of the social economy — 238
Max Weber and the German Historical School — 243
Problems of methodology: Menger and Weber — 248
The problem of rationality — 255
The marginalist foundations of Weber's sociology — 261
Economy and society — 265
The typology of action and the theory of society — 273
Capitalist rationality and the dilemmas of modernity — 286

9 Marx, Marginalism and Modern Sociology — **290**
The antinomies of sociology and the dilemma of liberalism — 290
The marginalist foundations of Parsonian functionalism — 298
Structure and action in 'Post-Parsonian' Sociology — 301
The limits of Marxism and the legacy of Marx — 306
Lukács and and the foundations of 'Western Marxism' — 311
The Dialectic of the Enlightenment — 318
The irrationality of capitalism and the alienation of labour — 323

Preface to the Second Edition

I originally wrote this book because I felt that it was important to take liberal social theory more seriously than did the 'radical' social thought of the 1970s. The main aim of the book was to develop a Marxist critique of liberal social theory, which could identify both the scientific strengths and the ideological limitations of such theories. The book was well-received, but critical responses made it apparent that the central argument had not been widely understood, particularly by those who could only read Marx through the eyes of his orthodox interpreters, and so missed the distinctiveness of the interpretation of Marx presented here. The book was also read as an historical study, because it did not include an explicit discussion of the liberal foundations of contemporary economic and social theory, ending with the marginalist revolution in economics and Weber's sociology.

Since the book was originally published the intellectual landscape has changed dramatically. An uncritical return to liberal social theory has replaced its uncritical rejection, while the collapse of state socialism, in both East and West, has inspired the proclamation of the 'death of Marxism'. I believe that these changes have made the argument developed in this book more, and not less, relevant than when it was first written. There is no better testimony to the inadequacy of the orthodox Marxist and radical critiques of liberal social theory than the recent resurgence of liberalism. The development of a theoretically sound critique is all the more urgent as liberalism once more comes up against its limits.

The recent strength of liberalism has owed much more to its critique of the theory and practice of Orthodox Marxism than it has to its own positive virtues. Despite the 'death of Marxism', the inhumanity of capitalism is as evident today as it was when Marx wrote. The central theme of this book is that nobody more

Preface

clearly grasped the source of this inhumanity, and the possibility of its overcoming, than did Marx. But at the same time we have to recognise the limits of Marx's achievement. Marx laid the foundations of a critical social theory but, contrary to Marxist orthodoxy, he did not provide an all-encompassing world-view. Marx marked out a critical project, which was to understand and to transform society from the standpoint of the activity and aspirations of concrete human individuals. Marx's critique of liberalism sought to recover, both in theory and in practice, the constitutive role of human subjectivity behind the immediacy of objective and constraining social relations within which our social identity confronts us in the form of an external thing. This insight is as much a critique of the metaphysics of orthodox Marxism as it is of liberalism, a critique which I have sought to bring out in this second edition of the book.

Although the central argument of the book is unchanged in this edition, the miracles of modern technology have made it it possible substantially to revise and expand the text. The main additions are in Chapter Three and at the beginning of Chapter Four, where I have related my interpretation of Marx to those which dominate the secondary literature, and the additional Chapters Seven and Nine, which sketch the implications of the critique of marginalism and of Weberian sociology for the critique of modern economics, orthodox Marxism and modern sociology. As with the original edition, I have tried to write the book in such a way that each chapter can be read independently of the whole.

I am very grateful to Chris Arthur, Tom Bottomore, Gillian Rose, and particularly Bob Fine, for their comments on drafts of parts of this new edition, and to those many colleagues and students with whom I have had the pleasure of discussing the issues over the years.

1
The Origins of Modern Sociology

Talcott Parsons and the voluntaristic theory of action

Fifty years ago Talcott Parsons isolated what he called a 'voluntaristic theory of action' in the work of writers as diverse as Marshall, Pareto, Durkheim and Weber. In *The Structure of Social Action* Parsons argued that the voluntaristic theory of action was the basis of a fundamental reorientation of the social sciences, marking a decisive advance in the development of sociology as a response to the 'problem of order'.

Parsons contrasted the voluntaristic theory of action with the theories that it superseded, the *positivistic theory of action* and the *idealistic theory of action*. The positivistic theory of action 'treats scientifically valid empirical knowledge as the actor's sole theoretically significant mode of subjective orientation to his situation' (Parsons, 1949, p. 79). In other words the positivistic theory treats the actor as a subject whose course of action is chosen on the basis of a rational evaluation of alternative means to given ends. The archetypal positivistic theory of action is that formulated by utilitarianism and classical political economy. It culminated in the sociology of Herbert Spencer and Social Darwinism, and the historical materialism of Marx.

An idealistic theory of action is contrasted with the positivistic theory in stressing the normative orientation of action at the expense of any recognition of the objective constraints imposed by the conditions of action. The conditions of action have no objective reality, but can only be constraining to the extent that they are given subjective meaning by the actor. Thus 'in an idealistic theory "action" becomes a process of "emanation", of "self-expression" of ideal or normative factors' (Parsons, 1949, p. 82). The archetypal idealistic theory of action is found in the German tradition deriving from Kant and Hegel.

While the positivistic theory ignores the role of normative elements in the determination of action and the idealistic theory ignores the role of conditional elements, the voluntaristic theory of action adopts the happy mean of according full recognition to both, explaining action as the result of the interaction of normative and conditional elements, recognising that the subjective orientation of action cannot be reduced to the rational adaptation of means to ends, while also recognising that the situation in which action takes place may impose objective constraints on the course of action adopted. Its superiority over the positivistic and idealistic theories seems self-evident, for it reconciles the valid elements of both within a broader synthesis.

In *The Structure of Social Action* Parsons was concerned to establish that the voluntaristic theory of action was indeed to be found in the work of the writers whom he identified as its pioneers, and to defend the claim that its emergence marked a genuine scientific advance. While he recognised that the development of the voluntaristic theory of action probably was 'in considerable part simply an ideological reflection of certain basic social changes', he postulated that 'it is not less probable that a considerable part has been played by an "immanent" development within the body of social theory and knowledge of empirical fact itself'. The observation that 'it would scarcely be possible to choose four men who had important ideas in common who were less likely to have been influenced in *developing this common body of ideas* by factors other than the immanent development of the logic of theoretical systems in relation to empirical fact' persuaded Parsons that the voluntaristic theory of action was indeed a scientific achievement, and not merely the expression of a common ideological perspective: 'the concepts of the voluntaristic theory of action must be sound theoretical concepts' (Parsons, 1947, pp. 5, 14, 724).

Parsons was not concerned to write the history of social thought, but to invent a genealogy and an ancestral authority for his own conception of sociology. While he did establish the presence of a voluntaristic conception of action in the work of his chosen authors, there was only a very limited sense in which Parsons's often idiosyncratic interpretations were able to establish the presence of a more substantial 'common body of ideas' in their work. Moreover in a book of almost 800 pages he devoted fewer than forty pages to the development of the positivistic theory of action and fewer than thirty to the idealistic tradition. Most of those few pages are at such a high level of generality that it is difficult to know what particular authors and works he had in mind. Had Parsons paid closer attention to the earlier traditions he would have found the 'voluntaristic theory of action' no less prominent than it was in the work of his chosen authors.[1] As we will see below, Adam Smith's theory of the 'moral sentiments' played a central role in his liberal economic theory, while the balance between 'self-love' and 'social-love' lay at the heart of Comte's sociology. If Parsons established the existence of the voluntaristic theory of action in the work of his chosen authors, he certainly did not establish its originality.

The weakness of Parsons's interpretation should not lead us to reject it out of hand. There is no doubt that the end of the nineteenth century did see a fundamental reorientation of social thought on the basis of which modern sociology has been built. There is no doubt that Parsons's chosen authors played a part in that reorientation, and that the idea of a voluntaristic theory of action throws some light on the change. Moreover the question posed by Parsons still remains to be answered: is the conception of society on which modern sociology is based an achievement of a new science of society, or does it after all have an ideological foundation? One purpose of this book is to take up Parsons's challenge.

The problem of order and the theory of action

Parsons's interpretation is determined by his focus on the 'problem of order' and on the 'theory of action'. For Parsons the problem of order was the fundamental practical problem faced by any society, and so was the defining conceptual problem for any theory of society.

Parsons defined the problem of order in essentially Hobbesian terms as an abstract problem posed by the anti-social character of human nature. The positivistic theory of action naïvely postulates a spontaneous harmony of interests, and so ignores the need for normative regulation as a response to the problem of order. Enlightened self-interest is a sufficient guide to action and a sufficient condition for a harmonious society. Social conflict arises from ignorance and irrationality and can be remedied by education and science. The idealistic theory of action recognises the inadequacy of this assumption and takes full account of the Hobbesian problem, but it divorces the values that determine the subjective orientation of action from the context of action so that values belong to a supra-individual and supra-empirical

---

[1] Parsons's interpretation of the sociological tradition has recently been developed in a somewhat modified form by Jeffrey Alexander (1982–4).

order of reality. Both the positivistic and the idealistic theories of action resolve the problem of order by referring beyond action, the former explaining order by reference to the external conditions of action, the latter by reference to the external system of values. Only the voluntaristic theory of action is able to resolve the problem of order within the framework of the theory of action.

However, the problem of order is not an abstract problem; it is a concrete historical problem whose terms are defined by the character of the society within which it arises, as the problem of resolving the conflicts to which that society gives rise. The 'problem of order' presupposes that conflict is a potential problem and so only arises within a theory that defines the 'problem of conflict'.

The problem of order is also not a problem that is amenable to a single solution. The terms on which conflict is resolved cannot be taken as given, for the imposition of order must resolve that conflict on terms favourable to one or the other party to it. In so far as a theory of society can be considered to be a response to the problem of order, every such theory defines its own problem of order, while we have to ask of that theory for whom is order a problem?

Parsons's formulation of the problem presupposes that 'a social order is always a factual order in so far as it is susceptible of scientific analysis but ... it is one which cannot have stability without the effective functioning of certain normative elements' (Parsons, 1947, p. 92), but this is not a formulation which is self-evident: it is one that expresses Parsons's conception of human nature and of the nature of society. In particular, it rests on the belief that the problem of disorder derives from a conflict of material interests, while this conflict can be resolved within an appropriate normative framework. It therefore presupposes a theory which defines material interests as conflicting but reconcilable. In a capitalist society, in which economic activity has come to be dissociated from other forms of interaction, such a theory is provided by the theory of the economy.

In the nineteenth century it was classical political economy which provided the theory on the basis of which both the problem of order and the possibilities of its resolution were theorised. The classical theory of production, based on the model of the division of labour, established the complementarity of interests of social classes defined by their ownership of the co-operating factors of production. The classical theory of exchange established that voluntary exchange must be to the benefit of both parties, so that restrictions on the freedom of exchange could only restrict the opportunities for self-improvement. Conflicts of economic interest only arose when consideration of the distribution of the benefits of economic growth was introduced. These interests were defined by the distinct laws which determined the revenues accruing to the various social classes, on the basis of their ownership of the distinct factors of production. Thus the key to the resolution of the problem of order was the identification of the relationship between the interests of particular classes and the general interest of society as a whole. For political economy it was the common interest in the growing prosperity of the nation which provided the criterion against which distributional conflicts could be resolved.

The problem of order so defined was that of constructing a constitutional and moral order which would ensure that the common interest prevailed over the superficial conflicts of individual and class interest which threaten disorder. For Adam Smith order would be secured by an appropriate constitution, supported by proper relations of deference and authority, in which justice guaranteed the security of property and the person, whose normative conditions would be underpinned by the moral sentiments fostered by a wide circle of social contacts while ignorance, which was the source of disorder, would be dispelled by an enlightened educational system. Comte did not share Smith's confidence that an appropriate moral order could emerge spontaneously from the interaction of conflicting interests, and proposed that the religion of positivism would be required to enforce the normative conditions of order. The German Historical School, for similar reasons, called on the state to perform the same role.

These various theories offered a range of diagnoses of, and solutions to, the conflicts endemic to the new society, which gave greater or lesser weight to normative elements in the resolution of the problem of order. However, they all rested on the common foundation of a liberal rationalism, which they inherited from the political theories of the Enlightenment. They were all *rationalist*, in the sense that the appropriate constitutional and moral framework was determined by a rational evaluation of the benefits of such an order, and not by the desirability of order for its own sake. They were all *liberal*, in the sense that the benefits of this framework were defined solely in relation to the ends of individuals: moral and political institutions did not constitute ends in themselves. However the rational individual, who defined the conditions of constitutional and moral order, could not immediately be identified with the concrete individuals, burdened with ignorance and superstition and motivated by narrow self-interest, who inhabited the real world. The rational individual was a theoretical construct, which defined an ideal world against which mundane reality could be judged, and in whose likeness it could be reformed.

The weakness of these theories lay in the abstract character of their liberalism. Although they proclaimed the freedom of the individual, they also insisted that order and prosperity depended on confining individual freedom within a constitutional, political, legal and normative framework defined by their economic, moral or historical laws. This weakness came to the fore with the rise of an independent working class in the third quarter of the nineteenth century, which based its demands not on the ideal rationality of the abstract individual, but on the concrete aspirations of a particular social class, aspirations which could no longer be rebuffed in the name of abstract laws. It is in this sense that an adequate liberal theory of society had to be formulated on the basis of a voluntaristic theory of action, which could derive the conditions of order not from the theoretical evaluation of the hypothetical interests of the rational individual, but from the actual aspirations of the concrete individuals who make up society, and it was in this sense that Parsons was correct to judge nineteenth century social theory as deficient. However Parsons saw this defect as deriving from an inadequate theory of action. Marx, by contrast, had seen it as inherent in the liberal project itself.

Marx's critique of political economy

Parsons followed the orthodox interpretations of Marx, which assimilate his theory of capitalist society to the utilitarianism, the historical materialism, and the class theory developed by classical political economy. These interpretations of Marx's work are quite inadequate, in failing to grasp the power and significance of Marx's *critique* of political economy. The key to this critique is to be found in Marx's early theory of alienated labour, which was later developed in his theories of the value-form and of commodity fetishism. These theories have conventionally been interpreted as a quasi-Hegelian philosophical critique of political economy, from the point of view of the human essence in the theory of alienation, and from the point of view of the historical specificity of capitalism in the theory of commodity fetishism. The interpretation of Marx presented here is very different from those which dominate the literature.

The central argument of this book is that Marx offers a simultaneous critique of political economy and of Hegelian philosophy which rests on his critique of the concept of private property, which is the presupposition on which liberal social thought constitutes the rational individual as its primitive theoretical term. This critique was first developed in Marx's theory of alienated labour, in which Marx argued that private property is not the foundation of alienated labour but its result. Capitalist private property presupposes the development of a system of social production in which the products of labour are exchanged in the alienated form of the commodity. The relation of private property, as a relation between an individual and a thing, is therefore only the juridical expression of a social relation, in which the products of *social* labour are *privately* appropriated. This critique of private property immediately implies that the abstract individual of liberal social theory is already a socially determined individual, whose social determination is implicit in the proprietorial relation between the individual and the things which define that individual's mode of participation in society. This critique cuts the ground from under the feet of liberal social theory, in making it impossible to relate social institutions back to their origins in some pristine individual instrumental or normative rationality. The only possible foundation of social theory is the historically developed social relations which characterise a particular form of society. Social theories could not be derived from *a priori* principles, but could only be developed through painstaking empirical investigation and conceptual elaboration.

Marx's intellectual achievement was to develop a theory of the economic forms of the social relations of capitalist production, which laid the foundations on which a properly historical social theory could be built. However Marx's social theory also provided the basis for a moral and political critique of capitalism, in establishing that the evils of capitalism were not merely the contingent effects of human greed, ignorance and superstition, but were necessary aspects of the social form of capitalist production. Thus Marx's theoretical critique of private property was at the same time a critique of the society on which it was based, and in particular of the impoverishment and degradation of the working class. However it was not Marx's theoretical critique, but the practical critique of the working class which led to the overthrow of political economy and provoked the reorientation of social thought at the end of the nineteenth century.

From social reform to modern sociology

Political economy recognised the poverty which was the lot of the working class in a capitalist society, and recognised that employers might abuse their powers to drive down wages, but poverty was in general not the result of any such exploitation, but of the limited development of the productive forces, on the one hand, and the excessive pressure of population, on the other. The general condition of the working class could therefore not be ameliorated either by trade union pressure or by political intervention, beyond that required to check the abuse of the employers' power, but depended on the development of the productive forces, through the productive investment of capital, and on restricting the growth of population by the exercise of 'moral restraint'. The political implication of such an analysis was that the working class did not constitute an independent interest, its improvement depending on the economic and moral progress of the nation as a whole.

This denial of the independent interest of the working class could not survive the growth of trade unionism, working class political agitation, and the wider movement for social reform. A more pragmatic approach to the problem of order was called for than was allowed by political economy, and this approach was provided by various schools of sociology and historicism. However the abandonment of the laws of political economy removed any coherent basis on which to address the 'problem of order', and so to evaluate proposed reforms. Political economy had provided a model of the ideal society, based on the rational individual, against which to judge misguided reformist schemes. The pragmatic approach to social reform provided no means of setting limits to the demands for reform, which escalated with the legalisation of trades unions, the extension of the franchise, and the growth of working class parties. Without an adequate liberal solution to the 'problem of order', which could recognise the necessity for social reform while confining reformist ambitions within appropriate limits, there appeared to be nothing to stop the inexorable advance of social reform towards socialism.

The liberal response to the socialist challenge was provided by the marginalist revolution in economics, which set political economy on a rigorously subjective and individualist foundation. The basis of the marginalist revolution was the replacement of the classical cost of production theory of value with a subjective theory of value. The primary significance of this change was to undermine the classical theory of distribution, according to which the revenues of different classes were determined by different laws, and were evaluated in terms of their contribution to the growth of production. For marginalism the determination of revenues was integrated into the theory of exchange, as revenues were identified with the prices of the commodities from which they derived. The question of distribution was then a question of the initial allocation of resources, which was not a concern of the economist but a matter for moral and political judgement. Thus marginalism rescued political economy from the socialist challenge by removing questions of distribution from the domain of economics. The rationality of capitalism no longer lay in its dynamic efficiency as a system of production, based on the productive employment of the surplus product, but in its allocative efficiency as a system of provision for human needs. The 'problem of order' was therefore redefined as the problem of reconciling the efficiency of capitalist relations of production and exchange with the equity of capitalist relations of distribution.

Marginalism derived the rationality of capitalism from the subjective rationality of the economic actor. However the abstraction of the economic actor from the social relations of production continued to rest on the liberal theory of private property, the naturalistic conception of production, and the rationalistic conception of exchange, which had been the objects of Marx's critique of political economy. Thus marginalist economics is as vulnerable as was classical political economy to Marx's critique — all that the marginalist revolution achieved was to reformulate the theory at a higher level of abstraction.

The marginalists were quite conscious of the abstract character of their economic theory, and took pains to make the basis of its abstraction explicit. While this allowed the marginalists to claim the universal applicability of their economic laws, it also created the space within which complementary disciplines, appropriate to other orientations of action, could develop. Thus, where classical political economy claimed to offer a social theory adequate to the reality of capitalist society, marginalist economics self-consciously developed a theory that abstracted from the particular social and historical context within which economic activity takes place. In this sense marginalism claimed to offer not a social theory but a pure theory of rational choice.

The investigation of concrete economic and social problems

introduced social and historical considerations. *Social economics* qualified the optimistic conclusions of pure theory, analysing the extent to which inequalities of economic power, the development of monopoly, the imperfect exercise of rationality and the intervention of the state distort the harmonious equilibrium defined by pure theory and introduce economic conflict into the model of perfect competition.

While social economics continued to be a branch of economics, in presupposing the rational pursuit of material self-interest to be the only basis of social action, marginalist economics also left a space for sociology. Within the framework of the theory of action, economics is defined as only one branch of the social sciences, the science that studies the consequences of rational economic action. Sociology is then the discipline that studies the consequences of non-rational action and of action oriented to other than economic goals, the discipline that takes account of the normative orientation of action and so that locates economics within the framework of the voluntaristic theory of action.

The task of developing such a sociology fell to Max Weber, who is the most important figure in *The Structure of Social Action* and who took it upon himself to formulate a systematic typology of action as the basis for the social sciences. Weber classified social actions according to the ends to which action was addressed and the values that oriented the action. Within his typology economic theory had a place as the theory that develops the ideal-typical forms of rational economic action, while sociology develops ideal-types corresponding to all other forms of action. Within this framework Weber was able to locate capitalist society not in economistic terms, as a society which is subordinated to the pursuit of economic ends, but sociologically, as a society characterised by a particular value-orientation of action, a rational orientation. This rationality is characteristic not only of economic action, but also of political action and of the value system of modern capitalism. The 'rational economic action' whose implications the economists have uncovered is not an ahistorical universal, but is an historical result of the wider cultural process of the rationalisation of Western society.

Although Weber developed his sociology as a critique of marginalist economics, he did not challenge the adequacy of the marginalist characterisation of the rationality of the economic institutions of capitalist society, but sought only to locate marginalist economics within a wider cultural theory, based on the 'voluntaristic theory of action'.

From social reform to modern sociology

This wider theory provided the ground on which Weber could criticise economic liberalism from the perspective of higher moral values, which for Weber established the 'substantive irrationality' of capitalism, in contrast to the 'formal rationality' of capitalism as an efficient system of provision for human needs.

Weber's 'voluntaristic theory of action' did not resolve the problem of order, but presented liberalism with an irresoluble dilemma, for considerations of equity and efficiency, of substantive and formal rationality, pulled in opposite directions. Moreover the fragmentation of modern society, which was the inevitable result of its rationalisation, meant that liberal individualism could not provide any basis on which this dilemma could be resolved. The freedom of the individual was irreconcilable with the resolution of the problem of order, the formal rationality of capitalism irreconcilable with its substantive irrationality. It is this liberal dilemma which defines the antinomies on which modern sociology is based, and from which it cannot escape so long as it presupposes the marginalist demonstration of the formal rationality of capitalism, based on the marginalist abstraction of the property-owning individual from the social relations which define that individual as a social being.

Although Marx's critique of political economy cut away the foundations of liberal social theory, and provided an alternative basis on which to develop a more adequate social theory, the dominant currents of Marxism have signally failed to build on Marx's critique, reducing Marxism to a system of historical laws akin to those of political economy and/or to a philosophical critique of capitalism akin to that of romantic idealism. Marx's critique of liberalism has been used not as a means of transcending liberalism by replacing liberalism's abstract individual with the real individuals whose concrete collectivity makes up society, but as a means of suppressing the liberal dilemma by suppressing the individual in the name of abstract collectivities. The interpretation of Marx's work presented in this book is as much a critique of 'Orthodox' and 'Western' Marxism as it is of liberal social theory. The hope which this book expresses is that the 'death of Marxism' can also be the condition for its re-birth.

2

Classical Political Economy

A theory of society

Nineteenth-century social thought was dominated by classical political economy, a set of doctrines that served as a negative point of reference where it did not act as a positive inspiration. For this reason classical political economy has to be the starting point for any serious study of Marxism or of modern sociology, for both were born out of debates that surrounded classical political economy.

The term 'classical political economy' refers to theories developed between the seventeenth and nineteenth centuries that sought to conceptualise the structure of society on the basis of an understanding of society's economic foundation. The starting point of these theories was the abstract individual property-owner of liberal political theory, but the new theories sought to advance beyond this abstraction by locating the individual socially, distinguishing the interests of different social classes determined by the qualitatively different forms of property which they owned. The basis of this qualitative distinction was the economic functions performed by the three factors of production, land, labour and capital, and the correspondingly distinct laws which determined the contributions to production of the different factors, and the revenues accruing to the owners of those different forms of property. Thus the abstract juridical relations of 'civil society' of liberal political theory were given a substantive content, defined by economic interest.

Classical political economy saw society as being composed of social classes, which were defined on the basis of different economic functions, and whose social and political interaction was oriented by their economic interest and structured by the development of their economic relationships. The main concerns of classical political economy from Petty to J. S. Mill were to identify the social classes that comprised society, to define the economic relationships between these classes and to discover the laws that governed the development of these relationships. In a very literal sense classical political economy saw its task as being the construction of a science of society. However the economy was not seen as a realm independent of society. For classical political economy the economy was the heart and soul of 'civil society'.

The history of classical political economy is the history of the attempt to develop this model of the economic foundation of society, in abstraction from those causes 'that depend on the mutable minds, opinions, appetites and passions of particular men' (Petty, 1963 p. 244), finding the 'inner physiology of *bourgeois* society', as Marx called it, in the economic relations between classes (Marx, TSV, II, p. 165). This depended on isolating the economic foundations of social relations from extraneous moral, political or religious considerations. The most complete and satisfying development of political economy is to be found in the work of Adam Smith, which located the analysis of economic relationships within a comprehensive theory of society, while its most rigorous economic development is found in the work of David Ricardo.

The materialist conception of society

Classical political economy sought to develop a model of the ideal harmonious society within which every form of property would have its proper place. However, the purpose of describing the contributions of different forms of property to the well-being of society as a whole was not so much to develop theoretical models, as to set politics on a rational foundation, the ideal society defining an appropriate form of constitution, and appropriate forms of legislation, taxation and economic and social policy, whence the term 'political' economy. While the ideal was to construct an harmonious society, the different theories of political economy attached different degrees of importance to different forms of property, and so inevitably favoured one class against another. However disinterested a particular thinker might be, political economy could not avoid being an intensely political field of study.

The theories of political economy were based on the principles of eighteenth century materialism, which had developed within the broader framework of the intellectual and ideological revolution of the Enlightenment, which laid the foundations of modern bourgeois thought. The Enlightenment expressed a direct challenge to the fundamental principles of political and moral authority which underlay the absolutist order. It replaced God by Reason and Nature as the regulative principle of the moral, social and political order, it replaced divine revelation by scientific inquiry as the source of Truth, and it replaced the priest and philosopher by the scientist as the arbiter of propriety. The revealed truths of religion stood condemned as the false judgements of passion and ignorance. However, while it challenged the principles of absolutism, the Enlightenment by no means challenged the authority of the state, but rather sought to re-establish that authority by setting it on more secure foundations, appropriate to the new form of society which was emerging.

The legitimation of the absolutist state rested on a modified version of the medieval conception of a society based on status and organised into estates, held together by relations of spiritual and temporal authority. The medieval conception of society was that of a patriarchal hierarchy based on the model of the household. Within the household order was maintained by the exercise of patriarchal authority, and this patriarchal model was extended to the social relations between households, the sovereign being ultimately under the authority of God. Thus every member of society was subject to spiritual and temporal authority, within a framework of mutual rights and obligations defined in terms of personal status.

In the new society that was emerging, most dramatically in the towns, social position and social relations were defined not by divinely sanctioned status, but increasingly by property and by occupation, which was in turn seen as a form of property: as the ownership of the skills and tools of a trade. Property was not initially an homogeneous concept, to be attached uniquely to an individual and captured in a quantitative measure. It was differentiated, so that consideration of the rights and obligations of the individual came to revolve around consideration of the rights and obligations attached to different forms of property, in relation to one another and to the sovereign. Thus consideration of property was not initially opposed to the consideration of society in terms of status, but status was progressively detached from the person and embodied instead in property.

As relations based on personal status were progressively eroded with the growth of commercial relations, so the conception of society as a network of relations between persons gave way to a conception of society as a network of relations between different forms of property. Similarly the state came to be seen increasingly as a juridical body, sustaining the established order by regulating the relationships between the various forms of property. This 'dehumanisation' of society undermined the self-evident sanctity of the established order, and called for new ways of understanding the possibility of a stable and harmonious social order, on the one hand, and of justifying the political reforms required to achieve that order, on the other. Thus the medieval conception of society was modified firstly by providing a rational foundation for the authority of the sovereign over his subjects and of the patriarch over his dependent household, and secondly by recognising the jural and moral rights and obligations entailed in the establishment of contracts as the typical form of social relation between property-owners. Society thus came to be conceptualised as a political order whose foundation was some form of real or implied contract. The juridical relations of right and obligation that bound the members of society together, under the superintendence of the sovereign, were no longer defined and differentiated according to personal status and sanctioned by God, but came to be conceived in terms of the 'natural laws' that accorded with reason, that governed the rights and obligations of individuals as property-owners, and that guided sound government.

This view of society as a juridical order, regulated by a sovereign subject to the obligation to respect the natural laws embodied in the rights and obligations of the individual as a property-owner, dominated the political theories which emerged in the second half of the seventeenth century. While those theories challenged the absolutist principles of divine right and arbitrary authority, they retained the absolutist conception of the state as the integrating centre of society, so that the differential rights and obligations of different forms of property were defined in terms of their contribution to the stability of the political order. Thus, for example, the constitutional privileges of landed property were defended by reference to the relations of deference and authority which landed property embodied, and which the state was called on to enforce, while the commercial privileges of mercantile property were defended by reference to its contribution to the coffers of the state.

The various theories proposed sought to establish the authority of the state on a rational foundation. The principal problem was that of the relationship between 'law' and 'authority', between the 'natural rights' of the individual property-owner and the delegated authority of the sovereign. This problem was defined by a particular philosophical conception of human nature, which determined the potential challenge to the social and political order presented by unregulated human inclinations, and so the extent to which the authority of the state was called on to impose the rule of reason on human passions. However, different thinkers had different conceptions of human nature, according to the form of constitution they sought to defend. The ultimately arbitrary foundation of these juridical theories became increasingly apparent in the course of political debate, so that it became imperative to find a more secure foundation on which to build social and political theory. This was the achievement of eighteenth century materialism.

Eighteenth century materialism sought to replace philosophy by science as the means of uncovering the natural laws of society. It was able to do this because it no longer sought to criticise the political order from the standpoint of an abstract human nature, but from the more mundane standpoint of the economic and moral progress of society, to which the corruption and parasitism of the state presented an increasingly serious barrier. That political order was best which was best adapted to the moral, intellectual and material progress of society, while the foundation of moral and intellectual progress was firmly identified with material progress. Thus materialism diverted attention from the philosophical investigation of human nature to the scientific investigation of the laws that governed the economic progress of society. Different forms of property were henceforth to be evaluated not according to the natural rights of property, although the sanctity of property continued to be presumed, nor according to their contribution to the state, but according to their contribution to material progress. Thus attention moved to what we now recognise as economic questions, and political philosophy gave way to political economy as the cornerstone of the theory of society.

Society was no longer seen as an expression of human nature, but as an order regulated by its own laws that were not the result of human design and that could not be modified by human intervention. These laws were generally considered to be divinely inspired, but they were no more amenable to divine than to human intervention. They could therefore be known scientifically, whether through experiment (Smith) or through the exercise of reason (Physiocracy), and they had to be respected if harmony were to prevail. Thus 'nations stumble upon establishments, which are indeed the result of human action, but not the execution of any human design' (Ferguson, 1966, p. 122).

Society is governed by 'natural laws'. 'All men and all earthly powers ought to be subject to these sovereign laws instituted by the Supreme Being. They are immutable and indisputable and the best laws possible; thus they are the foundation of the most perfect government, and the fundamental rule for all positive laws' (Quesnay, 'Natural Right', in Meek, 1963, pp. 53–4). However, although these laws are 'self-evident', they are not necessarily known or observed. It is essential that 'the nation should be given instruction in the general laws of the natural order, which constitute the form of government which is self-evidently the most perfect', hence education of the public and enlightenment of the sovereign is the prime condition for good government (Quesnay, 'General Maxims', in Meek, 1963, p. 231).

Eighteenth century materialism was *naturalistic*, but by no means *fatalistic*, for it introduced a fundamental distinction between the external world of physical nature, which was governed by immutable and irresistible laws, and the internal world of human nature, which was characterised by a division between the psychological faculties of reason and passion, intellect and emotion. While the primaeval instincts of passion expressed the continued subordination of Humanity to Nature, Reason enabled Humanity to transcend the constraints of its internal Nature. 'Nature' became an external world, which provided no more than the raw material which Humanity could appropriate, intellectually and practically, in order to subordinate Nature to its own intellectual and material needs. 'Progress' was measured precisely by the extent to which Humanity had freed itself from Nature by subjecting Nature to its own intellectual and practical rule. This subordination of Nature was achieved by the progressive realisation of the rule of Reason. For the materialists the development of the forces of production was both the measure of the progress of practical reason, and the means by which humanity freed itself from the constraint of natural scarcity to subordinate ignorance and passion to intellectual and moral reason. This development was neither an intellectual nor a political enterprise, but could only be achieved in and through 'civil society', which was established as the mediating term between Reason and Nature.

The divorce between Reason and Nature constituted human society as a self-sufficient realm, and so as the potential object of a new 'historical' science. The historical development of civil society, embodied in the practical mastery of natural forces in production, became the measuring rod of progress and, in particular, of the appropriate forms of 'manners and morals', of the constitution, legislation and public policy. At the same time this intellectual revolution shifted the focus of reformist projects. Against the absolutist belief that civil society had to be moulded in accordance with the will of God, the needs of the State and the dictates of Human Nature, the Enlightenment insisted that the State and Human Nature had to be adapted to the needs of civil society, according to the rule of Reason.

Nature defined the external limits to the rule of Reason: Reason could harness the laws of Nature, but it could not override them. However, the foremost barrier to progress lay not outside humanity, but within, in the residual power of the passions and of ignorance which impede and subvert rational judgement. Progress then lay in the imposition of the intellect on natural inclinations. '*Differences in intellect* which we observe among (men) depend on the *different circumstances* in which they find themselves placed, and the *different education* which they receive', while 'all our *false judgements* are the effect either of our *passions* or of our ignorance' (Helvétius, *De l'Esprit*, quoted Meek, 1976, pp. 92–3). Reform is both possible and necessary, and is to be guided by the exercise of reason that will dispel the prejudices of passion and ignorance that are the source of bad government. The basis of rational reform can only be the scientific understanding of the causes of the progress of society.

The physiocratic theory of society

The materialist conception of society emerged in the mid-eighteenth century as thinkers throughout Europe sought to discover an objective foundation for morals and for social and political institutions. It is difficult to disentangle influence from independent conception, so rapid was the development, but it is generally agreed that the decisive moment was the publication of Montesquieu's *Spirit of the Laws* in 1748, which offered the most influential early formulation of a materialist conception of society. For Montesquieu the natural factors determining the forms of law, manners and customs in a society were the geographical factors of the soil and the climate, but he also considered the independent influence of the mode of subsistence, the form of government and the 'spirit' of the nation. Helvétius soon noted the empirical inadequacy of the climatic explanation and invoked population pressure as the primary source of progress, but it was the

The physiocratic theory of society 19

Physiocrats and Adam Smith who first systematically related political and social institutions and the 'moral sentiments' to the mode of subsistence, probably reaching their conclusions independently around 1750–1.[1]

The Physiocrats theorised the contribution of large-scale agriculture to the well-being of society, and in so doing developed a model of society as a whole. This theory was opposed primarily to the mercantilist doctrines which had been dominant hitherto. Like the mercantilists, the Physiocrats identified national wealth with the formation of a surplus, and evaluated particular forms of property by their contribution to that surplus. However the importance of this surplus was not identified directly with its contribution to the reserves of the state, as it had been by mercantilism, but more broadly with the provision of a fund which could be mobilised alternatively in unproductive expenditure, whether by the state or by individuals, or in fostering economic development by improving agriculture. This meant that the Physiocrats did not conceive of the surplus only in terms of money, as had the mercantilists, but primarily in physical terms, as a surplus of produce, distinguishing the sterility of money-lending from the productivity of agricultural investment. More fundamentally, the physiocratic theory immediately meant that the evaluation of forms of property was no longer confined within the limits of the existing political order, as it was for mercantilism, but was conceived more broadly in terms of their differential contributions to the well-being of society. This in turn led the Physiocrats to construct a model of the flow of goods between different classes, without the intermediation of the state, and so led them to develop the first rigorous theory of the economic foundations not only of the state, but also of the emerging civil society.

The Physiocrats divided society into the 'productive class', the 'proprietors' and the 'sterile class'. The productive class represented agricultural producers, and was divided into wage-labourers and entrepreneurs. The proprietors were the class of landowners, while the merchants and manufacturers made up the sterile class, within which wage-labourers and entrepreneurs were not systematically distinguished. Manufacture is sterile because it simply transforms existing products, in the form of agricultural foodstuffs and raw materials, into

---

[1] Although Smith probably identified the determining role of the mode of subsistence independently, he drew very heavily on the Physiocrats in the development of his theory.

manufactured goods without producing any surplus. Agriculture, by contrast, produces a net product, which is attributed to the powers of nature and which accrues to the proprietors in the form of rent.

The implication of this model is that rent is the sole form of the surplus, so the maximisation of the surplus is identified with the maximisation of rent, which is achieved by augmenting the productivity of agriculture. Although some used the model to defend landed property, it is not landed property but agricultural enterprise which is productive, landed property simply appropriating the god-given benefits of nature by virtue of its engrossing the land. The most productive form of agricultural enterprise was identified by the Physiocrats as large-scale, and increasingly capitalist, farming. Thus the general conclusion drawn was that progress depends on fostering the growth of large-scale farming through the concentration of enterprises and through agricultural investment, which could best be achieved by a regime of *laissez-faire* that provides the basis for the expansion of markets.[2]

The identification of the interests of the large-scale farmer with those of society as a whole by no means implied that the Physiocrats were simply the ideological representatives of a particular class. Their primary concern was with the stabilisation of the political regime, and their primary appeal was to the Statesman, proposing that the power of the state should be strictly limited by the fact that it has to respect the natural laws of the economy if it is not to impede progress. This implied that the state should not interfere with those laws, restricting itself to the protection of the realm, of individual liberty and of property and, in the case of Quesnay, diverting some of the net product to agricultural investment. Constitutionally this implied that the state should be disengaged from all forms of class representation, to take the form of an enlightened despotism, guided by the divinely ordained natural laws discovered by the Physiocrats, whose foundation would be best secured by a system of education to propagate the principles of Physiocracy.

The political programme of Physiocracy had a growing appeal in mid-eighteenth century France. It certainly was the case that commerce

---

[2] The Physiocrats did not see profits as an independent form of revenue. Entrepreneurial profits were seen as a form of wage, although exceptional profits might be earned by increasing productivity or reducing costs, while commercial profits were a diversion from rent based on monopoly power. Manufacturing investment was considered as a diversion not from the surplus but from consumption, as entrepreneurs saved from their normal revenue.

was stagnating, while agriculture was the most dynamic sector of the economy, its development impeded by taxation, proprietorial privileges and commercial regulation. The rapid development of capitalist agriculture would favour not only the emerging class of agricultural entrepreneurs, but also offered a way of resolving the growing social and political problems confronting the state, by expanding the available surplus and so promising to ameliorate the growing conflict over rent and taxation that set the peasantry against both landed proprietors and the state. However the contradiction inherent in the physiocratic programme was that the development of large-scale capitalist farming could only be at the expense of the small-holding peasantry, so that the physiocratic solution could only exacerbate social tensions in the short-term.

The theoretical limitations of Physiocracy lay in its continued adherence to natural law doctrines and to Cartesian rationalism, on the one hand, and in its insistence that agriculture alone was productive, on the other.[3] It was Adam Smith who overcame these limitations, rejecting the 'self-evidence' of the truths of Physiocracy, replacing Cartesian rationalism with the empiricism of his friend David Hume,[4] and recognising the productivity of manufacture by introducing the concept of capital, or 'stock', independent from land and labour. In modifying the fundamental assumptions of Physiocracy in this way the division of society was changed from that between agriculture, manufacture and the proprietors, to that familiar today between the landed class, the capitalist class, and the labouring class.

Smith's Theory of Moral Sentiments

Smith's theory of society is to be found in three works: *The Theory of Moral Sentiments*, *The Lectures on Jurisprudence* and *The Wealth of Nations*. Although Smith is thought of today as an 'economist', the three books form a whole.

---

[3] The later Physiocrats did abandon this insistence, to recognise the productivity of manufacture, without systematically developing its theoretical implications.

[4] The extent to which Smith's work remains within the framework of natural law doctrines is a question of interpretation that is still hotly disputed. On the one hand, the difference between Smith's appeal to reason as a psychological propensity, as opposed to the Physiocrats view of reason as an *a priori* truth, is purely rhetorical, the evidence for both resting on intuition. On the other hand, Smith did not follow the Physiocrats in regarding intuition as the conclusive proof of his theories, but sought instead to establish their truth through extensive comparative and historical investigation.

The historical framework for Smith's analysis of his own society is provided by what Meek has called the 'four-stages theory' (Meek, 1976). According to this theory the mode of subsistence is the fundamental determinant of the forms of property and government, social institutions and moral sentiments current in a society. There are four fundamental modes of subsistence underlying the four types of society: hunting, pasturage, agriculture and commerce. These stages are arranged in an ideal evolutionary succession of material, and corresponding moral, political and intellectual progress. The basis of this progress is the extension of the division of labour which gives rise to growing social differentiation: between town and country, arts and manufacture, different occupations and professions, and different social classes. The extension of the division of labour increases the social surplus which, if properly applied, furthers the division of labour and leads to a diffusion and proliferation of property. This in turn provides the foundation for the growing independence of the state, set up to defend property, from any particular interest, and for the progress of the moral sentiments.

In *The Theory of Moral Sentiments* Smith explored the material foundation and social development of the moral sentiments. Smith's starting point was the materialist assertion that 'the understandings of the greater part of men are formed by their ordinary employment'. However Smith did not adopt the utilitarian thesis, advanced later by Bentham, that people were guided by pure self-interest, nor even Hume's limited identification of utility with pleasure. For Smith the moral sentiments were formed socially and the basis of the moral judgement was the sense of 'propriety', of the beauty of a well-ordered whole. The basis of judgements of propriety was 'sympathy', the ability to adopt the position of the 'impartial and well-informed spectator' in relation both to our own and other people's conduct and it was sympathy that conditioned our approval of 'benevolence', of conduct that was conducive to the well-being of society. For example, people did not desire wealth for its own sake, for Smith had a puritanical scepticism about the pleasures to be derived from wealth, but for the sake of the social approbation that was attached to the possession of wealth. The source of the moral sentiments was passion and not reason, but the effect of the mechanism of sympathy was that socially beneficial passions were endorsed while harmful passions were condemned. Thus the empirical principle of sociability replaced the natural-law principle of obligation.

Sympathy is not sufficient to restrain the negative impulses that express 'self-love'. A degree of self-love is necessary for every individual to fulfil her social role so that in seeking to achieve her own interests social benefits ensue. However, unmoderated self-love could have harmful effects when not restrained by benevolence, as selfishness led the individual to seek her ends by anti-social means. Such selfishness could be the result either of inadequate moral restraint, as when the individual had only a restricted circle of social contacts, or of ignorance, where individuals were inadequately aware of their own best interests. Moral education and a wide circle of social contacts, such as were provided by an extended division of labour, would contribute to the perfection of the moral sentiments.

Smith's theory of moral sentiments provided a neat account of the moral order of society such as would be recognizable to any modern sociologist. But for Smith this moral order was strictly subordinate to the economic order whose reproduction it served. Thus it was not the basis of his theory of society, but provided only a link in the explanation of how a society based on the pursuit of self-interest could be sustained. Moreover the moral sentiments alone were not sufficient for the maintenance of good order in society. Above the moral sentiments stood the state, and beneath them lay the division of labour.

In Smith's *Lectures on Jurisprudence* he examined the nature and functions of the state, part of which discussion was resumed in *The Wealth of Nations*. The state was seen as a set of institutions which had a strictly limited, and largely negative, role in preserving a good social order. The state was the repository of *law* rather than of *authority* and its primary function was to protect the rights of the individual as a man, as a member of a family, and as a member of society. Smith argued that 'justice ... is the main pillar that holds the whole edifice' (Smith, 1976, p. 86). This was not because justice could ordain the propriety of social relationships, for benevolence could not be enforced, but because only justice could preserve the rights of the individual to life, liberty and property and so guarantee the framework of civil society within which benevolence can moderate the abuses of misguided self-love. This framework was provided by the relationship of the individual to his (not usually her, because the woman was a dependent member of a patriarchal family) legally acquired property and by the relationships established by the division of labour that were mediated by the free and equal exchange of property.

The Wealth of Nations

Both the theory of moral sentiments and the theory of the state depended on Smith's identification of the moderated and restrained pursuit of self-interest with the improvement of social well-being. It was this identification that was first systematically theorised in *The Wealth of Nations*, which was the foundation of Smith's entire social and political theory.

For Smith, progress was identified with the extension of the division of labour, including the application of machinery, that was the foundation of the increasing productivity of labour.

> This division of labour ... is not originally the effect of any human wisdom ... It is the necessary, though very slow and gradual consequence, of a certain propensity in human nature which has no such extensive utility; the propensity to truck, barter and exchange one thing for another (WN, I, p. 12).

This propensity, Smith argued, was probably 'the necessary consequence of the faculties of reason and speech', rather than being a mere natural instinct, through the rational consideration that if I want the help of others I do better to interest their self-love in my favour than to appeal to their benevolence alone (WN, I, p. 13). Thus each, in rational pursuit of her own ends, achieved spontaneously the progressive extension of the division of labour. The extension of the division of labour was limited by the extent of the market. The expansion of production enlarged the market, providing the basis for an extension of the division of labour, and so for a further expansion of production. The extension of the division of labour, if confronted by no 'unnatural' barriers, was thus a cumulative process.

Any barriers to the freedom of exchange restricted the possibilities of self-improvement available to the individual, and so restricted the progress of society. Thus Smith established that free exchange was the condition for the most rapid development of the division of labour and so of the wealth of nations. However it is not sufficient to consider only the production and exchange of wealth. The problem of the proper regulation of society is raised most particularly by the question of the distribution of the product. Smith's great originality lay in his development of a theory of distribution that enabled him to conceptualise the different interests of the different classes of society and so to identify the best means of reconciling their interests. It was Smith who first systematically introduced into social theory the fundamental distinction between the three component classes of capitalist society, the owners of 'stock', the landowners and the wage-labourers. He achieved this by means of an analysis of the component parts of the price of a commodity.

Smith's analysis of class rests on the observation that production depends on the technical co-operation of the three distinct factors of production, land, labour and 'stock'. These factors of production are the property of individuals, who sell the services of their appropriate factor in exchange for a revenue. Thus the distinction between land, labour and 'stock' defines the distinction between the corresponding revenues, rent, wages and profit, which accrue to the owners of the appropriate factors of production. It is these three revenues which constitute the component parts of the price of a commodity. The laws which govern these revenues accordingly define the distinctive interests of the three classes, corresponding to the factor of production which constitutes the source of each class's revenue. Moreover, since these three revenues exhaust the product there can be no other source of revenue, all other revenues deriving ultimately from one of these sources, so that the interest of every member of society is ultimately attached to one of the three classes.

Smith's account of the component parts of the price of a commodity was notoriously ambiguous. On the one hand, he argued that profit and rent in some sense represented deductions from the product of labour: the labourer now had to share her product with the capitalist and landowner. If this were the case then the value of the commodity would be the amount of labour bestowed on it and it would not be self-evident that the interests of the labourer coincided with those of the capitalists and landowners, since profits and rent could increase, given the productivity of labour, only at the expense of wages. On the other hand, Smith argued that profit and rent did not represent deductions from the product of labour, but corresponded in some way to the original contributions made to the product by capital and land. Thus profit, rent and wages were independent component parts of the value of a commodity and there was no reason to conclude that increasing rents and profits were at the expense of wages. This latter is the argument that Smith typically adopted in *The Wealth of Nations*. Thus, for example, he tended to argue that an increase in money wages would not lead to a fall in profits but to an increase in prices. He then introduced the distinction between the producer and the consumer, so that price increases were passed on to the consumer, failing to recognise that the consumer could ultimately only be the wage-labourer, capitalist or landowner wearing another hat. The introduction of this device of the consumer frequently prevented Smith from following through the logic of his arguments in a systematic investigation of the social relations between the component classes of society.

The purpose of the examination of the component parts of price was not to lead into an examination of prices but to establish the basis on which the national product is divided between the component classes of society: 'wages, profit and rent, are the three original sources of all revenue as well as of all exchangeable value. All other revenue is ultimately derived from some one or other of these' (WN, I, p. 46). In particular, interest is a deduction from profit and taxation is a drain on revenue. Smith turned to the examination of the determination of the different forms of revenue, and so to the material foundation of the interests of the different social classes that comprise society.

It is in considering the different forms of revenue independently of one another that Smith definitively abandoned the *embodied labour* theory of value in favour of a theory of the independent component parts of value. He retained a labour theory of value only in the sense that he uses *labour commanded* as the most convenient measure of value, because he believed that this provided the most stable standard of value (although it should be added that he was not altogether consistent in this). Thus the labour value of a commodity was not the number of hours of labour entailed in its production, but the number of hours of labour that could be commanded by its price. The latter would be greater than the former to the extent of profit and rent. Thus the theory of value analysed the independent component parts of the *real price* of a commodity, only introducing the labour standard in order to facilitate long-period comparisons that abstracted from the changing value of money. Smith's labour theory of value served not as the basis of his analysis of social relations between the classes, but only as a convenient accounting device.

The rapid abandonment of the embodied labour theory of value had important implications, for it meant that the revenues of the different classes could be considered independently of one another. This meant in turn that Smith was not compelled to consider systematically the relation between these revenues, nor the social relations between the classes that comprise society. Smith considered the three original sources of revenue not in relation to one another, but in relation to their independent contributions to, and benefits from, economic growth. The interdependence of these classes was located only in the technological interdependence of the factors of production to which the revenues correspond, as an aspect of their co-operation in the division of labour. Land, labour and stock are the universal foundations of social differentiation and are considered on a par with other functional distinctions, such as that between agriculture and manufacture, as aspects of the technical division of labour characteristic of any developed society. This is why Smith could not conceive of any but the simplest society except in terms of the categories appropriate to his own, and this is why he proceeded immediately from 'that early and rude state of society' to a society in which stock has accumulated in the hands of particular persons who 'will naturally employ it to set to work industrious people' (WN, I, p. 42).

Wages are determined by the balance between the supply of and the demand for labour. However 'there is a certain rate below which it seems impossible to reduce, for any considerable time, the ordinary wages even of the lowest species of labour' (WN, I, p. 60). In the wage bargain the masters have the upper hand, so the tendency is for the wage to fall to this minimum. However an increasing demand for labour, associated with an increasing revenue in the form of profit and rent which constitutes the fund out of which wages are paid, enables the labourers to 'break through the natural combination of masters not to raise wages'. 'The demand for those who live by wages, therefore, necessarily increases with the increase of the revenue and stock of every country and cannot possibly increase without it'. Hence the labourers have an interest in the progressive increase in rent and profits since this alone can secure increased wages for them. Moreover the 'liberal reward of labour' is socially beneficial: 'No society can surely be flourishing and happy, of which the far greater part of the members are poor and miserable'. More to the point, the liberal reward for labour encourages the growth of population and encourages the 'industry of the common people'. The effect of accumulation on wages is beneficial to the workers, to the masters and to the nation (WN, I, pp. 58–61, 70–73).

Profits are necessary to encourage the owner of stock to hazard his stock by employing labourers. The size of profits, however, is determined by the relation between the size of stock and the opportunities for its employment. Although the opening of new investment opportunities may lead to an increase in profits, Smith assumed that the general tendency is for the increase of stock to lower profit as competition between the owners of stock for investment opportunities increases. Thus accumulation tends to increase wages but to lower profits. However it is not the former that causes the latter, although low wages can be a source of high profits and *vice versa*, but rather it is the independent relationship between the supply of investment funds and the opportunities that confront them that determines the decline in profits. Thus in a society in which opportunities are so exhausted that accumulation reaches its limits, both wages and profits will be low.

Accumulation, although it increases the mass of profits, tends to lower the rate of profit. This means that the owners of stock have an ambiguous interest in economic progress, and are tempted to seek to increase the rate of profit artificially. Such measures are, however, extremely harmful to society. 'In reality, high profits tend much more to raise the price of work than high wages' (because high wages encourage industriousness and growth of population). Thus high profits restrict the growth of the market and so the extension of the division of labour.

> Our merchants and master-manufacturers complain much of the bad effects of high wages in raising the price, and thereby lessening the sale of their goods both at home and abroad. They say nothing concerning the bad effects of high profits. They are silent with respect to the pernicious effects of their own gains (WN, I, pp. 87–8).

Smith's analysis of rent is even more ambiguous than his analysis of profit. On the one hand, rent is seen not as an independent component of the price but as whatever is left over after normal wages and ordinary profits have been deducted. An increase in rent can therefore only be at the expense of wages or profits. Rent is not a form of profit, due as a result of investment of stock in the land, but is a 'monopoly price' determined by 'what the farmer can afford to give'. Thus

> rent ... enters into the composition of the price of commodities in a different way from wages and profits. High or low wages and profit are the causes of high or low price; high or low rent is the effect of it (WN, I, pp. 131–2).

However, if rent is a deduction from price the question arises of what determines the price: it cannot be determined by the sum of profits, wages and rent if rent depends in turn on price. Smith's answer was to follow the Physiocrats in relating rent to the natural fertility of the soil. Thus the total product is fixed and rent is what remains after the deduction of wages and profits. It arises because the natural powers of the soil make agriculture more productive than manufacture. Clearly, however, rent depends not on the size of the product, but on the value (price) of the product. Thus Smith went into an extended investigation of the relationship between the prices of agricultural produce, of other raw materials, and of manufactured goods. The basic conclusion is that the relative prices of non-food raw materials rise and those of manufactures fall in relation to the prices of foodstuffs, so that 'every improvement in the circumstances of society tends either directly or indirectly to raise the real rent of land, to increase the real wealth of the landlord' (Smith, WN, I, p. 228).

This argument may explain why rent should increase, but it does not provide any explanation either for the existence or the level of rent. However the conclusion that Smith had reached is the one that was essential to him, for it enabled him to identify the interest of the landowner with the general improvement of society, for the landowners gain from 'every improvement in the circumstances of the society', and this was of fundamental importance in the constitutional circumstances of Smith's time.

Smith concluded his investigation of rent by examining the interests of the 'three different orders of people': 'those who live by rent', 'those who live by wages', and 'those who live by profits'. The interest of the first order, the landowners, 'is strictly and inseparably connected with the general interests of society', as is that of the labourer. Those who live by profit are those 'whose stock puts into motion the greater part of the useful labour of every society'. But the rate of profit tends to fall with progress and the great merchants and manufacturers, although they have 'more acuteness of understanding' than the landowners, are concerned with their own particular interests rather than with those of society. 'The interest of the dealers ... is always in some respects different from, and even opposite to, that of the public', and they have exercised their own abilities to impose on the gullibility of the other orders of society, having 'an interest to deceive and even to oppress the public' by narrowing competition (WN, I, pp. 230–2).

The constitutional conclusions that Smith reached are developed later in *The Wealth of Nations* and elsewhere, but they can be summarised as the need for a balanced constitution, in which the oppressive dangers of 'monarchy' are balanced by 'democracy', the parliamentary representation of property, and the need for public education, to which Smith attached great importance. Public education is desirable because the state of society does not 'naturally form' in the people 'the abilities and virtues which that state requires' so 'some attention of government is necessary in order to prevent the almost entire corruption and degeneracy of the great body of the people', so making them 'the less liable ... to the delusions of enthusiasm and superstition, which, among ignorant nations, frequently occasion the most dreadful disorders ... less apt to be misled into any wanton and unnecessary opposition to the measures of government' (WN, II, pp. 263–9). However, Smith was not too confident of the powers of reason in the face of the persuasive power of the merchants and manufacturers. Smith's conclusion was that

> all systems of either preference or of restraint ... being thus completely taken away, the obvious and simple system of natural liberty establishes itself of its own accord. Every man, as long as he does not violate the laws of justice, is left perfectly free to pursue his own interest his own way, and to bring both his industry and his capital into competition with any other man, or order of men. ... According to the system of natural liberty, the sovereign has only three duties to attend to ... first, the duty of protecting society from the violence and invasion of other independent societies; secondly, the duty of protecting, as far as possible, every member of the society from the injustice or oppression of every other member of it, or the duty of establishing an exact administration of justice; and, thirdly, the duty of erecting and maintaining certain public works and certain public institutions (WN, II, p. 180).

The good order and progress of society depends on the existence of a state that will maintain justice, and so the rule of competition, and on the development of the moral sentiments that will be advanced by the growth of industriousness and the extension of the division of labour, and that will be endorsed by the development of education.

Smith's contribution to social theory

Smith is best remembered today as an economist and as the theorist of economic liberalism. However, as economics his work is eclectic and unsystematic. His theory of wages derives from the Physiocrats, his theory of rent still rests on physiocratic prejudice and his theory of profit at best rests on an implicit extended physiocratic identification of profit with the productive powers of stock. His account of the interests of the fundamental classes of society is equally unsystematic. He recognised the morally harmful effects of large-scale industry and of the division of labour on the working class, so his identification of the interests of the workers with those of society rests wholly on the postulate that accumulation, and accumulation alone, can increase wages. His identification of the interests of the landowners in the improvement of society is equally tenuous, depending on an intuitive, if not wholly implausible, analysis of the relations between prices of foodstuffs, minerals and manufactured goods. His identification of the relation of the owners of stock to accumulation rests on the neglect of any systematic investigation of the fundamental relationships between profits, rent and wages, and between the rate of profit and the rate of accumulation. In short, his defence of economic liberalism rests more on faith than on any systematic analysis.

However the fundamental importance of Smith's work is not its technical contribution to economics, but the fact that it opens up an entirely new approach to society which earlier writers had partially anticipated, but which Smith first presented as a systematic and relatively coherent whole. Smith's contribution can be summed up under three headings. Methodologically he was the first systematic social theorist to break definitively with the natural-law tradition. In this he replaced the rationalistic foundation of Physiocracy with the empiricism of his friend David Hume, so separating social theory from philosophy in subjecting theoretical laws to empirical evaluation. Theoretically, he was the first to develop a systematic materialist conception of history based on the determining role of the mode of subsistence. Finally, the originality of his contribution is consummated in his theory of social class, for he was the first to analyse systematically the emerging capitalist society in terms of the fundamental class division between capitalists, landowners and wage-labourers.

To many it may seem strange that Adam Smith, who is best known as the theorist of liberal individualism, should be acclaimed for his contribution to the class theory of society. However, there is no paradox here, for in Smith's work there is no conflict between individual aspiration and class affiliation. Smith's conception of social class is quite different from the medieval conception of an *estate*, a corporate body of which membership entails differential rights and obligations. Social classes are not corporate entities in this or in any other sense.

Social classes arise because of the functional differentiation, established in the course of development of the division of labour, between labour, land and stock as factors of production. All means of subsistence derive from the collaborative employment of land, labour and stock, and all revenues derive ultimately from one or other of these factors of production. In the 'early and rude state of society' the same person owned all three factors of production, and so appropriated all three revenues. With the development of the division of labour their ownership becomes differentiated, so that the distinct revenues accrue to different people, thereby defining their different class interests.

The interests of different members of society depend on the ultimate source of their revenues. Because the different forms of revenue are determined differently, the three factors of production which constitute the ultimate sources of all revenues define three differential class interests. However much they may conflict with each other in competition, capitalists, for example, have a common interest as owners of stock in relation to the owners of land and labour. Moreover, because there are ultimately only three sources of revenue in society there are only three social classes. All 'intermediate strata', such as lawyers, priests, or government employees, must ultimately belong to one or other of these classes, depending on the ultimate source of their revenues. It is possible to straddle the classes, as does the independent artisan who is both labourer and owner of stock, but it is not possible to belong to society except through assimilation into its class system, for it is only as a member of a social class that it

Smith's contribution to social theory

is possible to acquire access to a revenue with which to secure the means of subsistence.

Although class interests are defined objectively, the members of those classes may not be aware of their interests, and may not act in accordance with them. The capitalists have an acute awareness of their own interest, since their very survival depends on their paying the closest attention to it. However, as we have seen, their interest is at variance with that of society, and so they seek constantly to deceive the public. The landowners, by contrast, are 'too often defective' in their knowledge of their own (and thus the public) interest.

> That indolence, which is the natural effect of the ease and security of their situation, renders them too often, not only ignorant, but incapable of that application of mind which is necessary in order to foresee and understand the consequences of any public regulation ... The interest of the second order, that of those who live by wages, is as strongly connected with the interest of society as that of the first ... But though the interest of the labourer is strictly connected with that of the society, he is incapable either of comprehending that interest or of understanding its connection with his own (WN, I, pp. 230–2).

The labourer is only heard on particular occasions 'when his clamour is animated, set on, and supported by his employers, not for his, but for their own particular purposes'. It is this ignorance which political economy must dispel.

It is through his theory of class that Smith opened up the possibility of a systematic social science. Earlier students of society, most notably Gregory King, had entertained the idea of social classes, but had not established a rigorous foundation for their class distinctions. King, for example, identified twenty-six ranks of the population, differentiated on the basis of status, which could be classified in turn as belonging to the 'poorest sort', the 'middle sort', and the 'better sort', but the classification had no principled foundation. Political theorists, on the other hand, had approached society more systematically, but had tended to rely on a much more abstract conception of society, attempting to reduce the heterogeneity of statuses and of forms of property in order to establish the common foundation of the polity in the abstract individual.

Smith made it possible to bridge the gap between the empirical and the theoretical approaches to society by making it possible to locate the political theorists' individual within a systematically organised society. He could do this because the systematic distinctions in society no longer depended on inherent differences in personal status, but rather on the material basis on which the individual participated in society, although he still recognised the existence of gradations of rank and status. Thus social differentiation was reconciled with the uniformity of human nature that had become the foundation of liberal political theory and continued to underlie the materialism of classical political economy. Moreover the new theory was able to justify and reconcile both social differentiation and the freedom and security of the individual.

Social and political differentiation was justified on the basis of the differential contributions of land, labour and stock to the product and to the growth of the economy, while the freedom and security of the individual was justified by the need to give the individual the means and incentive to pursue her own ends in order to contribute to the betterment of society. Thus the theory of class, far from compromising the individualism of liberal theory, makes it possible to rest the latter on a much more concrete foundation. Because it is possible to explore much more systematically the participation of the individual in society, it is possible to provide a defence of liberalism no longer solely on the basis of claims about human nature but more practically in terms of the material benefits to which a liberal regime will give rise.

In locating the individual socially and historically Smith opened the way to an empirical social science, and his lead was soon followed in Scotland by Adam Ferguson and John Millar. However Smith's approach continued to harbour fundamental weaknesses that also marked the work of the other members of the Scottish Historical School. Despite its apparent concreteness Smith's theory still rests on the speculative definition of a 'natural' order of society against which real societies and real history are measured. Smith was not really concerned with how particular societies actually work, but was much more concerned with how the ideal society would work, in order that he could measure his own and other societies against that ideal. This focus explains Smith's failure, on the one hand, to offer any adequate account of the relationships between the fundamental classes of society and, on the other, his failure to reconcile his materialism with any adequate conception of history.

The failure to provide an adequate account of the relationships between the fundamental classes of society rests on the absence of any coherent theory of value, not in the narrow technical sense of a standard of price, but in the more fundamental sense of a theory that can account for the revenues of the different classes of society. Smith related wages, profits and rent to labour, stock and land, but he had no adequate theory of the relations between each of the terms. This weakness is not only of economic importance, for wages, profit and rent are not simply economic categories. More fundamentally they determine the interests of, and the relations between, the fundamental classes of society and, arising out of these interests and social relations, they determine the form of government and the moral sentiments appropriate to the society. They determine not only the pattern of economic development, but also the moral, political and intellectual development of society. The absence of a coherent theory of value means that Smith's entire social theory is ultimately based on anecdote and assertion.

The weakness of Smith's theory of value could be remedied within the framework of his social theory, and indeed the history of economics is, as we shall see, primarily the history of the attempt to remedy this weakness. However the lack of an adequate conception of history was a more serious deficiency, one which was not unique to Smith, but which derived from the theoretical perspectives of the Enlightenment on which he drew, and which define the character and limits of liberal social thought.

The limits of Enlightenment

As we have seen, the fundamental concepts of the Enlightenment were those of Reason and Nature. However Nature appeared in a dual guise. On the one hand, there was the world of 'external' Nature, whose Laws could be known but could not be modified by human intervention. On the other hand, there was the world of 'internal' Nature, of human impulses, passions, and emotions, which could be modified by their subordination to the human intellect, so that human morals, conduct and institutions could be rationally adapted to human aspirations, subject to the constraints imposed by the immutable world of external Nature. The dividing line between 'internal' and 'external' Nature marks the limits of Reason. Those human institutions are rational which are based on the mastery of 'internal' Nature, within the limits of the constraints of 'external' Nature. These limits mean that the world which results is not the best of all *conceivable* worlds, but it is the best of all *possible* worlds.

The Enlightenment made Reason its watchword. However reason was not an invention of the Enlightenment: previous philosophies had been equally committed to rational argument. What distinguished the Enlightenment was the conception of the world to which reason should be applied. It is not so much its commitment to rational criticism which distinguishes the thought of the Enlightenment, but rather its dualistic conception of Nature, which defines the possibilities and limits of rational criticism in radically distinguishing 'internal' from 'external' Nature, Subject from Object, Mind from Matter. The dividing line between subject and object, between 'internal' and 'external' Nature, between the mutable and the immutable, between the 'conceivable' and the 'possible', is the basis of Enlightenment thought, and presented that thought with its central philosophical problem, that of providing a rational foundation for its conception of the world. For empiricism this conception of the world was impressed on Reason by the unmediated experience of the externality of Nature. However rationalism insisted that concepts cannot derive from immediate experience, but can only be imposed on experience by Reason. In either case 'enlightenment' consists in laying bare the truths imposed on immediate experience, whether by Nature or Reason (or both), by analytically stripping that experience of the supervening layers of myth and superstition.

Both rationalism and empiricism remained transcendental philosophies, unable to provide a rational foundation for the Enlightenment's view of the world because each had to postulate an unknowable Nature or Reason as the condition of experience of that world. Hegel sought to overcome this dilemma by locating Reason historically, so that the Enlightenment view of the world is not imposed on human experience by an external Nature or an external Reason, but is one which has been constructed by the historical development of Reason, through its progressive mastery of 'internal' Nature, as it displaces the superstition which attributes a 'supernatural' origin to human institutions. History can still only be understood retrospectively, from the vantage point of a Reason which stands outside the historical process, but Hegel's historicist perspective can at least account for the fact that Reason only emerges to human consciousness at the end of History.

The implication of all these philosophies, made explicit by Hegel, is that the concrete human understanding of history is always provisional, confined within the limits of the historical achievements of Reason, limits expressed in the historically developed conceptions of the distinction between 'external' and 'internal' nature, between 'matter' and 'spirit', between 'object' and 'subject'. The critical power of rational thought depends on its being aware of its provisional character as an historical product. However Enlightenment thought abandoned its critical project at just this point, representing its own reason not as an historical product, the intellectual expression of a particular stage of human development, but as Reason itself, the creative power and culmination of History. In so doing it presented bourgeois thought, and the bourgeois society depicted as rational by that thought, as the culmination of the self-realisation of Reason. Thus Enlightenment thought does not escape from the superstition which it sought to surpass, for like its predecessors it attributes a 'supernatural' origin to human institutions, which are not explained as the concrete result of human practical activity, but as the product of a transcendent Reason.

In its idealist versions the metaphysical character of this Philosophy of History is plain to see. However Smith's materialist conception of history is no less metaphysical in 'naturalising' the progress of Reason by attributing it to the advance of the division of labour. Reason for Smith is not a transcendental principle, but a human faculty. However, ignorance and immoderate self-love are barriers to the realisation of this faculty, barriers which are overcome as the development of the division of labour leads to the formation of the socially beneficial 'moral sentiments' of moderated self-love, and a growing awareness of the benefits of specialisation. It is the self-evident rationality of the division of labour, and of the associated social institutions of capitalist society, which underlies the historical process. It is the natural foundations of these institutions which places them on the side of immutable 'external' Nature to which Reason must conform. It is this 'naturalisation' of bourgeois social institutions which constitutes Smith's theory, for all its strengths, as bourgeois.

The rationality of the social institutions of capitalist society is determined by their rational conformity to the natural laws of production, distribution and exchange. Smith's account of history is the story of the self-realisation of this rationality. This means that for Smith human institutions can have only one of two origins: either they correspond to the order of reason, or they are the results of misguided and misdirected human intervention. History is the study of the barriers to progress thrown up by the abuse of power motivated by pride, greed, vanity, prejudice and ignorance. This history has a certain rationale, in that the unsavoury characters who litter its pages were formed primarily by the circumstances of their material existence, but the more fundamental rationality of history lies outside history in the natural advance of the division of labour, accumulation of stock and improvement in the productive powers of labour. Capitalism marks the end of this history not because it abolishes want, or brings production under human control, but because it marks the limits of human perfectibility as the advance of Reason comes up against the constraints imposed by the immutability of Nature.

> Economists have a singular method of procedure. There are only two kinds of institutions for them, artificial and natural. The institutions of feudalism are artificial institutions, those of the bourgeoisie are natural institutions ... the relations of bourgeois production ... therefore are themselves natural laws independent of the influence of time. They are eternal laws which must always govern society. Thus there has been history, but there is no longer any (Marx, PP, p. 116).

Smith's conception of history as the self-realisation of reason rests on his naturalistic conception of capitalist social relations of production. The foundation of this naturalistic conception of bourgeois society lies in his account of the formation of revenues, which is the basis of his theory of class. Smith did not account for the formation of revenues as a social process, appropriate to a particular form of society. Instead he referred these revenues back to a natural origin. Thus wages were referred back to the physiological subsistence requirements of the worker. Rent was determined by the natural productivity of land and profit was, at least implicitly, related to the productive powers inherent in the forces of nature, including the division of labour, set in motion by stock. Thus the formation of wages, rent and profit could be considered independently of the form of society since their 'natural' rates correspond to the natural properties of the universal categories of labour, land and stock. The system of *natural liberty*, which is supposed to be the most conducive to social progress, is that in which, within the framework of justice that protects the 'sacred and inviolable' rights of property, the natural order of society can assert itself for the benefit of humankind.

Since this order of society is so obviously natural, rational and ideal, any interference with this order can only be seen as unnatural, irrational and pernicious. Smith could not recognise that different modes of subsistence can give rise to different social relations; indeed he could not recognise that the relations between the classes are *social* relations at all, for class membership is defined exclusively by the *property relation* between the individual and the factor of production which constitutes her revenue source. He had, therefore, no conception of history as the history of social relations in a continuous process of change. History begins with 'the accumulation of stock and the appropriation of the land' and it ends with 'the system of natural liberty'. Between the two is merely the progressive advance of the division of labour, checked from time to time by the vices and ignorance to which man, in his imperfection, is heir.

Ricardo's completion of the system

The technical weaknesses of Smith's theory were no barrier to its political and ideological success. *The Wealth of Nations* was, after all, a political tract as much as a work of science, and it was one that so accorded with the spirit of the times that it was greeted largely uncritically by those favourable to Smith's point of view.[5] Smith's work was not universally accepted, nor did it immediately supplant all other works of political economy. For example, David Hume offered a much more sophisticated theory of money and a correspondingly more powerful critique of mercantilism. However, Smith's work immediately came to dominate political-economic thought and continued to do so for decades to come. Moreover Smith's work had an impact that went far beyond the policy-oriented debates of political economy, providing a framework that was taken up by social theorists and philosophers throughout Europe, as a point of reference if not a direct inspiration, to the extent that the specifically Smithian origins of the framework were soon lost to view.

The technical weaknesses of Smith's system only began to become apparent when his sanguine assumptions about the natural harmony of class interests came to be challenged politically, so reopening consideration of the basis of class relations. The question of the relation between the fundamental classes of society was reopened

---

[5] I have discussed the the role of political economy as a political ideology at length in Clarke, 1988, Chapters 2 and 3.

in Britain by consideration of the economic and social dislocation precipitated by the Napoleonic Wars. The Wars had been a sharp increase in the price of grain, and so of agricultural rents, at the expense of wages and profits, and were followed by a serious recession. Although the War was not the only source of strain in a period of rapid capitalist expansion, the increased price of grain created real hardship for large sections of the population and, even if it was not the cause, could easily be made the scapegoat for successive waves of working class radicalism. Moreover, the price of grain, inflated by the Corn and Poor Laws and by the debasement of the coinage, on top of a heavy burden of taxation, could easily be blamed for the recession through its impact on profits. Thus widespread grievances surrounding the price of corn, monetary policy, the Corn Laws, the Poor Laws and the burden of taxation directed attention to the impact of economic policy on the level of wages and profits, and so on the distribution of the product among the component classes of society.

Consideration of these questions of economic policy was not simply an economic concern. In France, failure to deal adequately with similar grievances had precipitated a revolution, and radical agitation in Britain was sufficient to make the threat real at home. Thus the point at issue was that of the proper organisation of society, and particularly of the relations between the classes, and this had fundamental constitutional and political as well as economic significance. Thus questions were raised that Smith's system could not answer. It fell to David Ricardo to bring the classical system to completion.

Ricardo's starting point in his *Principles of Political Economy and Taxation* was to observe the inadequacy of the work of his predecessors 'respecting the natural course of rent, profit and wages', identifying the determination of the 'laws which regulate this distribution' as the 'principal problem in Political Economy' (Ricardo, 1971, p. 49). Although Ricardo also modified the Smithian theory of money and of foreign trade, his major contribution to political economy as a theory of society was in addressing this problem, and in his realisation that the key to the solution of the problem lay in the theory of value.

Ricardo took as his starting point the embodied labour theory of value, according to which the value of a commodity corresponded to the amount of time taken to produce it. The great advantage of such a theory for Ricardo's purpose was that the value of a commodity was given independently of the determination of wages, profit and

Ricardo's completion of the system

rent. Wages, profit and rent could then be considered as proportionate shares of a fixed sum of value. Once any two of the revenues were determined, the third would be simply the remainder. For Ricardo it was profit that was residual in this way, so to determine profit he required only adequate theories of wages and of rent.

Ricardo adopted the theory of differential rent already developed by Anderson, West and Malthus. According to this theory rent was determined by the differential fertility of different pieces of land and not, as Smith had thought, by the absolute fertility of the soil. Thus the worst piece of land in use would pay no rent, while rent would arise on more fertile pieces of land in token of the extra profits that could be earned by the farmer because of the greater productivity of the soil. The greater the difference between the productivity of the best and worst land under cultivation, the greater would be the rent. Rent would be determined by the fact that succeeding pieces of land are progressively less fertile.

Wages were determined for Ricardo, as for Smith, by the supply of and demand for labour, gravitating around the 'natural price of labour' which corresponded to the cost of the necessary means of subsistence, a sum which depended, following Malthus, on the 'habits and customs of the people'. Ricardo went further than Smith, however, in offering an explanation for the fact that wages correspond to this subsistence minimum and the basic explanation was again owed to Malthus. According to the Malthusian doctrine, if wages rose above the subsistence minimum, as a result of legislative or charitable intervention or as a result of an increased demand for labour, there would be an increase in population as more affluent workers would marry earlier and have more children and more of these children would survive. This population increase would increase the supply of labour until the wage was forced back to the subsistence minimum. The only way in which the wage could remain above the minimum would be by the demand for labour running permanently ahead of its supply as a result of the rapid accumulation of capital.

This theory clearly only applies in the long run, since the labour supply will take some time to adapt to the change in wages. In the short run a different mechanism, that of the wages-fund, is operative. According to this doctrine the demand for labour was determined by the fund available to capitalists for the payment of wages. An increase in wages would reduce the demand for labour until the natural rate of wages has been restored. The implication of the two doctrines taken together is, of course, to reinforce Adam Smith's conclusion that the demand for labour, and so wages, can only increase as a result of increased capital accumulation. Wages cannot be increased by the Poor Law, by charity, by trade unions or by co-operation. The reactionary implications of the theory at a time of considerable distress among the working class were clear and were especially attractive to politicians whose instinctive response to the problems so caused was repressive rather than reformist.

Having determined the level of wages, and armed with the theory of differential rent, Ricardo was in a position to determine the rate of profit. Rent can be excluded from consideration by considering the situation of the capitalist on the marginal piece of land that bears no rent. The value of the commodity will be determined by the amount of labour embodied in the product of the marginal piece of land. On superior pieces of land less labour will be required to produce an equivalent quantity of product because the land is more productive. Thus the value of commodities is determined by the 'quantity of labour that will suffice for their production ... under the most unfavourable circumstances' (Ricardo, 1971, p. 37), and rent is determined by the difference between this value-determining quantity of labour and the lesser quantity actually bestowed on the product of the more fertile land.

Having excluded rent by focusing on the marginal piece of land, Ricardo identified the share of the product that accrues to labour, that share being determined by the 'natural price' of labour, while the residue accrues to the capitalist as profit. Thus for Ricardo, although rent and wages are determined independently, the fact that the total available for distribution is given meant that he could theorise the dependence of profit on rent and wages, and so the relation between classes, in a way that Smith could not. The function of the 'labour theory of value' in Ricardo's theory is to give conceptual precision to the idea that the national product available for distribution is a given magnitude, limited by the productivity and availability of labour, that is divided up amongst the classes of society. In particular it carries over to the determination of the component parts of the price of the individual commodity the idea that the size of the national product is independent of its distribution.

The independence of production from distribution that underlies Ricardo's theory of value does not carry over into a dynamic context, and Ricardo's main concern was not to study distributive shares for their own sake, but to consider the implications of changes in the pattern of distribution for the subsequent development of production, and the consequent implications of accumulation for the pattern of distribution. Within this dynamic context he was concerned above all with the implications of changes in the price of corn and of the incidence of taxation on the pattern of accumulation.

Ricardo's analysis of accumulation was centred on his account of the impact of accumulation on the rate of profit. As the economy developed and population grew it became increasingly necessary to bring less fertile land into production, so increasing rent and, through the rising cost of corn, wages. Thus the proportion due to capital would decline in the course of accumulation, in the absence of countervailing factors that could only slow the decline, while the capital required for a given level of production would rise with rising costs of production. Thus the rate of profit would decline continuously in the course of accumulation, and the prospect was one of rent absorbing more and more of the net product until eventually the rate of profit fell so low that further investment would cease.

For Ricardo the ultimate barrier to progress was seen not as the monopoly privileges of the large capitalists that boosted profits, but as the declining natural fertility of succeeding portions of land. This natural barrier could not be circumvented, but it was exacerbated by two factors that could be modified. One was the effect of the Corn Laws, which prevented the importation of corn and so kept corn prices high and less fertile land in production. The other was the Poor Law, which inflated the demand for corn and gave an unnatural stimulus to the growth of population, so undermining the positions of both capital and, by slowing accumulation, labour.

Conservatism, radicalism and socialism

Ricardo's theory of value gave classical political economy an analytical rigour and a cutting edge that Smith's formulation lacked. However Ricardo did not supplant Smith as the theorist of liberal capitalism. Ricardo's *Principles* is essentially an extended commentary on *The Wealth of Nations*, lacking the breadth of the latter work and concentrating on its technical deficiencies. This has led to the view of Ricardo as the man who reduced political economy to the status of 'the dismal science'. Thus Marx in his earliest writings condemned 'the cynical Ricardo' for whom 'economic laws blindly rule the world. For Ricardo men are nothing, the product everything' (Marx and Engels, *CW*, 3, pp. 192, 256).

This interpretation of Ricardo is misleading in being much too narrow. The importance of Ricardo's work for his contemporaries and for his classical successors was not primarily that it perfected the analysis of the economic machine, but that it provided an account of the proper regulation of the class relations of his society that was more appropriate to the post-Napoleonic political conflicts than that of Adam Smith. The adherents of classical political economy were not especially impressed by Ricardo's concern for rigour, they were much more impressed by the results that he achieved.

Ricardo modified Smith's analysis most particularly in the status he accorded to the landowner. For Smith the landowner's interest was identified with the general interest, while for Ricardo 'the interest of the landlord is always opposed to the interest of every other class in the community' (Ricardo, 1951, IV, p. 21). Such statements have led to another misleading interpretation of Ricardo that sees him as the radical theorist of the industrial bourgeoisie, arming itself for a decisive struggle with landed property. Such an interpretation considerably overemphasizes Ricardo's radicalism and the distance that separates him from other, and more conservative, political economists from Smith to Malthus and McCulloch.

Ricardo's attack on the landlords was confined to his attack on the Corn Laws and the Old Poor Law. He did not attack landed property as such, indeed he was himself a landed proprietor. For Ricardo rent was determined not by the existence of landed property, but by the differential fertility of the soil, while the barrier to accumulation was not landed property but the niggardliness of nature. It was because rent was spent unproductively that it restrained accumulation, and in this Ricardo simply followed Smith, drawing Smith's conclusion that landed property should bear the brunt of taxation.

Ricardo's analysis stands out from that of all his contemporaries in its rigour, and in the starkness and clarity of his conclusions. However, although Ricardo's analysis eventually prevailed in Britain, it also met with fierce opposition. Rigour was no virtue if it led to unpalatable conclusions. Thus many preferred the vagueness and ambiguity of Smith, Say or Sismondi to the harsh rigour of Ricardo. Nor did Ricardo's attack on the landed class go unchallenged. Malthus defended the landed interest against Ricardo, asserting that the unproductive expenditure of the landed class is a virtue in averting the dangers of over-production, while Sismondi extended the critique to the principles of *laissez faire*. Nevertheless, while these various thinkers differed in the emphasis and detail of their analyses, which led to often very different political conclusions, they all developed their analyses on the common basis of the naturalistic theory of class, within the framework of the materialist philosophy of history, handed down by Smith. Thus, while they may have differed in their assessment of the proper relation between rent and profit, and of the role of the state in regulating that relation, they were in complete and unshakeable agreement that capitalist class relations rest on a rational foundation and they were in complete unanimity as to the proper role of the working class within society. All agreed that the working class should remain subordinate; the issue was to whom should it be subordinated. While Smith had drawn the constitutional conclusion from his analysis that the foundations of a sound constitution lay in the allied interests of the landed gentry and the emerging proletariat, the conclusion could be drawn from Ricardo's work that a sound constitution could only be based on the allied interests of agrarian and industrial capitalists and the proletariat. Thus Ricardianism was turned into a radical weapon in the agitation leading up to the 1832 Reform Bill.

Ricardo's theory could be developed in an even more radical direction that Ricardo himself would never even have contemplated. Although Ricardo established an inverse relation between wages and profits, he did not imagine for one moment that such a relation implied a conflict of interest between capital and labour. Wages were determined by the necessary means of subsistence, and could only rise above this level as a result of the rapid accumulation of capital on the basis of healthy profits. The Malthusian and wages-fund doctrines ensured that any unnatural increase of wages, whether secured directly through trades union agitation or indirectly through poor relief, would inevitably prove self-defeating by stimulating population growth and retarding accumulation. The inverse relation between wages and profit did not refer to an exploitative relation between worker and capitalist, but to the mechanism by which an increase in the price of corn, by raising money wages, eroded profits. However, the labour theory of value could easily be turned from a convenient analytical device into a moral statement about the rights of labour, so turning Ricardo's theory from an apologia into a critique of capitalism. If the worker was entitled to the full fruits of her labour, Ricardo's theory clearly showed that profit represented a deduction from the worker's entitlement. While Ricardian radicalism bound the worker to the capitalist in opposition to the landlord, Ricardian socialism incited the worker to turn on the capitalist too.

Ricardo's theory was not only vulnerable to a socialist re-interpretation. Even in its own terms it provided a very inadequate basis on which to defend capitalism. In abandoning the physiocratic foundations of Smith's theory, Ricardo also abandoned the justification of rent and profit. In Ricardo's system rent and profit no longer corresponded to any real contribution to production. Rent was a deduction from the profit of the farmer that accrued to the landlord as an expression of the declining fertility of the soil that was the greatest barrier to human progress: the landlord benefited from increasing human misery. Profit was a deduction from the product of labour, a simple residue. Insofar as Ricardo defended profit he referred to the reward for the capitalist who had foregone consumption for a period as the reward for waiting, but this defence is not very persuasive in the absence of any analysis that relates the supposed sacrifice of the capitalist to the size of his profit: indeed the greater his sacrifice the faster the rate of profit falls. The idea that profit and rent are deductions from the product of labour could easily be transformed by the emerging socialists into a moral theory that saw profit and rent as unjust deductions made by parasitic landlords and capitalists.

Smith's moral justification of capitalism was based fundamentally on the progressive character of the capitalist system. This too was seriously compromised in Ricardo's account, for Ricardo showed that both land and capital are ultimately barriers to progress. Land acts as a constant drain on profit, directing funds from investment into unproductive expenditure and so slowing accumulation. Capital too acts as a barrier to progress, since investment will only be made in so far as it yields a profit and as profits inevitably fall, investment will be curtailed.

Ricardo's theory thus abandoned any foundation on which capitalism could be justified morally. For Ricardo there was no need to do so: Smith's struggles against the remnants of feudalism had been all but won, even the defence of landed property by writers such as Malthus now taking place within the framework of capitalism. The working class critique of capitalism in the name of a different, co-operative rather than competitive, form of society had not yet become a powerful independent force. Thus for Ricardo the existence of capital, landed property and wage labour was simply an inescapable fact of life, the natural foundation of any developed society. For Ricardo, as for Smith, the self-evident evils of other forms of society flowed 'from bad government, from the insecurity of property, and from a want of education in all ranks of the people'. It was 'essential ... to the cause of good government that the rights of property should be held *sacred*' (Ricardo, 1971, p. 120).

But the socialist movement that began to emerge just as Ricardo was writing was beginning to question not simply the constitutional arrangements of contemporary society, but the sanctity of property and the naturalness of competitive capitalism, generating instead a vision of a society based on property held in common and on co-operation. Once the naturalness of capitalism and the sanctity of property were questioned, Ricardo's theory could be given a radical twist that sharply counterposed the interests of labour to those of both capital and landed property. Capitalism then came to be seen not as a natural, but as an historical form of society, a particular form of society that has not always existed and that is destined to be replaced. This was the direction in which Marx developed the initial insights of the 'Ricardian socialists', to develop a critique not only of political economy, but of the very foundations of liberal social theory. I will examine this critique in the next two chapters.

Meanwhile the rise of an independent working class, and particularly the development of Ricardian socialism at the end of the 1820s, had precipitated an ideological crisis in political economy. Although Ricardo's theory was technically far superior to Adam Smith's, the Ricardian labour theory of value, on which the potentially subversive deduction theory of profit rested, was technically deficient and could easily be abandoned by those who sought to evade the unacceptable conclusions that the socialists began to draw from the Ricardian system.

The technical weakness of Ricardo's theory of value becomes apparent as soon as it is realised that relative prices do not in fact correspond to the amount of labour embodied in different commodities. If the sum of profit earned by a capitalist were equal to the number of labourers employed, multiplied by the unpaid labour of each, the rate of profit would depend on the number of labourers set to work by a particular capital, and the rate of profit on a capital that mobilised a large number of workers and little fixed capital would be higher than that on a capital that employed a large quantity of fixed capital, and so employed relatively few labourers. However, the mobility of capital, fostered by the credit system, means that the rate of profit on different capitals tends to be equalised as capitals flow from the less towards the more profitable outlets. Hence profit is related to the size of capital and not to the number of labourers employed.

Ricardo realised that the employment of fixed capital, and the varying turnover times of different capitals, modified his theory of value in this way, but it did not trouble him because he was interested not in relative prices, but in problems of growth and distribution. Thus he sought to develop an 'invariable measure of value' that would enable him to consider problems of growth and distribution without having to worry about divergences due to differences in the proportions of fixed capital employed. However the 'contradiction' at the heart of the Ricardian theory of value provided a strong lever for those who wished to reject the labour theory of value and the associated deduction theory of profit. Even Ricardo's closest followers, James Mill and McCulloch, modified Ricardo's theory to incorporate the independent contribution to value made by fixed capital, while the 'vulgar economists' abandoned the labour theory altogether, to return to Smith's theory of revenues as the independent component parts of price, an approach which was to be rigorously developed by the marginalist school of economics which emerged in the last quarter of the nineteenth century.

3
Alienated Labour and the Critique of Political Economy

Marx developed his theory of capitalist society through a critique of the theories of classical political economy. However, many features of Marx's work that are commonly identified as its central themes were already commonplace in political economy. Thus Adam Smith had a thoroughgoing 'materialist' conception of history, in which class relations emerge out of the mode of subsistence, the development of these relations is conditioned by the development of the forces of production and the state is introduced to preserve the rights and property of the rich. Ricardo provided a more rigorous analytical foundation for this model and in so doing produced a theory that could easily be interpreted by the Ricardian socialists as a theory not of class harmony, but of class conflict, in which profit derives from the exploitation of the labourer and the development of the forces of production is held back by capital and landed property, just as in feudal society it had been restrained by the political power of landed and mercantile property. Thus Marx relied heavily on Smith and Ricardo in his condemnation of the capitalist system in his *Economic and Philosophical Manuscripts* and *The Poverty of Philosophy*. Clearly what sets Marx apart from the political economists is not simply a 'materialist conception of history' nor a 'class conception of society', for versions of these are already to be found in classical political economy.

According to the dominant interpretations, Marx's theories supposedly integrate the critical historicist perspectives of utopian socialism and of Hegelian idealism with the bourgeois materialism of Feuerbach's philosophy, in the early works, and of political economy, in the works of his maturity. Marx's critique of political economy is then seen as an 'extrinsic' philosophical critique, expressed from the standpoint of 'human nature' in the early theory of alienation, and from the standpoint of the economic interests of the working class in the mature theory of surplus value, so that the development of Marx's critique is seen as a move, for good or ill, from 'philosophy' to 'economics'.[1]

These interpretations can certainly find some textual justification, for Marx borrowed from a wide range of sources, so that his early works, in particular, can easily be dismissed as an eclectic and contradictory mixture of borrowings and original insights. It is also true that the young Marx used the materialism of political economy as a stick with which to beat the idealism of Proudhon and the Young Hegelians, at the same time as using the utopian communism of the latter as the basis of a critique of the 'cynicism' of political economy. However these interpretations isolate Marx's texts from the intellectual and political project which underlies them and gives them their coherence in relation to his work as a whole, whether to dismiss Marx's early work as incoherent and unoriginal, or to appropriate his work for quite different projects. My aim in this chapter is to cut through this confusion, to locate Marx's early works in relation to his overall project. While the *exposition* of Marx's early work in this chapter is close to that of the few commentators who have stuck to Marx's text (see particularly Cornu, 1934; Mészáros, 1970; Arthur, 1986; and the exposition, although not the interpretation, of McLellan, 1970), the *interpretation* is very different from those which dominate the literature.

The assimilation of Marx's works to other projects is not surprising when we remember that the founders of 'Marxism' all came to the works of Marx from quite different intellectual backgrounds, and saw Marx's work as the means of resolving intellectual and political problems which they brought with them. Moreover the publication of Marx's texts was in the hands of his 'orthodox' interpreters (first Kautsky, and then the Communist Party of the Soviet Union), so that those texts which did not endorse the orthodox interpretations were only published in the 1930s, as part of the still (unfinished) project of publishing Marx's complete works, and even then were not widely disseminated. The appearance of these 'subversive' texts did not immediately lead to a re-examination of Marx's work as a whole,

---

[1] The interpretation of Marx's work as the *synthesis* of contending schools of thought derived from Plekhanov, and was shared by Lenin (1913) and Lukács (1971).

but rather to the reinforcement of the orthodox opposition of Marx's youthful romanticism to his mature economism.[2]

The re-interpretation of Marx's work is perfectly legitimate, and indeed is essential if Marx's work is to have a continuing relevance. However the dominant interpretations of Marx's work, far from revitalising Marxism, lose sight of the originality and critical power of Marx's critique of political economy, to reduce Marx to an ideologue of one or another brand of 'utopian' or 'scientific' socialism. But Marx's critique of political economy cannot be reduced to the simple task of reinterpreting the findings of classical political economy from a different class viewpoint, or situating them historically, or criticising them morally, all of which had been done by previous thinkers, let alone to the narrow technical amendment of certain aspects of the labour theory of value. Marx's critique is in fact a total critique in the sense that it is at one and the same time methodological, theoretical and political, attacking the very foundations of classical political economy in attacking the conception of society and of history on which it rests. Moreover it is not only a critique of political economy, it is a critique of liberal social theory in general, and at the same time a critique of the capitalist society which that theory serves to legitimate.

It was really only with the re-emergence of an independent socialist movement in the advanced capitalist countries in the 1960s that the orthodox interpretations of Marx's work began to be questioned. Much of this work of re-interpretation again involved absorbing Marx into contemporary academic debates within economics and sociology, as a means of introducing critical perspectives into a complacent conservativism. But Marx's texts also came to be seriously studied in their own right, and to be translated and published more widely.

---

[2] An important selection from Marx's early writings was published by Mehring in 1902, but the *Contribution to the Critique of Hegel's Philosophy of Right* was first published in 1927, while the *Economic and Philosophical Manuscripts* were only published in a Russian summary in 1929 and in German in 1932. The *Grundrisse* was published in a very limited edition between 1939–41, and only became more widely available in 1953. This did not mean that the early theory of alienated labour was not known. Although little interest was shown in Marx's early works, *The Holy Family*, published in 1845, included a summary of theory of alienated labour as the basis of the critique of private property (See Lenin's *Conspectus* (*CW*, 38, pp. 19–51) for an orthodox interpretation of this text). The origin of theory of commodity fetishism in Feuerbach's critique of religion as human self-alienation was also well-established (Hammacher[1909], quoted Rubin, 1972, pp. 53–5), but only to reinforce the orthodox identification of commodity fetishism with religious alienation as an ideological inversion of a deeper reality.

(Selections from the early writings appeared in 1956 (Bottomore and Rubel, 1956). The *Grundrisse* only appeared in French in 1968 and in English in 1973.) Lost traditions of Marxism (lost because annihilated by Hitler and Stalin), embodying alternative political and ideological perspectives, began to be recovered (Korsch, 1970; Rubin, 1972; Hilferding, 1975; Pannekoek, 1975; Grossman, 1977; Mattick, 1978; Bottomore and Goode, 1978; Smart, 1978; Pashukanis, 1978) and Marx's work restored to the context of his own intellectual and political project, which had long been submerged beneath the polarisation of social democratic reformism and Marxism-Leninism (Colletti, 1972, 1975; Draper, 1977–8; Mattick 1983). It is these developments which have made it possible to recover the intellectual power and revolutionary significance of Marx's critique of political economy and, more generally, of liberal social theory, to resolve this paradox of a critique which is both total, and yet retains so much from what is criticised.

The critique of Hegel's theory of the state

The first phase of Marx's critique of political economy was inaugurated by his *Economic and Philosophical Manuscripts*. However the foundations of this critique were laid in his *Critique of Hegel's Philosophy of Right*.[3]

Hegel's theory of the state starts from the observation that civil society is marked by egoism, by the particularity of individual interests. This raises an immediate problem, for civil society seems to lack any principle of cohesion, it is merely a collection of individuals all pursuing their own ends and none with any immediate interest in the fate of the whole. Within civil society individual existence alone is the goal, while social relations are simply a means. Among all the contending interests of civil society there is no body that can rise above particular interest and represent the general interest of society as a whole. Indeed any such body would be a contradiction in terms, for as a part of civil society it could express only particular interests. The principle of cohesion of society, the expression of the universal

[3] The interpretation of Hegel's work, as of that of Marx, is a matter for continuing debate, which I do not intend to enter here. In his early critique Marx treated Hegel's philosophy as the summation of bourgeois thought. When he returned to Hegel at the end of the 1850s it was to recover the critical power of Hegel's dialectic. In this sense the work of the mature Marx is much more Hegelian than that of the young Marx.

The critique of Hegel's theory of the state

interest of all members of society and of their social character, can, therefore, only be something external to the particular interests of civil society and that something is the state. The state stands above all particular interests as the embodiment of the universal.

It was this principle which guided Hegel's search for the ideal form of the state. The ideal form of the state is the one which most perfectly achieves the dissociation of the universal from the particular. The state will therefore be the embodiment of universality, detached from the particular needs and interests expressed in civil society and so able to act as the disinterested regulator of the whole.

Hegel posed the problem in essentially logical terms, for the ideal form of the state is that form which is the most perfect embodiment of the logical category of universality. Thus Hegel tried to deduce the most perfect form of the state by the application of his dialectical logic. The state so discovered is then the rational, and so ideal, form of the state. It just so happens that the form of the state that Hegel deduced in this way was a modified version of the Prussian state. Universality is personalised in the hereditary monarch and formalised in the constitution. The universality of the state is then mediated with the particularity of civil society through the system of representation.

The starting point of Marx's critique of Hegel is his rejection of the conception of the individual on which Hegel's theory is based. Hegel sought to locate the individual socially and historically. However his solution merely synthesised theories he sought to transcend, in seeing the historical development of the social individual as the outcome of a dialectic between an abstract individuality and an abstract sociability. For Marx the individual is a social animal in a much more fundamental sense than this. For Marx the individual is only a *human* individual within society, so that human individuality is a form of sociability. This does not mean that the individual is simply the creature of society, for Marx rejects the categorical opposition of individual and society. 'Above all we must avoid postulating "society" ... as an abstraction *vis-à-vis* the individual. The individual *is the social being*' (*CW*, 3, p. 299). Hegel's individual is not a real person, but is a philosophical abstraction which destroys that which it seeks to understand by taking away from the real person all those social qualities which make that person a human being.

The other side of the abstraction of the individual from society is the abstraction of society from the individual. For Hegel human sociability is not a property of real human beings, but is an attribute of reason. For Marx, by contrast, neither individuals nor society exist in the abstract. All that exist are concrete human beings, interacting in historically developed social relations, through which they define both their individuality and their sociability. The philosophical categories of 'individual' and 'society' are only the reflection of concrete historical categories, whose relationship can only be understood historically. Thus Marx's critique immediately points away from philosophy, towards the study of historically developed social relations.

Hegel's philosophical inversion of the relation between the abstract and the concrete means that his theory of the state inverts the true relationship between the state and civil society. Universality is imposed on civil society by the state instead of being imposed on the state by civil society. Thus for Hegel the universality of the sovereign and of the constitution derive not from their really expressing the universality of human sociability, but from the logical category of the universal. Having taken away the social qualities of real human beings, Hegel imposed those qualities on them as an attribute of the state. Human nature is then a realisation of the state, itself only the embodiment of logic, instead of the state being a realisation of human nature.

Hegel not only inverted the true relationship between the human individual and her social nature, between civil society and the state, between existence and reason, between the particular and the universal. In doing so he reduced the particular to the universal, existence to reason, and so made the state into a purely formal principle, the expression of the logical category of the universal and not of the real social needs of individual human beings. Thus the universality of the state is purely formal, entirely abstract, and has no relation to the real content of society, human social needs.

Hegel's argument is entirely spurious, for the particular cannot be deduced from the universal without specifying its particularity. 'An explanation which fails to provide the *differentia* is no explanation at all ... the real subjects ... are and remain uncomprehended because their specific nature has not been grasped.' For example, it is impossible logically to deduce hereditary sovereignty from the principle of universality: what Hegel really did was to describe a particular state of affairs, on the one hand, and then assign logical attributes to this state of affairs, on the other. He thus idealised existing reality, in the double sense that he made reality the embodiment of the idea, and in so doing made the world as it actually exists into the only world that could rationally exist. 'Thus empirical reality is accepted as it is; it is even declared to be rational.' This is a travesty of reason, for 'the rational is seen to consist not in the realisation of the reason of the real person but in the realisation of the moments of the abstract concept.' Thus Hegel's theory of the state is an *'uncritical mysticism'* that does not understand the state as the expression of the social quality of human existence, but simply endorses the state as it exists. 'At every point Hegel's political spiritualism can be seen to degenerate into the crassest *materialism*' (Marx, 1975, pp. 67, 63, 84–5, 149, 174).

Hegel's philosophical inversion, that reduces the state to an empty formal abstraction, was not for Marx merely an error of reasoning, for the state that Hegel describes really is only formally universal: the universality expressed by the constitutional state really is empty and abstract, for it does not emerge from the social needs of real human individuals. Thus:

> Hegel should not be blamed for describing the essence of the modern state as it is, but for identifying what is with the *essence of the state*. That the rational is real is *contradicted* by the *irrational reality* which at every point shows itself to be the opposite of what it asserts, and to assert the opposite of what it is (Marx, 1975, p. 127).

Hegel's error is to see the constitutional state as rational. The contradiction comes to a head, both in Hegel's theory of the state and in the constitutional state itself, in the system of representation. The system of representation gives the lie to the claim of the constitutional state to be the embodiment of universality.

The system of representation is the focus of the contradiction inherent in the constitutional state because it mediates between the state and civil society. The representatives can express only particular interests: the mere fact of representation cannot transform these particular interests into universal interests. Thus, if the state is to represent the universal as opposed to the particular interest, the representatives cannot appear as representatives of particular interests but only in their capacity as abstract individuals. Thus, insofar as the state is the expression of the universal interest, it can only be such by ignoring all particular interests, all real human needs. 'This point of view is ... abstract' and 'atomistic' because 'the *political state is an abstraction* from civil society'. Thus if the state is to be a true state, that is a true expression of the *social quality* that defines the human essence and not simply an abstraction that is opposed to real human beings, the separation of the state from civil society must be overcome (Marx, 1975, pp. 145, 78).

The implication of Marx's analysis is that if human social qualities can be expressed only in the abstract and alien form of the constitutional state, this must be because they do not express themselves in civil society. It did not take Marx long to draw out this implication.

From political philosophy to the critique of private property

In looking at Hegel's theory of the state we seem to be a long way from political economy. At first sight Hegel's idea of civil society might seem to have more in common with Hobbes than with Smith, while Smith has a materialist theory of the state, which far from being the embodiment of the principle of universality has a mundane origin in the desire of the rich to protect their property. However, for Marx there was a very close convergence between Smith and Hegel that belies the apparent differences.[4]

Smith and Hegel were both concerned to discover the foundation of society in order to reform their own society so that it would accord with the dictates of reason. Both observed that civil society is based on egoism, albeit moderated for Smith, so that the coherence and unity of society, its inherent harmony, is not immediately apparent. Thus for both Smith and Hegel the rationality of society could only be imposed on society from outside. While Hegel looked to the idea of universality to provide the rational principle of unity, Smith looked for the roots of reason in nature. Thus while Hegel wanted to show the nation state as the self-realisation of the Idea, classical political economy strove to see the capitalist economy as the self-realisation of Nature. While Hegel established the rational necessity of the constitutional state, classical political economy established the natural necessity of the capitalist economy. Both Smith and Hegel thereby abolished society, Hegel absorbing it into an absolute Reason, Smith into an absolute Nature. Thus in each case society is abstracted from humanity and attributed to some external force.

[4] On the relationship between Smith and Hegel see particularly Lukács, 1975; Hyppolite, 1969; Colletti, 1975; Arthur, 1988.

It might seem that there is a world of difference between nature, which is after all something tangible, and Hegel's Idea. But this is not really the case, for, as we saw in the last chapter, Smith's 'nature' is not the tangible reality of nature, it is a pure abstraction, an abstraction in particular from the social relations within which human beings appropriate nature. Thus Smith's 'nature' is as far from the everyday world of nature as Hegel's Idea is from the everyday world of ideas; his 'materialism' is purely abstract, and is ultimately as idealistic as Hegel's philosophy.

Against the common interpretation of Marx as a 'materialist', it is essential to be clear that Marx did not oppose materialism to idealism.[5] Marx, following Hegel, believed that the opposition was a false one, since 'matter' is no less idealist a concept than is the 'idea', so that '*abstract materialism* is the *abstract spiritualism* of matter'. However, Marx rejected Hegel's attempt to overcome the opposition by absorbing nature into reason just as much as he rejected Smith's attempt to absorb reason into nature.

Marx sought to overcome the opposition by focusing on *society* as the mediating term between the 'material' and the 'ideal', but society understood not as yet another abstraction, but as the everyday practical activity of real human beings. It is the divorce of individual from society which underlies the false antitheses of the Enlightenment, in eliminating the mediating term between humanity and nature, between the ideal and the material, between subject and object. Thus in his early works Marx criticised materialism and idealism alike from the standpoint of '*human sensuous activity*, practice ... practical-critical activity ... human society or socialised humanity' (First Thesis on Feuerbach), characterising his own position not as a materialism but variously as a humanistic naturalism, or a naturalistic or real humanism: 'Consistent naturalism or humanism is distinct from both idealism and materialism, and constitutes at the same time the unifying truth of both' (*CW*, 3, p. 336). Similarly Marx rejected the equally

---

[5] The identification of Marxism as a philosophical materialism derives from Plekhanov, and was made the touchstone of orthodoxy by Lenin. In the *German Ideology*, and elsewhere, Marx characterised his starting point as 'materialist', but the term referred not to a philosophical materialism, but to the premise of 'real individuals, their activity and the material conditions under which they live' which can 'be verified in a purely empirical way' (GI, p. 31), a perspective which Marx identified as that of the '*practical* materialist, i.e., the *communist*' (GI, p. 56). Engels typically characterised Marx's work as 'materialist', but in the sense of assimilating it to the movement of modern science, which 'no longer needs any philosophy standing above the other sciences' (Engels, 1962, pp. 39–40).

false antithesis between humanity and nature: '*Society* is the complete unity of man with nature ... the accomplished naturalism of man and the accomplished humanism of nature' (*CW*, 3, p. 298), a formulation which should not be interpreted as proposing 'Society' as the solution to a philosophical problem, but as transforming the problem from a philosophical to a socio-historical one, and so defining a quite different project of investigating the relation between individual and society, and between humanity and nature, within the framework of the historical development of concrete social relations.

Marx's critique of both Smith and Hegel is that their theories are equally idealist in resting on the categorical oppositions of matter and idea, individual and society, humanity and nature, oppositions which Marx argued were empty abstractions, empty because they are concepts which do not correspond to any determinate existence, and so can have no determinate effects. However this is not only a critique of Smith and of Hegel, for these conceptual oppositions are constitutive of bourgeois thought in general, as that has come down from the Enlightenment.

In Hegel's work bourgeois reason finds its summation and its most systematic expression. The great merit of Hegel is that he has pushed bourgeois reason to its limits, so that its speculative foundations stand out starkly in the contradiction between the universal and the particular, which Hegel can only resolve speculatively in the dialectical development of Reason. In exactly the same way Smith, and later Ricardo, recognised the real contradictions between universal human needs and aspirations and the particular social relations of the capitalist system of production, but again resolved these contradictions speculatively, in the dialectical development of Nature. Whether the supra-human force which makes history is called Reason or Nature is neither here nor there. Thus Marx's critique of Hegel can be translated immediately into a critique of political economy because it is a critique of their common ideological foundations. These ideological foundations lie in their attempt to present bourgeois social relations as the culmination of the history of the synthesis of Reason and Nature, and it is precisely this that characterises them as bourgeois. This is why Marx regarded Hegel's philosophy as the culmination and limit of bourgeois thought, and why his critique of Hegel is a critique of the ideological foundations of all forms of bourgeois social thought.

Marx could apply the method developed in the critique of Hegel's abstract spiritualism to the critique of political economy because the theories were two sides of the same coin. Like Hegel, political economy is content to describe the alienated forms of social existence, attributing their social character not to their human origins but to an alien power: on the one hand, the Idea, on the other, Nature.

The origin of this alienation is in both cases the same. Smith and Hegel looked for the key to society outside the individuals who comprise it because the immediate relations between those individuals appear as the antithesis of society. These relations are not truly human social relations because they are based on the opposition of private interests. The focus of Marx's critique is this conception of private interests, which underlies the categorical opposition between individual and society which, for Marx, is the hallmark of bourgeois social thought and the underpinning of bourgeois philosophy.

For Marx the opposition of private interests is not an expression of an atomistic individualism inherent in human nature. Human existence is only possible on the basis of co-operation, so that human interests are necessarily social interests, and human individuals necessarily social individuals. 'Private' interests can therefore only be an expression of the 'privatisation' of socially defined interests.

The opposition of privatised interests is constructed socially, as the individual expression of a *social* institution, the institution of *private property*. It is the *private* appropriation of the means and products of *social* production which constitutes interests as private, exclusive, and opposed. Smith and Hegel, developing Locke's theory of private property, conceal the social foundations of private property in conceiving of private property as ultimately deriving from a primitive proprietorial relation of the individual to her own body and, by immediate extension, to the things produced by the exercise of her physical and mental powers. It is only by uncovering the origins of private property in human social activity that the alienation expressed by Hegel's idealism and by Smith's materialism can be traced back to its source. The critique of private property provides the key to the critique both of political economy and of Hegelian philosophy.[6]

---

[6] But what would old Hegel say if he learned, on the one hand that the word "Allgemeine" [the General] in German and Nordic means only "common land", and that the word "Sundre, Besondre" [the Particular] only meant the particular owner who had split away from the common land? Then, dammit, all the logical categories would proceed from "our intercourse" (Letter to Engels, 25th March, 1868).

Proudhon, Engels and the critique of political economy

In turning to political economy Marx was not simply trying to solve a philosophical riddle. His critique of political economy flowed from the same political inspiration that led him to the critique of Hegel's theory of the state. However this political inspiration had acquired a new dimension. In the *Introduction to the Critique of Hegel's Philosophy of Right*, written after the *Critique* itself, Marx concluded that human liberation was not a philosophical task, but could only be achieved when philosophy became a 'material force', when 'theoretical needs' correspond to 'practical needs'. The theoretical need identified in the critique of Hegel was for the universal interest to conquer all particular interests in civil society. The 'practical need' that corresponds to this is the need of a 'universal class', a class whose interest is opposed to all particular class interests, 'a class of civil society that is not a class of civil society, an estate which is the dissolution of all estates', and this class is the proletariat. Thus the proletariat, in liberating itself, liberates all humanity (*CW*, 3, pp. 155, 182–3, 186).

This philosophical conclusion coincided with Marx's discovery of, and involvement in, the real movement of the working class and it was through this involvement that Marx came upon political economy. Within the working-class movement a critique of political economy was already emerging that showed some similarity to the form of critique that Marx had applied to Hegel. In France Proudhon, in *What is Property?* (1840), had identified private property as the contradictory foundation of political economy. For Proudhon, political economy took private property for granted and tried to establish the rationality of a society based on private property. However at every stage political economy itself shows that private property undermines economic rationality by introducing inequality and monopoly. Thus private property undermines the equality of the wage bargain and, indeed, of all exchange relations. Proudhon argued that there is no moral or practical justification for this inequality and concluded that a rational and just society could only be based on the establishment of equality by the equalisation of property.

The limitations of Proudhon's approach for Marx were that he isolated only one element of political economy for criticism, failing to recognise the connection between private property and the categories of wage-labour, exchange, value, price, money, etc. Therefore Proudhon wanted to abolish private property without abolishing the society which was based on it. The equalisation of property remains a form of property, a form, moreover, which is inconsistent with the continued existence of such phenomena as wage-labour and exchange. Thus, as Marx wrote in *The Holy Family* (1844), 'Proudhon makes a critical investigation — the first resolute, pitiless, and at the same time scientific investigation — of the foundation of political economy, *private property*', but it is still 'under the influence of the premises of the science it is fighting against'. Thus 'Proudhon's treatise ... is the criticism of *political economy* from the standpoint of political economy' (Marx, 1956, pp. 46, 45).

The work that first went beyond Proudhon in attempting to develop the critique of private property into a critique of political economy, and which had a dramatic impact on Marx's own thought, was Engels's *Outlines of a Critique of Political Economy* (1843–4). Engels, following Proudhon, identified private property as the uncriticised premise of political economy. The development of political economy has revealed ever more clearly the consequences of private property, but 'it did not occur to economics to question the *validity of private property*'. Engels therefore sought to criticise this premise 'from a purely human, universal basis'.

Although Engels took up Proudhon's starting point, he developed a much more radical analysis than that of Proudhon, in trying to show not simply the evils to which private property gives rise *within* an economy based on exchange, but in trying to show how private property underlies the entire economic system. Engels argued that 'the immediate consequence of private property is *trade*', which is immediately and necessarily antagonistic, based on 'diametrically opposed interests' and giving rise to 'mutual mistrust'. Thus although Smith preached the humanity of trade in the mutual benefits arising out of peaceful trade, the bases of trade remain egoism and distrust, and morality is subordinated to self-interest.

From trade emerges the category of *value*, which is determined under the rule of private property by the conflict between producers and consumers, competition being the only way of relating utility to costs. The economists' concept of value tries to conceal the dependence of the category on private property by isolating value from exchange, reducing it either to production costs or to subjective utility, whereas the concept has no meaning in abstraction from the relation between the two in exchange. In the same way the Ricardian theory of rent claims that rent derives from differences in the productivity of the soil, whereas it is in fact determined by 'the relation between the productivity of the land, the natural side ... and the human side, competition'.

The division between capital and labour likewise derives from private property, for capital is merely stored up labour, the two being reunited within production only to be divided with the appropriation of the product. Capital is further divided, again on the basis of private property, into capital and profit, and profit splits into interest and profit proper. Moreover the distribution of the product among these categories is not carried out according to some 'inherent standard; it is an entirely alien, and, with regard to them, fortuitous standard, that decides — competition, the cunning right of the stronger'.

Engels's conclusion was that all the categories of political economy presuppose competition and therefore exchange and private property. Private property splits 'production into two opposing sides — the natural and the human sides' as the land is appropriated by landowners. Human activity itself is divided between capital and labour, which confront one another antagonistically. Within these categories too, private property introduces fragmentation, setting capitalist against capitalist and worker against worker. 'In this discord ... is consummated the immorality of mankind's condition hitherto; and this consummation is competition' (*CW*, 3, pp. 419, 421, 422, 429, 431, 432).

Engels finally returned to the standpoint of political economy, showing that the 'contradictions' of the competitive society arose out of competition, and so private property: the growth of monopoly, the disproportions between supply and demand, the coexistence of overwork and unemployment, the centralisation of property and the impoverishment of the worker are all the results of the system of competition based on private property. In abstracting from competition the different schools of political economy abstract from the private property on which the system is based, and conceal the roots of the contradictions inherent in the system. These contradictions are then either denied, or attributed to external natural forces, as in the 'law of population'.

Alienated labour and the critique of capitalism

Marx's *Economic and Philosophical Manuscripts* (1844) transformed Engels's critique from the perspective opened up by Marx in his critique of Hegel. Engels had shown how the categories of political economy and the realities to which they correspond presuppose competition and so private property, but he had not established the foundations of private property by showing how private property emerges out of human social existence. It is this critical task that Marx undertook. The key to this undertaking was the relationship between private property and exchange. For Proudhon private property subverted the essential equality of exchange. For Engels private property and exchange were inseparable, but property remained the foundation of exchange. Marx inverted the relationship between the two, arguing that *social relations of exchange are the basis of modern private property*. This is the significance of Marx's famous theory of alienated labour.

The interpretation of Marx's theory of alienation is not made easy by the fact that the *Manuscripts* do not represent a completed work, but a series of notebooks in which Marx developed his own ideas alongside his earliest readings in political economy.[7] Moreover only the last four pages of the 43-page second manuscript, which immediately follows the first sketches of the theory of alienated labour at the end of the first manuscript, survive. There is therefore ample scope for creative interpretation of the theory of alienated labour. Nevertheless, when this theory is set firmly in the context of Marx's developing critique of political economy, its fundamental significance becomes clear.

The bulk of the first *Manuscript* is confused, unoriginal, and based on a very limited acquaintance with political economy. In this part of the work Marx adopts 'the standpoint of the political economist' and does not advance significantly beyond Proudhon in pointing out, through extensive quotation from the political economists, the negative implications of the market society for the worker, whom political economy treats only as a 'commodity', 'it does not consider him when he is not working, as a human being' (*CW*, 3, pp. 239, 241). Marx also noted the power of capital over labour; the fact that it is only competition that defends society against the capitalists while competition necessarily gives way to monopoly through the concentration of capital; and Marx took great pleasure in attacking Smith's (and Hegel's) defence of landed property.

---

[7] On Marx's reading see Evans, 1984, Hennings, 1985. On the influences on Engels see Claes, 1984.

It was in the last section of the first manuscript that Marx turned from political economy to its critique, and the basis of the critique is the alienation of labour. Within a system of commodity production 'the worker becomes all the poorer the more wealth he produces ...Labour produces not only commodities: it produces itself and the worker as a *commodity*'. The reason for this is that the product of labour has become '*something alien* ...a *power independent* of the producer'. The more the worker produces, the greater the power that confronts her. This alienation of the product of labour is the expression of the alienated form of the activity of labour, something which political economy conceals because it does not look at 'the direct relationship between the worker (labour) and production' (*CW*, 3, pp. 271–3).

The activity of labour is alienated in the sense that 'it is ...not the satisfaction of a need; it is merely a *means* to satisfy needs external to it'. It is, therefore, '*forced labour* ...not his own, but someone else's'. This is labour as '*self-estrangement*'. From this follows the 'estrangement of the *thing*', that is, from nature as the product and as the object of production (*CW*, 3, pp. 274–5). Since labour does not flow from the needs of the individual it seems to be imposed by nature, in the form both of the object on which the labourer works, and of the means of subsistence that impose the need to labour. Moreover labour as naturally imposed individual labour is estranged from the species, from participation in the conscious human transformation of the world of nature and from conscious collaboration with other human beings.

This first attempt to apply theory of alienation, which Marx derived from Feuerbach and Moses Hess, to the critique of political economy is familiar, and has been the focus of almost all the commentaries on Marx's *Manuscripts*. Marx condemns alienated labour from the perspective of the needs of the labourer as an individual and as a member of the human species. It is therefore very easy to interpret the theory of alienated labour as a direct development of the ideas of Feuerbach and Hess, proposing an 'anthropology of labour' which criticises capitalism from the perspective of a particular conception of human nature, expressed in human needs.

The modern versions of this interpretation derive from Lukács's theory of reification, written before the publication of the *Manuscripts*, according to which the dehumanisation of 'rationalised' labour is confronted by the human aspirations deriving from the manual worker's 'humanity and his soul' (HCC, p. 172) (an argument which Lukács later rejected as a 'purely metaphysical construct' (HCC, p. xxiii)). This idea was developed by Marcuse in his early review of the *Economic and Philosophical Manuscripts* (Marcuse, 1932, see also Marcuse, 1973), which Marcuse assimilated to Heidegger's existential anthropology. Marcuse's interpretation of Marx was rapidly taken up by existentialist writers as the basis of a 'humanistic' interpretation of Marx, which became very popular in the 1950s and 1960s, although since Marcuse such an interpretation has become increasingly detached from Marx's text, turning more to Nietzsche and Kierkegaard as sources of inspiration. For Heideggerians, from Marcuse to Sartre, the soul is found in the remaining traces of authenticity, whether rooted in the unconscious, in the human will, in marginalised strata, or in the remoter realms of culture, which have thus far evaded the embrace of reification.[8] More mundane developments of theory insisted that the evaluation of the subjective experience of the labourer is not a metaphysical but an empirical question, an observation which leads directly into social psychological interpretations of the theory of alienation (Blauner, 1964; Naville, 1957).

Marcuse's anthropological interpretation of Marx's early works was extremely influential not only amongst those who shared his existentialist perspective, but also amongst many of the critics of humanistic Marxism, who were led to reject Marx's early works as the products of an adolescent 'romantic individualism', or, even worse, of an Hegelian 'essentialism', to be replaced by the 'materialism' which underpinned the work of the mature Marx (Feuer, 1962; Althusser, 1969). Horkheimer, Adorno and Habermas shared this interpretation, rejecting both the supposed anthropological perspective of the early Marx and the supposed 'positivism' of his mature works.

The main problem which this interpretation faces is that Marx's critique of Feuerbach lay precisely in his rejection of any such essentialist anthropology, on the grounds that the human 'essence' is developed historically and is not to be found in the individual psyche, underpinning a romantic yearning for a 'truer' form of society, but in the form of historically developed social relations, however alienated

---

[8] An alternative interpretation of alienation combines Weber not with Nietzsche or Heidegger but with Husserl, seeing the recovery of intentionality as the means to overcome alienation. Thus John O'Neill argues that 'social institutions become instruments of estrangement only when they fail to achieve purposes which the participants intended. Estrangement is primarily a phenomenon of the ideological superstructure' (O'Neill, 1982, p. 74), which he goes on to attribute to a conflict between the 'economic means-value system' and the 'end-value system'.

may be the form in which they appear. As Marx noted in the sixth of his *Theses on Feuerbach*, 'the human essence is no abstraction inherent in each single individual. In its reality it is the ensemble of the social relations'. Marcuse attempted to overcome this objection by locating the human essence historically. However this attempt could not but fail, for Marcuse's human 'nature' is only a critical force to the extent that it is *not* subsumed in the historical process. Thus Marcuse's anthropology rests on the transformative power of human potentialities and human needs which are unfulfilled by capitalism, and which stand outside history. In sharp contrast to Marcuse's anthropological interpretation, Marx saw the unfulfilled human needs and aspirations which lead to the overthrow of capitalism not as qualities hidden in the human soul, but as the creation of capitalism. For Marx capitalism creates the means and possibility of liberating humanity from the rule of natural necessity, while making humanity the slave to a social necessity imposed through the alienated form of the rule of the commodity. There were certainly elements of romanticism in the young Marx's critique of alienated labour, but even in his early works Marx focussed as much on the evils of overwork, of poverty and of exploitation as on the spiritual degradation of the labourer.

Marx's first *Manuscript* offers a powerful description of the dehumanisation of labour under capitalism, but his brief discussion of alienation at the end of the manuscript is a slender basis for an interpretation of Marx which contradicts almost everything else he wrote! Marx's description of alienation still begged the fundamental question, which was to get behind this alienation, to understand its foundations.

Alienated labour and the critique of private property

The power of alienated labour cannot be a power inherent in the thing that is alienated. Ultimately 'only man himself can be this alien power over man' (*CW*, 3, p. 278). Thus the power of alienated labour, its *alien* as opposed to its purely *objective* character, derives from the fact that it expresses a particular form of social relationship.

It is at this point in his analysis, at the very end of the first manuscript, that Marx takes the decisive step, one which has bewildered most of those commentators who have not simply passed it by. Thus far Marx has *described* the forms of alienated labour characteristic of the capitalist mode of production. He now seems

Alienated labour and the critique of private property

to be moving smoothly to an *explanation* of alienated labour as the *consequence* of private property. In alienated labour a social relation between people appears in the form of the subordination of a person to a thing. This social relation is the relation of private property, in which the capitalist appropriates the means of production as his private property, so permitting him to subordinate the labourer to his own will (Bell, 1959, pp. 933–952; Schacht, 1971, p. 107; Oakley, 1984, pp. 63, 66). Thus we find again the 'hidden premise' of political economy, already identified by Proudhon and by Engels.

This explanation would be entirely in accord with the orthodox interpretation of Marx's 'historical materialism', for which capitalist social relations are defined by the private ownership of the means of production, which implies that property relations are prior to production relations (and which also has the very embarrassing implication that 'juridical relations' are prior to 'economic relations' (Plamenatz, 1954, Chap. 2; Cohen, 1970)) However this is not the step that Marx takes. He is quite clear that alienated labour is the *cause* and not the consequence of private property. Before labour can be appropriated in the form of property it must *first* take the form of alienated labour. Thus the proprietorial relation between a person and a thing expresses a more fundamental social relation between people. The legal form of private property presupposes the social relation of alienated labour:

> Thus through estranged labour man ...creates the domination of the person who does not produce over production and over the product ...The relationship of the worker to labour creates the relation to it of the capitalist ...*Private property* is thus the product, the result, the necessary consequence, of *alienated labour* (*CW*, 3, p. 279).

Marx recognised that this argument may seem paradoxical, but he was unequivocal:

> True, it is as a result of the *movement of private property* that we have obtained the concept of *alienated labour* (of *alienated life*) in political economy. But analysis of this concept shows that though private property appears to be the reason, the cause of alienated labour, it is rather its consequence ...Later this relationship becomes reciprocal (*CW*, 3, pp. 279–80).

Marx's argument has certainly seemed paradoxical to his orthodox readers. Feuerlicht notes that 'one of the most conspicuous contradictions lies in the fact that young Marx considers private property sometimes as the cause and sometimes as the effect or symptom of alienation' (1971, p. 130). Dick Howard tells us that in the passage quoted above Marx recognises that the argument 'seems to be circular' (1972, p. 155). John Elliott follows David McLellan (1970, p. 174) in telling us that Marx's argument is 'generally recognised as a *petitio principii*', insisting that alienated labour and private property enjoy a mutual and indissoluble relationship, Marx here proposing a 'reciprocal influence, demonstrating, as in so many other instances, his commitment to mutual inner-penetration (sic) rather than linear causation as his basic methodological perspective' (Elliott, 1979, p. 332). If this were the case 'alienated labour' and 'private property' would be the same thing, and Marx's theory would be vacuous, as many of his critics have claimed. However Marx was quite clear what kind of relationship he was proposing, concatenating the terms 'reason', 'cause', 'consequence', 'product', 'result', 'necessary consequence' to drum into the heads of his readers that he is talking about causal relationships, not the mish-mash of 'mutual inner-penetration'.

Many commentators rely on Marx's supposed postulation of 'dialectical' relations of mutual interdependence to explain away what Marx actually says, and suggest that Marx later reversed the position he took in the *Manuscripts*. Ernest Mandel relates alienation in Marx's early works to the 'constant interaction between commodity production, division of labour, and private property' (1971, p. 33) and to the division of society into classes (1971, pp. 160, 181), arguing that the mature Marx finally settled on private property as the foundation of alienation. Mandel follows Jahn (1957) in explaining away the quoted passage by arguing that 'Marx is not dealing here with the problem of the *historical origins* of private property, but rather with the problem of its nature, and of how it reappears daily in a mode of production based on alienated labour' (Mandel, 1971, p. 161n), ignoring the fact that it is precisely the 'nature' of private property that is in question. Maurice Dobb similarly argues that 'the treatment of alienation is double-sided, and it is a mere question of emphasis as to whether commodity production *per se* or appropriation of the product by the capitalist is regarded as the crux of the matter. Later the emphasis is undoubtedly shifted to the latter' (Introduction to Marx, 1971, p. 8). The emphasis is undoubtedly not shifted to the latter. In *Capital*, Vol. I, which begins with the analysis of the commodity, Marx is quite clear that private property is only the expression of the alienated form of exchange of the products of labour as commodities. The property relation 'whose form is the contract ...is a relation between two wills which mirrors the economic relation ...Here the two persons exist for one another merely as representatives, and hence owners, of commodities' (*Capital*, Vol. 1, pp. 178–9).

Mészáros tries to resolve the paradox by distinguishing the historical origins of alienation from its subsequent reproduction. He explains the alienation of labour in terms of a primitive division between 'private property and its owner' and 'wage labour and the worker', arguing that such 'institutionalised second order mediations' as 'exchange, money, etc.' are 'already implied' in this primitive division (Mészáros, 1970, pp. 108–9). This leads him into an historical account of the development of alienation on the basis of the historical development of private property. Thus he refers to a 'three-way interaction' between the division of labour, exchange and private property (Mészáros, 1970, p. 143), although he goes on to recognise that 'private property is considered only as the *product*, the necessary consequence of alienated labour' because it presupposes that the worker is 'alienating himself from himself in the very *act of production*' (Mészáros, 1970, p. 147). However, such an act presupposes the social relations of alienated labour, which brings us full circle. Mészáros fails to resolve the problem because he interprets Marx within an Hegelian perspective which views society as a self-reproducing totality, driven forward by the dialectical development of the contradiction between wage labour and private property, i.e. *within* the alienated forms of labour, which makes it impossible for him to see anything but mutual dependence between alienated labour and private property.

Chris Arthur, in his rigorous commentary on the *Manuscripts*, follows Mészáros in seeing private property as historically prior to alienated labour, while arguing that 'study of the movement of private property itself leads Marx to conclude that in its reciprocal relationship with labour it is ultimately best understood as the consequence rather than the cause of alienated labour. The state of estrangement between labour and private property is developed, historically and conceptually, to a process of *active alienation of labour from itself*' (Arthur, 1986, p. 25). Like Mészáros, Arthur does not explain *why* the relationship between alienated labour and private property 'is ultimately best understood as the consequence of alienated labour'. Certainly estrangement results from the 'active alienation of labour from itself', but for Arthur it seems that this active alienation in turn results from private property. Mészáros and Arthur do not penetrate beneath the alienated form of labour to see the fundamental contradiction between labour, as the active agent of production, and its alienated (commodity) form which explains both its foundation and the possibility of its overcoming.

Although Marx's theory of alienated labour has been wilfully or unwilfully misinterpreted by almost all the commentators, it is the very foundation not only of his critique of political economy and of Hegel's philosophy, but also of his critique of the presuppositions of liberal social thought in general. It was this insight which, Marx later acknowledged, 'served as a guiding thread for my studies' (Marx, 1968, p. 181). Private property is the hidden presupposition of liberal social thought because it is private property that constitutes the abstract individuality of the bourgeois subject, the individual having been isolated from society through her *private appropriation* of the conditions and products of her *social* existence.

If Marx's critique had remained a critique on the basis of private property, as the orthodox interpretations would have it, it would have remained, like that of Proudhon, a critique on the basis of political economy and, more generally, within the limits of bourgeois social thought. But if the relation of private property between a person and a thing is only the juridical expression of a social relation between people, the abstract individual subject of bourgeois social theory is found to be only a philosophical abstraction, expressing particular social relations of production. The starting point of philosophy and of social theory has to be not the abstract individual, whose social qualities are concealed behind a property relation between the individual and a thing, but the historically developed social relations which characterise a particular form of society. Marx's apparently innocent argument that private property is the result of alienated labour has devastating implications, for it undermines the apparently *a priori* character of the fundamental categories of bourgeois thought.

Alienated labour and the critique of money

The conclusion that Marx immediately drew from his critique of private property is fundamental, and it moves a long way from Proudhon. If alienated labour is the basis of property, the abolition of property can only take the form of the abolition of alienated labour. Thus

> the emancipation of society from private property, etc., from servitude, is expressed in the *political* form of the *emancipation of the workers*; not that their emancipation alone is at stake, but because the emancipation of the workers contains universal human emancipation (*CW*, 3, p. 280).

Thus the problem that arose out of the critique of Hegel's theory of the state finds its practical solution.

Having discovered the essence of private property in the alienation of labour Marx argued that every category of political economy is 'only a *particular* and *developed* expression of these first elements' (*CW*, 3, p. 281). However Marx did not follow up this suggestion immediately, not least because at this stage he had a very limited knowledge of political economy. (The evidence suggests that it was at precisely this moment that Marx turned to the serious study of political economy for the first time.) Instead Marx turned to the most fundamental question of all. If private property is the consequence of alienated labour, we have to look elsewhere for the cause of the latter. 'How, we now ask, does *man* come to *alienate*, to estrange, his *labour*?' (*CW*, 3, p. 281). However it is at just this point that forty pages of Marx's manuscript are missing, freeing creative commentators from the inconvenience of pinning their interpretations to Marx's text.

Almost all those who accept Marx's argument that alienated labour is the basis of private property go on to argue that the foundation of alienated labour is to be found in the division of labour, which would imply that alienation is a universal phenomenon. Bert Ollman tells us that 'the division of labour occurs and ... it brings alienation in its wake. The further it develops ... the more alienation approximates the full blown form it assumes in capitalism ... For Marx alienation exists in all societies where the division of labour is the operative principle of economic organisation' (Ollman, 1971, p. 161). Walter Weisskopf (1971) offers the same interpretation, as does John Maguire (1972, p. 69). It is picked up in almost identical terms in a recent textbook: 'the root of all forms of alienation he considered to be alienated labour caused by the specialisation of activity' which is 'most intense in systems based upon commodity production, and especially in capitalism' (Howard and King, 1985, p. 18). Others include the division of labour among a number of different causes of alienation (e.g. Ernest Mandel, 1971). John Elliott adds the division of labour, 'mutually interwoven' with private property, to the 'inner-penetrating' causes, while characteristically quoting a passage which says the opposite: 'the *division of labour* is the economic expression of the *social character of labour* within alienation' (*CW*, 3, p. 317, quoted Elliott, 1979, p. 345).

This last quotation makes it clear that Marx saw the division of labour as an *expression* of alienation, not as its cause. The confusion arises from a mis-reading of Marx's use of the term 'labour' in his early works. In the early works Marx consistently used the term 'labour' as synonymous with alienated labour (Arthur, 1986, pp. 12–19), and 'division of labour' as synonymous with the fragmentation of alienated labour, so that the identification of alienated labour with the division of labour is a tautology, not the expression of an explanatory link. More generally, far from contradicting essential human needs, the division of labour is for Marx the manifestation of the human sociability which Marx regarded as humanity's defining feature, even when the division of labour appears only in an alienated form. Thus it is quite clear in Marx's account that it is not the division of labour that is the source of alienation, but the social form of the division of labour in which the social character of labour is only realised through the form of the exchange of labour-power and its products *as commodities*. It is the analysis of the commodity that is the key to the explanation of alienation.

Despite the gap in the *Manuscripts*, we do have another text which, the evidence strongly suggests, was written after completion of the first of the *Manuscripts*, and before Marx got to work on the second. This text is made up of Marx's excerpts and *Comments on James Mill*. Although the *Comments* were first published alongside the *Manuscripts* in 1932, they did not appear in English until 1967, and have received little critical attention.

Marx's earliest references to alienation had focused on money as 'the estranged essence of man's work and man's existence', arguing that 'this alien essence dominates him and he worships it' ('On the Jewish Question', *CW*, 3, p. 172), an idea which derived from Moses Hess's conception of money as 'the alienated power of man, the product of the mutually alienated men, the alienated man', through which 'the human potential is alienated and degraded to a mere means of making a living' (quoted Feuerlicht, 1978, p. 137).

Alienated labour and the critique of money

The *Comments* return to the crucial category of money, and start by taking up Mill's account of money as a means of exchange, which for Marx 'very well expresses the essence of the matter' in emphasising that the essence of money is not that it is a form of private property, but that it is a medium of exchange which embodies, in an alienated form, the mutual complementarity of the division of labour:

> The essence of money is not, in the first place, that property is alienated in it, but that the *mediating activity* or movement, the *human* social act by which man's products mutually complement one another is *estranged* from man and becomes the attribute of money, a *material thing* outside man (*CW*, 3, p. 212).

It is only on the basis of this role of money as means of exchange that money acquires its '*real power*' over what it mediates to me' so that 'objects only have value insofar as they *represent* the mediator, whereas originally it seemed that the mediator had value only insofar as *it* represented *them*. This reversal of the original relationship is inevitable. This *mediator* is therefore the lost, estranged *essence* of private property' (*CW*, 3, p. 212). It is only because money is constituted as the abstract form of alienated labour in its role as means of exchange that alienated labour can take on the independent form of private property as money. Private property is therefore no more than the juridical expression of the mutual recognition of commodity producers in the exchange relation.

The significance of this apparently simple observation can be best brought out by contrasting it with Engels's analysis of exchange. Engels saw the exchange relation as a conflict between two wills, and so a transparent relation that political economy had distorted by concealing its presupposition in private property. Moving the focus from money as a form of private property to money as a means of exchange, which was achieved within political economy by Hume's critique of mercantilism, leads to a quite different view of exchange as a *mediated* relationship in which the exchange is effected not directly, but through the medium of money. Seen in this light private property is no longer the presupposition of exchange, but is rather its result. It is only when the activity of social labour is expressed in the alienated form of money that the product of that labour is detached from the human activity that produced it and assumes the form of a thing which can be appropriated as private property. Thus the problem of explaining private property becomes the problem of explaining the alienation of labour in the form of money.

In the rest of the *Comments* Marx develops the implications of this fundamental insight, deriving the categories of political economy *not* from private property, as Engels had done, but from capitalism as a form of social production whose social character is only expressed in the alienated form of the exchange of commodities under the rule of money. In the society based on exchange the '*human community* ... appears in the form of *estrangement* ... To say that *man* is estranged from himself, therefore, is the same thing as saying that the *society* of this estranged man is a caricature of his *real community*' (*CW*, 3, p. 217).

On the basis of commodity exchange an individual comes to assess all her capacities not in their own terms but in terms of money. In the same way the significance of others for the individual is assessed in money terms. Thus all human qualities are reduced to qualities of the thing, money, which detaches them from the individual and makes them into an objective power. As human qualities are reduced to things, so human relations are reduced to relations between things (*CW*, 3, pp. 212, 213, 217–8).

In the system of exchange human needs are not related to one another directly, but the relation is mediated through the alienation of human activity in the form of money, which thereby acquires an independent existence as private property. I do not orient my activity to the needs of another, thereby directly expressing my awareness of my social nature; instead my need is related to a thing that is the private property of the other, and the need of the other is related to my private property. Thus my social need for the other is expressed in the form of my need for the thing that the other possesses. In this way the essential social relationship between people, their mutual need for one another, appears in the alienated form of a relation between things, and my social dependence on the other person appears in the alienated form of my dependence on things.

With the extension of exchange and the division of labour the activity of labour becomes an alienated activity, for the thing that the labourer produces has no inherent connection with the needs of the labourer: the labourer does not produce the particular object because it responds either to her need to engage in a particular form of activity, or to a need for that particular product, or to a recognition of the need of another for that product. The labourer produces simply in order to exchange the product for another product, in order to earn a living.

Thus the product as an indifferent *thing* comes to dominate labour.

All the misunderstandings of Marx's theory of alienated labour derive from the failure to grasp the insight first achieved in Marx's *Comments on James Mill*. The orthodox commentaries identify alienated labour as the expression of an *unmediated* relation of labour under the domination of another, whether in capitalist production or through the division of labour, instead of locating alienated labour as a specifically *capitalist* form of labour, which is marked precisely by the fact that the worker has been freed from immediate relations of domination. Thus capitalist private property is distinguished from feudal landed property by the fact that capitalist exploitation is not *direct*, but is mediated by the commodity-form of labour and its products. It is only this mediation of social relations by things that defines the alienation of labour and constitutes the product of labour as private property. Consequently the worker does not 'alienate himself from himself in the very act of production', but in selling her labour-power as a commodity.

Alienation is not simply an ideological or psychological phenomenon, through which the power of private property is concealed behind the things which are the substance of that property, to be overcome by the acquisition of a true consciousness of class exploitation. In a capitalist society things really do have the power attributed to them by the alienated consciousness. What has to be understood is not *who* is hidden behind the mask of the commodity, but *how* commodities acquire social powers as the alienated power of social labour. This is why it is only on the basis of the analysis of the commodity-form that it is possible to understand the more developed forms of private property, in particular money and capital.

The *Comments on James Mill* provide only an indication of the direction in which Marx's thought was moving. In particular, the analysis remains at the level of commodity, and does not have any account of the social relations of capitalist production. Thus, although Marx indicates that the 'relationship of alienated labour reaches its highest point only when ... he who *buys* the product is not himself a producer' (*CW*, 3, p. 219), he still seems to follow Smith in seeing this relationship as a linear development of the division of labour, so that the domination of capital over labour is not a qualitatively different social relation from that of commodity exchange, but only the culmination of the domination of money: 'The complete domination of the estranged thing *over* man has become evident in *money*' (*CW*,

3, p. 221). Nevertheless in the *Comments* we can see Marx taking the decisive step which enabled him to get beyond Proudhon's 'critique of political economy on the basis of political economy' by discovering, in his analysis of the form of commodity exchange as the act of alienation, the secret of private property. From this point onwards the emphasis of Marx's account of alienated labour shifts, from the subjective experience of alienation in the relationship between the individual and private property, to its historical foundation in the relationship between the 'real community' and its 'estranged form', from a philosophical critique of capitalism to an historical critique.[9]

This perspective informs the bulk of the third *Manuscript*, which is made up of a critique of those forms of communism that have not been able to go beyond private property because they have not grasped its essence, and of a polemical discussion of the dehumanisation of alienated labour, the division of labour and money. This discussion brings out the powerful moral dimension of Marx's critique of political economy. Political economy offers a theory of capitalist society that rests on a resolutely naturalistic materialism for which the human being is reduced to an animal stripped of all human qualities, whose needs are reduced to the biological need for subsistence. It does not concern itself with human moral qualities, but it still 'expresses moral laws *in its own way*' (*CW*, 3, p. 311).

These are the moral laws of the society that it describes, and for Marx, at this stage in his thinking, political economy gives an accurate account of the reality of capitalist society. The critique of political economy, which shows that it is on the basis of the particular social form of alienated labour, and not of an impoverished human nature, that this dehumanising society arises, is therefore at the same time a moral critique of capitalist society. However this is

---

[9] The dating of the *Comments* is complicated because Marx kept his excerpt books separate from his substantive notebooks. Evans, 1984 and Hennings, 1985 itemise the contents of the various notebooks and the hard evidence of dating. There are no references to Mill before the second manuscript, nor to any of the other texts which follow the excerpts from Mill in Marx's notebooks (the references to Buret in the first manuscript, which Oakley (1983, p. 27) cites as evidence for the prior completion of these notebooks, are *not* those which appear in the notebooks subsequent to the comments on Mill — I am very grateful to Chris Arthur for clearing up this crucial point). It is only at the end of the first manuscript that it occurs to Marx to make the connection between alienated labour and political economy which dominates his comments on Mill. The editors of the *Collected Works* suggest that the *Comments on James Mill* 'anticipated the thoughts expounded in the missing pages of the second manuscript' (*CW*, 3, n. 48, p. 596). Colletti (1975, p. 53) also suggests the significance of the *Comments* for the theory of alienated labour.

Alienated labour and the critique of money

not an abstract moralism, referring back to moral truths hidden in an unrealised human nature. The moral critique is only an expression of the contradictory form of capitalist social relations as the estranged form of human sociability, an estrangement which is already expressed theoretically in the contradictions inherent in political economy, which both recognises and denies the human foundation of society in social labour. Within the reality of capitalist society true human needs remain which will and must express themselves in the overthrow of capitalism and its replacement by a society in which labour will be immediately social, in which the state, as the alienated form of sociability, will be abolished, and in which religion will be superfluous.

This moral critique is interesting, if very abstract. More significant from the point of view of the development of Marx's critique of political economy is the theoretical conclusion he draws at the beginning of the third *Manuscript*.

We have seen that Engels's critique of political economy stopped short of an analysis of private property and criticised political economy from the standpoint of the market. For Engels an adequate political economy must be based on the market, where object and subject, producer and consumer, objective costs of production and subjective utility, meet one another. What Engels offered was a synthesis of the competing schools of political economy (in this sense anticipating not Marx but Alfred Marshall), and not ultimately a critique at all. Marx, however, as soon as he had found the basis of private property in alienated labour, concluded that labour must be the basis of political economy, and so he came down firmly on the side of Ricardo and his labour theory of value.

It is significant that this is the first point in his work at which Marx had anything positive to say about Ricardo, whose 'cynicism' he had hitherto regarded with contempt, and whose work he had not thought it worth reading. Now Marx notes that 'there is not merely a relative growth in the *cynicism* of political economy from Smith through Say to Ricardo, Mill, etc., ...these later economists also advance in a positive sense constantly and consciously further than their predecessors in their estrangement from man. They do so, however, *only* because their science develops more consistently and truthfully' (*CW*, 3, p. 291). The attraction of the labour theory of value for Marx was not that it 'proved' that the labourer was exploited under capitalism, which it did not and could not do, but that it connected labour with its alienated forms.

For Marx the great advance of Smith over mercantilism was to recognise property not as something external, money, but as a form of labour, a view which is most rigorously developed by Ricardo. However political economy *inverts* the true relationship between labour and property because it does not recognise that labour is inverted, in the form of alienated labour. Instead of seeing alienated labour as the human essence of property, political economy sees labour as the natural form of property: 'they make private property in its active form the subject, thus simultaneously turning man into the essence ... the contradiction of reality corresponds completely to the contradictory being which they accept as their principle' (*CW*, 3, pp. 291–2). Thus Marx rediscovered the inversion that he found in his critique of Hegel's philosophy of the state, and it is not surprising that the final section of the *Economic and Philosophical Manuscripts* returns to the critique of Hegel.

Hegel and the critique of political economy

The *Economic and Philosophical Manuscripts* owe much more to Marx's engagement with Proudhon and Hegel than to any thorough exploration of political economy. However the insights gained in the critique of alienated labour laid the foundations on which Marx developed his mature critique of political economy. In this sense there is no break between the 'philosophical' works of his youth and the 'economic' works of his maturity, between the 'abstract' critique of 1844 and the 'historical' critique of 1867. To see how this can be, we need to go back to the question of the affinity between Hegel's philosophy and the doctrines of classical political economy, to which Marx returns in the final *Manuscript*.

Hegel's philosophy is 'mystical' for Marx because it presents the real as rational by suppressing the irrationality of reality. Thus Hegel describes real contradictions, but then dissolves these contradictions again in the development of self-consciousness by turning reality into an attribute of thought. Nevertheless the power of Hegel's system is that his ruthless attempt to reduce everything to reason leads him to uncover real irrationality, even if for him such irrationality is simply another logical problem. The 'rational kernel' can be extracted from Hegel's philosophy as soon as it is recognised that the contradictions he describes are real contradictions, which demand a real resolution.

Hegel and the critique of political economy

Thus his theory of the state recognises the contradiction between the particularity of interests in civil society and the universality supposedly embodied in the state, but treats this as a formal contradiction to which he provided a formal solution. For Marx this is a real contradiction which calls for a real solution: the abolition of a society based on the opposition of private interests. In exactly the same way political economy describes the real contradictions inherent in capitalist social production, between the enormous growth in the productive power of social labour and the social and material impoverishment of the labourer, which appears in the contradiction between the restricted value of labour-power and the value created by the expenditure of that labour-power, but even Ricardo, the most rigorous and honest exponent of political economy, provides only a formal solution to this contradiction.

The parallel between Hegel and political economy is not only methodological. The substantive connection between Hegel and political economy is, as we have seen, to be found in the common idea that private property is based on the private appropriation of the products of labour, so that labour is the substance of property. This is not an idea unique to Smith and Hegel, but one that is fundamental to liberal social thought, emerging with the development of bourgeois production relations as an aspect of the secularisation of bourgeois property. It is an idea that is developed first in political theory, classically in Locke's explanation of the origins and foundations of property. It is then taken up by classical political economy, which considers bourgeois social relations to be simply an aspect of the division of labour, participation in those social relations as labourer, landowner or capitalist depending on the form of property as labour, land or capital. The idea is given its most rigorous and abstract formulation in Hegel's *Phenomenology of Mind*.

For Hegel the private appropriation of the products of labour was the basis of property and therefore the basis on which social relations acquire an objective reality, embodied in things, beyond the immediacy of inter-personal relations. For Hegel the alienation of the object in exchange is simply the means by which the character of the product of labour as private property, already established in the act of labour, is affirmed by others. However, to become private property the object must be more than a product of labour. It must be an object which is detached from its producer, and so has acquired its independence, *before* it can be appropriated as property. Hegel's identification of alienated labour with objectified labour suppresses the real contradiction implied in the alienation of labour that underlies bourgeois property — the contradiction that explains how it is that the product of an individual's labour can be appropriated by another and turned into the means of subjection of the direct producer — to reduce alienation to the subjective recognition of the equivalence of the objects of exchange as private property. Marx's analysis in the *Manuscripts* starts with the real contradiction as the basis on which to develop his concept of alienated labour.[10]

Marx's critique of Hegel can be applied directly to classical political economy because the two theories of capitalist society rest on the same concept of property. Thus, as Marx noted in the *Manuscripts*, 'Hegel's standpoint is that of modern political economy' (*CW*, 3, p. 333). Engels had already brought the two together in his critique of political economy, which betrays a strong Hegelian inspiration in showing the dependence of all the concepts of political economy on this fundamental presupposition of private property. However Engels could not get beyond a moral critique that condemned bourgeois property for its inhuman consequences. Although Marx's critique retained this strong moral thrust, it also went beyond it to establish the socio-historical foundations of bourgeois property and so to reveal the real possibility of its historical supersession. Thus Marx's critique of political economy is a moral critique, but it is much more than a moral critique. It is a philosophical critique, but it goes beyond philosophy in revealing the real historical foundation both of bourgeois social relations and of the mystifications of bourgeois ideology.

Hegel's identification of alienated with objectified labour conceals the real foundation of bourgeois social relations and so is the basis on which those social relations are mystified. If private property derives from objectified labour, then it is the necessary consequence of the production of objects, it has a natural foundation and a universal existence. If private property derives from alienated labour, however, then it has a social foundation, in a particular social form

---

[10] Marx's critique of Hegel is not that Hegel *confuses* alienation with objectification, as most commentators believe, but that he *identifies* the two. The identification of alienation with objectification is not a 'false identification of opposed fundamental categories' (Lukács, 1971, p. xxiv), because for Hegel, as for the early Lukács, alienation and objectification are two sides of the same coin. This is equally true of Hegel's 'materialist' analysis in the early Jena manuscripts, in which he saw private property as the *expression* of the division of labour, as of his later works, in which he returned to the liberal conception of property as constituted in the relation between the will and the thing (Lukács, 1971, Chs 5, 7; Arthur, 1988).

of labour, and a purely historical, that is, transitory, existence. Where political economy naturalises bourgeois social relations by attributing them to the natural powers of objectified labour, Marx located them historically by attributing them to the social power of alienated labour. Behind alienated labour as a philosophical category lie particular social relations of production. Hence the philosophical critique immediately gives way to a socio-historical critique. It was this step that Hegel was unable to undertake.

> The outstanding achievement of Hegel's *Phänomenologie* ... is ... that Hegel conceives the self-creation of man as a process, conceives objectification as loss of the object, as alienation and as transcendence of this alienation; that he thus grasps the essence of *labour* and comprehends objective man — true, because real man — as the outcome of man's *own labour* (*CW*, 3, pp. 332–3).

The weakness of Hegel's work, however, is that

> all estrangement of the human being is therefore *nothing* but *estrangement of self-consciousness*. The estrangement of self-consciousness is not regarded as an *expression* — reflected in the realm of knowledge and thought — of the *real* estrangement of the human being (*CW*, 3, p. 334).

This means that Hegel's philosophy is ultimately an uncritical criticism, for, although it recognises the alienation of labour it does so only in a formal, speculative, alienated way. Thus 'Hegel's standpoint is that of modern political economy' in that 'he sees only the positive, not the negative side of labour' (*CW*, 3, p. 333). The critique of Hegel and the critique of political economy are ultimately one and the same: the critique of the constitutive presupposition of bourgeois thought.

Marx's early critique of political economy

The *Manuscripts* laid the foundations for a series of works produced in the 1840s, most of which were polemical in intent. Rather than go through these works in detail, I will summarise the achievements and limitations of Marx's early critique of political economy, as that was developed in the works written between 1844 and 1848, before the revolutionary upsurge in Europe interrupted his studies.

Marx's early critique of political economy was based on a philosophical critique of its fundamental concepts. However, even in the *Economic and Philosophical Manuscripts* it is clear that Marx was going beyond philosophy. The concept of 'alienated labour' is not simply a philosophical concept, nor is it seen primarily as a moral or psychological attitude to labour. Behind the abstract concept of 'alienated labour' is a real, concrete, specific historical form of labour. The critique of private property is not merely a philosophical critique, for it is clear that for Marx property develops historically on the basis of the development of alienated labour.

Marx's moral condemnation of the alienation and dehumanisation of labour was not based on his own beliefs about human nature and human dignity, but on human needs expressed in everyday human existence. In an alienated form these needs are expressed in religion and in politics, but they are expressed directly in the community. In the past the community provided a very narrow and limited response to these needs. For Marx the community that is emerging within capitalist society out of the association of the proletariat will be a universal community which will satisfy human needs directly and so, at last, the alien forms of politics and religion will disappear along with the narrowness of community. Thus even in the *Manuscripts* 'alienated labour' is not primarily a philosophical, moral or psychological concept, it is a socio-historical concept. It is in this sense there is no break between the *Manuscripts* and Marx's later work.

The later work develops directly out of the counterposition in the *Manuscripts* of the real world of human practical activity to the abstractions of bourgeois social thought, a counterposition that is expressed in the argument that alienated labour is the specific socio-historical foundation of bourgeois social relations. It was this perspective which informed Marx's reading of political economy between 1844 and 1848, and which underlies the critique of political economy to be found in the works of that period. The main contribution of the works of this period is that Marx develops a critique of the social relations of *capitalist* production.

The central theme of this critique is that political economy is based on the 'naturalisation' of historically specific social relations, and so its concepts are formulated in abstraction from the specific historical characteristics of capitalist society. In this sense they are 'formal abstractions'. Political economy abstracts from the social fact of landownership, to present rent as a quality of the land. It abstracts from the social form of wage-labour, to present wages as the recompense for labour. It abstracts from the social form of capital, to present profit as a quality of the means of production. It abstracts from the social form of exchange, to present exchange as an expression of a rational/natural propensity to 'truck, barter and exchange'.

However this is an illegitimate form of abstraction, for it is only in a particular form of society that land generates a rent, means of production a profit, and labour a wage. It is only in a particular form of society that the private labour of individuals is related through exchange. To treat these categories in abstraction from their social form is to deprive them of any content, to make them into purely formal categories that exist wherever there are land, labour, means of production or co-operation. Thus the categories of political economy are given an eternal status, and are even applied to societies within which neither wages, nor profits, nor rent, nor exchange, actually exist.

Marx's critique of political economy is not merely an historicist critique, which stresses the historical relativity of the concepts of political economy, such as was developed by the German Historical School. Underlying this historicist critique is a theoretical critique, whose foundation is the critique of private property. For political economy it is only private property that constitutes individuals as social beings by defining them socially as the *owners* of particular factors of production. Land, labour and capital are regarded as co-operative 'factors of production' distinguished from one another by their distinct functional roles in production, corresponding to the technological distinction between the object, instrument and means of labour. In the course of the development of the division of labour the functional roles of these factors of production are separated from one another, just as the functional roles of the butcher and the baker are separated. This separation corresponds to the appropriation of these distinct 'factors of production' as private property by different individuals, which establishes an immediate correspondence between the technically imposed relations of co-operation between the factors of production and the social relations between people. Private ownership simultaneously constitutes the factors of production as sources of revenue, and so defines the particular interests of distinct social classes, on the basis of the mode of their participation in the distribution of the social product. Thus wages flow from labour to the *owner* of labour, profits from the means of production to the *owner* of the means of production, rent from the land to the *owner* of the land.

Political economy can recognise that class interests conflict with one another, Smith providing a devastating critique of the anti-social instincts of the capitalist, and Ricardo of the regressive character of landownership. However this recognition is confined within the limits of political economy's 'naturalisation' of capitalist social relations of production, and the limits of capitalism are the natural limits of the diminishing returns to capital and land. Conflicts of class interest necessarily follow from the private appropriation of the means of production, but for political economy production relations are technically imposed co-operative relations between the factors of production, while class conflicts are confined to the level of distribution, and are resolved through competitive exchange.

The political economists' concepts derive from private property as a philosophical abstraction. For political economy private property cannot arise out of society, as the historical product of human sociability, since it is only private property that makes society possible. This means that the explanation for private property can only lie outside society, as an expression of natural inclinations, human rationality, or divine will. In this abstraction a particular form of property, capitalist property, is given a universal status. It is only through this universal category that the recipients of revenues are related to their sources of revenue. History is then simply the history of the liberation of private property from the unnatural fetters imposed by political power and by religious and sentimental prejudice, fetters that prevent revenues from flowing to their appropriate recipients. For example, in feudal society the landowner uses his political power to secure not only his rent, but also the 'profits' and even a portion of the 'wages' of the serf.

The effect of the formal abstraction of political economy, based on its concept of private property, is to attribute social powers to things, inverting the subject and the predicate. Thus, instead of seeing the machine as a particular embodiment of capital, political economy sees capital as a particular manifestation of the machine. Instead of seeing labour as the physical substance of the commodity wage-labour, political economy sees wage-labour as a particular manifestation of labour. Instead of seeing the 'propensity to truck, barter and exchange' as a need imposed by exchange, political economy sees exchange as an expression of this 'natural' propensity.

This formal abstraction cannot be reduced to a methodological error, for the inversion is something that really exists in capitalist society. The abstraction of political economy leaves out of account the social form within which things come to acquire a social power, and so it attributes this power to the things themselves, but in a capitalist society things really do manifest this social power. Thus workers really do find themselves slaves to their physiological needs and to the means of production; capitalists really do acquire profits in accordance with the productivity that they attribute to their means of production; landowners really do earn rents in accordance with the relative fertility of the soil; exchange of things really is the only way in which producers relate socially to one another. Political economy reproduces uncritically the alienated social forms of capitalist society within which social powers are mediated through things, so that social powers appear as the attributes of things. The mystifications of political economy do not simply represent an ideological inversion of reality, but the ideological expression of a real inversion. This is why the critique of political economy is not simply a critique of a mystificatory ideology, but of the alienated forms of social life which political economy describes but cannot explain.

It is because political economy is uncritical of its presuppositions, most fundamental of which is private property, that its analysis mystifies the foundations of capitalist society. In denying the social character of its fundamental categories political economy makes these categories into eternal truths that can be distorted by unwise political intervention, but that can never be suppressed. In turning its fundamental categories into eternal truths political economy makes the society to which these categories correspond itself an eternal truth. For political economy capitalist society is the best of all possible societies, because it is in terms of the categories of capitalist society that political economy evaluates all forms of society.

Marx's critique of political economy reveals the socio-historical content of the formal abstractions of political economy by revealing the socio-historical foundation of bourgeois property in alienated labour. Bourgeois property rests on the co-ordination of social production not through the self-conscious organisation of production on the basis of human need, but through the exchange of the products of private producers in the form of commodities. The commodity is thus a specific social form of the product of labour. Similarly wage-labour is a particular form of labour which corresponds to the dispossession of the labourer that forces her to work for another, who has appropriated the necessary means of production and subsistence in the form of capital. Thus wage-labour and capital are the complementary aspects of a particular social relation of production. It is only within this social relation that capitalist and wage-labourer relate to one another as independent commodity owners, and it is only within this social relation that the labourer is compelled to alienate her productive powers in exchange for a wage. It is only within this social relation of production that property based on labour is transformed into its opposite, the appropriation of the product of labour by the non-labourer.

The limits of the early critique

Although the *Manuscripts* defined Marx's intellectual project, it would be quite wrong to see Marx's mature works already present *in nuce* in the works of his youth. In the *Manuscripts* Marx had cut away the foundations of the old edifice, but the edifice itself remained intact. This explains why, in place of the intrinsic critique which his project mapped out, Marx fell back for polemical purposes on an extrinsic critique. In his polemical works Marx still tended to combine an Hegelian critique of the naturalistic empiricism of political economy, with a materialist critique of the speculative idealism of the Hegelians. This was almost inevitable to the extent that he had not yet shown concretely how the standpoint of alienated labour transformed the concepts of political economy, nor how the standpoint of human practical activity transformed the concepts of Hegel, by developing his own *historical* analysis of the development of capitalist social relations.

In his early works Marx did not contest the scientific adequacy of classical political economy as a theory of capitalist society. In the first *Manuscript* it is through the findings of political economy that he condemns capitalist society. In *The Holy Family* (1844–5) Marx used the findings of political economy against the Left Hegelians, while arguing that contradictory ideas express contradictions in reality, the contradictions developed by political economy expressing the contradictions introduced into the real world by private property, so that these contradictions cannot be overcome philosophically, but only by the real abolition of private property through the self-emancipation of the proletariat. In *The Poverty of Philosophy* (1847) he used Ricardo's proof of the futility of reform to berate Proudhon's reformism, arguing that 'Ricardo's theory of values is the scientific interpretation of actual economic life; ... Ricardo establishes the truth of his formula by deriving it from [from it?] all economic relations, and by explaining in this way all phenomena, even those like ground rent, accumulation of capital, and the relation of wages to profits, which at first sight seem to contradict it; it is precisely that which makes his doctrine a scientific system' (PP, p. 47).

The tension between political economy and its critique appears most clearly in *The German Ideology* (1845–6), in which Marx first attempted to present his conception of history as the history of private property. To be more precise, Marx offers three separate and rather different, but equally unsatisfactory, attempts. The problem is that Marx's approach to history remains abstract, for he has no coherent account of the historical development of alienated labour as the expression of different social forms of production. His 'historical materialism' tends to take the form of an abstract dialectic of labour underlying the historical process, manifested in the parallel and continuous, rather than contradictory and discontinuous, development of the division of labour and private property, in which all differences are accidental, to be shed in the unfolding of the dialectic which culminates in the final confrontation of labour and capital.

In the *Manuscripts* Marx still followed Hegel in seeing property as an abstract and homogeneous category which only reaches its developed form in capital. Thus 'landed property is private property — capital — still afflicted with *local* and political prejudices ... capital not yet *fully developed*' (CW, 3, pp. 288–9). This abstract conception of property persists in *The German Ideology*, combined with the idea, derived from Smith, of the history of society as based in the development of the division of labour. Instead of providing an analysis of the historical development of different *social forms of labour* as the foundation of the development of different forms of the division of labour and different forms of property, Marx tries to integrate the 'materialist conception of history' developed by the eighteenth century materialists, in which it is the progressive development of the *technical* division of labour that governs the historical development of society, with an idealist account of history as the development of property from its early forms, in which it continued to be restrained by political, communal and moral considerations, to its purest and most rational form as modern private property.

The problem with this attempt to integrate a quasi-Hegelian account of the development of property with the materialist account of the development of the division of labour is that of establishing the relation between the two. In the terms of subsequent Marxist debate the problem is that of the relationship between the development of the 'forces' and the 'social relations' of production.[11] In Marx's first account in *The German Ideology* he follows Smith in arguing that 'the existing stage in the division of labour determines also the relations of individuals to one another with reference to the material, instrument and product of labour' (GI, p. 32), but in practice does not establish any coherent connection between the two, forms of property being related to forms of social organisation ('tribal', 'ancient communal', 'feudal') with no reference to the division of labour (GI, pp. 33–6). This is a promising lead, which Marx immediately abandons, only taking it up again in the section on 'pre-capitalist economic formations' in the *Grundrisse*. In his second account he ties the development of forms of property more closely to the development of the division of labour, but loses sight of the social form of production, so reducing property to the 'identical expression' (GI, p. 44) of the division of labour.

It is the separation of town and country that gives rise to the separation of capital and landed property, while a class division arises in the towns 'which is directly based on the division of labour and on the instruments of production' (GI, p. 64). Thus Marx falls back into political economy's identification of forms of property not with social forms of labour, but with the physical substance in which property is embodied: land, labour and means of production, so that property remains an ahistorical abstraction, on the basis of which class relations follow directly from the division of labour, and property develops from 'naturally derived capital' to capital 'having its basis only in labour and exchange' (GI, pp. 67, 65). The result is that the critique of private property remains equally abstract and ahistorical, for the *contradiction* between private property and the division of labour, between the 'social relations' and the 'forces' of production, has disappeared. The third presentation does not escape from this perspective, but resurrects the contradiction, although in an entirely formalistic way. Thus Marx argues that 'private property was a necessity for certain

---

[11] An indication of the problem is that Marx does not clearly distinguish the two in *The German Ideology*. Thus the 'division of labour' is equated both with the 'forces of production' and with 'private property'. The 'mode of co-operation' is both a 'productive force' and a 'form of property'.

The limits of the early critique

industrial stages' but that 'in big industry the contradiction between the instruments of production and private property appears for the first time', because for the first time 'the totality of the productive forces' confront 'the majority of the individuals from whom these forces have been wrested away' (GI, pp. 81–2).

Arthur notes a difficulty which this account of the development of private property establishes for Marx's claimed analytical priority of alienated labour over private property, since feudal landed property is *not* based on alienated labour, but on relations of personal dependence (c.f. Mészáros, 1970, pp. 134–9). But this discontinuity in the history of private property is not so much a problem for Marx's theory of alienated labour as for the quasi-Hegelian idea of history as the unfolding of the dialectic between labour and private property, which Mészáros and Arthur draw from *The German Ideology*. Feudal landed property is manifestly not an impure or undeveloped form of capitalist property. It is a quite different form of property, expressing quite different social relations of production, a form of property which, far from being *private*, is encumbered with a network of social relations of dependence and obligation. Capitalist forms of private property did not emerge *out of* feudal forms, but in opposition to them, the struggle between the two being a long drawn out and bloody one.

Marx soon saw the way to move beyond the philosophy of history which informs *The German Ideology*. In a very important letter he wrote to Annenkov as early as 1846, in which he made it quite clear that the critique of private property was the key to the critique of both bourgeois society and bourgeois social thought, Marx stressed the *discontinuity* between bourgeois and feudal property, as expressions of quite different social relations of production:

> Property, finally, forms the last category in M. Proudhon's system. In the real world, however, the division of labour and all the other categories of M. Proudhon are social relations and their totality forms what is currently called "*property*": bourgeois property outside these relations is nothing but a metaphysical or legal illusion. The property of another epoch, feudal property, developed in a series of entirely different social relations. M. Proudhon, in establishing property as an independent relation, commits more than one methodological fault — he proves conclusively that he has not grasped the thread which connects all the forms of *bourgeois* production (Letter to Annenkov, 28 December 1846).

Similarly Marx soon recognised in his other works of the 1840s that his critique of political economy transforms the economists' categories. Thus 'money is not a thing, it is a social relation' (*CW*, 6, p. 145); 'machinery is no more an economic category than the bullock that drags the plough' (*CW*, 6, p. 183); 'rent results from the social relations in which the exploitation of the land takes place ... Rent is a product of society and not of the soil' (*CW*, 6, p. 205), but Marx did not follow this insight through. His critique of political economy remained an 'external' critique, which put political economy in its historical place, but which left the substance of political economy intact. 'Economists express the relations of bourgeois production, the division of labour, credit, money, etc. as fixed, immutable, eternal categories ... Economists explain how production takes place in the above-mentioned relations, but what they do not explain is how these relations themselves are produced' (*CW*, 6, p. 162). But Marx did not explain this either. The result was that the radicalism of Marx's theoretical critique was not realised in practice in his early works. Thus *The Communist Manifesto* (1848) still has remnants of the philosophy of history sketched out in *The German Ideology*, in proposing historical laws whose foundation appears to lie outside history. The 1859 Preface to the *Contribution to the Critique of Political Economy* contains a much quoted summary of the findings of Marx's early works which can easily be read in just such terms, which are also the terms of Engels's popularisation of Marxism in *Anti-Dühring*. In a different vein, the 'political writings' of the 1850s provide sophisticated journalistic accounts of historical events, with occasional programmatic asides, but without any systematic theoretical analysis.

The critique of political economy was incomplete until it had been transformed from an external philosophical and political critique, which establishes the limits of political economy by revealing its hidden presuppositions, into an internal theoretical and historical critique which could provide a more adequate theory of capitalist society. In order to lay bare the 'laws of motion' of capitalist society as an historically developed mode of social production, Marx had to reformulate the classical concepts of wages, rent and profits, and the classical laws of production, of population, of currency, of the determination of revenues, and of the falling rate of profit, in properly historical terms. Even in the 1840s Marx was well aware of the need to develop the positive side of his critique, but he repeatedly

The limits of the early critique

postponed writing his 'Economics', under the pressure of political and personal circumstances, until he returned to his 'economic studies' in 1857.

It was in the *Grundrisse* (1857–8) that Marx first began to develop his intrinsic critique of political economy.[12] From one perspective the *Grundrisse* is a thoroughly confused and eclectic mixture of philosophy and political economy. But within the context of the project mapped out in the *Manuscripts*, the *Grundrisse* provides the 'missing link' between Marx's early works and those of his maturity. The need to develop his analysis more rigorously arose out of the need to distinguish his own theory from Proudhon's eclectic synthesis of Hegel and political economy, and specifically out of the need to develop a rigorous analysis of money, which he had identified as the key to the critique of private property in his earliest works, to counter Proudhonian proposals for monetary reform. In order to give substance to his critique of Proudhon Marx took up the theory of alienated labour as the basis of a critique of the labour theory of value, which was the foundation of Proudhonian reformism, which brought him once more face to face with political economy. In the course of the *Grundrisse* Marx distinguished his own analysis from that of Proudhon by progressively filling his philosophical categories with social and historical content. The critique of political economy is no longer a philosophical critique, based on an extrinsic conception of human nature, but is an immanent critique, the contradictions of political economy being located within political economy. These contradictions can only be resolved by reformulating the concepts of political economy, whose contradictions can then be explained as the expression of the historically developed contradictions of the social form of capitalist production.

---

[12] The *Grundrisse* only became widely available in German in the 1950s, in French in 1968, and in English in 1973. We still lack an adequate commentary on the *Grundrisse*, but see Rosdolsky (1977), Negri (1984), Uchida (1988).

4

Value, Class and the Theory of Society

Marxism and the critique of political economy

Despite Marx's proclamation of the death of philosophy in his early works, his critique of political economy in those works remained essentially an extrinsic philosophical critique in the sense that it ultimately rested on an appeal to abstract categories of 'human nature', 'history' and 'society'. In *Capital*, by contrast, Marx abandoned such abstract categories, developing an analysis of capitalism as a form of social production which developed historically through the interaction of 'individuals, not as they may appear in their own or other people's imagination, but as they *really* are; i.e., as they operate, produce materially, and hence as they work under definite material limits, presuppositions and conditions independent of their will' (GI, pp. 36–7).

It is very easy to see this difference between Marx's early and mature works as marking a distinction between an early humanistic philosophy, based on the theory of an alienated human nature, and a later scientific economics, which formulates objective economic laws which operate independently of the human will. This distinction is sometimes seen as a distinction between two complementary, but separable, aspects of Marx's project: between his philosophical critique and his scientific theory, and sometimes it is seen as a radical opposition between two antithetical perspectives: between his youthful humanism and his mature naturalism. In either case *Capital* is read primarily as a work of technical economics, while Marx's critique of political economy is read as an extrinsic critique, based on a human nature which is denied by the subordination of human values to economic constraints, and/or on the objective material interests of the proletariat which is subordinated to the domination of capital, leading to the reinterpretation of political economy from a different perspective, whether that of an alternative conception of human nature, or that of a different class. In the former case Marx's mature works dilute, or even deny, his early critique to the extent that Marx looks to economic interests as the basis of human liberation. In the latter case his mature works overcome the immature romanticism of the early critique, for precisely the same reason.

Both of these interpretations lead to a distinction between Marx's 'philosophy of history', which defines the ontological primacy and historical variability of the social relations of production, his 'sociology', which considers historically specific configurations of these social relations, and his 'economics', which defines the underlying economic 'laws of motion' which determine the development of these social relations. Sweezy, in his classic exposition of *Capital*, stresses the historical character of Marx's method but goes on radically to distinguish the 'quantitative value problem' from the 'qualitative value problem'. Thus Smith saw, in the case of exchange value, 'the quantitative relation between products', while Marx saw, 'hidden behind this ... a specific, historically conditioned, relation between producers' (Sweezy, 1942, p. 25; c.f. Dobb, 1940; 1973, pp. 143–6). Ernest Mandel (1962) follows the orthodox tradition (Bogdanov, 1979; Kautsky, 1925) in locating Marx's 'economics' historically by prefacing his exposition with a summary of the historical origins of capitalism.

According to this interpretation the fundamental error of political economy lay not in its characterisation of the 'economic' laws of capitalism, nor even in its characterisation of the social relations of capitalist production, but in its philosophy of history, which ignored the historically specific character of the social relations of capitalist production, based on the private appropriation of the means of production. The failure of political economy lies 'in its failure to see and take account of the *historical character* of the facts on which it is based', so that the 'unhistorical and antihistorical character of bourgeois thought' is revealed as soon as 'we consider *the problem of the present as a historical problem*' (Lukács, 1971, pp. 6, 157).

This orthodox interpretation is clearly and concisely presented in a recent Soviet textbook, which tells us that the precondition of Marx's 'revolution in economic science' was 'a revolution in philosophy'. The 'application of the method of dialectical and historical materialism ... and a historical approach to the analysis of phenomena made it possible to define the true subject-matter of political economy and to reveal the laws of economic life'. This enabled Marx and Engels to identify the historically specific character of the social relations of production, which 'are determined primarily by who owns the means of production. *Ownership of the means of production* ... underlies the social relations between people at all stages of social development. It is the development of the means of production that necessitates changes in property relations and the sum total of social relations. Property relations, in turn, affect the development of the means of production. When the form of ownership corresponds to the given level of development of the productive forces, it facilitates their progress. If property relations are obsolete, they act as a brake on the development of the productive forces' (Kozlov, 1977, pp. 14–15).

The problem with this interpretation is that it makes Marx indistinguishable from Smith, Malthus and Ricardo (c.f. Colletti, 1972, pp. 65–6). Smith was quite clear that the social relations of production were determined by the form of ownership of the means of production, and that they develop historically, on the basis of the development of forms of property, which in turn express the development of the forces of production. He was equally clear that 'obsolete property relations act as a brake on the development of the productive forces', for this was the basis of his critique of feudalism and mercantilism. Smith also recognised the evils of capitalism, but regarded them as unavoidable features of the best of all possible worlds. Malthus was well aware of the possibility of replacing private property by forms of communal property, his law of population being designed precisely to establish that the co-operative schemes of Godwin would act as a fetter on the development of the forces of production by dissipating the surplus in the form of unproductive consumption. Ricardo described the contradictory character of capitalist production, on the basis of his unequivocal commitment to the labour theory of value but, like Smith and Malthus, believed that socialism would lead only to an equalisation of poverty. All that this interpretation leaves for Marx is his introduction of the distinction between labour and labour-power, which Ricardo had confused. This discovery enabled Marx to 'prove' his theory of exploitation by showing that profit derives from the surplus labour of the worker, appropriated by the capitalist without equivalent, and to complete the Ricardian system by resolving the contradictions inherent in Ricardo's exposition of the theory of value.

This orthodox interpretation of Marx is shared by the majority of Marx's critics, who assimilate Marx to classical political economy, and then condemn the two to the same fate. Thus Schumpeter

Marxism and the critique of political economy

distinguished Marx's sociological definition of capitalism, which located the institutional framework of capitalism historically, from his 'economic theory', which explained 'the *mechanics* of capitalist society', and which derived from Ricardo, whose theory of value is the cornerstone of Marx's *Capital* (Schumpeter, 1987, p. 20, a judgement approvingly quoted by Dobb, 1973, pp. 142–3). The result is that the work of Marx, as the last of the classical economists, stands or falls with Ricardo's labour theory of value, a theory which, argue the critics, was definitively superseded by the marginalist revolution in economics, whose critique of Ricardo was devastatingly applied to Marx by Böhm-Bawerk.[1]

The orthodox response to such criticism has been to defend the Ricardian theory against the marginalist onslaught, either on the 'scientific' grounds of the technical superiority of a properly corrected labour theory of value, or on the 'philosophical' grounds that the labour theory of value expresses a particular class perspective and/or expresses the ontological primacy of production over exchange. Thus the 'Marxist economics' of the 1970s was dominated by an increasingly sterile debate between the 'neo-Ricardians', who took the former view, and the 'fundamentalists', who took the latter.[2] In the same way the defence of 'historical materialism' is reduced to a defence of the 'mechanical materialism' of the Scottish Enlightenment, an interpretation developed by the 'Analytical Marxists', who try to reconstruct Marxism on the basis of Smith's individualistic and rationalist materialism (Cohen, 1978; Roemer, 1982; Elster, 1985).

The interpretation of Marx's early works developed in the last chapter implies a quite different view of Marx's mature works. There is a difference between the philosophical character of Marx's early critique of political economy and the historical character of the intrinsic critique developed in *Capital*, but the two are different stages of the same project, a project clearly mapped out in the early works. The philosophical character of the early works derives from the fact that

---

[1] Marxist 'economists' differ in their characterisations of the 'problem' which the labour theory of value solves. Dobb (1940) focuses on the theory of surplus value, although Dobb later assimilated Marx to Sraffa's interpretation of Ricardo, the theory of value providing a way of determining prices independently of distribution (1973, pp. 147–52). Meek (1973, Chaps 4 and 5), on the other hand, saw the theory of value as the solution to the problem of allocating social labour to the various branches of production. For a survey of such interpretation see Kühne, 1979, Chaps 1–2.

[2] Steedman (1977) and Fine and Harris (1979) are the most sophisticated exponents of the two sides to this debate.

Marx had not yet given his philosophical categories any historical content. The extent to which Marx abandoned these categories in his mature works does not mark the extent to which he had broken with his early project, but the extent to which he had fulfilled it.

At the heart of this difference in interpretation lies the role of the labour theory of value in Marx's mature work. In his early work Marx used his theory of alienated labour as the basis of a *critique* of Ricardo's labour theory of value. Yet, according to the orthodox interpretation, the labour theory of value is the foundation of Marx's mature theory of capitalism. Does this mean that Marx abandoned his early critique of the labour theory of value? Or does it mean that he retained it only to set the labour theory of value in its historical context? Or does Marx's critique transform the classical theory of value?

The critique of political economy and the labour theory of value

I argued in the last chapter that Marx's critique of alienated labour defines a quite different project from that of simply re-interpreting political economy from a different class viewpoint. Far from defining the historical form of the social relations of capitalist production on the basis of the private ownership of the means of production, Marx insisted clearly and unequivocally that this was precisely the source of the errors of political economy, which failed to see that private property was only the expression of alienated labour. Thus, far from Marx adopting Ricardo's labour theory of value, the key to Marx's critique of political economy was his critique of that theory.

Marx followed Ricardo in making labour the starting point of his theory of capitalist society, but Marx's 'labour' was quite different from that of Ricardo. Where Ricardo's labour was the labour-time of the individual embodied in the product of her labour, which thereby constituted that product as her property, Marx's labour was not individual but social labour, the attribution of that labour to the individual only appearing in the form of the attribution of a value to the commodity. It is only in the alienated social form of commodity production that the labourer's own activity, as a part of social labour, confronts the labourer in the form of a quality (value) of a thing (the commodity), which can thereby be appropriated as private property.

The critique of political economy and the labour theory of value 97

Thus Marx does not provide an external socio-historical critique of political economy, which leaves intact the field of the 'economy' as the object of analysis, alongside 'society' and 'history', for the 'economy', the world of quantitative relations between things, can only be understood as the alienated social form of the reproduction of social relations of production. Marx's critique of political economy does not create a space for a Marxist political economy since political economy can never do more than describe the alienated forms of social existence.[3]

Far from adopting the labour theory of value to 'prove' the exploitation of the working class, Marx's critique of Ricardo undermines any such proof, both philosophically, in undermining the liberal theory of property which sees labour as the basis of proprietorial rights, and theoretically, in removing the immediate connection between the expenditure of individual labour and the value of the commodity, so that the relationship between 'effort' and 'reward' can only be constituted socially. Thus Marx was harshly critical of 'Ricardian socialism' which proclaimed labour's entitlement to its product, arguing that such a 'right' was only a bourgeois right, expressing bourgeois property relations.[4] For Marx what was at issue was not ethical proofs of exploitation, whose existence requires no such proof since it is manifested daily in the contradiction between the growing wealth created by social labour and the relative impoverishment of the working population, but 'to prove concretely how in present capitalist society the material, etc., conditions have at last been created which enable and compel the workers to lift this social curse' (Marx, *SW*, p. 317).

The scientific achievement of Ricardo, for Marx, was that he

[3] This interpretation of Marx's theory of value derives from Hilferding's critique of Böhm-Bawerk [1904], which was based on the argument that Marx 'starts from labour in its significance as the constitutive element in human society' (Hilferding, 1975, p. 133), so that Marx's theory is not primarily an account of the formation of prices, but an explanation of value as the alienated form of appearance of social labour. The implications of Hilferding's account were developed by Rubin [1923], whose work offered a remarkable anticipation of the argument of the *Economic and Philosophical Manuscripts*, not only in grasping the source of the theory of commodity fetishism in the theory of alienated labour, but also in grasping the limitations of Marx's early theory (Rubin, 1972, pp. 55–60, see also Rubin, 1978). The analysis of the value-form was also emphasised by a few writers who sought to integrate the emphasis of the Frankfurt School of Critical Theory on social form with the Marxian theory of value (Sohn-Rethel, 1978; Grossmann, 1977; Backhaus, 1969, 1974–8). See also Elson, 1979; Clarke, 1980a.

[4] The contemporary school of 'Analytical Marxism', following Morishima (1973), has devoted much intellectual energy to the question of the 'proof' of exploitation (Roemer, 1982).

unflinchingly described the contradictions of the capitalist mode of production, recognising the pauperisation of the working class as the condition for the accumulation of capital, recognising the need for periodic crises, the tendency for the rate of profit to fall, and the creation of technological unemployment, as necessary features of capitalism. The weakness of Ricardo's theory lay precisely in his labour theory of value, which provided a basis on which Ricardo could *describe* the effects of alienated labour to the extent that he reduced the concepts of value, wages, rent and profit to labour, but provided no means by which he could *explain* them. Ricardo could not explain them because his theory identified labour *immediately* with its social forms, as value, wages, rent and profit. This was the source of the contradictions which his theory could never resolve, because he could not grasp the socio-historical foundation and limits of these social forms as forms of *alienated labour*. It was his critique of alienated labour which enabled Marx to overcome these limitations in his mature analysis of the value-form, because it is through the theory of value that labour is connected with its alienated forms.

Even in his lifetime Marx was constantly exasperated by the failure of his readers and critics to grasp the significance of his analysis of the value-form. His analysis was first developed in the *Grundrisse*, and was first published in *A Contribution to the Critique of Political Economy*. However the *Critique*, to Marx's distress, had little impact. Marx further developed his ideas in the manuscripts later published as *Theories of Surplus Value*. In the first edition of *Capital* Marx summarised the argument in the text, and at the last minute added a 'school-masterly' appendix which presented the argument 'as simply as possible' (Letter to Engels, 22nd June 1867). This met with an equal incomprehension, so that Marx integrated the appendix into a re-written first part for the second edition of *Capital*. This last attempt is the most confusing of all for the reader, because it separates the exposition of labour as the substance of value, with which the chapter begins, from the exposition of the form of value which follows, despite the fact that it is only through the value-form that labour is constituted socially as the substance of value. Thus the exposition can easily be read as radically distinguishing the 'quantitative value problem', constituted by the economic analysis of labour as the substance of value, from the 'qualitative value problem', constituted by the analysis of the historically specific form of value.

However, Marx insists that labour is not in itself value, nor is it in itself the source of wages, rent and profit. The relationship between labour and its social forms is not an *immediate* one. It is a relationship that is *mediated* by the particular social relationships within which the expenditure of labour-power and appropriation of the products of labour take place in a particular society.

The task of the critique of political economy is to go beyond the analytical moment of the classics in order to show how it is that in a particular kind of society labour appears in the alienated form of value. The foundation of the critique of political economy is, therefore, the investigation of the 'form of value' that the classics took for granted, for this is the fundamental social reality of the alienation of labour. On the basis of this investigation it becomes possible to locate the relations of the production, distribution and circulation of things in a capitalist society as the alienated forms of social relations between people.

The analysis of the value-form makes it possible to go beyond the 'external' critique of political economy of Marx's early works and of most of his interpreters. It does not simply add an historical and sociological dimension that was neglected by the classical writers. The substance of the classical theory is transformed through the critique, for the processes through which the economic categories are determined are no longer natural processes: of subsistence need, of fertility of the soil, of demographic increase. The economic categories are determined socially and so the factors involved in their determination are quite different from the factors identified by the classical writers. In revealing the social determination of these categories the critique of political economy uncovers the social foundations of the laws of development of capitaism. In so doing the critique of political economy is able to resolve the contradictions that plagued classical political economy. It does this by showing that these contradictions within theory arise from the attempt to deny the existence of real 'contradictions' in capitalist society, that is from the attempt to show the process of capitalist development as an harmonious and co-ordinated process. Correspondingly, once it is recognised that economic laws are not natural but social laws it comes to be recognised that these laws do not determine the fate of humanity, but only the fate of a particular form of society.

Marx's critique of political economy, centred on the critique of the labour theory of value, is the core of Marx's theory of capitalist society. It is not primarily a critique of the adequacy of classical political economy as economic theory, although it does give rise to important economic conclusions (and Marx anticipated most of the valid criticisms of the classical school that came to be formulated by later economists: of the wages-fund doctrine, the Malthusian law of population, the neglect of the role of the market, the theory of money, Say's Law, etc.). Above all it is a critique of the classical conception of society that rested on the naturalism of the classical theory of value. In *Capital* Marx laid the foundations of a quite different approach to capitalist society. It is this approach that I hope to elucidate in this chapter.

The magnitude of value and the form of value

According to Marx, Ricardo's great contribution to political economy was that he discovered the key to the 'obscure structure of the bourgeois economic system' in 'the determination of *value by labour-time*' (*TSV*, II, pp. 165–6). However, Ricardo's theory of value was formulated in abstraction from the social relations within which things come to acquire value as commodities. Thus the Ricardian theory of value is based on the 'formal abstraction' of 'production' in which the expenditure of labour-time is considered independently of the social form of production, as a technical characteristic of the production process. The value of a commodity is determined by the quantity of labour required for its production, given the knowledge, techniques and implements available, irrespective of the form of society within which the thing is produced. The concept of value is therefore essentially a technological concept, determined prior to, and independently of, the social relations between the producers, in accordance with the productivity of labour.

Ricardo's naturalistic theory of value overlooked the fact that it is only in a particular kind of society that the products of labour take on the form of commodities and appear as values. It is not labour in general that appears in the form of value, but commodity-producing labour. Thus Ricardo ignored the fact that value is only determined as such within particular social relations. Ricardo '*does not examine* the form — the peculiar characteristic of labour that creates exchange-value or manifests itself in exchange-values — the *nature* of this labour' (*TSV*, II, p. 164).

Marx did not simply *add* consideration of the *form* of value to

The magnitude of value and the form of value

Ricardo's labour theory of value. Once we consider the form of value we realise that the substance of value is not the labour embodied in the commodity.

> The materialisation of labour is not to be taken in such a Scottish sense as Adam Smith conceives it. When we speak of the commodity as the materialisation of labour — in the sense of its exchange value — this itself is only an imaginary, that is to say a purely social mode of existence of the commodity which has nothing to do with its corporeal reality; it is conceived as a definite quantity of social labour or of money ... The mystification here arises from the fact that a social relation appears in the form of a thing (*TSV*, I, p. 167).

The substance of labour is not embodied labour, but the labour-time socially necessary to produce the commodity.

The distinction between 'embodied labour' and 'socially necessary labour-time' appears at first sight to be a technical distinction of interest only to economists. However it is fundamental because it expresses the distinction between the naturalistic conception of value as the labour embodied in the commodity as a thing and the socio-historical conception of value as the labour that is socially attributed to the thing as a commodity. The labour that is the source of value is not embodied labour as a universal substance. Value is labour for others; labour in so far as it is socially recognised within a division of labour; labour whose social character has been abstracted from the activity of the labourer to confront the labourer as the property of a thing; labour whose human qualities have been reduced to the single quality of duration; dehumanised, homogeneous, in short *alienated* labour.[5] The social foundation of value is precisely the alienation of labour that Marx had analysed in 1844.

In 1844 Marx had shown that the hidden presupposition of classical

---

[5] This distinction between embodied labour and alienated labour appears to be contradicted by Marx's presentation of his theory of value in the first chapter of the third edition of *Capital*, on which the English translations are based, where Marx refers to the expenditure of human labour-power 'in the physiological sense' as the common property of commodities which is expressed in the form of value. This formulation replaced a very different passage in the first edition, where Marx had argued that 'commodities as objects of use or goods are corporeally different things. Their reality as *values* forms, on the other hand, their *unity*. This unity does not arise out of nature but out of society' (Marx, 1976, p. 9). It seems clear that the misleading formulation of the first part of Chapter One of *Capital* is the unfortunate result of Marx's attempt to simplify his exposition.

political economy was the concept of private property and that the foundation of private property was alienated labour. In the critique of the classical theory of value this argument is made more concrete. The social foundation of value is an extended division of labour within which social production is regulated through the exchange of commodities. The individual member of society does not produce directly for society according to some self-consciously regulated plan. Rather the individual produces privately. However, the product is not destined for the producer's own use. It can only function as a use-value within the system of social production. Despite its private production, therefore, it has been produced for the use of others and it is only as such that it can serve as a useful product. Thus the commodity is necessarily a social product, and the labour which produced it is necessarily a part of social labour.

As a thing the commodity is a useful object, product of the concrete useful labour of an individual producer. However the commodity cannot serve directly as a use-value. It can only become a use-value by being exchanged as a value. Hence, within a commodity-producing society the social production of use-values, and so the satisfaction of human needs, is only achieved in the alienated form of the private production of commodities as values.

The mysteries of the commodity arise because the social relations within which commodities are determined as values are not immediately apparent. Although value is attributed to a commodity within a social relation of exchange, it is a matter of accident with whom any particular exchange is made. The individual producer is not concerned who buys the product, but is concerned only to realise its value. The individual has a determinate relationship with the commodity as a value, but a purely accidental relationship with other producers. The value of the commodity then appears to be a property inherent in the relation between the private individual and the commodity as a thing.

As Engels argued in his early critique of political economy, the 'labour theory of value' derives the value of the commodity one-sidedly from the relationship between the commodity and the labourer as producer, the theory of utility derives it equally one-sidedly from the relationship between the commodity and the purchaser as consumer. In each case the value of the commodity appears to be independent of the social relations of production: the relations between people appear to arise because the commodity has a value, as product of labour, on the one side, and as object of desire, on the other. Hence the social powers of the commodity, that derive from the social relations of commodity production, appear to be inherent in the commodity as a thing. This is the origin of the 'fetishism of commodities'.

The failure of the classical political economists to investigate the connection between social labour and its alienated forms prevented them from penetrating the illusions of the fetishism of commodities. It was this failure to explore the social determination of value that led them to naturalise capitalist social relations:

> Even its best representatives, Adam Smith and Ricardo, treat the form of value as something of indifference, something external to the nature of the commodity itself. The explanation for this is not simply that their attention is entirely absorbed by the analysis of the magnitude of value. It lies deeper. The value-form of the product of labour is the most abstract, but also the most universal form of the bourgeois mode of production; by that fact it stamps the bourgeois mode of production as a particular kind of social production of a historical and transitory character. If then we make the mistake of treating it as the eternal natural form of social production, we necessarily overlook the specificity of the value-form, and consequently of the commodity-form together with its further developments, the money form, the capital form etc. (Marx, *Capital*, I, p. 174).

Commodity fetishism is the form of appearance of particular social relations of production, but it is not merely an illusion. It really is the case that the relations between individuals and things are determinate, while the relations between particular people are accidental. It really is the case that the social fate of the individual is determined by the fate of the commodities she possesses. Thus it really is the case that social relations are mediated by relations between things. The illusion lies not in the fact of the social power of the commodity, but in the belief that this social power derives from the commodity as a thing, rather than being seen as the particular form of alienated social relations. To understand the value-form we need to look more closely at the social form of commodity exchange, and in particular uncover the secret of money in which the power of the commodity is expressed in its most abstract and universal form.

Money as a social relation

Classical political economy failed to penetrate the fetishism of commodities and so it was unable to identify the specific character of exchange as a form of the social relation of commodity production. This underlies the failure of classical political economy to understand money as a form of social relation.

For classical political economy the exchange relation was essentially symmetrical. The two parties to an exchange each had commodities that were wanted by the other. Each could therefore satisfy his or her needs by exchanging commodities, and the rate at which they exchanged was determined by the amount of labour-time each had spent on acquiring the given commodities. Here a double exchange took place: on the one hand, one kind of use-value was exchanged for another, and this was the *form* of exchange; on the other hand, one private labour was exchanged for another, and this was the quantitative determination, the *content*, of exchange. Classical political economy was based on this picture of exchange as an essentially *private* relation of barter between *individuals*. The developed system of exchange found in a capitalist society is simply a generalisation of this elementary private barter, into which money has been introduced as a technical instrument to facilitate the coordination of needs.

For Marx this model of exchange was nonsense. Where isolated individuals made occasional exchanges, as in the parable of classical political economy, there was no reason why exchange ratios should correspond to the quantity of labour embodied in the particular commodities, for it was only within a competitive system of exchange that there was a tendency for exchange ratios to achieve such a quantitative determinacy. But within any *system* of exchange the

> private interest is itself already a socially determined interest, which can be achieved only within the conditions laid down by society and with the means provided by society; hence it is bound to the reproduction of these conditions and means. It is the interest of private persons; but its *content* as well as the *form* and means of its realisation, is given by social conditions independently of all. (*Grundrisse*, p. 156, my emphasis)

In any developed system of exchange the exchange relation does not comprise two separate exchanges, of use-values, on the one hand, and of labour-time (values), on the other. Rather there is a single but asymmetrical exchange. If I bring a commodity to market I am not concerned with the use-value of the commodity, but only with its value: for me the commodity is a means of acquiring other commodities. On the other hand, in making an exchange I seek to trade my commodity, which has no use for me, for another commodity which I can use. The other commodity therefore exists for me as a potential use-value. Thus in the process of exchange I seek to realise my commodity as a value in order to acquire another commodity which can serve as a use-value for me. The whole point of the system of exchange is that it does not, as in the classical parable, co-ordinate needs with one another through the direct exchange of use-values. Needs are related in an alienated form, only through the mediation of value. Thus, even within the direct exchange of commodities there is a fundamental asymmetry that already contains the possibility that exchange will not prove as harmonious as the classical parable would lead us to believe.

As soon as we move away from the classical parable and consider exchange as a social process it becomes clear that the process of exchange, even in its simplest form, cannot be reduced to the isolated exchange of one commodity for another. When I take a commodity to market I take the product of a certain quantity of concrete labour which I want to exchange. I hope that in exchanging my commodity I will be compensated for the amount of labour that I have actually expended. In other words I seek to represent my commodity as the embodiment of abstract, socially necessary labour-time and not simply as the product of my particular concrete labour. This is the key to the understanding of money.

In seeking to make an exchange in which another commodity will serve as equivalent for my commodity, I will not consider the amount of concrete labour actually embodied in that commodity, I will consider that commodity as an embodiment of abstract labour, of socially necessary labour-time. I will not be swayed by the observation that the producer of the other commodity has in fact taken much longer than the time socially necessary, for on entering the market the equivalent is detached from its concrete conditions of production.

Examination of exchange as a social relation makes it clear that the commodity which acts as the equivalent for my commodity does not appear as a particular commodity in the exchange relation, but represents the social world of commodities in which my commodity has to play its part. Thus the equivalent commodity appears in the exchange relation as the embodiment of abstract labour, a portion of the labour of society as a whole, and my commodity seeks to represent its value in the bodily form of the equivalent. It is only within the exchange relation, within which the other commodity acts as equivalent, that the latter has this social power. Outside that relation, and its role of equivalent, it is simply a particular commodity like any other. The conclusion of Marx's analysis of the equivalent form is that any commodity can act as equivalent, and that money is indeed simply a commodity like any other. However the properties that are attributed to money as the universal equivalent, the embodiment of human labour in the abstract, are not inherent in money as a particular commodity. They are properties that derive from money's social role as equivalent, as properties of the equivalent form.

If we consider money in isolation from the form of exchange we fall into the errors of the political economists. The mercantilists thought that gold embodied value in itself. For them, therefore, the exchange-value of a commodity was determined solely in the market by the relation established between the particular commodity and money as the substance of value: the value of a commodity was the amount of money for which it could be exchanged. Classical political economy ridiculed the monetarist superstition, noted that gold was a commodity like any other, and so argued that exchange-value is simply the ratio of the values of two particular commodities, one of which happens, for convenience, to be gold. For monetarism and mercantilism the exchange-value of a commodity was the accidental relationship established in the market. For the classical school value was immanent in the commodity, and the market was simply the arena in which value expressed itself.

Marx insisted that neither of these conceptions of exchange, and so of money, was adequate. Classical political economy was right to note that the money commodity was a particular commodity like any other. But the monetarists were right to note that money appeared in exchange not as a particular commodity, but as a universal, as the embodiment of value. The paradox is resolved when it is realised that money acquires its powers not through its own properties, but because of its social role in the system of exchange. It is only in its function as universal equivalent that money comes to acquire its power as embodiment of value. This power can consequently only be a social power, the relationship of the commodity to money can only express a social relation, and the development of money is the result of the development of the social relations of commodity production.

The social relation that is expressed in the form of money is the relation between the labour of the individual and the labour of society. It is by submitting the commodity to the test of the market that private labour is submitted to the test of its social usefulness and of its social necessity and that it seeks validation as abstract, social labour. In this relationship there is no guarantee that the individual labour will be validated in this way, so there is no guarantee either that the labour-time socially necessary will correspond to that actually expended or that the labour will prove socially useful in responding to social need as expressed in the market. It is only through the regular divergence of prices from values and of values from the labour-times embodied in particular commodities that the social regulation of production in a commodity-producing society is achieved. The divergence between price and value, which classical political economy treated as accidental and insignificant, is therefore a necessary characteristic of the alienated character of commodity production.

The formal abstractions of political economy, that lead it to treat money simply as a technical instrument, eliminate from view the contradictory foundation of a commodity-producing society that is the source of the crises that punctuate capitalist development. For political economy, which treats production in abstraction from its social form, the only barriers to the indefinite expansion of production are natural barriers, specifically the barrier established by the Malthusian relationship between the natural growth of population and the fertility of the soil. On the other hand, exchange, which is reduced to a purely formal transaction, is considered to be wholly unproblematic. Classical political economy could only conclude that periodic crises are accidental and irrational phenomena, expressing human imperfection, rather than expressing the normal operation of an alienated and irrational form of social production.

It is only when exchange is considered as a particular moment of the social relations of production that the exchange of the commodity for money becomes problematic. In a hypothetical society of petty commodity producers, in which the exchange of commodities is the exchange of things between individuals seeking to satisfy their needs, prices may rise and fall in response to accidental disruptions in the relation between demand and supply. However in a capitalist society, which is the only type of society in which commodity production exists in its developed form, exchange no longer co-ordinates social production with social need, but involves, on the one hand, capitalists who are seeking to produce and reproduce capital and surplus-value, and, on the other, workers who are seeking to reproduce themselves by selling their labour-power as a commodity in order to be able to purchase the means of subsistence from capitalists.

The breakdown of exchange is not simply a superficial disturbance in the relations between the producers and the consumers of things, but an inherent aspect of the regulation of social production. It arises because of the contradictory foundation on which that society is built — that things will only be produced and exchanged to the extent that they can play their part in the production of surplus-value and the reproduction of capitalist social relations. A crisis is not, therefore, simply an economic phenomenon: it is an interruption in the reproduction of the social relations of capitalist society. It is ultimately the neglect of the commodity-form that prevents classical political economy from uncovering the contradictions inherent in the value-form that come to a head in crises:

> If Ricardo thinks that the *commodity* form makes no difference to the product, and furthermore, that commodity circulation differs only formally from barter, that in this context exchange value is only a fleeting form of the exchange of things, and that money is therefore merely a formal means of circulation — then this in fact is in line with his presupposition that the bourgeois mode of production is the absolute mode of production, hence it is a mode of production without any definite specific characteristics, its distinctive traits are purely formal. He cannot therefore admit that the bourgeois mode of production contains within itself a barrier to the free development of the productive forces, a barrier which comes to the surface in crises. (*TSV*, II, pp. 527–8; c.f. III, pp. 54–5.)

The theory of value and the theory of society

The analysis of the value-form, and the demystification of money as the most abstract form of value, brought to fruition the critique of political economy inaugurated in the *Comments on James Mill*. However its implications are much wider than may appear at first

The theory of value and the theory of society

sight, for it is not primarily a critique of the adequacy of political economy as an economic theory, nor is it simply a critique that complements political economy in drawing attention to the social and historical context within which economic activity takes place. It is essentially a critique of the liberal conception of society on which classical political economy is based, and to this extent is a criticism of all bourgeois social thought. At the risk of repetition, it is worth recalling the theoretical structure of political economy.

Classical political economy develops a theory of society on the basis of the formal abstractions of the individual, private property, production and of exchange. The foundation of political economy is the conception of the private property owner as an abstract individual, unconstrained by imposed obligations, who is capable of making and of acting on her own rational judgements. The individual is inserted in relations of production, distribution and exchange, on the basis of her ownership of physical things which can serve as factors of production. Thus the social relations of capitalist production, distribution and exchange exist independently of persons, as relations between things.

Production is reduced to the technical process of the production of things, while exchange is treated as a mechanism through which those things are exchanged for one another on the basis of the physical labour-time embodied in them. These relations between things are expressed in the form of social relations between persons through the development of private property, by which persons are attached to those things as owners, and thereby enter social relations independent of their will. This leads to the fundamental conclusion of political economy, that the condition for the realisation of the productive potential inherent in the technical conditions of production, through the extension of the division of labour and the application of machinery, is the freedom of the individual property owner to dispose of her property according to private judgements of individual self-interest. Capitalist private property is therefore a juridical institution that imposes no social constraints, an expression of the reason that is the defining characteristic of human nature. Thus the social relations of capitalist production, embodied in the freedom and security of private property, are naturalised, and presented as the free expression of human rationality in the face of the objective constraints imposed by an external nature. Moreover these social relations also express the moral ideal, since they leave the individual to be the judge of her own interest while providing the means by which such interests can be optimally reconciled.

Classical political economy is not simply a theory of capitalist economic relations. The realisation of human rationality through capitalist relations of production, distribution and exchange presupposes the freedom and security of property, on the one hand, and the freedom of the individual from external moral and political constraint, on the other. It therefore defines the constitutional, legal and political circumstances within which rational judgements of self-interest can be made and acted on, and derives moral imperatives from the rational self-interest of the abstract individual that can serve as the basis of education, enlightenment and legal regulation. Thus classical political economy offers a liberal theory of the ideal society that can reconcile the necessity of legal, political and moral constraint with the freedom of the individual by establishing that such constraint corresponds to the rational self-interest of the enlightened individual. Classical political economy develops a complete model of capitalist society as the expression of human reason. It describes 'a very Eden of the innate rights of man. It is the exclusive realm of Freedom, Equality, Property and Bentham' (*Capital*, I, p. 280).

The coherence of this liberal model of society rests on the coherence of its starting point, the presupposition that capitalist social relations can be analysed as relations between 'private' individuals, related as property owners through the 'things' which they own. It is this presupposition that Marx undermined with his critique of alienated labour, which showed that private property is not a juridical relation between a person and a thing, but a form of social relation, in which the relation of the owner to the thing owned is subordinate to the social relations between commodity producers. It is this critique that is given positive substance by the development of the analysis of the 'fetishism of commodities' in *Capital*.

According to political economy the property relation is constituted in the act of production, as the producer appropriates nature through labour, and appropriates the product of that labour in the form of private property. In abstraction from the system of social production this property relation indeed appears to be a private relation between an individual and a thing. However this relation of appropriation is not a private relation, for the thing has not been produced with a view to its appropriation by its producer, but with a view to exchange. The individual produces the thing as a commodity, on the presupposition that others will also produce commodities and

The theory of value and the theory of society

that the respective products will be exchangeable as commodities. The individual act of (private) production is only undertaken on the assumption that the individual will find available in the market the things necessary to satisfy her subsistence needs and to sustain a renewed round of commodity production. The individual act of production and appropriation therefore presupposes a social division of labour expressed in the total process of production and exchange of commodities. It is only in relation to this system of social production that the individual act of production and appropriation has any significance, and it is only on that basis that the product takes the form of private property. The presupposition of private property is therefore the social relation of commodity production.

However private property not only *presupposes* these social relations, it is itself a *form* of the social relations of commodity production. Liberal social theory, and classical political economy, fail to see this because they fail to distinguish the commodity as a thing (a use-value), from the commodity as a social relation (a value), and correspondingly fail to distinguish the concrete labour embodied in the product from the abstract labour expressed in the form of the value of the commodity. The liberal theory of property is based on the immediate relation between concrete labour and the product as a thing, and it is this relation which is expressed in the Ricardian theory of embodied labour as the substance of value. However the value of a commodity is not determined in this private relationship, by the amount of labour concretely embodied in the product. It is only determined in the social relationship between producers, in which the commodity is attributed a value to the extent that it is recognised as the socially useful product of socially necessary labour. Outside this relationship the commodity has no value, and so does not exist as property.

Although the commodity that is appropriated as private property is indeed a thing, it is not as a thing that it is appropriated as private property, but as a value. The commodity has not been produced to satisfy directly the needs of the producer, and it is worth nothing to the producer as a use-value. It is only as the property of *another* that the commodity can be realised as a use-value. Thus it has been produced as a commodity not to serve directly as a *use-value*, but to be exchanged as a *value*, and it is only to the extent that it can achieve social recognition as a value that it is worth appropriating as private property. The property relation is not, therefore, a private relation between an individual and a thing, but a social relation between an individual and a sum of value embodied in a thing, a relation of *privatisation* of a portion of the social product, not a relation constructed in private.[6]

The relation of private property is the fetishised form taken by the relation between the individual and other producers within the social division of labour. The relation of exchange, within which the commodity is realised as private property, is the relation within which the social character of private labour is realised as a moment of the social division of labour. However, if the commodity is viewed as a thing, if its social character is considered to be inherent in it as a thing, the social relations between the producers appear as relations between things, and the social determinations of the individual appear as natural laws, impervious to the human will. Human subjectivity is thereby reduced to individual rationality in the face of a world of natural constraint. Thus the demystification of the fetishism of commodities is at the same time the demystification of the relation of private property, and the corresponding concept of the private individual, that is at the foundation of liberal social theory.

If the individual proprietor is necessarily a social being, with the social relations of production already presupposed in the property relation, the implication is that the theory of society must take as its starting point not the abstract individual, but the historically given social relations of production: 'Individuals producing in society — hence socially determined individuals — is, of course, the point of departure' (*Grundrisse*, p. 83).

Once it is recognised that the property relation is a social relation it also becomes clear that different forms of property express different forms of social relation. These differences are suppressed in the abstract consideration of the individual as a property-owner, a consideration which corresponds to the abstract model of an undifferentiated society of petty commodity producers, in which social relations are indeed relations of freedom and equality, however restricted their social and material base.

The analysis of capitalist society cannot stop with the analysis of the abstract commodity-form. It also has to understand how the relations of freedom and equality expressed in that form turn into their opposite. Thus we have to turn from the analysis of value

---

[6] The social determination of private property is most dramatically brought home by the *devaluation* of the commodity in the event of a crisis of overproduction, in which the commodity becomes worthless as private property, and may be discarded or destroyed.

and of money to the analysis of capital. However it is important to understand that in turning to capital we are not leaving the analysis of the commodity-form behind, for capital is only a further development of the contradictions inherent in the commodity form. Thus the classical failure to understand the commodity-form also explains the classical failure to understand the more developed form of value as capital.

The classical model of a society of freedom and equality is not only abstract, it is also purely hypothetical, for petty commodity production rests on contradictory foundations. The emergence of money as the universal equivalent forms the immediate basis on which money can be withdrawn from circulation, to become a store of value, whether as savings from normal revenues, or as a windfall deriving from particular good fortune. The accumulation of a monetary hoard gives the more frugal or the more fortunate a claim on the product of the less fortunate, and so becomes the basis on which inequalities will, unless checked by other social mechanisms, develop cumulatively. Money gives rise to credit, as those with money lend to those in need, and debt gives rise to dependence. The cushion of a monetary reserve ensures that good fortune becomes cumulative, allowing the wealthy to augment their hoards, while the poor fall ever-deeper into debt. The lever of debt than provides a means by which the rich can appropriate the products of the labour of the poor, and eventually, by foreclosing on their loans, reduce the poor to the status of wage-labourers. The freedom and equality of petty commodity production is transformed, according to the contradictory development of its own rationality, into the unfreedom and inequality of capitalism.

Capital as a social relation

In analysing the form of value Marx abstracted from the specifically capitalist form of production, although it is only under capitalism that commodity production is generalised. In the analysis of value Marx therefore made no reference to class relations nor to the distribution of the value produced among the social classes. This abstraction is legitimate because capitalism is a form of commodity production, on the one hand, and because recognition of the capitalist form of production does not *immediately* affect the analysis of the commodity and the form of value, on the other. However we now have to ask how the social form of capitalist production expresses itself in distinctively capitalist relations of production and exchange.

Marx introduced consideration of capital by examining capital in its most abstract form, its 'first form of appearance', as 'money capital' (*Capital*, I, p. 247). Money is not in itself capital, but only becomes capital when it acquires the power of 'self-expansion'. When money functions as the means of circulation of commodities it has no such powers of self-expansion, nor does it if it is accumulated in an idle hoard. A sum of money can only be increased by throwing it into circulation, by buying some commodities, and then withdrawing it again by selling commodities. Money therefore only becomes capital through this process in which it expands in the course of its circulation. 'Value therefore now becomes value in process, money in process, and, as such, capital' (*Capital*, I, p. 256).

In this process a sum of value in the form of money is expended in the buying of commodities, and commodities are later sold in order to realise a greater sum of value in the form of money. Thus a certain sum of value through this process begets a 'surplus-value'. The term 'capital' refers to this *process* in which a sum of value apparently acquires the power of expanding itself. Money and commodities are not in themselves capital, they are simply forms taken on by capital in the process of self-expansion. It is not the value of money nor that of the commodities that increases in the process, otherwise there would be no need for capital to go through these changes of form to expand itself. To believe otherwise is to identify capital with one of its forms, to see capital '*as a thing, not as a relation*' (*Grundrisse*, p. 258) and so to succumb to the fetishism of commodities.

Money and commodities only become capital when they participate in the process in which value expands itself. To understand capital we therefore have to understand this process of self-expansion of value. How does a sum of value, a quantity of abstract labour, manage to assimilate to itself more value in the course of its circulation? This is only possible if at some point in its circulation capital is able to appropriate labour without payment. The problem is where this occurs.

This appropriation cannot take place within exchange, at least as so far considered, because exchange does not *create* value, it merely changes its form. It is certainly the case that unequal exchanges could take place, but such exchanges could not yield a *surplus* value, they could only redistribute a portion of an existing sum of value as gains

Capital as a social relation

and losses balanced out. The early forms of merchants' and usurers' capital were based on such a redistribution of value.

New value can be added only by the expenditure of labour in production. Thus the source of surplus-value can only be a difference between the amount paid for the labour and the labour actively expended. However this in turn seems impossible to explain, for it implies that labour is a commodity paid below its value, which raises the question of what is special about labour that prevents it from being paid at its value.

Marx solved this problem by examining carefully the *social form* of capitalist production, concluding that the commodity purchased by the capitalist was not labour, but labour-power. When the capitalist employed the worker there was not a symmetrical relation of production in which the worker sold her labour and the capitalist his 'capital' to the enterprise and each then shared in the product according to the contributions of labour and 'capital'. What actually happened was that the worker sold to the capitalist her ability to work ('labour-power') for a certain length of time. The capitalist used his capital to buy this labour-power and the requisite means of production which he then set to work to produce commodities. In selling her 'labour-power' the worker had given up all rights to the product, so the entire product was appropriated by the capitalist. Thus the capitalist form of the labour process

> exhibits two characteristic phenomena. Firstly, the worker works under the control of the capitalist to whom his labour belongs ... Secondly, the product is the property of the capitalist and not that of the worker, its immediate producer. (*Capital*, I, pp. 291–2)

These characteristics derived from the fact that production was premissed on the purchase and sale of labour-power as a commodity.

The difference between the labour-power that the worker sells and the labour that the worker actually performs is the key to the understanding of surplus-value. As a commodity, labour-power has an unique characteristic in that the 'consumption' of labour-power is itself the expenditure of labour and so the production of value. Thus labour-power is paid for as a commodity at its value, like any other commodity, but having been purchased the labour-power can be set to work to produce value in excess of its own value.

The distinction between labour and labour-power is no pedantic terminological distinction, it is an aspect of the fundamental distinction between use-value and value, the confusion of which underlies the mystifications of political economy. Labour and labour-power are distinct concepts because they describe distinct objects, corresponding to distinct social relations, the relationship between which is only established through particular social relations of production. Labour is the realisation of the potential inherent in the capacity to labour. Where the labourers possess the requisite means of production and subsistence the realisation of this potential is subject only to the will of the labourers, individually and collectively. The historical separation of the labourer from the means of production and subsistence severs the immediate connection between labour-power and labour. Labour-power is now the object of an exchange relation between capitalist and wage-labourer, in which the labourer sells her labour-power in exchange for the value equivalent of the means of subsistence. In exchange for the wage the capitalist acquires a title to the entire product of labour. However, on completion of the exchange this product does not yet exist. It can only come into being through the subjective exercise of the will of the labourers in the production of commodities.

The contradiction which now arises is that the labourers have alienated all entitlement to the product of their labour to the capitalist, and so no longer have any interest in realising the potential inherent in their capacity to labour. The capitalist, on the other hand, has to ensure that the labourers produce a sum of value exceeding that which he has laid out as capital, and to do this he has to subordinate the will of the labourers to his own will. The relationship between labour-power and labour is only realised through this conflict of wills, which is fought out within the social relations which constitute the immediate production process. Ricardo's identification of labour-power with labour abstracts from the necessarily antagonistic character of these social relations.

It is important to notice that the theory of surplus value does not depend on the determination of value by labour-time, but on the analysis of the social form of capitalist production, based on the distinction between labour and labour-power, the value of which is determined quite independently of one another. Surplus value derives from the quantitative relationship between two quite distinct magnitudes, as the difference between the sum of value acquired by the capitalist for the sale of the product and the sum paid out in the purchase of labour-power and means of production. The latter sum has to be paid out as the condition of production. The size of the former depends on the ability of the capitalist to compel the workers to work beyond the time necessary to produce a product equivalent in value to the sum initially laid out, whatever may be the particular units in which value is measured. It is the capitalist form of the social determination of production which makes it appropriate to express the value of the product in terms of the expenditure of labour-time, since it is capital, not Ricardo or Marx, which subordinates the concrete activity of labour to the expenditure of labour-time. Thus the validity of the 'labour theory of value' is not the presupposition of the theory of surplus value, but is its result, to the extent that it is the adequate theoretical expression of the social form of capitalist production.

The distinction between labour and labour-power makes it possible to overcome the contradictions of political economy, by making it possible to reconcile the existence of profit with the equality of exchange. For Ricardo wages correspond to the value of labour, so that labour has not one but two values — the value it has in exchange and the value it contributes to the product. Thus its exchange-value does not correspond to its value. This led the Ricardian socialists to conclude that labour is paid below its value and that this is the source of profit. The implication is that the source of exploitation is the inequality of exchange between labour and capital and that exploitation can therefore be abolished by equalising that exchange. By introducing the distinction between labour and labour-power Marx resolves this contradiction and shows that exploitation is consistent with equality of exchange, so that the abolition of exploitation depends on the abolition of the wage-relation and not simply on its equalisation.

The social foundation of labour-power as a commodity is the separation of the labourer from the means of production and subsistence that compels the labourer to sell her labour-power as a commodity in order to participate in social production and so gain access to the means of subsistence. It is this separation that is consequently the social foundation of surplus-value and so of capital. Capital, like the commodity, is not a self-sufficient thing with inherent social powers, but a social relation that appears in the form of relations between things. The social relation that is concealed behind capital is, however, a new social relation, not the relationship between private producers concealed behind the commodity, but a relation between social classes. This *class* relation is the logical and historical presupposition of capitalist production, the social condition for the existence of individual capitalists and workers, and the basis on which the labour of one section of society is appropriated without equivalent by another. The foundation of this relation is the separation of the mass of the population from the means of production and subsistence.

The capitalist labour-process

Once the concept of capital is introduced our understanding of production and exchange is further developed. Production is no longer under the control of the direct producer. The social presupposition of capitalist production is the separation of the direct producer from the means of production, so that the direct producer can only work under the direction of another, the capitalist. For the capitalist the aim of production is not the production of use-values, but the production of value and of surplus-value. The capitalist production of use-values is only incidental to the capitalist production of surplus-value. The capitalist labour-process is no longer a process in which workers produce use-values by setting the means of production to work. It becomes the process in which capital sets labour to work to produce value: 'It is no longer the worker who employs the means of production, but the means of production which employ the worker' (*Capital*, I, p. 425).

This domination of the worker by the thing in the labour-process, which first acquires a 'technical and palpable reality' with the coming of machinery, should not be seen as a feature of the labour-process as a technical process. The thing in this, as in other cases, can only acquire its social power within particular social relations. The power of the machine over the worker in the labour-process is therefore only a form of the power of capital. The power of capital is in turn the power of alienated labour, of labour appropriated by the capitalist in the form of surplus-value and turned, as capital, into the means of appropriating more labour. 'Hence the rule of the capitalist over the worker is the rule of things over man, of dead labour over living, of the product over the producer' (*Capital*, I, p. 990).

It is only within the capitalist labour-process that the process of production is completely subordinated to the production of value. For the independent commodity producer the labour-process can still be endowed with some human qualities. In the capitalist labour-

The capitalist labour-process

process the only criterion is labour-time and the attempt to reduce the labour-time spent to a minimum. It is this unqualified subjection of production to the production of value and of surplus-value that characterises the capitalist labour process. Production is therefore not in any way the technical arena of co-operation in the production of use-values presented by classical political economy; it is a constant arena of struggle over the length of the working day, over the intensity of labour, over the degradation and dehumanisation of labour through which the worker seeks to resist her complete subordination to capital.

The class struggle over production is not a matter of the subjective motivation of the capitalist, but is imposed on every capitalist by the pressure of competition, which is the expression of the tendency for capitalism to develop the forces of production without regard to the limits of the market. Capitalist production is not marked by the subordination of social production to social need, even as that is expressed in the restricted form of 'effective demand' in the market, for the purpose of the capitalist is not to meet social need, but to expand his capital. The pressure of competition forces every capitalist constantly to develop the forces of production, which leads to the general tendency for capital, in every branch of production, to develop the forces of production without limit and, in particular, without regard to the limits of the market. This tendency to the overproduction of commodities and the uneven development of the forces of production is only overcome by the expansion of the world market and the development of new 'needs', and by the regular destruction of productive capacity and redundancy of labour in the face of crises of overproduction. The development of capitalist production is subject neither to the needs of the associated producers, nor to the needs of the latter as consumers, but to the contradictory logic of the production and accumulation of surplus value.

The tendency for capitalist competition to impose on every capitalist the need to reduce labour-time to a minimum gives rise to the two fundamental features of capitalist development: on the one hand, the tendency to increase the productivity of labour to an extent never before seen; on the other hand, the tendency to increase productivity not for the benefit of, but at the expense of, the mass of the population. Thus the increased productivity of labour is not expressed in a growing abundance of goods for the mass of the population, nor in a reduction in the burden of work. Instead it is expressed in a growing accumulation of capital at one pole of society and growing poverty (relative if not absolute) at the other. It is expressed in an increased burden of work for those with jobs, alongside a growing 'reserve army of labour' who have been made redundant and are condemned to idleness. The depreciation of machinery in the course of accumulation is matched by the throwing of workers onto the scrap heap. The more rapid is 'progress' the more rapidly is work dehumanised and workers degraded, exploited and cast aside.

Capitalism makes possible unprecedented increases in the productive powers of labour. These increases are associated with an increasing scale of production, the application of machinery and the application of science. These are characteristics of the greater socialisation of production achieved under capitalism. But this socialisation only takes place under the direction of capital, and the product of socialised labour is appropriated by the capitalist. Thus the social powers of labour, which appear only when labour is organised socially, appear to be the powers of capital. Moreover, since capital in turn is seen as a thing and not a social relation, these powers of capital seem to be inherent in the means of production, so that productivity appears as a technical characteristic of the means of production and not as a social characteristic of the labour process.

> The *social configuration* in which the individual workers exist ...does not belong to them ...On the contrary, it confronts them as a *capitalist arrangement* that is *imposed* on them ...And quite apart from the combination of labour, the social character of the conditions of labour — and this includes machinery and *capitale fixe* of every kind — appears to be entirely autonomous and independent of the worker. It appears to be a *mode of existence of capital* itself, and therefore as something ordered by *capitalists* without reference to the workers. Like the *social character* of their own labour, but to a far greater extent, the *social character* with which the conditions of production are endowed ...appears as capitalistic, as something independent of the workers and intrinsic to the conditions of production themselves ...In the same way, *science*, which is in fact the general intellectual product of the social process, also appears to be the direct offshoot of capital (*Capital*, I, pp. 1052–3, c.f. *TSV*, I, pp. 377–80).

The capitalist process of exchange

Classical political economy considered exchange as a formal abstraction. The exchange relation was treated as a self-sufficient relation whose content was reduced to its formal properties. As such a formal abstraction the exchange relation is a relation between free and equal individual property-owners who enter a voluntary contract in pursuit of their own self-interest. The exchange relation in itself makes no reference to the circumstances in which the individual seeks to exchange, nor to the characteristics of the commodity offered for exchange, nor to the means by which the individual came upon that commodity. Since every exchange is freely entered by both parties it must be to the advantage of each and the conclusion is therefore that unfettered exchange can only serve the common interest. In this simple form of exchange:

> all inherent contradictions of bourgeois society appear extinguished ... and bourgeois democracy even more than the bourgeois economists takes refuge in this aspect ... in order to construct apologetics for the existing economic relations. Indeed, in so far as the commodity or labour is conceived of only as exchange-value ... then the individuals, the subjects between whom this process goes on, are simply and only conceived of as exchangers. As far as the formal character is concerned there is no distinction between them, and this is the economic character, the aspect in which they stand towards one another in the exchange relation; it is the indicator of their social function or social relation towards one another ... As subjects of exchange, their relation is therefore that of *equality*. It is impossible to find any trace of distinction, not to speak of contradiction, between them — not even a difference. Furthermore, the commodities which they exchange are, as exchange values, equivalent, or at least count as such (*Grundrisse*, pp. 240–1).

If we look outside the act of exchange we still cannot find any class relations, for according to this model the relation of exchange brings together individuals who exchange a natural product in accordance with their natural needs:

> As regards the content outside the act of exchange ... this content, which falls outside the specifically economic form, can only be:

(1) The natural particularity of the commodity being exchanged. (2) The particular natural need of the exchangers ... The content of the exchange ... far from endangering the social equality of individuals, rather makes their natural difference into the basis of their social equality ... In this respect, however, they are not indifferent to one another, but integrate with one another ... so that they stand not only in an equal, but also in a social, relation to one another ... In so far as these natural differences among individuals and among their commodities ... form the motive for the integration of these individuals ... there enters, in addition to the quality of equality, that of *freedom* (*Grundrisse*, pp. 242–3).

If we turn our attention from a society of independent commodity producers to a capitalist society in which labour-power has become a commodity there appear to be no significant changes in the exchange relation. The form of property remains apparently unchanged, exchange still appears to relate free and equal commodity-owners. Every exchange is voluntarily contracted and is, at least ideally, an exchange of equivalents. It would therefore seem to be legitimate to apply the liberal model of the free and equal society, based on the freedom and equality of exchange, to the capitalist society as much as to the society based on simple commodity production. The only difference now is that one more commodity has come onto the market, the worker selling not the products of her labour, but her labour-power, but this commodity, like any other, is exchanged freely and voluntarily.

However, if we look at the process of exchange not from the mythical point of view of the isolated individual, but in terms of the social relations that exchange articulates, matters appear very differently: 'The illusion created by the money-form vanishes immediately if, instead of taking a single capitalist and a single worker, we take the whole capitalist class and the whole working class' (*Capital*, I, p. 713).

If we isolate distinct acts of production and exchange from one another we abstract them from the system of social production within which they take place. Such an abstraction would be forced, for to separate these acts from one another is to deprive them of any meaning. Each act of production or exchange only makes sense as a moment of the total process of social production, so the motive of each exchange can only be found in the process as a whole. The examination of the social form of capital has revealed the social foundations of capitalist production to lie in the class-relation between capital and wage-labour.

This class-relation is the presupposition of every individual act of production and exchange, and alone gives meaning to those acts. If the act of exchange is isolated from the reproduction of capitalist social relations of production of which it is but one moment, the act itself becomes irrational. Thus, for example, the capitalist, as a capitalist, does not purchase labour-power in order to enjoy the use-value of that commodity directly, for labour-power has a use-value for the capitalist only in the process of production of surplus-value. The capitalist does not produce commodities in order to satisfy his own consumption needs, but in order to expand his capital. Labour-power is not a commodity like any other:

> Here ... we are not concerned with the merely *social division of labour* in which each branch is autonomous, so that, for example, a cobbler becomes a seller of boots but a buyer of leather or bread. What we are concerned with here is the *division* of the *constituents of the process of production* itself, constituents that really belong together (*Capital*, I, p. 1015).

This division, which is the basis of the class-relation between capital and labour, represents a completely different social relation from that effected between independent commodity producers by the social division of labour, and so the production of capital expresses a completely different social relation from the production of commodities.

> In the actual *commodity-market*, then, it is quite true that the worker, like any other owner of money, is a buyer and is distinguished by that fact alone from the commodity-owner as seller. But on the *labour-market*, money always confronts him as *capital* in the form of money, and so the owner of capital appears as capital personified, as a *capitalist*, and he for his part appears to the owner of money merely as the personification of labour-power and hence of labour, i.e. as a *worker*. The two people who face each other on the market-place, in the sphere of circulation, are not just a *buyer* and a *seller*, but *capitalist* and *worker* who confront each other as buyer and seller (*Capital*, I, p. 1015).

Thus nobody enters exchange as a pre-social individual. We are from the beginning concerned with society, social relations based on class antagonism. These relations are not relations between individual and individual, but between worker and capitalist, between farmer and landlord, etc. Wipe out these relations and you annihilate all society (*CW*, 6, p. 159).

When we look at the process of capitalist production as a whole we find that the class relations are not only its *presupposition* but also its *result*. The worker

> emerges from the process as he entered it, namely as a merely subjective labour-power which must submit itself to the same process once more if it is to survive. In contrast to this, capital does not emerge from the process as it entered it. It only becomes real capital ... in *the course* of the process. It now exists as capital realised in the form of the aggregate product, and as such, as the property of the capitalist, it now confronts labour once more as an autonomous power even though it was created by that very labour ... Previously, the conditions of production confronted the worker as capital only in the sense that he *found* them existing as *autonomous* beings opposed to himself. What he now finds opposed to him is the product of his own labour. What had been the premiss is now the result of the process of production ... Therefore it is not only true to say that labour produces on a constantly increasing scale the conditions of labour in opposition to itself in the *form* of *capital*, but equally capital produces on a steadily increasing scale the productive wage-labourers it requires. Labour produces the conditions of production in the form of *capital*, and capital produces labour, i.e. as wage-labour, as the means towards its own realisation as *capital* (*Capital*, I, pp. 1061–2).

The result is that the capitalist production process as a whole, seen as a social process which embraces both production and exchange, produces not only use-values, but values; not only values, but surplus-value; not only surplus-value, but the social relation of production between capital and labour. The capitalist form of property is both the premiss and the result of capitalist production and exchange. 'This incessant reproduction, this perpetuation of the worker, is the absolutely necessary condition for capitalist production' (*Capital*, I, p. 716, c.f. pp. 723–4, 1065).

The capitalist process of exchange

The capitalist form of property is still based on the freedom and equality of every commodity owner, and so is still compatible with the legal form of private property appropriate to simple commodity production, although it is the negation of freedom and equality:

> Each individual transaction continues to conform to the laws of commodity exchange, with the capitalist always buying labour-power and the worker always selling it at what we shall assume is its real value. It is quite evident from this that the laws of appropriation or of private property, laws based on the production and circulation of commodities, become changed into their direct opposite through their own internal and inexorable dialectic. The exchange of equivalents, the original operation with which we started, is now turned round in such a way that there is only an apparent exchange, since, firstly, the capital which is exchanged for labour-power is itself merely a portion of the product of the labour of others which has been appropriated without an equivalent: and, secondly, this capital must not only be replaced by its producer, the worker, but replaced together with an added surplus. The relation of exchange between capitalist and worker becomes a mere semblance belonging only to the process of circulation, it becomes a mere form, which is alien to the content of the transaction itself, and merely mystifies it. The constant sale and purchase of labour-power is the form; the content is the constant appropriation by the capitalist, without equivalent, of a portion of the labour of others which has already been objectified, and his repeated exchange of this labour for a greater quantity of the living labour of others ... The separation of property from labour thus becomes the necessary consequence of a law that apparently originated in their identity ... To the extent that commodity production, in accordance with its own immanent laws, undergoes a further development into capitalist production, the property laws of commodity production must undergo a dialectical inversion so that they become laws of capitalist appropriation ... This *dispels* the illusion that we are concerned here merely with *relations between commodity-owners*. This constant sale and purchase of labour-power, and the constant entrance of the commodity produced by the worker himself as *buyer of* his labour-power and as constant capital, appear merely as *forms which mediate* his subjugation by capital (*Capital*, I, pp. 729–30, 733–4, 1063).

The 'trinity formula' and the theory of class

On the basis of his investigation of the social form of the commodity Marx was able to establish the historical specificity of capitalist social relations and so to undermine the abstract naturalism of classical political economy. Marx's critique of political economy in *Capital* culminates in the critique of the classical theory of class, a theory that Marx characterised by its reliance on the 'trinity formula': land—rent; labour—wages; capital—profit.

The classical theory of class is very different from that developed by Marx. Classical political economy constructs the theory of class, like the rest of its social theory, on a naturalistic foundation. Classes arise on the basis of a differentiation of functions in the technical division of labour. Thus the 'factors' of production — land, labour and capital — are each considered to make specialised contributions to production, so that the social differentiation between the owners of these commodities is an expression of a supposedly technical differentiation between the factors of production. The existence and specific social functions of the three social classes — landowners, was–labourers and capitalists — are then considered to be the inevitable consequence of the existence of land, labour and means of production as 'factors' of production and 'sources' of revenue.

The starting point of the trinity formula is the perfectly accurate observation that revenues accrue to the owners of particular commodities. Thus profit is the revenue that accrues to the owner of means of production; interest, the revenue that accrues to the owner of money, wages the revenue that accrues to the owners of labour-power and rent the revenue that accrues to the owner of land. However, the theory then abstracts from the social relations within which these things function as commodities and within which alone they appear as sources of revenues, to postulate that it is the things themselves that give rise to the revenues in question. Things acquire miraculous social powers as soon as they come into the possession of their owners. This is the culmination of the fetishism of commodities: 'The form of revenue and the sources of revenue are the *most fetishistic* expression of the relations of capitalist production. It is their form of existence as it appears on the surface, divorced from the hidden connections and the intermediate connecting links' (*TSV*, III, p. 453).

However much the trinity formula might accord with the illusions of the individuals engaged in capitalist social relations, it does not stand up to serious analysis. In the first place, it is not clear what properties of the commodities that serve as revenue-sources give rise to their corresponding revenues. Thus different versions of the theory attribute profit to 'capital', to 'money' or to the 'means of production'. The source of profit is alternatively the 'abstinence' of the capitalist; the labour of superintendence; the productive powers of the means of production, the 'roundaboutness' of capitalistic methods of production, the taking of risks or simply the passage of time. The source of wages is variously the subsistence needs of the worker, the unpleasantness of work or the productive powers of labour. The source of rent is variously the fertility of the soil, the progressive infertility of the soil or the scarcity of land. There are, therefore, not one but many different versions of the trinity formula, none of which can provide a satisfactory definition of the source of the revenue in question.

More fundamentally, the formula is irrational, for things cannot have social powers unless those powers are bestowed on them by their insertion in particular social relations. It is only within particular social relations that things become commodities and are able to function as sources of revenue. Labour can only appear as the source of wages in a society in which labour-power has become a commodity. In such a society it is labour-power, and not labour, whose sale gives rise to wages, and wages are determined in a competitive struggle between capitalists and workers whose social identity is constituted by the class relation between a class that is able to monopolise the means of production and subsistence and a class that is deprived of access to the means of production and subsistence except through the sale of labour-power. It is, therefore, only on the basis of the class-relation between capital and labour that labour-power becomes a commodity and so a potential (and not necessarily actual) source of wages. The commodity labour-power whose value appears in the form of the wage has nothing to do with the labour that is engaged as a 'factor' in the production process. The labourer sells her labour-power, not the product of her labour, and the capitalist is contracted to pay for that labour-power for so long as he has it at his disposal, however he may employ it.

The same is true of capital:

> capital is not a thing, but rather a definite social production relation, belonging to a definite historical formation of society,

which is manifested in a thing and lends this thing a specific social character. Capital is not the sum of the material and produced means of production. Capital is rather the means of production transformed into capital, which in themselves are no more capital than gold or silver in itself is money. It is the means of production monopolised by a certain section of society, confronting living labour-power as products and working conditions rendered independent of this very labour-power, which are personified through this antithesis in capital (*Capital*, III, pp. 794–5).

The same is true of land. Rent, as a share of the social product, is supposed to derive from the natural properties of the soil. Land certainly contributes to the production of things, the fertility of the soil being a major determinant of the productivity of labour, but the soil cannot claim back 'its' share. The share of rent can only be determined within definite social relations, and the share of rent will differ according to the form assumed by those relations.

The capital relation and its forms

The trinity formula is irrational because it isolates the individual act of exchange, within which the service of a productive factor is exchanged for a revenue, from the system of social production of which it is necessarily a part. However this irrationality is not just the irrationality of the theories of political economy, for political economy merely expresses the irrationality of the fetishised forms in which capitalist social relations of production present themselves to individual experience. The individual act of exchange is indeed the basis and the limit of the immediate experience of the members of a capitalist society. However, in abstraction from the system of social production, the isolated act of exchange is *irrational*, so any attempt to explain the source of the revenue on the basis of that act can only be irrational in its turn. Nevertheless, however irrational it may be, the trinity formula accords accurately with a commonsense interpretation of individual experience. The irrationality of the trinity formula is therefore not merely the irrationality of political economy, but it reflects the alienated form of capitalist social relations. The critique of the trinity formula has not simply to criticise it as illusory and irrational, but also to show how it arises as the culmination of the

The capital relation and its forms

fetishism of commodities.

In competitive exchange the social character of the commodity is effaced, as a social relation is mediated through the exchange of things between private individuals. In the form of the commodity a social relation assumes an objective and coercive power which is fetishistically attributed to the commodity itself. This is as true of the relations within which the elements of production are exchanged as it is of the relations of exchange between commodity-producers.

The foundation of the illusion of the trinity formula is the 'wage-form', which is the form in which labour-power is purchased and sold as a commodity. Since the worker is employed by the day, the week or the year it appears as though the worker is being paid the full price of her labour and not for her labour-power.

> The wage-form thus extinguishes every trace of the division of the working-day into necessary labour and surplus labour, into paid labour and unpaid labour. All labour appears as paid labour ... We may therefore understand the decisive importance of the transformation of the value and price of labour-power into the form of wages, or into the value and price of labour itself. All the notions of justice held by both the worker and the capitalist, all the mystifications of the capitalist mode of production, all capitalism's illusions about freedom, all the apologetic tricks of vulgar economics, have as their basis the form of appearance discussed above, which makes the actual relations invisible, and indeed presents to the eye the precise opposite of that relation (*Capital*, I, p. 680).

The wage-form is the basis of all the other illusions of the trinity formula. These illusions arise because it appears that labour has already been rewarded for its contribution in the form of the wage. If the value of labour-power is attributed to labour as a factor of production and that value is less than the total value of the commodity, then the remainder of the value must have some other source than labour:

> the other portions of value, profit and rent also appear independent with respect to wages, and must arise from sources of their own, which are specifically different and independent of labour; they must arise from the participating elements of production, to the share of whose owners they fall; profit arises from the participating

elements of production, the material elements of capital, and rent arises from the land, or Nature, as represented by the landlord ...Because at one pole the price of labour-power assumes the transmuted form of wages, surplus-value appears at the opposite pole in the transmuted form of profit (*Capital*, III, pp. 805, 36).

The capitalist receives a profit as a return on his capital, and consequently the capital itself appears to be the source of that profit. In the transformation of surplus-value into profit the illusion arises that it is the entire capital that gives rise to surplus-value and its specific origin, in the extraction of surplus-labour, is concealed. Moreover, in the course of the production and realisation of surplus-value capital takes on various forms — money capital, productive capital, commodity capital — and the functions that fall to each of these forms in the reproduction of capital may be taken on by specialised capitals — money-lenders' capital, industrial capital and commercial capital. Each of these capitals must be compensated by receiving a share of the surplus-value and this gives rise to the distinctive forms of surplus value — interest, the 'profit of enterprise' and commercial profit, each of which appears to have a distinctive source. Finally, barriers to the equalisation of the rate of profit give rise to rent, which is not a product of the land, but a form of surplus-value.

The relationship between surplus-value and the forms in which it appears as interest, commercial profit, the profit of enterprise and rent is a complex and mediated relationship in the development of which the nature and determinants of surplus-value are systematically obscured. All the phenomena that appear in competition

> *seem* to contradict the determination of value by labour-time as much as the nature of surplus value consisting of unpaid surplus labour. *Thus everything appears reversed in competition.* The final pattern of economic relations as seen on the surface, in their real existence, and consequently in the conceptions by which the bearers and agents of these relations seek to understand them, is very different from, and indeed quite the reverse of, their inner but concealed essential pattern and the conception corresponding to it (*Capital*, III, p. 205).

For each individual capitalist the given pre-conditions of capitalist production are wages, the costs of raw materials and means of

The capital relation and its forms

production, and the rent and interest payable. In setting the price at which he will sell his commodity the capitalist adds to these costs of production, which make up the 'cost-price' of the commodity, his expected rate of profit, which corresponds more or less to the normal profit of enterprise. The 'portions into which surplus-value is split, being given as elements of the cost-price for the individual capitalist, appear conversely therefore as creators of surplus-value, creators of a portion of the price of commodities, just as wages create the other'. The result is that

> profit seems to be determined only secondarily by direct exploitation of labour, in so far as the latter permits the capitalist to realise a profit deviating from the average profit at the regulating market prices, which apparently prevail independent of such exploitation. Normal average profits themselves seem immanent in capital and independent of exploitation; abnormal exploitation, or even average exploitation under favourable, exceptional conditions, seems to determine only the deviations from average profit, not this profit itself (*Capital*, III, pp. 249, 806).

Thus the theory embodied in the trinity formula corresponds exactly to the experience and the everyday conceptions of the individual capitalist.

The appearance of capitalist social relations in the form of the trinity formula is consistent with the reality of the class-relation between labour and capital because it really is the case that the value of labour-power and surplus-value appear in the forms of wages, profit and rent and these forms therefore really are the starting point of the economic activity of the individual member of capitalist society.

> These ready-made relations and forms, which appear as preconditions in real production because the capitalist mode of production moves within the forms which it has created itself and which are its results confront it equally as ready-made preconditions in the process of reproduction. As such, they in fact determine the actions of individual capitalists, etc., and provide the motives, which are reflected in their consciousness (*TSV*, III, p. 485).

The capitalists are not aware that in producing commodities in order to make a profit they are also producing and reproducing capitalist social relations. To the individual the appearances seem natural and rational, for the individual takes for granted the social relations within which things acquire their social powers. The need to reproduce capitalist social relations does not immediately enter into the consciousness of the individual capitalist, yet in fulfilling his role in the capitalist production of commodities this is nevertheless what the individual capitalist achieves.

So long as political economy does not question the naturalness of capitalist social relations it is unable to get beyond the illusions of the trinity formula and it can do no more than present in a more or less systematic fashion the irrational forms in which capitalist social relations appear. The critique of political economy depends on a critique of the apparently natural foundations of capitalist social relations in order to establish that those social relations express a particular social form of production. This is what Marx achieved in his critique of the trinity formula as the fullest development of the fetishism of commodities.

The Ricardian contradiction

I have argued that the foundation of Marx's critique of political economy is not the 'labour theory of value', but the theory of alienated labour. The 'labour theory of value' is thus not the foundation but the result of Marx's analysis of the social forms of value and of surplus value. It is only on the basis of this analysis that it is possible to pose the problem of the quantitative determination of value and of price. The key to the solution of this problem is provided by Marx's critique of the trinity formula.

The trinity formula corresponds to the form in which social relations appear to the members of society, as relations in which things are exchanged by private individuals. It therefore. expresses in the most developed form the alienated character of commodity production within which social relations appear in the form of relations between things. It represents the culmination of the fetishism of commodities and the basis on which bourgeois social theories achieve the naturalisation of capitalist class relations.

We have already seen that the Physiocrats identified the natural fertility of the soil as the source of rent, and that Adam Smith at times seemed to be extending the physiocratic theory to capital. The generalisation of the physiocratic theory of distribution, which became the basis of subsequent vulgar economy, was completed by J.-B. Say, for whom the revenues accruing to the different factors of production corresponded to the productive contributions of each factor. The problem with this sort of theory, as we have seen in the case of Smith, is that it is not only irrational, in attributing social powers to things, but it is also indeterminate. Since wages, rent and profit are determined independently of one another, in accordance with the respective productive contributions of labour, land and capital, the price of the commodity is simply the sum of wages, rent and profit. However, wages, rent and profit are themselves prices, so, in the absence of a general equilibrium within which all prices and revenues are determined simultaneously, 'vulgar economy' lacks any determinate theory of distribution.

Smith and Say made important contributions in elucidating the relations between land, labour and capital, on the one hand, and rent, wages and profit, on the other, as they appeared on the surface of capitalist society. However they were unable to penetrate to the 'obscure structure of the bourgeois economic system' beneath its 'externally apparent forms of life' because they had no theory of value that would enable them to explore the relations between the classes.

The labour theory of value is the basis on which 'Ricardo exposes and describes the economic contradictions between the classes — as shown by the intrinsic relations — and that consequently political economy perceives, discovers the root of the historical struggle and development' (*TSV*, II, p. 166). However, class-relations disappear 'in the phenomena of competition', for here members of classes relate to one another as individuals and each class appears to have an independent source of revenue. Thus Smith noted that quite different factors appear to regulate wages, profits and rent respectively. Moreover, price bears no apparent relation to labour-time, being (tautologously) the sum of costs, which Smith reduces to wages, profit and rent. Finally, in relation to individual commodities there is no necessary relationship between wages and profits: an increase in wages being associated sometimes with a rise in profits. Thus Smith abandoned the labour theory of value as soon as he moved beyond the 'early and rude state of society' to adopt an 'adding up' theory of price that corresponded to the apparent relations expressed in the trinity formula.

Ricardo insisted on retaining the labour theory of value despite the fact that it apparently contradicted the determination of prices in the individual relations of competition. Ricardo was well aware of the contradiction, but he could not afford to abandon the labour theory of value because without it he could not explore the relations between classes. He therefore sought to reconcile the theory of value with the determination of price. He did this through the misguided search for a formalistic solution to the problem that prices are affected by the distribution between wages and profits. This was his search for an 'invariable measure of value'. The defenders of Ricardo sought similar formalistic solutions to the contradictions to which the Ricardian theory of value gave rise. These contradictions the later Ricardians

> attempt to solve with phrases in a scholastic way. Crass empiricism turns into false metaphysics, scholasticism, which toils painfully to deduce undeniable empirical phenomena by simple formal abstraction directly from the general law, or to show by cunning argument that they are in accordance with that law (*TSV*, I, p. 87).

The obvious alternative to such metaphysics was to return to the approach of Smith and Say which derived the revenues of the different factors of production independently of one another. Such an approach had the merit of constructing a theory of distribution that accorded with the commonsense experience of the members of capitalist society. The 'vulgarisation' of political economy could claim a certain descriptive validity, so that 'vulgar economy' could present itself as an empirically grounded doctrine against the dogmatic abstractions of Ricardian political economy. Moreover it had the added ideological appeal of a theory that determined distributive shares independently of one another, and so dissolved the conflicts that were inherent in the Ricardian theory. However, to abandon the labour theory of value was to abandon any attempt to penetrate the illusions of the fetishism of commodities in order to establish a determinate theory of class relations. Thus for Marx the vulgarisation of political economy marked the abandonment of any scientific pretensions.

> Whereas the classical, and consequently the critical, economists are exercised by the form of alienation and seek to eliminate it by analysis, the vulgar economists, on the other hand, feel completely at home precisely with the *alienated form* in which the different parts of value confront one another (*TSV*, III, pp. 502–3).

It is clear that the contradiction between price and value is potentially fatal for the Ricardian system, but to abandon the labour theory of value would be to abandon any attempt to develop a determinate theory of class relations. The theories of vulgar economy are, trivially, consistent with the observed tendency for prices to be formed in accordance with the equalisation of the rate of profit on capital, but are indeterminate. The Ricardian theory of value gives a determinate theory of distribution, but one which does not accord with observed tendencies. The contradiction can only be resolved by distinguishing clearly between the formation of surplus-value, on the basis of the expenditure of surplus labour, and the formation of profit, on the basis of the equalisation of the rate of profit, and by investigating more closely the relationship between the two in order to show that the contradiction is 'an *illusion* which arises from the development of the thing itself' (*TSV*, II, p. 32). This must involve a repudiation of the formal abstraction of Ricardo's attempt to derive prices *immediately* from values, in order to uncover the real movement in which surplus labour takes the form of surplus-value and surplus-value is transformed into profit.

Ricardo cannot do this because his method of formal abstraction leads him to ignore the specific features of the social form in which prices diverge from values and so from the specific determinants of price in a particular form of society. It is because he cannot see capitalism as a particular form of society that he identifies the exchange value of the commodity immediately with the concrete labour embodied in it, and so seeks to secure the immediate reconciliation of value and price. Thus he

> wants to show that the various economic categories or relationships *do not contradict the theory of value*, instead of, on the contrary, *developing* them together with their apparent contradictions out of this basis or presenting the development of this basis itself ... Hence the contradiction between the general law and further developments in the concrete circumstances is to be resolved not by the discovery of the connecting links but by directly subordinating and immediately adapting the concrete to the abstract (*TSV*, II, p. 150; III, p. 87).

The reconciliation of surplus-value and profit can only be achieved by an analysis of the real social processes through which each is formed. Prices are not relations between things, but are the expression of social relations of production. The price of any commodity, however, will express not one but a number of social relations. The commodity is produced by a set of workers, under the direction of a particular capital, in competition with other capitals, selling perhaps to yet other capitals or perhaps to workers. The commodity therefore exists at the point of intersection of a series of social relationships between and within classes. Fluctuations in the prices of individual commodities are the means by which a range of social relations are regulated.

The framework within which prices regulate the social relations of production is that of the material and social reproduction of capitalist society. The price-mechanism is the means by which the conditions for the expanded reproduction of capital, without which no material production would take place, are imposed on particular capitals as an external constraint. An analysis that ignores the social form of price, and so does not concern itself with social relations, will abstract the formation of price from this context, within which alone it has any social significance, to construct scholastic formulae, or sets of simultaneous equations, that will accurately predict the price of a commodity. The more complex are such formulae the more accurately will they be able to achieve their predictive task and the less they will illuminate.

A more adequate theory will have to analyse the formation of prices within the framework of the expanded reproduction of capital and make this the basis of its abstractions. Within this framework the most abstract level of analysis is that of the reproduction of the class relation between capital and labour since this is the fundamental social relation of a capitalist society, whose reproduction is the condition for the reproduction of all other social relations. In Volume One of *Capital* Marx was concerned to explore this aspect of capitalist reproduction alone. The labour theory of value provides an appropriate and an adequate basis on which to investigate the relationship between capital and wage-labour in the exchange of capital for labour-power and in the production of value and of surplus-value, and so Marx's analysis was conducted on that basis.

We have already seen that the theory of surplus-value does not depend on the assumption that commodities exchange at prices corresponding to their labour-values. The assumption of equivalent exchange in this sense is an assumption appropriate at this level of abstraction, not because 'production' is, in some ontological sense, 'prior' to exchange, but because it adequately expresses the social relation under investigation, the class relation around which capitalist production as a whole revolves. The theory of surplus-value depends on the distinction between labour and labour-power, that defines the social form of the relation between labour and capital, and it is on this basis that the theory establishes that the source of surplus-value is the unpaid labour of the wage-worker. Whatever the prices at which commodities exchange, the *source* of surplus-value remains the surplus labour of the wage-worker. It is therefore appropriate to conceptualise the relation between capital and labour within which surplus-value is produced on the basis of the labour theory of value, since this eliminates all extraneous considerations at this level of abstraction.

Many commentators have recognised that the theory of surplus value does not depend on the assumption that commodities in practice exchange at prices corresponding to labour-values, only to claim that it rests instead on the moral argument, derived from a reading of Locke, that labour is entitled to its full product. This claim is also fallacious. The entitlement of labour to its full product is not a moral argument propounded by Locke or any other philosopher. It is a description of the social and juridical reality of a commodity-producing society. Such a society has eliminated the compulsory obligations laid on the slave and the serf to labour for another and has established the unchallengeable right of the labourer to the full fruits of her labour. However it has also given the labourer the unchallengeable right to assign her right to the product to another and so to enter into the wage-contract by which she will labour for the benefit of another. The philosophers have not invented these rights, they have merely sought to reconcile the contradictions to which they give rise. The illusion of the wage-form is the illusion that the worker receives the full fruits of her labour. By contrast, Marx's analysis of exchange as a moment of the reproduction of capitalist social relations, establishes that surplus-value is the value-form of labour that is appropriated without equivalent.

In the analysis of the transformation of surplus-value into profit — and of profit into its fragmented forms of interest, commercial profit, the profit of enterprise and rent — we have to move beyond consideration of the class relation between capital and labour to consider the relations between capitalists. In looking at these relations we are no longer concerned with the social relation within which surplus value is produced, but are now looking at relations within which existing surplus-value is distributed amongst the individual capitalists. The analysis of these relations within the capitalist class presupposes the analysis of the class relation between capital and labour, both formally, in that capitalists can only exist on the basis of the existence of a class of wage-labourers, and substantively, in that exchange can only redistribute commodities that have already been produced and appropriated within the capitalist class-relation. The mechanism by which shares in the total surplus value are allocated to individual capitals is that of the formation of prices through capitalist competition, and the theoretical problem at this level of abstraction is to specify the law of that competition.

Within the system of petty commodity production Marx assumed that the law of competition was that of the exchange of commodities at prices corresponding to their labour-values. This law is determined by the requirements of the material and social reproduction of a society of petty commodity producers. On the basis of such exchanges labour will tend to be allocated to various branches of production in accordance with the requirements of the material reproduction of that society. If too much labour is allocated to a given branch of production the price of the commodity will fall below its value and some producers will transfer their production to underpopulated branches. The social co-ordination of production is thus achieved through the equilibration of competitive markets at prices corresponding to labour-values. However, the exchange of commodities at prices corresponding to their values is not an inexorable law; it is the social law of competition appropriate to a particular (hypothetical) type of society.

Within a capitalist society such a law of competition would be inappropriate since it would not permit the material reproduction of society. If it were the case that individual capitals appropriated surplus-value in accordance with their contribution to its production the result would be that only industrial capitals would earn a profit, while the rate of profit on different industrial capitals would be different, depending on the organic composition and the turnover time of the individual capital. Within a capitalist society the *law of motion* of capital is the need for capital constantly to expand itself, a need that is enforced through the competition between capitals in which the less successful are destroyed. Thus, if commodities exchanged at their values, every capital would be applied in the most profitable branch of production and nothing else would be produced. The law of capitalist competition is not, therefore, the tendency for commodities to exchange at prices corresponding to their values, but

The Ricardian contradiction

is the tendency for commodities to exchange at prices corresponding to the equalisation of the rate of profit. The material reproduction of capitalist society requires that commodities exchange at prices that, in general, diverge from values in such a way as to equalise the rate of profit on different employments of capital.

This does not mean that the material reproduction of capitalist society is guaranteed by the regulatory role of competition. The driving force of capitalist accumulation is the uneven development of the forces of production, which underlies the tendency to the overproduction of commodities and the uneven development of the forces of production, as each capitalist seeks to steal a competitive advantage. The tendency to the equalisation of the rate of profit only acts as a *counter-tendency* to the underlying tendency to uneven development, which does not act smoothly, but only through commercial crises and 'revolutions in value'.

It is quite possible that the transformation of values into prices in the course of capitalist competition might have an effect on the quantitative determination of the rate of surplus-value through its effect on the value of labour-power.[7] However any such quantitative modification of the determination of the rate of surplus-value has no implications for the analysis of the *social form* of the production and appropriation of surplus-value, nor for the conclusion of that analysis that the basis of surplus-value is the social relation of capitalist production and its source is the unpaid labour of the working-class. Thus the distributional impact of the transformation of values into prices is an aspect of the redistribution of value, that can only be adequately conceptualised on the basis of the prior theory of value and surplus value, and is not an aspect of its production and appropriation.

Classical political economy could not resolve the Ricardian contradiction between value and price because it failed to distinguish the social processes of the production and appropriation of surplus-value, on the one hand, and the redistribution of surplus value, on the other. Marx's critique of political economy, in explaining the social form of capitalist production and reproduction, was able finally to resolve this contradiction by establishing that value and price are concepts that are both valid, but that are appropriate to the investigation of different social processes which have to be analysed at different levels

---

[7] This is the basis of the so-called 'transformation problem', which seeks to derive prices from values not through the examination of the social relations within which prices are formed, but by importing the Ricardians' 'scholastic formulae' into Marxism.

of abstraction. Thus Marx was finally able to reconcile a theory of the class-relationship of capitalist society with the determination of revenues in exchange.

Formal and determinate abstraction

Marx's analysis of the social formation of value and surplus value, of prices and of revenues, on the basis of his progressively more concrete analysis of the social relations of capitalist production enabled him to establish the concrete social forms through which the fundamental tendencies of capitalist reproduction, which he had already identified in his early works, were expressed in, and mediated by, the most superficial and fragmented forms of capitalist social relations. Although Marx's analysis was no less abstract than that of political economy, the form of his abstraction was quite different. Political economy abstracted its concepts immediately from the fetishised forms of appearance of capitalist society, and specifically from the relations of commodity exchange, in which prices and revenues appeared to derive from the inherent qualities of things — in Ricardo's case as the products of useful labour, in the case of Say as the products of the three 'factors of production', in the case of 'vulgar economy' as the objects of subjective valuations of utility. However this method of 'formal abstraction' is incoherent and irrational.

The 'formal abstractions' of political economy are not gratuitous inventions, but express real abstractions in a mystified form. Thus the 'abstract individual' really exists in a capitalist society. However the individual is a 'formal' abstraction when it is considered in abstraction from its historical foundation, which lies in the separation of the labourer from the means of production. In abstracting its fundamental concepts from the social forms of capitalist production and reproduction, political economy abstracts from the social relations which alone determine the qualities which it calls on to give its concepts their explanatory powers. The private individual, private property, the value-creating power of labour, the 'productivity' of capital, the formation of rent, the 'tastes' of the consumer, have no determinate existence outside the social relations of capitalist production, and so the causal relations proposed by political economy equally have no determinate existence. Political economy could at best *describe*, but it could not *explain*.

Formal and determinate abstraction

Marx's abstraction, by contrast, is a method of 'determinate abstraction', in which his abstractions correspond not to 'essential qualities' embodied in things, but to determinate social processes.[8] The distinction between the abstract and the concrete, for Marx, therefore corresponds not to the distinction between the 'essential' and the 'inessential', but to the distinction between the general and the particular. The theory of value, for example, expresses the generality of the social relations through which social labour is expressed in the form of the value of the commodity, and the generality of the social processes through which the allocation of social labour is regulated through the exchange of commodities. The abstraction 'value' corresponds to, and is only appropriate to, a society in which such processes have become generalised.

> Indifference towards any specific kind of labour presupposes a very developed totality of real kinds of labour, of which no single one is any longer predominant. As a rule, the most general abstractions arise only in the midst of the richest possible concrete development, where one thing appears as common to many, to all. Then it ceases to be thinkable in a particular form alone. On the other side, this abstraction of labour as such is not merely the mental product of a concrete totality of labours. Indifference towards specific labours corresponds to a form of society in which individuals can with ease transfer from one labour to another, and where the specific kind is a matter of chance for them, hence of indifference (*Grundrisse*, p. 104).

The law of value is only valid to the extent that the features of the social processes depicted by the law pertain to every particular example of those processes. At the same time every particular example will add other determinations, which have to be conceptualised at progressively lower levels of abstraction, so that 'the concrete ... is the concentration of many determinations' (*Grundrisse*, p. 101). Thus the theoretical analysis of the social forms of capitalist production developed in *Capital* does not provide any kind of eternal truth, but only the analytical foundation on which to develop comparative

---

[8] There is nothing particularly original about this form of abstraction — it is no more and no less than the method of modern science, whose abstract laws do not depict 'essential relations' but concrete generalisations, which describe the common feature of a multiplicity of particular relations, and are applicable to the extent that they are manifested in those particular relations (c.f. Dobb, 1940, Ch. 5; Sayer, 1979).

and historical analyses of the more concrete (and complex) particular forms in which capitalist social relations are expressed and develop. Similarly, the concrete investigation of any of the 'laws of motion' of the capitalist mode of production will show how 'like all other laws, it is modified in its working by many circumstances' (*Capital*, I, p. 798).

The economists' model of capitalism was an abstract model which described an ideal world of perfect rationality, perfect knowledge, and perfect foresight, which expressed the perfectibility of Man, within the limits of Nature. Even the most optimistic of the political economists had to acknowledge that their world of harmony and prosperity hardly corresponded to the reality of capitalist society. However the other side of political economy's method of 'formal abstraction' was its attempt to derive reality immediately from its fundamental concepts. The ideal model grasped the 'essence' of reality. It depicted the possibilities of material and spiritual emancipation which economic and political liberalism offered to humanity. The perfection of the abstract model showed that the source of the acknowledged evils of capitalism could not be private property, wage labour, or unrestrained competition. If reality did not correspond to this ideal it was not the ideal which was at fault, but human intellectual and moral weaknesses which prevented humanity from living up to the abstract ideal. Thus the divergences of reality from the ideal model were explained in terms of human frailty and human imperfection. The appropriate methods of social reform were correspondingly identified as the moral and intellectual elevation of the species. Thus the method of 'formal abstraction', which was the source of the scientific weakness of political economy, was also the source of its ideological strength.

For Marx, by contrast, the evils of capitalism were inseparable from its progressive characteristics. While capitalism undoubtedly developed the forces of material and intellectual production to an unprecedented degree, it did so within social relations in which the production and appropriation of the social product was subordinated not to human need but to the accumulation of capital. The alienated form of social labour under capitalism was not a technical necessity, imposed by the development of the division of labour, but a specific, historically developed, form of social production, based on specific social relations of exploitation and domination. These relations of exploitation and domination were not simply the result of the contingent abuse of capitalist power, but were the necessary form of the social relations of capitalist production, imposed on every capitalist by the pressure of competition through which every capitalist was compelled to subordinate all human considerations to the production of surplus value. Far from expressing the possibilities of human intellectual and material freedom, the social relations of capitalist production increasingly subject humanity to domination by an alien power, the power of capital. The development of human productive and intellectual capacities serves only to increase the power which stands over humanity. At the same time, however, the socialisation of production leads to the development of new social collectivities, in the form of working class organisations, which contest the power of capital and which provide the foundation on which a new form of society can be built.

5

Political Economy and its Sociological Critics

Classical political economy and the labour theory of value

It has become the Marxist orthodoxy to identify classical political economy with the labour theory of value. However, of all those who could be called classical political economists only Ricardo adhered (almost unequivocally) to the labour theory of value. As we have seen, Smith had proposed a labour-commanded theory, but this was largely for methodological convenience. Say, who first systematised Smith's theory, adopted a theory of supply and demand. Malthus, Bailey, Senior and many other leading economists rejected the Ricardian theory of value altogether, while Ricardo's closest followers, James Mill and McCulloch, followed in turn by John Stuart Mill and Cairnes, all modified the labour theory in order to accommodate the awkward inconsistency between price and value. Even Ricardo himself at times indicated a willingness to abandon the labour theory. If we take the labour theory of value as the defining feature of classical political economy we reduce it to a system that had but one adherent.[1]

The importance of the labour theory of value for Ricardo was not that it connected labour with its alienated forms, but that it provided the basis of a rigorous theory of distribution, which made it possible

---

[1] This interpretation is implicit in most orthodox Marxist periodisations of the history of political economy, which identify the transition from the scientific perspective of classical political economy to the ideological perspective of 'vulgar' economics with the abandonment of the labour theory of value in the early 1830s. Bourgeois periodisations, on the other hand, identify the transition with the replacement of a cost of production theory by a subjective theory of value in the marginalist revolution of the 1870s, when 'political' economy was purged of extraneous political concerns, to become a scientific economics. If the transition is neither from science to ideology, nor from ideology to science, but from one ideology to another, as I would argue, then the ideological transition is best identified with the 1870s, for the abandonment of the labour theory of value compromised the scientific claims of classical political economy, but only to strengthen it ideologically in the face of the challenge of the working class.

to identify the ultimate impact of particular economic policies, and especially of taxation, in order to evaluate their impact on productive investment. From this point of view Ricardo's followers were content to regard the inconsistency between the determination of prices and the theory of value as a minor technical problem, to be resolved by various *ad hoc* expedients, that did nothing to undermine the validity of Ricardo's theory of distribution (in much the same way as friction affects the motion of falling bodies without invalidating the law of gravity). Ricardo himself did not dismiss the problem as inconsequential, for he devoted a great deal of energy to devising the 'scholastic formulae' that could resolve it. Although he did not achieve this, it is in fact the case that the problem can be solved if an appropriate standard of measurement is chosen. Ricardo's early followers and popularisers, James Mill and McCulloch, were more cavalier, explaining the divergence in terms of the independent addition of labour by machines, anticipating John Stuart Mill's abandonment of the labour theory of value in favour of a cost of production theory within which direct labour was only one component part of value.

The abandonment of the labour theory of value was not a result of its technical deficiencies, but of its ideological weakness. It was perfectly rational for Ricardo to adhere to the labour theory of value, and to seek to accommodate it to the reality of price formation through secondary adjustments, for the alternative was to return to the indeterminacy of the theories of Smith or of Say according to which prices are determined by supply and demand, which in turn depend on prices. On the other hand, such indeterminacy could prove very attractive to those who found the Ricardian conclusions unpalatable. Thus the fate of the labour theory of value was not determined by the internal logic of the Ricardian system, but by the ideological demands that were made on it.

The essential ideological weakness of the Ricardian system was that it did not provide a satisfactory basis on which to defend profit. Although Ricardo made vague reference to profit as the reward for 'waiting', the essence of his theory is to determine profit as a deduction from the product of labour, while its proportionality to capital is a contingent empirical characteristic of profit that conflicts with its essential relationship to labour. The ideological defence of profit, however, required that the proportionality of profit to capital, and so to the magnitude of the capitalist's contribution, was not simply a contingent empirical phenomenon, but was rather its essential characteristic; it could hardly be claimed convincingly that profit was some kind of reward for capital if the size of the profit did not correspond in its essence to the size of the capital.

The inconsistency at the heart of the Ricardian system only came to acquire decisive significance when the proportionality of profit to capital came to acquire a decisive ideological and political importance. It was only then that the deviation of the rate of profit from the rate of surplus labour came to have a systematic significance greater than that, for example, of the 'market' rate of profit from the natural rate. It was the ideological challenge to profit presented by the growth of an independent working-class movement and by its socialist propagandists that was the circumstance that elevated a technical problem into a fatal contradiction and led economists away from the labour theory of value following an apparently purely intellectual logic.

The context of the modification, or in some cases abandonment, of the labour theory of value was the period of growing social tension in the early 1830s as the working class, that had been mobilised in part by a bourgeois leadership within the reform movement, began to follow co-operative and socialist agitators such as Owen and Hodgkin. The debate was initiated in 1825 by Samuel Bailey, who rejected the very idea of a theory of 'absolute value', and was pursued most intensively in the Political Economy Club through the first half of the 1830s. The upshot of the debates was a nearly universal rejection of the labour theory of value in favour of some kind of 'adding up' theory, according to which the revenues of land, labour and capital could be determined independently of one another, somewhat in the manner of Adam Smith, Malthus and Say, by the interaction of supply and demand. Various theories of profit were proposed that gave profit an independent justification, either as the reward for the capitalist's abstinence and labour of superintendence (Senior, Scrope) or as a reward corresponding to the contribution of capital to the value of the final product (Read, Gray, Longfield). Longfield also followed up Say's suggestion that the reward for labour could likewise be related not simply to the subsistence needs of the labourer, but more fundamentally to the productive contribution made by labour.

The most energetic opponents of the labour theory of value, such as Cazenove, Scrope, Read and Longfield, were quite explicit about the need to repel the socialist attack and their prime motivation was clearly to provide a secure justification for the powers and privileges of capital. A similar concern to rebut the socialist interpretation of the deduction theory of profit clearly motivated Carey in the United States, Bastiat in France and Roscher and Knies in Germany in rejecting the labour theory of value. However, their criticisms of Ricardo's theory of value did rest on an undeniable inconsistency in the theory, so it was perfectly possible for more disinterested thinkers to reject or modify the labour theory of value for what to them might seem purely intellectual reasons.

The abandonment of the labour theory of value was primarily of ideological importance, for its implication was that profit was no longer seen as a deduction, but as an independent revenue with its own source, which could now be defended against socialist attack. The revenues accruing to each factor of production could now be justified, on the supply side, by the 'trouble and toil' incurred by labour or abstinence, and, on the demand side, by the contribution to production made by the relevant factor. Thus the theory of distribution could be assimilated to the theory of production, distribution relations expressing the cooperative interdependence of the factors of production. However, in Ricardo's system it was only the labour theory of value that made it possible to establish a determinate relationship between wages, rent and profit. Thus the price that had to be paid for the vulgarisation of political economy was that the system became indeterminate; in particular it became impossible to determine the rate of profit. To abandon the labour theory of value was to abandon the Ricardian ambition of providing a rigorous analysis of the relations between the classes. Thus Marx was right to criticise the vulgarisers for abandoning science for ideology. When the vulgar critics of Ricardo were resurrected by historians of economic thought it was as 'some neglected British economists' (Seligman, 1903), and their scientific neglect was fully justified.

Classical political economy was far from destroyed by the abandonment of the labour theory of value. James Mill and McCulloch had already relaxed the theory, without forswearing any of Ricardo's conclusions. John Stuart Mill, in his *Principles of Political Economy* (1848), completed the assimilation of the vulgar criticisms into the Ricardian framework, but in order to reaffirm Ricardo's theory of distribution. Mill's cost of production theory of value retained the Ricardian relationship between wages, rent and profit as an approximate account of the relations between the classes. The abandonment of the labour theory of value meant that the rate of profit became indeterminate, and so the impact on profit of an increase in wages or in rent could not be rigorously explored, but the cost of production theory of value did give the system the appearance of rigour and coherence and so served to renew the scientific authority of classical political economy.

The classical economic laws

While the theory of value was an object of some debate, there was almost universal agreement among economists over the classical laws of political economy. In the most general terms political economy provided a theoretical framework within which to understand the social relations of capitalist society and within which to formulate the problems raised by the regulation of those social relations. The basis of this framework was the 'trinity formula' that defined the fundamental component classes of capitalist society and within which the relations between those classes could be conceptualised. The theory of production established the fundamental harmony of class-relations on the basis of the complementarity of the different factors of production. The theory of exchange imposed a commitment to *laissez-faire* in the regulation of economic relations, on the basis of the liberal principle of individual self-determination, subject to the obligation to respect life, liberty and property. Within this liberal framework any intrusion on the freedom of the individual to be the best judge of her own interests could only be justified on the grounds of the individual's ignorance or insanity, or on the grounds that the action of the individual impinges on the life, liberty or property of others. The theory of distribution was the means by which the distinctive interests of the component classes of society were defined and related to one another.

Within this framework political economy can be defined by the economic laws on the basis of which it defended its fundamental political principle, the principle of *laissez-faire*. Following Gide and Rist we can identify seven fundamental laws of classical political economy (Gide and Rist, 1948, pp. 359–71). The first four derive from the theory of exchange, and characterise any liberal economic theory, whether 'classical' or 'vulgar'. These four are: first, the *law of self-interest*, which in its most general form states that individuals tend to pursue their economic ends in accordance with their rational self-interest. Economics is concerned to elucidate the implications of

The classical economic laws

action performed on this basis, the most optimistic theories claiming to show that in a world of perfect liberty the pursuit of self-interest spontaneously gives rise to social harmony and social progress. However such bland optimism was by no means generally characteristic of classical political economy, as we have seen. Second, the *law of free competition*, which again cannot be reduced to the doctrine of spontaneous harmony, but which states that competition will secure prosperity and progress, in the absence of barriers to its operation. The recognition of such barriers is the only basis on which political or moral intervention in the competitive process can be justified. Third, the *law of supply and demand*, according to which market prices fluctuate around an equilibrium value in response to the interaction of supply and demand. Most of the classical political economists, and their marginalist successors, complemented this with Say's *law of markets* according to which supply created its own demand so that crises and unemployment could only be the result of impediments to the smooth operation of markets, set up, for example, by restrictions on the supply of money and credit. Fourth, the *law of international exchange* according to which both parties gain, although not necessarily equally, from international trade conducted according to the law of free competition. Again this law was not absolute, for it came to be recognised that in some circumstances, particularly in the case of goods in monopoly supply or in the case of an 'infant industry', there may be grounds for intervention in the market.

These four laws were regarded as almost self-evident. If individual capitalists pursued their own self-interest a regime of economic freedom would maximise their incentives and their opportunities and so result in the maximisation of profits and of economic growth. Any infringement of such freedom could only be justified to the extent that the abuse of economic power infringed the freedom and opportunities of others. However it was not so self-evident that the interests of capitalists in economic freedom was shared by the other classes of society, the landed interest and the working class. Economic conflict between these classes over the determination of rent and wages was a feature of capitalist society that could hardly be ignored. The classical theory of distribution was an attempt to theorise this conflict in order to establish the relationship between the capitalist interest and the interests of society as a whole, and so to establish a proper basis on which to achieve the harmonious integration of capitalist society. Although Ricardo formulated the theory of distribution within the framework of the labour theory of value, the economic laws that defined the theory of distribution could equally be presented on the basis of other theories of value.

The first such law was the *law of rent*, according to which rent was determined by the difference in costs of production between the least and the most productive enterprises. The specific twist given to this law by Ricardo was to combine it with the law of diminishing returns in agriculture, from which he deduced the secular tendency for rents to rise at the expense of profits. The rigorous formulation of this law did depend on the labour theory, but it was also espoused by those who adopted a cost of production theory, in which case it could be held as an approximation and not as an exact law. The law of rent could be rejected within the framework of classical political economy by rejecting the law of diminishing returns in agriculture or, as was done by Bastiat and Carey, by identifying rent with the return to capital invested in the land and so assimilating rent to profit. On the other hand, the apparent conflict of interest between land and capital that was implied by the law of rent could be dissolved by arguing that unproductive expenditure, characteristic of the landed class, was necessary to stave off the threat of underconsumption, as was argued by Malthus.

The interest of the working class was defined not by the theory of value, which appeared to establish a conflict of interest between capital and labour, but by the *law of population* and the *law of wages*, which established the identity of interests of the working class and capital on the basis of their common interest in maximising the rate of growth, which depended on maximising the funds available to capital. As we shall see, it was the collapse of faith in these laws that destroyed classical political economy.

The law of population, derived from Malthus, was supposed to establish that population would tend to grow more rapidly than the supply of the means of subsistence, so that the latter would act as a check on the growth of population. The law of wages relied over the long-term on the law of population, as wages would be held down to the historically and customarily determined subsistence level by the operation of Malthusian checks. The law of population was supplemented in the short-term by the mechanism of the wages-fund.

The wages-fund doctrine postulated that the demand for labour was set by the supply of capital, in the form of the means of subsistence, that comprised the wages-fund. Any increase in wages meant that

The classical economic laws

the wages-fund had to be spread over fewer workers, and so would give rise to unemployment, which would exert downward pressure on wages. Any permanent increase in the wages of one set of workers, achieved, for example, through the use of trade union power or through legislation, could only be at the expense of other workers, whose wages would correspondingly be reduced by the overall limit set by the wages-fund. Wages could only be increased by increasing the size of the wages-fund through the accumulation of capital, or by reducing the supply of labour by practising moral restraint. Any encroachment of wages on profits would only curtail the demand for labour further. Thus the inverse relation between wages and profits, which appeared to establish a conflict of interest between labour and capital, in practice served, within the framework of the wages-fund doctrine and the theory of accumulation, to establish their identity. In fact the wages-fund doctrine was very shaky, and political economy never satisfactorily reconciled the long-term Malthusian mechanism with the short-term wages-fund mechanism to establish that the latter would necessarily impose subsistence wages. However the law of wages, although theoretically the weakest link in the classical system, was its ideological lynch-pin, for it provided the main weapon against both conservative and socialist opposition to the rule of capital.

Against conservatives the law of wages established that the privileges of the landed class, and their paternalistic benevolence towards the poor, only served to undermine national prosperity by inflating the price of corn, and so eroding profits. Against socialists, the law of wages established with the imposing rigour of science that neither the combination of workers nor Mr Owen's co-operatives could alleviate the general condition of the working class. The call for combinations and co-operatives served only as the rallying cry of demagogues seeking to secure the support of the ignorant mob in pursuit of their own sectarian ends. Combination may have had a limited value in correcting specific evils, caused for example by unscrupulous employers, and may even have had a positive value in encouraging the prudent provision for distress in periods of unemployment, sickness or old age, so that responsible trade unionism could be welcomed, but the general combination of the workers against their employers was an unqualified evil.

In the same way private charity and the Old Poor Law could not mitigate the evils they were supposedly designed to combat. They could only discourage the prudent provision of the workers for the future of themselves and their families and so intensify the misfortunes to which the working class was inevitably subject. They were merely the deceitful means by which ancient privilege sought to reproduce its hold on the working class. Neither paternalism nor socialism, neither charity nor combination, could improve the lot of the working class. Their only prospect of general improvement was through moral restraint and submission to the law of the market, while their political interests were best served by the representation of property, whose own interest in its unfettered expansion could best secure the conditions for the workers' well-being.

The great strength of classical political economy was that it could reconcile the apparent distributional conflict between labour and capital with a more fundamental community of interests based on a common interest in the accumulation of capital. Vulgar economy, which rejected the classical laws of distribution in favour of a theory of distribution according to which revenues were determined independently of one another by the interaction of supply and demand, provided a much weaker foundation on which to reject the claims of labour because it depended on the bland assertion that distributional conflict did not exist, the market serving spontaneously to assign appropriate rewards to the factors of production, an assertion that could be countered by the equally confident claim of the socialists that the unequal market was the means by which capital appropriated the product of labour.

Early working-class agitation could be put down to the actions of a misguided mob, so that vulgar assertions of the harmony of class interests might be sufficient. However, the persistence of working-class demands, and the development of trade unions to further those demands, forced political economy in Britain to sharpen its ideological defences in the name of its natural laws, in order the better to rebuff demands for reform. Thus classical political economy survived the criticisms of the 1830s; was reformulated by Mill in the 1840s; was vindicated by the period of unprecedented prosperity and social peace that followed the repeal of the Corn Laws in 1846, and was constantly reinvigorated by resistance to the exaggerated claims of trade unionism and social reform through the 1850s and 1860s. In Europe, however, where effective trade unionism developed later than in Britain and where the major challenge to the rule of capital was a political and ideological one, vulgar economy, in one form or another, reigned supreme.

Classical political economy and the birth of sociology

In the hands of Smith and Ricardo political economy had been a weapon with which to attack the privilege and corruption of the old order, and it was as such that it was taken up by radical and revolutionary liberals throughout Europe. However, once the liberal battles were won, political economy rapidly degenerated into an apologetic role. Political economy did not necessarily endorse the *status quo*, for it could hardly deny the suffering which was associated with the generalisation of capitalist relations of production, nor the increasingly severe crises which punctuated its advance, nor the growing class conflict to which it gave rise. However political economy insisted that exploitation and periodic crises, poverty and distress, class conflict and civil disorder were not inherent in capitalism, but were the result of human failings. Distress and disorder were the results of the ignorance of politicians, the abuse of privilege, the irresponsibility of bankers, or the moral and intellectual failings of the working class. It was not capitalism which failed to meet human aspirations, but human weakness which prevented the realisation of the rational ideal.

The faith of the political economists (both classical and vulgar) in the adequacy of the market as the means of regulating the class relations of capitalist society was by no means universally shared, particularly in Continental Europe, where capitalist development was associated with much more serious economic and political dislocation than it was in Britain. To many the unfettered rule of capital appeared to be a prescription not for prosperity and social peace but for exploitation and social conflict.

Criticism of political economy came from three major directions. First, political economy had to face conservative critics who believed that the development of capitalism was undermining the established order and creating a society which would inevitably be marked by conflict and moral degeneration. Second, it had to face socialist critics who believed that exploitation was inherent in the inequality of the capitalist system and who proposed reform on the basis of co-operation. Third, it had to face criticism from those who accepted the fundamental social relations of capitalist society, but who could not accept that such social relations could be regulated solely by the free play of the market.

Conservative critics did not share the economists' faith in the power of the hidden hand of the market to achieve social harmony and social integration. They pointed to the costs of capitalist development: crises, unemployment, undermining of paternalistic authority, class polarisation, socialist agitation, the destruction of cultural values and national spirit, and the erosion of the moral and political authority of the state, the church and the ruling class. Political economy neglected the spiritual, moral and aesthetic qualities of the human species and underestimated the importance of the essential ties of deference to and respect for authority that had held the medieval economy and society together, and that were being destroyed by the advance of capitalism. Capitalism was an unviable form of society.

Conservatives counterposed organic theories to the liberalism of political economy, calling for a restoration, in one form or another, of the medieval order, enforced by Church and State and governed by an hereditary ruling class. While such a romantic reaction was strong in the face of the French Revolution, and enjoyed occasional resurgences thereafter in periods of acute social tension, it gradually declined in power and influence in the wake of the post-Napoleonic stabilisation of capitalist society. It did, however, provide resources, in its emphasis on moral, cultural and national values and on the need for the moral and political regulation of social relations, for later critics of the economists' preoccupation with economic interest.

While conservative critics tended to reject political economy *in toto*, the theorists of socialism accepted some parts of political economy while rejecting others. Thus they tended to accept the theory of production, that defined the functional interdependence of labour, land and capital, while rejecting the theories of distribution and exchange, in which conflictual relations of competition were 'unnaturally' imposed on the co-operative relationships inherent in production. Some socialists drew on Ricardo's deduction theory of profit, while rejecting the law of population and the law of wages, and so developed an exploitation theory of society within which profit derived from the monopoly power of capital. They also drew on democratic political theory and on Sismondi's criticism of the crises, unemployment and class polarisation that accompanied capitalist development. For socialists, exchange gave rise to inequality, which was the basis of exploitation as the rich abused their economic powers, and society became increasingly polarised. They therefore proposed the equalisation of property and the regulation of competition to prevent such polarisation, and proposed that production should be organised co-operatively.

Classical political economy and the birth of sociology

Although the early socialists criticised the optimism and the fatalism of political economy, they nevertheless remained largely within the liberal framework that saw the free market as the necessary basis of liberty, equality and fraternity, believing that only the equalisation of property would make it possible to achieve those ideals. Thus the socialist criticism of political economy inspired not only Marx, who carried it much further, but also liberal reformers, such as Comte, drawing on St Simon, and John Stuart Mill, who incorporated many socialist ideas into his own political economy, recognising a role for co-operation in reducing inequality and the abuse of economic power.

The third major direction of criticism of political economy lay between the two just considered. On the one hand, it shared the conservative rejection of the 'dogma of self-interest' and the claim of political economy that a regime of *laissez-faire* could best ensure social harmony, while retaining a commitment to political liberalism against reactionary romanticism. On the other hand, it shared the socialist emphasis on the need for co-operation and for moral and political regulation to restrain the conflicts emerging out of competition, but rejected socialist projects to equalise property, seeing the defects of capitalism as deriving primarily from the unregulated market, rather than from its underlying inequality. Often drawing on the romantic and socialist critiques in stressing the limitations of *laissez-faire*, this kind of liberal reformism was directed at the over-abstraction of political economy, at its reliance on the deductive method, its cosmopolitanism and its universal claims. Some critics accepted the laws of political economy, but insisted that they were time- and space-bound, appropriate perhaps to nineteenth-century Britain but inappropriate elsewhere. Others denied any possibility of formulating economic laws, insisting that economics be absorbed into sociology or history, disciplines that could perhaps formulate evolutionary or statistical laws. These criticisms were developed particularly in France and Germany, countries in which the liberal opposition to conservatism had increasingly to secure its flanks against the threat of socialism. Comtean sociology and the German Historical School both defined themselves in sharp opposition to political economy, but both remained within a liberal framework. They sought not to reject the liberalism of political economy but rather to make it appropriate to domestic political reality, supplementing or replacing the market by more self-conscious forms of regulation of capitalist production relations.

The Positivist critique of political economy

The ideas of economic liberalism had been popularised in France through Garnier's translation of Adam Smith and through Say's systematic exposition of Smith's principles in his *Traité d'économie politique* (1803). Say is best remembered for his law of markets, *Say's law*, but from the present point of view his work is important for four other reasons. First, Say decisively rejected the priority given to agriculture by Smith and the Physiocrats, to bring industry into the front rank. Second, Say introduced the distinction between the capitalist, who lent capital at interest, and the entrepreneur, who hired capital, land and labour to undertake production. Third, on this basis Say first developed the 'trinity formula' as a systematic theory of distribution, according to which the revenues accruing to the owners of the factors of production corresponded to the contribution to production of the relevant factor. The entrepreneur was the intermediary who organised the co-operation of the factors of industry, capital and land in production. The labour, or 'productive services', of these factors were hired by the entrepreneur who paid a suitable price, determined by supply and demand, for those services. Thus the intermediation of the entrepreneur and the vulgarisation of the theory of distribution dissolved any essential conflict of interest between capital and labour. Fourth, Say introduced a clear distinction between economic theory and economic policy, insisting that political economy offered an abstract theoretical discourse that could not give rise to policy prescriptions. Economic policies had, therefore, to be evaluated on their merits, political economy offering only one means of evaluation.

Say's formulation of Smith's theory proved especially appropriate to the circumstances of France. French capitalism was still struggling to emerge from underneath the burden of feudal privilege, despite the advances made by the Revolution. Thus political conflict did not yet centre on the proper balancing of class interests within an accepted framework of capitalism, as it did in England, but rather on the conflict between the productive character of capitalist enterprise and the classes corresponding to it, on the one hand, and the unproductive character of the parasitic Church and State that carried over from the *ancien regime*, on the other. Say's separation of economic from political questions, his stress on the harmonious relations between the productive classes and his emphasis on the productive role of industry alongside that of agriculture were themes that fed directly into the political debate and were taken up by liberal and socialist reformers alike.

The restoration of 1830 gave a renewed impetus to these political debates, but the Lyons weavers' risings of 1831 and 1834 also resurrected, in a new form, the spectre of the revolutionary mob that haunted all liberal reformers in France, driving a wedge between liberalism and socialism. Comte, initially influenced by the socialist St Simon, developed his system as much as a critique of socialism as of the political regime he sought to displace. The socialism of St Simon derived very directly from the class model developed by Say, proposing to sweep away the barriers to the advance of productive enterprise and to replace the tyranny of a parasitical ruling class. However, St Simon rejected Say's faith in the market as an adequate means of regulating production, and proposed instead the functional administration of a co-operative society. Comte took many of his ideas from this scheme, believing in the necessity of completing the overthrow of the old regime and of establishing society on the basis of industrial co-operation, believing in the essential harmony of interests of the productive classes, and believing that the unfettered pursuit of self-interest would lead capital to abuse its powers and undermine social harmony and equity by economic exploitation. However, Comte rejected the socialist belief that the alternative to unfettered capitalism was political regulation, insisting that the problem was more fundamentally a moral one.

Comte formulated his system within the framework developed by Say and St Simon of the co-operation of labour and capital on the basis of the complementary contributions of each factor to production. Comte defined capital as 'every permanent aggregation of material products' arising from the 'natural excess of production over consumption'. Capital is therefore identified with Smith's 'stock', the accumulated surplus product necessary for the expansion of production and the extension of the division of labour. Thus 'the institution of capital forms the necessary basis of the Division of Labour', and capitalists 'ought to be regarded simply as public functionaries, responsible for the administration of capital and the direction of industrial enterprise. But at the same time we must be careful not to underrate the immense value of their function, or in any way obstruct its performance'. Capitalists should therefore be well remunerated for their arduous and responsible tasks. Capitalists should also be responsible for setting the wages of the workers, 'for no others can properly estimate the value of each special service', although they should not abuse this privilege. Against the socialists Comte insisted that wages should not be seen as the recompense for labour, since they 'really pay nothing but the material portion of each man's labour replacing the waste invariably required by the organ, and sometimes by the function it performs', the surplus over subsistence being required to provide the fund for further accumulation (Comte, n.d., II, pp. 129, 134, 135; I, p. 300, II, pp. 335, 332).

Although he accepted the basic class model of capitalist society proposed by political economy, Comte rejected the economists' belief that class relations could be harmoniously regulated on the basis of the competitive pursuit of individual self-interest. Political economy 'pretends that the general laws of Material Order can be studied, apart from other laws' (Comte, n.d., II, p. 329), but the rule of self-interest creates not harmony but conflict as opposed interests clash in the market. It may be the case that the present economic relations were based on the pursuit of self-interest, but such a condition was merely transitional, a symptom of the decline in the moral regulation of social relations in accordance with earlier forms of religion and law. It was a condition that was unstable, as the new forms of moral regulation associated with the Positivist doctrines took effect, regulating the conflicts to which an inadequate moral regulation gave rise by subordinating 'self-love' to 'social-love' in order to reconcile progress with order.

Comte insisted that socialism was not the solution to the conflicts of capitalist society, but was itself a symptom. As the employers were uncontrolled in the system of 'modern anarchy', the workers fell prey to absurd Utopian schemes. Comte endorsed the critique of socialism proposed by classical political economy (indeed that of the archliberal Dunoyer), for despite their differences 'Positivists adopt substantially the strictures which they have passed upon Communism'. Communism ignores the need to accumulate capital, it ignores the need for direction and co-ordination of production, and it ignores the fact that individualistic instincts still prevail. The imperative task is not to change the existing relations of production, which are the condition for industrial progress, but to impose a moral regulation on them.

> Without a sufficient concentration of material power, the means of satisfying the claims of morality would be found wanting, except

The Positivist critique of political economy

at such exorbitant sacrifices, as would soon be found incompatible with all industrial progress. This is the weak point of every plan of reform which limits itself to the mode of acquiring power, whether public or private, instead of aiming at controlling its use in whosoever hands it may be placed (Comte, n.d., I, pp. 127–8).

Reform must be a moral reform before it can be political, for it is unimportant who holds power, what counts is how that power is exercised.

Comte reconciled the fundamentally harmonious character of the class-relations of capitalist production with the conflict to which the development of capitalism gave rise by developing an evolutionary theory within which the deficiencies of capitalism as it then existed were explained as the results of the process of transition, from the period of the moral regulation of social relations on the basis of law and politics, to the period of regulation on the basis of scientific knowledge embodied in the positivist religion of humanity. Positivism extended human knowledge from the natural to the social domain, and it is on the basis of the growth of knowledge of human interdependence that social-love would come to replace self-love. Comte made it clear in his later work that he was not offering an idealist theory according to which the progress of knowledge would determine the progress of society. He insisted that positivism subordinates intellect to instinct, the development of moral precepts resting on individual and social nature and the development of social sympathies. The growth of positivism was directly related to the growth of capital, and the associated development of the division of labour, within which the individual worked for others and property acquired a social character. It was on the basis of this interdependence that sentiments of altruism arose, an argument similar in many respects to Smith's theory of moral sentiments. Positivism hastened the advance of altruism by bringing to light the general interdependence of individuals, thus establishing the essentially harmonious character of capitalist social relations both in theory and, through the process of moral education, in reality.

Although Comte counterposed his Positivism to the religion of self-interest proposed by political economy, his theory of society nevertheless rested on the foundations laid down by political economy, particularly as developed in the work of Say. It was political economy whose theory of production defined the interdependence of the productive classes which was the basis of social-love, and it was Say's theory of distribution that defined the appropriate rewards for capital and labour. Comte's critique of political economy was confined to its theory of competition, as Comte rejected the possibility that the harmony defined by political economy could be provided by the mechanism of competitive exchange of which political economy avails itself, for the economists' analysis of exchange illegitimately abstracts from the dimensions of power, knowledge, and morality. In practice capitalists use their economic and political power to seek unjustifiable gains, while workers organise in opposition to capitalists and fall prey to socialist propaganda. Thus the realisation of social harmony could only be based on the replacement of self-love by social-love that would prevent the powerful from abusing their position for their own advantage.

Even in the analysis of the market the distance between Comte and political economy is not unbridgeable. Those political economists who regarded a utilitarian ethic as a sufficient foundation for political economy were few in number: as I have noted, Comte's theory of social-love is very similar to Smith's theory of the moral sentiments, and the importance of scientific and moral education was a central plank of the programme of political economy. The real issue was not that of the opposition of social-love and self-interest, but that of the point at which the latter becomes subversive of the former. For political economy the general well-being was achieved by each individual pursuing her own moderated self-interest, within the framework of the law, and it was this coincidence that established the moral value of self-interested action. Thus political economy established the moral duty of the individual to pursue her own self-interest: social-love conveniently decreed the pursuit of self-interest.

Comte's critique of political economy engaged at the point at which the pursuit of self-interest is subversive of the general well-being, for this is the point at which social-love must qualify self-interest. The problem with Comte's sociology is that it had no means of specifying when that point is reached since Comte, 'disregarding all useless and irritating discussions as to the origin of wealth and the extent of its possession, proceeds at once to the moral rules which should regulate it as a social function' (Comte, n.d., I, p. 131). But without such irritating discussions there was no rigorous way of determining the content of those rules. Comte could offer his utopian schemes, but on what rational grounds could he defend the claim that his society would be any more prosperous and harmonious than the capitalism he sought to replace? As John Stuart Mill argued, how could the *limits of laissez-faire* be defined, other than on the basis of political economy?

Precisely the same problems confronted Durkheim's later attempt to purge Comte's positivism of its speculative elements in developing his critique of Spencer's liberalism. Durkheim too contrasted the 'anomie' of egotism with the moral individualism of a properly regulated capitalist society, which he saw as a spontaneous development of the division of labour, to be fostered by institutional and educational reforms. Although he eliminated the religion of positivism, to put more faith in institutional reform, his critique of liberalism remained as superficial as that of Comte, and his reformism no less utopian, in seeking an *immediate* reconciliation of conflicting economic interests.

Classical political economy and the German Historical School

In Germany, as in France, liberalism still had political battles to fight, but these were concerned with building a national state, rather than transforming an existing one. Thus, while Comte criticised political economy for neglecting the moral dimension of social regulation, the German Historical School was more concerned by its neglect of the political dimension, although the two questions were not mutually exclusive.

Germany at the beginning of the nineteenth century was politically fragmented and economically backward. Internal trade was restricted by innumerable local tariff barriers, and industry hampered by state regulation, while agriculture remained the dominant sector of the economy. In such a context the economic doctrines of political economy had a great appeal to those seeking to break down domestic barriers to capitalist expansion. Rau performed for Germany the role that Garnier and Say performed for France, popularising and interpreting the theories of Adam Smith. Rau, like Say, emphasised the distinction between theory and policy, the latter varying with local conditions giving liberalism an adaptability that the German situation required.

The immediate pressure was for economic unification. However the economic unification of Germany was not sufficient to ensure the progress of German capitalism. Germany continued to be dominated politically by the landowning Junkers, while internationally the weakness of German capitalism in the face of foreign competition meant that protection and state assistance was required to foster the growth of German industry. This was the context within which the distinctive theories of the German Historical School were developed.

The main contribution of the Historical School was its concept of the *national economy*. It was clear that Germany's national prosperity depended on the formation of a national state that could foster the development of industry. Correspondingly, the strength of such a state would depend on the strength of the German economy. The inappropriateness of political economy in this context was one of the major factors underlying the growth of the Historical School, which situated questions of economic policy within their historical, and especially their political, context. The concept of the national economy therefore embraced much more than economic questions, incorporating also a concern with the political and institutional framework which could provide the basis of national power and prosperity.

For conservatives the problem of the state was posed in the traditional romantic terms of the cultural unity of the *Volk*. However the members of the Historical School were not conservatives, but liberals, prominent among the revolutionaries of 1848 and suffering for their liberalism. Their emphasis on the role of the state did not derive from any specially authoritarian sentiments, but from the practical concerns of German unification and of the pursuit of the German national interest against the interests of the other European powers. Thus, although the Historical School drew on the Romantic, Hegelian and Cameralist traditions, it vigorously rejected the reactionary elements in the work of such writers as Adam Müller, who subordinated the individual to the state in defining the state as an end in itself. For the Historical School the role of the state was still to be defined in liberal terms, as an essential condition for the well-being of the individual, and it was in such terms that it developed its analysis of the role of the state in the reproduction of capitalist social relations. It was in this context that Friedrich List developed his theory of the national economy.

List argued against the cosmopolitanism of political economy that the prosperity of the individual depended on the ability of the state to pursue appropriate policies to further the national well-being. These were policies that would foster the growth of the productive forces, including not only the material capital of the nation, but also its 'spiritual capital', identified by List with the freedoms of political liberalism. In the development of the productive forces a nation would go through a series of stages, which Adam Smith had already identified, namely the savage, the pastoral, the agricultural, the agricultural-manufacturing and the agricultural-manufacturing-commercial stages. This was a progressive development, the height of which would be reached with the predominance of trade and manufacture. A nation at a superior state would be more powerful and more prosperous than a nation at an inferior stage, so free international trade would permit it to prevent the more backward nation from advancing in the face of foreign competition. Protection would be required to enable Germany to emerge as a fully fledged industrial power that could hold its own in the world market. The liberal cosmopolitanism of classical political economy was, within this context, simply the abstract expression of the British national economic interest in gaining free access to foreign markets to prevent the emergence of foreign competitors. The more backward position of German industry required a different political economy.

While economic liberalism might be appropriate to a more advanced stage of capitalist development, in the German context it was the condition for the continued dominance of foreign capital. On the other hand, state regulation continued to be distorted by the economic and political dominance of the landowning class, which List's theory identified with an inferior stage of capitalist development.

The conflict between the politically dominant Junkers and the economically ascendant bourgeoisie came to a head in the revolutions of 1848. The defeat of the revolutionary forces did not imply the subordination of the bourgeoisie to the Junkers, but their reluctant accommodation to Junker rule, complemented by a Junker recognition of the bourgeois economic interest. The need of the state for a strong economic base, and the development of capitalism in the German countryside, provided the basis for a pragmatic resolution of the divisions within the dominant class in Germany as in England, a resolution provisionally achieved under Bismarck. Although the studies of the Historical School retained, in a rather empty rhetorical form, the liberal spirit of 1848, the main concern came increasingly to be with the social conflict associated with the development of German capitalism: not only the direct conflict between capital and labour, but also the social and political dislocation threatened by the destruction of the petty producers.

Roscher, Hildebrand and Knies, the older generation of the Historical School, all took up List's emphasis on the national economy, formulated within an evolutionary theory that sought empirical laws of development, in order to situate German economic and social development within a national and historical context. However, their fear that the subordination of economic activity to self-interest would give rise to growing class polarisation led them to criticise more sharply the economists' preoccupation with purely economic motives. 'Industrial feudalism' and the growth of an agricultural proletariat would foster the growth of socialism and so had to be restricted by the State. They therefore laid an increasing emphasis on the need to consider the pursuit of economic goals within a broader social context, within which self-interest would be subordinated to morals, religion, custom and standards of propriety. The development of society could not be reduced to its economic development, for its moral development was equally important. Nor could policy by subordinated solely to economic ends, for the state had a primary concern with the conditions of social integration and national unity. Thus the Historical School became increasingly critical of any attempt to formulate general economic laws, or general laws of historical development, coming to emphasise the uniqueness of time and place and the necessarily pragmatic and empirical orientation of economic studies.

While Roscher followed List in regarding classical political economy as a theory appropriate to a particular stage of capitalist development, stressing only the need to temper the classical doctrines with a concern for the national particularities of historical development, Hildebrand and Knies carried the criticism of political economy further, arguing that history did not simply introduce qualifications into the laws of political economy, but that political economy had to be reformulated on an historical foundation. Hildebrand continued to believe that it was possible to formulate historical laws, distinguishing the phases of natural economy, money economy and credit economy. In the latter, access to credit would give workers and petty producers parity with capitalists and so would eliminate class conflict. Knies went further still, condemning the labour theory of value and the utilitarian orientation of political economy for playing into the hands of socialism. Although he believed in progress, Knies claimed that it was a moral rather than an economic category, so that laws of development were always moral laws that could not be formulated quantitatively and which could only provide a basis for analogical comparison.

Despite their criticism of political economy the older generation of the Historical School continued to fall back on its doctrines when convenient, supplementing them with an emphasis on the ethical orientation of economic activity, and with a plethora of historical illustrations demonstrating the divergence between theory and reality. Despite the claim of the Historical School to be counterposing reality to theory, a claim that became even more insistent among the younger generation, the Historical School nevertheless formulated its investigations within the framework of a particular conception of society. Although it rejected the economic laws of classical political economy, its essential framework was still that of political economy, being based on the theory of production that conceptualised the fundamentally harmonious character of capitalist social relations in terms of the co-operative division of labour between agriculture and industry and between land, labour and capital, and on the theory of distribution that denied any necessary conflict of interests between capital and labour, locating capitalism historically within Adam Smith's stages theory.

The distance between political economy and its historicist critics was exaggerated in their own eyes, and those of subsequent commentators, because the conception of capitalist society which they had in common had by now acquired the self-evidence of common sense. Comte and the German Historical School conceptualised the essential harmony of capitalist social relations on the basis of the model of the mutual co-operation and interdependence of the division of labour. However this conception accords with commonsense only because commonsense is ensnared in the illusions of the trinity formula:

> The more the vulgar economists in fact content themselves with translating common notions into doctrinaire language, the more they imagine that their writings are plain, in accordance with nature and the public interest, and free from all theoretical hairsplitting. Therefore, the more alienated the form in which they conceive the manifestations of capitalist production, the closer they approach the nature of common notions, and the more they are, as a consequence, in their natural element

wrote Marx of Roscher (TSV, III, p. 503). The Historical School, like Comte's sociology, rested on the same ideological foundations as political economy, and its critique of political economy was confined within the same ideological limits.

The critique of the Historical School, like that of Comte, was limited in attributing the conflict endemic in capitalism to the self-interested orientation of economic activity that is an essential characteristic of capitalist social relations. They therefore sought reforms that would regulate this conflict of interest to bring the social relations of distribution and exchange into harmony with the social relations of production. However, like Comte, the Historical School had no coherent theory that could specify the limits of self-interest, and so provide a rational definition of the content of the necessary moral and political regulation, because they had no alternative economic theory to that proposed by political economy, on the basis of which to define the extent to which self-interest and the hidden hand of the market were insufficient to secure economic prosperity and social harmony, and so to define the extent and content of necessary reforms. In general they saw the appropriate distribution as that defined by vulgar economy, according to which the just reward accruing to each factor of production would correspond to its contribution to production, on the one hand, and to the sacrifices made by its owner, on the other. However, neither Comte nor historicism could explain how, in the absence of a market, such a distribution could be determined.

In the end both schools of thought rested on a speculative philosophy of history that postulated the essential harmony of capitalist relations of production, which they combined with a purely pragmatic approach to the solution of particular social and political problems. Both schools of thought proposed a reformed capitalism as an alternative to socialism. But how far should such reform go? Taken to their limits Comte's positivism led to the socialist Commonwealth, while Roscher's historicism threatened to lead inexorably to State Socialism.

This is not to deny the practical and theoretical importance of Comte's sociology or of German historicism. Both took the threat of social dislocation much more seriously than did classical political economy, recognising the need for the moral and political regulation of social relations that the classical economic laws excluded. However their inability to specify the limits of *laissez-faire* rigorously meant that they were unable to provide any rigorous definition not only of the extent, but also of the limits of moral and political regulation. It was the failure to define such limits that proved their fatal weakness.

Herbert Spencer's liberal Sociology

It is essential to remember that both historicism and positivism were proposed as *liberal* critiques of political economy, as strongly opposed to the organicism of conservative theories as they were to the rampant individualism of political economy. The nation state and the moral order were not designated as ends in themselves, as they were by conservatives, but only as means to the fulfilment of individual needs and aspirations. The fundamental weakness of these theories, from their own liberal point of view, was their failure to provide a secure liberal foundation for their critiques of political economy, a failure which was expressed in the dualism of individual and society which they were never able to overcome. It is this dualism which explains what Parsons saw as the defining weakness of these theories, their failure to develop a 'voluntaristic theory of action' which could reconcile the need for the moral and political regulation of social relations with the freedom of the individual. Thus the temptation was always to attribute a spurious objectivity and a spurious authority to the state and to the system of morality because the theories did not relate these institutions back to the individual needs and aspirations to which they should, in liberal eyes, respond.

This weakness was not exclusive to sociology and historicism. The liberal credentials of political economy also came into question as the century wore on. The problem was that according to the laws of political economy the fate of the individual was inexorably tied up with the fate of her class. The simple class model may have been appropriate to the great constitutional conflicts of the first half of the nineteenth century, but these conflicts were largely resolved by the compromises which followed 1848. The 1850s and 1860s saw a realignment of the social and political relations between the classes and, correspondingly, of the terms within which capitalist society was considered, the class model of society proposed by political economy being progressively diluted as class boundaries were increasingly blurred.

The constitutional, political and legal reforms of the 1830s and 1840s and the increasing mobility of capital had considerably softened the opposition between the capitalist and landed interests so that land was becoming merely a form of capital, while capitalist wealth gave access to land and to political privilege. The economic distinction between rent and profit was progressively less adequate as the basis for distinguishing between discrete social classes. The theory of rent, correspondingly, lost its political centrality, becoming the basis on which some radical reformers proposed the taxation or even the nationalisation of land without necessarily implying any constitutional transformation.

While land was being progressively assimilated to capital, a more complex social differentiation was emerging lower down the social scale. On the one hand, a specifically capitalist middle class of shopkeepers, petty producers and professional people was growing fast and seeking to establish its own place in capitalist society. On the other hand, a clearer differentiation was beginning to develop within the working class, particularly between the skilled and unskilled, the respectable and the rough. This increasing complexity led to a blurring of the sharp class boundaries of the classical model and to the ideological resurgence of models of a hierarchical gradation of rank and status that corresponded not only to economic conditions, but also to personal moral qualities and educational achievements.

This hierarchical model provided a basis on which the priority of individual over collective, and moral over material, achievements could be asserted. A more fluid social structure provided the opportunity to preach the possibility of individual self-improvement within the hierarchy, and the means to achieve such self-improvement was by moral and intellectual elevation. The message of self-help was conveyed through the popular press and improving literature, through political propaganda and from the pulpit, through educational institutions and the public libraries. Even trade unionism, when properly conducted, had a part to play, fostering the moral qualities of the working class by making provision through mutual benefit funds for sickness, unemployment and old age and by providing workers' education. The working class was no longer an anonymous mass to be feared, but a collection of individuals to be enlightened and assimilated to the established order. Thus the emphasis on the moral qualities of the individual gradually displaced the political economists' emphasis on class as the determinant of the individual's fate.

This growth of a meritocratic individualism was above all expressed in the social philosophy of Herbert Spencer, which returned to many of the themes already developed by Adam Smith. Spencer conceptualised capitalist society within the framework of a speculative philosophy of history that presented *laissez-faire* capitalism as the culmination of the evolutionary process. Society was conceived on the model of the division of labour, expressed within an organic analogy, understood as the interdependence of the functionally differentiated parts of an increasingly complex whole, whose development could be understood within the framework of a theory of cosmological evolution. He saw the development of society as progressive, manifesting the fundamental cosmological law of the increasing differentiation and integration of functions, and the mechanism of evolution as the quasi-Darwinian competitive struggle for existence in which 'survival goes to the fittest'.

Spencer saw capitalism as the stage at which industry finally replaced war as the basis of society. This development was marked by the progressive differentiation of the economy from the state and the subordination of the state to the economy, instead of the subordination of the economy to the state characteristic of a military society. Within the economy this evolution was marked by the development from slavery, through serfdom, to wage-labour. The differentiation of capital and wage-labour corresponded to the differentiation of functions within production between capital, whose function was the regulation of labour, and wage-labour, whose function was to conduct the specialised tasks defined by the division of labour under the supervision of capital. More fundamentally the distinction between labour and capital was simply an aspect of the functional differentiation of mental and manual labour. Economic activity existed within a wider co-ordinating structure defined by the family, political and ecclesiastical organisation, the system of law and the cultural institutions of language, knowledge, morals and aesthetics. Each part of the whole had its part to play in the functioning of the system, and each part was adapted to its function through the evolutionary process governed by natural selection. The complexity of the system, and the ultimate beneficence of the law of evolution, militated against any attempt to intervene consciously to mitigate social evils, for any such attempted reform was as likely to interrupt as to accelerate the course of progress. Thus Spencer came to recognise that wage-labour 'amounts in practice to little more than the ability to exchange one form of slavery for another', but he did not propose any remedy, merely observing that 'it seems that in the course of social progress, parts, more or less large, of each society are sacrificed for the benefit of society as a whole' (Spencer, 1896, 3, p. 516).

Spencer's social philosophy was in one sense a generalisation of the optimistic perspectives of political economy, extending the belief in the inevitability of progress from the economy to all social institutions and glorifying the achievements of the mid-Victorian bourgeoisie. Spencer took for granted the virtues of economic liberalism and the impossibility of a general improvement in the condition of the working class, while his theory of evolution depended as much on the theory of the division of labour and of the beneficent operation of the market as it did on biological organicism and the Darwinian theory. His theory was essentially a completion of the ideology of political economy, that reformulated its optimistic conclusions within the framework of a speculative philosophy of history, presenting the existing order as the culmination of history and the realisation of rationality. The philosophy rested entirely on the plausibility of the application of the biological and economic analogy to society as a whole, so that Spencer's works amounted to little more than compendious illustrations of the fundamental cosmological principles of evolution. However, his work was enormously influential in England and the United States until the end of the century, and has inspired successive waves of optimism since. Moreover in his emphasis on the individual, in his demotion of the concept of class, and in his emphasis on the co-ordination of the division of labour rather than on the maximisation of the rate of growth of production, his work prefigured and inspired developments that were to come.

The decline and fall of political economy

The individualism of Spencer's social philosophy apparently conflicted with the class model on which political economy was based, just as the growing emphasis on moral improvement, expressed by evangelical, positivist and liberal reformers, conflicted with the uncompromising materialism of political economy. Nevertheless there was no other rigorous basis than political economy on which to defend the truths of liberalism. So long as there was a political resistance to the claims of the working class, political economy had an ideological function to perform, however far from reality its categories might appear to be. In particular, and above all else, political economy established the impossibility of a general improvement in the material condition of the working class, and so of the alteration of the existing class structure. It therefore continued to constitute the bastion of the ideological defence of the established order, which defined the ultimate limits of social and political reform.

John Stuart Mill showed how political economy could accommodate these developments. Mill espoused more and more reformist causes without his reformism undermining his confidence in the ultimate validity of the truths of political economy. Those truths may

The decline and fall of political economy 171

have been abstract, but they were nevertheless constraining:

> Howsoever we may succeed in making for ourselves more space within the limits set by the constitution of things, those limits exist; there are ultimate laws, which we did not make, which we cannot alter, and to which we can only conform. (Mill, 1965–77, II, p. 199)

Within this framework Mill was ready to concede that values other than those of material interest might prevail; that moral, educational and cultural improvements should be fostered, even at the expense of economic gain; and that the state might intervene to protect the ignorant and the weak, in providing a more just relationship between effort and reward by restricting the power of monopoly, and by the taxation of inherited wealth and unearned incomes. Nevertheless such reform could not violate the truths of political economy.

These truths were finally shattered by the resurgence of working class political agitation. The 1850s had been a period of unprecedented prosperity and social peace that appeared completely to vindicate the liberal optimism. However towards the end of the decade, changes began to take place that again gave the concept of class an ominous ring. These were the developments that led up to the 1867 Reform Bill.

The reform movement was predominantly extra-parliamentary and comprised an alliance of parts of manufacturing capital, the middle class and the organised elements of the working class. The essential condition for success was the suppression of the differences between the working class and Radical elements, and the acceptance by the working class of middle-class leadership. The basis of this acceptance was recognition by the middle class of the legitimacy of trade unionism. Thus the growing strength of the trade unions, and their active political involvement in the reform movement, were of fundamental significance for political economy.

On the one hand, whereas the rhetoric of class had played a major role in the agitation of 1832, the reformers of the 1860s were concerned above all to play down the class issue. The extension of the franchise was not intended to admit the working class to the constitution, but to bring into the electoral game those who exhibited moral reliability and political responsibility, qualities measured by respect for property and the constitution and found among the more affluent, and correspondingly improved, sections of the working class, but which were defined in moral and not in economic terms. *Citizenship*, and not *property*, was to become the basis of political representation. The extension of the franchise was seen as the necessary framework for political alliances that would transcend class, and so as the only viable alternative to class struggle. The dangers of refusing such an extension were clear:

> The struggle may cease in the end to be one between parties in Parliament and become one between classes, the class represented by the House of Commons, on the one side, and the class represented by the trade unions on the other ... The true stateman would almost rather drag the working men within the pale of the constitution by force than suffer them thus to organise themselves into a separate community outside it (Smith, 1866).

On the other hand, despite the political economists' inviolable laws, the working class persisted in pressing its independent interests through its own class organisations. In 1832, and again in 1846, the radical middle class had been able to mobilise sections of the working class, without making substantial concessions to the latter. However in each case the 'betrayal' of the workers' demands by the Radicals was followed by a short burst of intense working class political activity. By 1867 the working class was better organised and was more wary of the terms on which it forged alliances. If Radicals and Liberals were to secure working class support for reform, substantial concessions would have to be made, particularly in relation to trade union rights, and so the existence of independent working-class interests would have to be recognised, whatever political economy might say. If this was the case in the reform movement, it was even more the case after reform, when the existing Parties found themselves competing for the electoral support of the enfranchised sections of the working class. Thus the reform movement, and the subsequent admission of sections of the working class to the franchise, implied the acceptance of the legitimacy of the aspirations of the organised working class and recognition of the need to establish a framework within which trade unions could operate to further the collective interests of workers. Class conflict was assimilated into the constitution by separating the political activity of the working class, channelled through the electoral system, from its economic activity, conducted through the trade unions. Political reform was followed almost immediately, and quite inevitably, by trade union reform.

The recognition of independent working-class interests, and of the right of workers to organise themselves to pursue those interests within the limits of the constitution, undermined the most fundamental principle of political economy, the law of wages, by which it had denied the existence of any such interest for half a century. The law of wages was already under considerable pressure. On the one hand, the Malthusian law of population had to be reconciled with the fact that there was no clear empirical relationship between level of income and size of family. Indeed the poor tended to have larger families than those with more money. Thus moral qualities rather than economic condition appeared to be the main determinant of population growth. On the other hand, the wages-fund doctrine was contradicted empirically by the existence of considerable and persistent wage-differentials. Most fundamentally, the law of wages conflicted sharply with the doctrine of self-help, for the latter stressed the relationship between the fate of the individual and her moral qualities, while the law of wages stressed the levelling effect of competition, so that the fate of the individual was inexorably tied to the fate of the class: there is no point in practising self-help and moral restraint if others are breeding profligately, increasing the supply of labour, and dragging down wages for all. Mill and Cairnes had patched the wages-fund doctrine up with their 'theory of non-competing groups', but the law of wages was on such shaky ground by the 1860s that, in the face of the challenge of reform, it simply collapsed.

The wages-fund doctrine was demolished in England in 1868 by Cliffe Leslie and Fleeming Jenkins. In 1869 Thornton published his book *On Labour* and Mill, in his review of the book, conceded the fallaciousness of the doctrine, recognising that

> there is no law of nature making it inherently impossible for wages to rise to the point of absorbing not only the funds which he [the employer] had intended to devote to carrying on of his business, but the whole of what he allows for his private expenses, beyond the necessaries of life. The real limit to the rise is the practical consideration [of] how much would ruin him, or drive him to abandon the business, not the inexorable limits of the Wages Fund (Mill, 1965–77, V, p. 645).

Although Mill reissued his *Principles* in 1871 with only minor alterations and Cairnes persisted through the 1870s, and although the wages-fund doctrine has been repeatedly resurrected as a weapon against trade unionism, classical political economy was to all intents and purposes killed by this admission. Without the theory of the wages-fund it had no law of wages. Without the law of wages it could not pretend to have a theory of profit. Classical political economy could hardly provide an adequate theory of capitalist society without being able to offer a theory of distribution. 'It was the labour question, unsolved by that removal of restrictions which was all deductive political economy had to offer, that revived the method of observation. Political economy was transformed by the working classes' (Toynbee, 1969, p. 11).

Such residual appeal as political economy did have was soon eroded by the experience of the Great Depression that set in at the beginning of the 1870s. Growing foreign competition precipitated demands for the state to intervene to strengthen British capital at home and abroad. The 'law of international exchange' was forgotten as the cry for 'Fair Trade' and imperialist annexation replaced the classical demands for 'Free Trade' and colonial freedom. The law of free competition was forgotten as cartels and monopolies arose and State and municipal enterprises were formed to organise and finance the railways, coal, gas and public utilities. The law of self-interest was forgotten as growing concerns about the physical, moral and educational standards of the working class motivated increasing public provision and regulation of standards of housing, education and public health. Political economy had no way of dealing with such questions.

> The *a priori* reasoning of political economy, orthodox and unorthodox alike, fails from want of reality. At its base are a series of assumptions very imperfectly connected with the observed facts of life. We need to begin with a true picture of the modern industrial organism, the interchange of service, the exercise of faculty, the demands and satisfactions of desire (Booth, 1887, p. 7).

Social reform and the limits of Sociology

The changing economic, ideological and political circumstances of the 1860s and 1870s put classical political economy to the test and found it wanting. A new theory of capitalist society was urgently needed that could respond to the practical and ideological demands of a new era.

The first reaction to the collapse of political economy in Britain was to adopt a pragmatic approach that could give a truer picture of the 'observed facts of life'. What was needed was a theory that could look beyond the pursuit of self-interest to set economic relations within their institutional, political and moral context, and replace the dogmatism and abstraction of political economy with a more flexible and more realistic approach. What was needed was 'a scientific sociology comprehending true economic doctrine, but comprehending also a great deal more' as Ingram argued in his enormously influential presidential address to Section F of the British Association in 1878. Spencer had already indicated the importance of non-economic institutions in his sociology and Spencer continued to be influential among the opponents of reform. However his optimism became less and less appropriate as the need for social reform became more pressing. Thus there was a turn to foreign sources, and above all to France and Germany, to find theories that could fill the gap. Thus Ingram was a follower of Comte, while Arnold Toynbee and Thorold Rogers drew most heavily on the Historical School. Subsequently LePlay was a major influence. His theory, which had stressed the importance of the family and community in achieving social integration, stimulated a mass of family-oriented poverty studies and community investigations, and gave British sociological reformism a distinctive emphasis on the use of social policy to mould the family and the use of town planning to mould the community.

In similar circumstances in Germany the younger generation of the Historical School, dominated by Gustav Schmoller, established the *Verein für Sozialpolitik* in 1873, which built on the earlier tradition. The *Verein* sought to stimulate academic research that could serve as a guide for reform, and in its early years played a central role in the reform movement. The emphasis of the *Verein* was on discovering the means to ameliorate or abolish class conflict. This was recognised to involve assigning a high priority to economic expansion, but the *Verein* insisted that questions of economic policy should nevertheless be subordinated to ethical and political considerations. Economic development should be regulated in accordance with national political needs, and in particular the strengthening of the State domestically and internationally.

In France LePlay still had some following, but he was eclipsed by the rise of Emile Durkheim, who founded the French school of sociology. Durkheim drew heavily on Comte, Spencer and the German

Historical School to develop a comparable evolutionary theory within which social disorder was attributed to a failure of moral integration that had caused selfishness and ignorance to prevent the emergence of a properly regulated moral individualism (an individualistic reformulation of Comte's social-love). Such moral integration was to be achieved by the formation of associations, for example of producers and consumers, within which would be generated solidaristic sentiments based on the moral appreciation of interdependence. The Durkheimians also placed considerable emphasis on the development of a national system of secular education.

The last quarter of the nineteenth-century was a period in which there was a considerable cross-fertilisation of ideas throughout Europe as liberalism confronted the challenge posed by the institutionalisation of class conflict associated with the growth of an organised working class, on the one hand, and the centralisation and concentration of capital, on the other. Similar schemes for the amelioration of the condition of the working class, the regulation of capital, the protection of petty producers and the conciliation of class conflict were proposed throughout Europe. These schemes were formulated within a very similar theoretical framework, inspired largely by Comte, the German Historical School and, rather ambivalently, Spencer. The concerns of the last decades of the nineteenth-century were more pragmatic than had been those of the earlier writers, and speculative evolutionary schemes were largely displaced by a greater emphasis on detailed empirical investigation, but the essential features of the earlier theories were retained. We can sum these up under four headings.

First, the social theories of the late nineteenth-century stressed the need for the moral and political regulation of capitalist social relations, to moderate the conflicts that arose out of the unfettered pursuit of economic interest. Thus the radical individualism of political economy was tempered by a concern with the needs of society or of the nation, imposed morally or politically on the individual. Political economy was criticised for its abstraction, and the distinction between economic and moral questions was rejected. However the critics retained the harmonism of the materialist theory of society on which political economy was based. The problem was to realise this harmony socially. Thus the conflicting economic interests of opposed classes had to be seen within a broader context of communal interest in which class conflict was a sign of a failure of proper social regulation.

Second, although these theories uniformly stressed the socio-historical character of capitalist social relations, against the economic reductionism of political economy, this historical relativism was quite different from that of Marx's critique of political economy. The specific historical character of capitalist social relations was conceptualised within a naturalistic evolutionary framework that governed the development of the relations of production, only distribution relations being subject to historical change, these changes being seen as changes in the form of property, without being traced to their origins in different social forms of labour. This separation of relations of distribution from relations of production had its origins within political economy, being formulated first by Say and subsequently adopted by most political economists as the framework within which the economic laws of capitalist society were developed. John Stuart Mill classically stressed the historical variability of the laws of distribution, as opposed to the laws of production:

> The laws and conditions of the production of wealth, partake of the character of physical truths. There is nothing optional, or arbitrary in them ... It is not so with the Distribution of Wealth. That is a matter of human institution solely. The things once there, mankind, individually or collectively, can do with them as they like (Mill, 1965–77, II, p. 199).

Thus Mill distinguished petty proprietorship, slavery, *métayage*, cottagers, wage-labour and co-operation as different forms of the relations of distribution. Richard Jones, in relation to India, and Sir Henry Maine, in relation to Ireland, had likewise developed a framework within which to understand the changing forms of property that underlay different forms of the relations of distribution.

The distinction between the theories of production and distribution was the basis on which Mill assimilated the insights of sociology and historicism to recognise the possibility and limits of social reform. However, once the historical variability of relations of distribution is admitted, these possibilities are very wide indeed. Mill tempered his 'socialist' inclinations with a resolute defence of the inviolable rights of private property, but others were willing to go much further down this road. Not without reason were Schmoller and his associates referred to as the 'socialists of the chair', while in England the Comteans were among the staunchest defenders of trade unionism and in France the Durkheimians were closely associated with socialists. While for all these groups social reform was a vital means of staving off the socialist threat, the Fabians proposed the transformation of private into state property as the means of resolving the irrationalities of capitalism.

The third essential feature of the theories with which we are concerned was their emphasis on the need for empirical research. On the one hand, they stressed the importance of comparative and historical study as the only proper basis on which to develop evolutionary laws, thus replacing, so they believed, the speculative philosophies of history of the older generation by empirically based historical schemes. On the other hand, contemporary empirical investigation was required to measure the divergence between reality and the theoretical ideal of a just, harmonious and prosperous society so as to offer guidelines for reform. Thus empirical research was conducted not naively, but on the basis of a particular conception of capitalist society which defined the normal condition of such a society as one of justice and social integration. Injustice and social conflict were considered to represent departures from the normal condition, the consequence of evolutionary lags that were a part of the process of social change from old, paternalistic, forms of social regulation to new, co-operative, forms. Comparative and historical research was directed at vindicating this conception of capitalist society by identifying the different historical forms of social integration and by drawing the lessons from history of the unfortunate consequences of the unregulated exercise of economic and political power.

For all its empiricist criticisms of speculative Philosophies of History, not least directed at Marxism, this approach did not get away from speculative evolutionism, for empirical investigation could never contradict the claimed normality of social integration. Empirical investigation, specifically directed to the discovery of conflict, injustice and distress, in no way invalidated the conception of society as essentially harmonious, but merely pointed to the failure of evolution to complete its course. Empirical investigation explored the deviations of reality from the speculative ideal not in order to test the evolutionary theory empirically, but to evaluate reality in the light of the ideal. Instead of adapting theory to reality, the task of empirical investigation was to provide the basis on which social reform could make reality conform to the theory.

The fourth respect in which late nineteenth-century social thought built on the earlier traditions was in attempting to incorporate a concern with the political and moral regulation of social relations into a liberal framework. Thus, unlike conservative thinkers, they did not see either the state or morality as ends in themselves. Their critique of political economy was a critique from a liberal individualist direction, pointing to the ways in which the abuse of economic power and the socially conditioned existence of ignorance and irrationality enabled some individuals to intrude on the freedom and opportunities of others. Thus the moral and political regulation of social relations, and the development of an appropriate institutional framework within which such regulation could take place, were seen as an essential presupposition for the harmonisation of interests of the individual members of society. For example, Durkheim, far from being a conservative or a collectivist, was essentially seeking a sociological reformulation of social contract theory that could legitimate a greater degree of social and political regulation than had been appropriate to the 'age of reason' or the 'age of utilitarianism'.

The fundamental theoretical problem which such an attempt confronted was the familiar one of establishing the relationship between the individual interest and the general interest, and of identifying the point at which the unrestrained pursuit of self-interest became subversive of the general interest and so subject to regulation. We have seen that classical political economy had such a theory, expressed in its economic laws that set very narrow limits to social intervention. Vulgar economy and Herbert Spencer likewise defended a regime of *laissez-faire* on the basis of little more than liberal optimism. Comte and the German Historical School offered a moral and political critique of the implications of *laissez-faire*, but they had no means of rigorously establishing its limits, nor, correspondingly, the possibility and limits of intervention.

The sociology of Durkheim, the investigations of the Historical School, British empirical sociology and Oxford idealism equally rested on purely pragmatic foundations. While the principle of self-interest was rooted in the aspirations of the individual, the principles of moral and political regulation were located beyond the individual, in society, the state or religion. But in rejecting political economy, these critics were not rejecting liberalism. Thus they were not prepared to fall into the arms of the conservatives in subordinating the individual to supra-individual principles. The result is that in all of these theories we find a constant dualistic tendency with the individual, on the one hand, and the state or society, on the other, appearing as complementary ends without any rigorous theory of the relations between the two.

This absence had enormous practical consequences, for it meant that there was no principled basis on which to evaluate reforms, in which the rights and freedoms of the individual were restrained or violated in the pursuit of moral or political ends, because there was no way of systematically assessing the impact of such reforms. Conflict, injustice, poverty and distress could be discovered by empirical investigation, and *ad hoc* reforms proposed to deal with them, but how was the reformer to know what would be the effect of such reforms, how would the reformer know that the reforms might not exacerbate rather than solving the problem? How were the benefits gained by some to be weighed against the losses incurred by others? How was the reformer to weigh social benefits against the violation of individual rights?

Spencer repeatedly railed against vain attempts to treat social problems on the basis of an estimate of 'immediate benefits and costs' rather than on the basis of a more profound investigation.

> The politician will spend his energies in rectifying some evils and making more — in forming, reforming and again reforming — in passing acts to amend acts that were before amended; while social schemers will continue to think that they have only to cut up society and rearrange it after their ideal pattern and its parts will join together again and work as intended (Spencer, 1896, 3, p. 318).

Spencer believed that sociology was a 'moral science' whose task was to

> deduce, from the laws of life and the conditions of existence, what kinds of actions necessarily tend to produce happiness, and what kinds to produce unhappiness. Having done this, its deductions are to be recognised as laws of conduct; and are to be conformed to irrespective of a direct estimation of happiness or misery (Spencer, 1904, 2, p. 88).

Spencer's liberal optimism was acceptable to some, but the growing pressure for reform in the last decades of the nineteenth-century made it increasingly apparent that some more rigorous sociological theory was needed that could establish the possibilities and limits of reform and provide a means of evaluating alternative proposals. Foremost amongst the problems, once again, was the problem of labour.

With the collapse of classical political economy the right of the working class to organise in trade unions in order to pursue its economic aspirations was widely recognised. Historicism and sociology were brought into play to underscore the importance of trade unionism in rectifying the imbalance of power in the market between labour and capital, and in establishing a framework within which harmonious class relations could be established. Thus in the match-girls' strike of 1888 and the London dock strike of 1889 middle-class reformers vied with socialists to endorse the workers' claims and to subscribe to their support-funds. But how far should such claims go? What would be the effect of an increase in wages for the workers, for their employers and for the economy as a whole? At what point does trade unionism become an intolerable violation of the freedom of employers or of individual workers, rather than an essential agent of social justice? How should the state respond to the agitation to limit further the length of the working-day? How should it respond to demands to alleviate the condition of the unemployed? How should it respond to demands for social insurance, for the provision of public housing, for the establishment of municipal enterprises and the taxation of land and inherited wealth? All these were questions to which political economy had been able to give clear answers, even if those answers were no longer acceptable. A reformulation of political economy was imperative as demands for social reform and for workers' rights proliferated and escalated.

The need for a more rigorous theory was not only practical, but also ideological. With the development of monopoly capital and of imperialism the state was increasingly compelled to intervene domestically and internationally on behalf of capital, threatening intensified class struggle at home and colonial and inter-imperialist wars abroad. On the other hand, the rise of socialism carried with it the alternative threat that the state would become the agency through which the organised working class would nationalise capital and land. The socialist threat, on the one hand, and the resistance of monopoly capital, on the other, showed up the inadequacy of a pragmatic approach to social reform and produced an urgent need for a theory that could both recognise the necessity of reform and also set limits to such reform.

6

The Marginalist Revolution in Economics

The 'marginalist revolution in economics' is acclaimed by bourgeois economists as the theoretical revolution which freed political economy from extraneous political considerations, and so founded modern 'scientific' economics. The orthodox Marxist characterisation of the marginalist revolution inverts the bourgeois interpretation. For orthodox Marxism the marginalist revolution marks the final step in the ideological degeneration of political economy (Bukharin, 1927; Dobb, 1940, 1973; Meek, 1973).

The marginalist revolution in economics cannot be reduced either to the purely scientific revolution of the bourgeois interpretations, or to the purely ideological revolution of its Marxist critics. The pioneers of the marginalist revolution were neither disinterested scientists, nor were they mere apologists for capitalism. They certainly posed new scientific questions, which they sought to answer according to the normal canons of scientific procedure. These new questions were not posed in a scientific vacuum, but nor was their motivation purely apologetic. They were primarily an attempt to provide rational solutions to the new problems presented to the state by the maturing of the contradictions of capitalist accumulation, problems presented by the growth of an independent working-class movement, by the growing monopolisation of capitalism, and by the intensification of the crisis tendencies of accumulation. These were real problems, which could not be resolved by a purely apologetic ideology, but which had to be approached scientifically.

The ideological limitations of the new economics were no different from those of classical political economy. They lay not in the apologetic character of its answers, but in the restricted character of its questions. Like classical political economy, the new economics recognised the deficiencies of actually existing capitalism. But like classical political economy, it did not see these deficiencies as being inherent in the social form of capitalist production, but in the gap which separated the mundane reality of capitalism from its ideal model, a gap which, like political economy, it attributed to human intellectual and moral weakness which could be remedied by appropriate institutional reform. Marginalist economics was no more and no less ideological than had been classical political economy. The fundamental change lay not in the motivation of its proponents, or in the scientific status of its procedures, but in the questions which it posed.

If the marginalist revolution is not simply an ideological revolution, the orthodox Marxist critique, which reduces marginalist economics to its apologetic function, cannot be regarded as satisfactory. In this chapter I will explore in more detail the relationship between science and ideology in marginalist economics, in order to establish the continuity underlying the apparently radical break between marginalism and classical political economy. In the next chapter I will argue that Marx's critique of political economy provides an intrinsic theoretical critique of the ideological limitations of the new science of economics.

The marginalist revolution

The marginalist revolution was pioneered by three writers who initially worked independently of one another, but whose work had many convergent features. They were Jevons in England, Walras in Switzerland and Menger in Austria. The revolution is conventionally dated at 1870, but its roots go back into the 1860s and the new methods of economic analysis did not achieve general recognition until the 1880s and 1890s. It is therefore necessary to distinguish between the achievements of particular individuals in pioneering new techniques of analysis, on the one hand, and the adoption of the new system of economics based on the application of those techniques, on the other.

The particular motives of Jevons, Walras and Menger in developing the new approach did not necessarily coincide with the reasons for its achieving sweeping, if belated, recognition. Thus the initial problems that Jevons, Walras and Menger set themselves were apparently rather idiosyncratic and could not immediately be located within a general intellectual movement. On the other hand, the fact that three thinkers independently raised similar questions and reached very similar conclusions should indicate that their concerns were not as devoid of general significance as might appear at first sight.

Of the founding fathers, only Jevons defined his project directly in opposition to classical political economy. Walras worked within the French tradition of utility theory going back to Say and Smith, while Menger saw his task as being one of bringing some rigour into the German tradition of 'vulgar economy'. Moreover, as we saw in the last chapter, classical political economy was not immediately replaced by the method of marginal analysis. For about two decades the historical and the empirical methods were dominant, for the questions raised by the marginalists only became central political issues some twenty years after they were first raised by the pioneers.

Technically the marginalist revolution is defined by a new method of economic analysis which applies the calculus to the problem of the determination of prices. The new method of analysis did not involve any substantial technical innovations, for once the question of the determination of prices in the market had been posed as a topic for rigorous investigation the techniques required for solving the question fell almost immediately to hand. The pioneers all posed the question within the framework of a theory of utility and this in many ways made their approaches to the question, and their solutions, extremely cumbersome. However the essence of the problem, and of its solution, was relatively straightforward. Thus the methods of calculus had been applied to economic problems before, by such thinkers as Gossen and Cournot, and to analogous problems by Bernoulli, but the earlier attempts had been ignored, not because of a blindness to genius, but because the questions that were posed did not at the time seem particularly significant.

The new methods of analysis arose out of a new concern with the problem of prices. Economists had always sought to explain the determination of prices as part of their enterprise. What the marginalists introduced was an emphasis on the need for a *rigorous* theory of price determination. For classical political economy the determination of prices was a subordinate concern. The central theoretical issues were those of the constitutional order within which capitalism could best develop to the advantage of the nation as a whole, and of the relations between the classes proper to such a development. This led classical political economy to pose questions of distribution within the framework of a theory of growth, within which the rigorous determination of individual prices was of little concern, so long as the determination of prices could be assumed not to conflict too seriously with the theory of distribution. For the marginalists this order of priorities was inverted, and the central concern became one of developing a rigorous theory of price determination.

Within classical political economy the determination of prices was subordinate to the problem of distribution and prices were the by-product of the theory of distribution. Once wages, rent and the rate of profit had been determined, prices could be derived by adding together the component parts. However the contradiction between the classical theory of production and the Ricardian theory of distribution meant that the resultant prices did not coincide with the values according to which the distributive categories were determined. Hence within the Ricardian system the determination of prices was always subject to the qualifications that this divergence necessarily introduced. The vulgar critics of classical political economy had exploited this contradiction to reject the classical theory of distribution and the theory of value on which it was based. However, although they asserted the priority of price over value or even the exclusive reality of price as against value, they could offer no rigorous theory of price determination, nor did they seriously seek to develop such a theory.

The marginalists followed the vulgar economists in their concern with the question of prices, but they did not follow them in rejecting the need for a theory of value. For the marginalists a theory of value was essential to any attempt to develop a rigorous theory of price, and the scientific weakness of the classical theory of value was that it could not achieve this. The task the marginalists set themselves was to develop a rigorous theory of price determination on the basis of the subjective theory of value, the basis of the marginalist theory of value was initially defined as 'utility'.

The problem of prices and the problem of reform

In order to understand the marginalist revolution we have to understand why questions about the rigorous determination of prices came to replace questions about economic growth and distribution as the central concern of economists. An obvious answer is that questions about economic growth and distribution led too easily to socialist conclusions so that a new 'apologetic' theory was needed. Marginalism neatly avoided the major questions about class relations and the constitution in order to pose questions about utility, efficiency and the formation of prices. Thus the marginalist revolution removed the politics from political economy — precisely its strength as far as bourgeois economists are concerned. Marginalism thus narrowed the field of economics, made it into a technical rather than a political discipline and asked innocuous questions while still providing a naturalistic and rationalist justification for capitalist social relations.

In very general terms such an answer has some validity. However, it will not do as an account of the marginalist revolution. Firstly, as we have already seen, classical political economy had shown itself quite capable of defending capitalism, expressing Burke's dictum that 'the laws of commerce are the laws of nature, and consequently the laws of God' (Burke, 1907, VI, p. 22). Its deficiencies were its inability to accommodate the possibility of reforms to deal with the labour question and the increasingly apparent unreality of its fundamental premises. Secondly, the mantle of classical political economy was not immediately taken over by marginalism. Popularisations of economics relied on the relativism of the Historical School and on the vague notions of vulgar economy and continued to borrow ideas from the classical school. The directly apologetic development of marginalism had to wait until the 1890s.

It is also very far from being the case that in the last quarter of the nineteenth-century classical political economy was contrasted with marginalism as political rather than technical. Classical political economy had played a central role in the political conflicts of the first three or four decades of the century, but from the late 1840s it had progressively lost its radical veneer. The final break was marked in Britain by the repeal of the Corn Laws in 1846, and corresponded politically to the development of the Anti-Corn Law League from an organisation that sought to contest the privileges of landed property to an organisation that sought to preserve the working class from radical influence by persuading the workers of the futility of reform and of their common interest with their employers. On the Continent the break was similarly marked by the class compromise which followed the defeat of the Revolutions of 1848. Although the class model of society in a sense had radical possibilities inherent within it, and the classical framework was one within which fundamental constitutional and political issues could be raised, these issues were regarded by mid-century as having been definitively settled. Classical political economy, far from providing a framework within which to question capitalism, purported to show definitively and conclusively that liberal capitalism was the best of all possible worlds.

The problem of prices and the problem of reform 187

Marginalism, by contrast, was born in a period of fundamental political change and matured in debates whose motivation was intensely political. If classical political economy had degenerated by the 1860s, marginalism came upon the public stage in the last two decades of the century in a much more militant and aggressive garb, playing a central political role in the debates within the emerging labour movement between reformist and revolutionary factions, serving not simply to defend capitalism but also to show the necessity and the possibility of reforms within the capitalist order. It would be quite wrong to take marginalism at face value and to see it merely as a method of technical analysis that is devoid of any particular conception of society. Marginalism embodied a particular theory of capitalist society no less than did classical political economy, and it is our task in this chapter to disentangle that theory.

Although it presented itself as a positive science, and insisted on the strict separation of facts from values (in which it followed and was influenced by John Stuart Mill), the new economics arose directly from a concern with evaluation. The evaluative orientation of the new approach to the economy stands out very clearly when we consider just what were the prices to be explained. The marginalists were no more concerned with the determination of the actual prices that ruled on the market than were the classical economists.[1] All the innovators emphasised the abstract character of pure economic theory, in which the intervention of chance and uncertainty, of specific historical institutions or political interventions, could all be ignored and their consideration deferred to subordinate empirical and policy studies. Pure theory was not concerned with the determination of actual prices but with their determination in an ideal world of perfect knowledge, perfect foresight, perfect competition and pure rationality. It is against this ideal world that the real world, and proposed reforms in the real world, are to be measured.

The questions that gave rise to a demand for a pure theory of price were questions about the proper prices of commodities. Jevons, for example, was especially concerned with the problem of scarcity (in particular the scarcity of coal) and with the role of prices in allocating resources. The problem he posed was that of determining what prices would achieve the optimal allocation of resources. The solutions that

[1] Indeed marginalist economics is less able to explain actual market prices than is the classical approach since its reliance on subjective evaluation, rather than objective laws, deprives it of any means of investigating systematic divergences of market prices from equilibrium prices.

were reached would then serve as the basis of policy prescriptions about the proper role of state intervention in the formation of prices in order to achieve such an allocation.

This example may seem relatively insignificant, a slender basis on which to build a revolution in economics as opposed to, say, a branch of public administration. But the question had a much more general significance and the solution a much more fundamental application. The more general context of the marginalist revolution was a concern with understanding the possibilities and limits of state intervention in the regulation of economic relations, including in particular the resolution of the labour question. The general background of this concern was the increasing role of the state in economic and social life. This role involved not only increasing state provision of public utilities, and of limited education, health and welfare services, but also increasing pressure on the state to intervene in the regulation of the private sector: to protect domestic producers against foreign competition, to intervene abroad to secure foreign markets and investment outlets, to regulate financial markets and to stimulate domestic investment, to regulate the national transport system and above all to intervene directly or indirectly to regulate the relations between capital and labour.

All these actual and proposed forms of state intervention contravened the pure principles of economic liberalism. In order to evaluate them rationally a more rigorous theory of the consequences of a liberal economic regime was required. Such a theory would then provide a basis on which proposed intervention in the economy could be judged by providing a bench-mark against which it could be evaluated. Thus Menger developed his version of marginalism from a dissatisfaction with the empiricism of the German Historical School, that was unable to provide any principled basis on which the possibilities and limits of State intervention could be evaluated.

Walras sought to establish rigorously the results of economic liberalism in order to locate its limits:

> how could these economists prove that the results of free competition were beneficial and advantageous if they did not know just what these results were? ...the fact that economists have often extended the principle of free competition beyond the limits of its true applicability is proof positive that the principle has not been demonstrated (Walras, 1954, pp. 256–7).

Jevons too was quite explicit about his motivation: 'If such a thing is possible we need a new branch of political and statistical science which shall carefully investigate the limits of the *laissez-faire* principle, and show where we want greater freedom and where less' (Jevons, 1883, p. 204).

The context of the marginalist revolution was the rapidly growing movement for social reform. The specific motivation for the development of a rigorous theory of price determination was the concern to be able to achieve some basis on which to evaluate proposed reforms. This concern brought people of very different political persuasions into a common enterprise. Thus, while most of the marginalists were committed to some degree to social reform, some saw the new methods as a means of tempering reformist demands.

Menger saw in the new economics a means of setting conservatism on a rigorous foundation by showing the precise mechanisms by which organic social institutions, such as prices and money, emerge from the pursuit of individual self-interest and come to express the collective wisdom of society. Menger therefore lumped together classical political economy and the German Historical School as exponents of a one-sided rationalistic liberalism that paid insufficient attention to the value of organic social structures in their enthusiasm for reform. Menger saw himself as bringing to fruition the tradition of Burke and Savigny that the historical school had betrayed, in aiming at a

> full understanding of existing social institutions in general and of organically created institutions in particular, the retention of what had proved its worth against the one-sidedly rationalistic mania for innovation in the field of economy. The object was to prevent the dissolution of the organically developed economy by means of a partially superficial pragmatism, a pragmatism that contrary to the intention of its representatives inexorably leads to socialism (Menger, 1963, p. 177).

The marginalist theory of price

The starting point of the marginalist economic analysis is the possession by individuals of goods in conditions of scarcity. The economic activity of these individuals consists in exchanging these goods for other goods in such a way as to maximise the total utility that they derive from them. Thus the analysis focuses on the elementary form of exchange and asks how prices emerge on the basis of such elementary exchanges. The exact terms in which each writer proposed the solution differ, but the essential principles are common to all.

Exchange brings together individual owners of goods. When such owners meet in the market they have to decide which goods to sell, and at what price, and which goods to acquire, and at what price. It seems self-evident that the price an individual will be prepared to pay for a given good will depend on what she thinks it is worth to her. Yet for the classical political economists this always gave rise to the paradox that the highest prices are paid for the most worthless goods, such as diamonds, while the most useful goods, such as air, are free. The marginalists solved this paradox by noting that the price did not correspond to the total utility of the good, but to the utility of the last unit of the good that was acquired. They also observed that as an individual acquired more of a given good the utility of the marginal unit tended to diminish. Because air is available in unlimited quantities we are profligate in its use, so that the utility of the last unit of air used is nil, while because diamonds are very scarce the marginal utility of diamonds is high. Goods therefore only have value in conditions of scarcity, and the task of economics is to establish the value of scarce goods. The price an individual will be prepared to pay for a good will correspond not to the total utility of that good, but to the utility of the marginal unit of the good that is acquired.

The individual will take up the opportunity to exchange if by so doing she can achieve an increase in the sum of utilities at her disposal. Faced with given exchange ratios (prices) the individual will choose to exchange goods until the relative marginal utilities of the goods possessed at the end of the transaction correspond to the exchange ratios in which they stand. In any other situation the individual could improve her position by exchanging goods of relatively low for goods of relatively high marginal utility. Thus at every possible set of exchange ratios the demand for and supply of each good on the part of each individual can be specified. If individual demand and supply functions are aggregated, total demand and supply functions can be specified. It can be shown that under appropriate assumptions (including the absence of ignorance, inconsistency and uncertainty) the interaction of demand and supply will give rise to a unique set of stable equilibrium prices that clear all markets by equalising supply and demand. These prices are those that correspond to the free and

The marginalist theory of price

rational choices of all the individual members of society seeking to achieve their own optimal solutions in conditions of scarcity.

The analysis so far is based on the interaction of a series of individuals each endowed with a fixed and given supply of goods. The initial allocation of goods is taken as given historically and so is no matter for the economist to investigate. However an adequate economic analysis must take account of the fact that goods are produced, and so are not in fixed supply. Production is considered to be beyond the area of concern of economics and is seen as a purely technical process within which factors of production are employed in certain technically determined proportions to produce goods. If there is a range of techniques available to produce a given good then the economist will be concerned to explain which technique will be employed, but otherwise the 'hidden abode of production, on whose threshold there hangs the notice "No admittance except on business"' (*Capital*, I, pp. 279–80) is no business of the marginalist. The recognition of the fact that goods are produced does, however, have important implications. If we move from the level of abstraction at which production is considered to be undertaken by individuals, the introduction of production introduces a distinction between two different kinds of economic units: on the one hand, households, which are the units of consumption; on the other hand, firms, which are the units of production. Households supply the services of productive factors to firms and purchase from firms the goods that are produced with those productive services.

This recognition of production introduces two further distinctions. Firstly, the motivation of firms cannot be identified immediately with the motivation of households. The household aims to maximise utility, but utility is a subjective concept and a firm is not a subject. Thus the firm seeks to maximise profits. This introduces a complication into the theory that can only be resolved by formulating a theory of profit which can establish that profit corresponds to the return to the owner of capital, so that the maximisation of profit corresponds to the maximisation of utility on the part of the owner of capital. Secondly, a distinction is introduced between goods and productive services (the Austrians distinguished between goods of different orders). Productive services differ from the goods so far considered in having no utility as such, for they are only useful when they are applied to the production of useful goods. The utility of productive services is therefore a derived utility, as is that of intermediate products that never enter final consumption.

The fact that productive services can be said to have a derived utility makes it possible, under certain restrictive conditions, to derive prices of these productive services from the estimations of utility expressed in the prices of final products. If the factors of production are in fixed supply and if the same factors are used in different combinations in different productive activities, the marginal contribution of each factor to final utility can be derived and this will correspond, in equilibrium, to the price of the factor. Thus wages, rent and profit can be derived as the revenues accruing to the factors of production — labour, land and means of production — without making any reference to labour-time or to costs of production.

Such a result was gleefully proclaimed by the early marginalists as a demonstration of the falsity of the classical doctrines. However, their elation was premature since the assumption of fixed factor supplies on which the result depended was either meaningless, if it referred to the aggregate supply of each factor (because it could not specify the basis on which heterogeneous qualities of labour, land and means of production should be aggregated), or grossly unrealistic, if it referred to the fixed supply of each quality of labour, land and means of production taken separately.

More sophisticated developments of marginalism recognised the role that costs had to play in the determination of prices by recognising that factor supplies were not fixed. The prices of the factors of production are then determined by the interaction of demand and supply. The demand for each factor will be dependent on its *marginal productivity*, which is the monetary expression of its marginal contribution to utility. Since factors will be used in the most productive outlets first, the marginal productivity of each factor will decrease as relatively more of that factor is used. Thus the demand for the factor will be a decreasing function of its price.

The supply of each factor can be determined in one of two ways within the marginalist framework. On the one hand, on the basis of a *real cost* theory, such as that of Alfred Marshall and of the classical tradition, the supply of a factor of production will be dependent on the *marginal disutility* incurred in offering it for sale. For the labourer this is the marginal disutility incurred in having to work rather than enjoy the time at leisure; for the capitalist it is the marginal disutility involved in abstaining from immediate consumption in favour of consumption in the future. On the other hand, on the basis of a theory of *opportunity cost*, such as the Austrian theory of

The marginalist theory of price

utility cost, the supply of the factor of production will be dependent on the utility that could be gained by employing the marginal unit of the factor elsewhere. In the end the two theories come to much the same thing, although the opportunity cost theory is marginally less tendentious in being less reliant on the direct subjective estimation of utilities. All that matters is that either version can establish that in equilibrium the price of the factor of production corresponds to its marginal productivity, on the one hand, and to its utility cost or marginal disutility, on the other. Moreover it can be shown that the sum of wages, rent and profit derived in this way, subject to certain not unrealistic conditions, will exhaust the total product. Thus the marginalist analysis of prices can give rise to a theory of distribution, given the initial distribution of resources, by explaining the returns to the various factors of production.

The marginalist analysis of the pricing of products and of productive services is conducted at a level of abstraction that excludes consideration of an historically specific framework of social relations. However the proper realisation of the principles of economic rationality does require the institutional separation of households from productive enterprises as budgetary units, the existence of a free market, in both products and the factors of production, as a means by which individual evaluations of utility can be related to one another, and the freedom and security of property as the basis of free exchange. Within this framework the prices that arise are then the results of the spontaneous and unconstrained expression of individual rationality. Since the institutions of production and exchange are simply technical instruments by means of which individuals may rationally pursue their economic ends, it should not be surprising that the marginalist analysis offers not simply an abstract account of the formation of prices in conditions of perfect competition, but also purports to establish the social rationality of a society based on competitive exchange by establishing that the prices reached, and the consequent allocation of resources, are in some sense optimal. It is in this supposedly rigorous demonstration of the allocative efficiency of capitalist society that the originality of marginalism lies.

If product prices correspond to marginal utilities, and marginal utility is a diminishing function of the supply of the product, then no re-allocation of the products can achieve an increase in total utility, for the increase in utility corresponding to the new use of any good cannot be greater than the loss of utility corresponding to its old use.

Likewise, if factor prices correspond to marginal productivities, and marginal productivity is a diminishing function of factor supply, then the re-allocation of factors can only reduce the total product, measured at current prices, and so the total utility. Thus any intervention in the pricing or allocation of factors or products that disturbs the attainment of competitive equilibrium is bound to reduce (or at least cannot increase) total utility. This result is subject only to the qualification that the initial distribution of resources is given. Judgements about the equity of this distribution are outside the domain of economics. Thus Jevons: 'so far as is consistent with the inequality of wealth in every community, all commodities are distributed by exchange so as to produce the maximum of benefit' (Jevons, 1970, p. 171); Walras: 'the consequences of free competition ... may be summed up as the attainment, within certain limits, of maximum utility' (Walras, 1954, p. 255) and Wieser: 'Where the general conditions are considered socially satisfactory and morally and legally correct, the general price is found also to be the just, or equitable, price' (Wieser, 1927, p. 184). Needless to say this fundamental qualification, that the desirability of the competitive allocation of resources was conditional on the desirability of their distribution, was almost universally ignored by those who seized on marginalism as the basis for a new apologetic for capitalism.

The marginalist theory of society

In economics textbooks the marginalist revolution is usually described in terms of the technical innovations that made possible a more rigorous economic analysis. Economics is presented as the marginalists themselves presented it, as a natural science of the economic dimension of society, analysing economic phenomena in abstraction from any particular social or institutional arrangements. As such, economics is not about any particular society, and its laws can be considered to be applicable in the consideration of any economic problem, which is defined as any problem concerned with the allocation of goods in conditions of scarcity.

However, marginalism does not simply offer a theory of rational choice. The theory also purports to explain the rationality of the fundamental social relationships of capitalist society, by deriving those institutions from the rationality of the individual: property,

The marginalist theory of society

exchange, money, the division of labour and the separation of the labourer from the means of production are all explained not as forms of historically specific social relations, but as technical instruments that facilitate the most perfect realisation of individual rationality. It is only on this basis that marginalist economics abstracts the economic institutions of capitalist society from their social and historical context, reducing them to the rationally developed instruments appropriate to the optimal allocation of scarce resources. It can only make economics a 'natural science' because it 'naturalises' the fundamental economic relationships of capitalist society.

The starting point of the marginalist analysis is the isolated utility-maximising individual, endowed with given tastes, skills and resources, and making rational decisions in conditions of scarcity. The analysis asks how this typical individual would behave, on the assumption that the individual will seek to satisfy a 'desire for the most complete satisfaction of needs possible' (Menger, 1963, p. 63). At this level the method of analysis is psychological, but it does not depend on any particular psychological theory, although it was originally formulated in terms of a utilitarian psychology. The starting point is the 'practical consciousness of economic relations' (Wieser, 1927, p. 4). However, the method is not that of an 'intuitionist' psychology, but of the deductive reconstruction of the behaviour of a rational individual. Thus the Austrians considered economics to be a branch not of psychology, but of *praxiology*, the science of rational action. The analysis implies no assumptions either about how individuals actually behave or about how individuals should behave. On the one hand, it is an abstract analysis considering the hypothetical consequences of rational economic action. On the other hand, the assumption that the individual seeks to maximise the satisfaction of needs implies no particular assumption about the content of those needs, which may as well be moral or aesthetic as material needs. The theory requires only that the individual should have a set of preferences and act consistently on those preferences.

The elaboration of marginalist economic theory is an attempt to show that its essential results can be extended from the case of the isolated individual making subjective private decisions about the management of her scarce resources to the case of an exchange economy considered as a whole. The method generally adopted was to consider firstly the simple case of barter of two goods between two individuals and then progressively to elaborate the model to include many individuals, many goods, money, the production of goods on the basis of fixed and then variable technical conditions, and of fixed and then variable factor supplies to show that the essential results continued to hold throughout this elaboration, on certain not unrealistic assumptions about technical conditions and the ordering of preferences.

This extension of the analysis from the abstract and isolated individual to the exchange society depends on establishing the neutrality of the institutions of exchange by showing that the market provides the means by which individual preferences can be realised, without imposing any external constraints on individual choice. In this sense it depends on establishing that the market is a rational instrument through which human beings can achieve economic self-realisation, rather than a social institution that structures particular social relations and subjects individuals to particular forms of constraint. This is achieved by establishing the formal rationality of the institutions of exchange.

Many of the marginalists simply assumed the rationality of capitalist economic institutions, for it was an assumption that was one of the self-evident liberal truths handed down from classical political economy in all its variants. However marginalism took up these truths when they had been thrown more fundamentally into question than at any time in the previous century. Socialists and reformers alike were no longer prepared to accept their self-evidence, let alone their sacred character. Thus marginalism had to go much further than earlier versions of liberalism in attempting a rigorous, and thoroughly secular, demonstration of these truths and, indeed, of their limits. It was the Austrians, and in particular Menger, who undertook this demonstration.

Menger was insistent on the need to relate social institutions, such as money, prices and exchange, back to their origins in individual action in order to establish their foundations in the natural and spontaneously evolved needs and aspirations of individuals. He was also quite explicit about his motives for doing this, for his invective was not directed at the conservative organicism of Burke and Savigny, which he believed to be legitimate within limits, but at the relativistic approach of Schmoller and his associates in the Historical School, an approach that, for Menger, could only lead to socialism. Thus his confrontation with what he considered to be the blind radicalism of Schmoller led Menger to formulate much more clearly than did

The marginalist theory of society

his contemporaries the necessary foundation of marginalism in the radical distinction between the rational foundations of the economy and the social and institutional framework within which the economy operated, and correspondingly to offer a rationalistic and individualistic derivation of those foundations. Methodologically, Menger presented the issue as one of pure theory against singular explanation, but the substantive issue underlying this was the fundamental one. The possibility of a pure economic theory depended on the possibility of a rationalistic conception of economic relations, and this rationalistic conception could in turn set limits to the reformist ambitions of radicals and socialists.

The institutions for which he had to account were the institutions of property, exchange, money and capital. The first precondition for exchange is private property. Menger rejected the classical theory of private property, which saw the origins of private property in labour, for very good reason, to offer instead a teleological explanation, which related the institution of private property to the rationality of the system of exchange which it underpinned. It is only the protection given by the institution of private property that can prevent the scarcity of goods in relation to human needs from giving rise to open conflict:

> Thus human economy and property have a joint economic origin since both have, as the ultimate reason for their existence, the fact that goods exist whose available quantities are smaller than the requirements of men. Property, therefore, like human economy, is not an arbitrary invention but rather the only practically possible solution of the problem that is, in the nature of things, imposed on us by the disparity between requirements for, and available quantities of, all economic goods (Menger, 1950, p. 97).

The security of private property ensures the peaceful resolution of the problem of scarcity, which is the economic problem confronting any society.

The economic problem facing the isolated individual is a relatively simple one, of employing her resources so as to attain the maximum possible degree of satisfaction, but this problem is not essentially altered when another individual is introduced with whom it is possible to exchange. Since each individual is free to exchange or not, the only significance of exchange is to increase the possibilities available, and so to make it possible to achieve a higher level of satisfaction. Thus the institution of exchange is simply a further development of the rational attempt to maximise utility, spontaneously evolved by the action of self-interested individuals. Thus Menger, after establishing that exchange is not an end in itself, concluded that 'the effort to satisfy their needs as completely as possible is therefore the cause of all the phenomena of economic life which we designate with the word "exchange"' (Menger, 1950, p. 180).

Within exchange the marginalist analysis establishes that exchange ratios express nothing but the private evaluations of goods, hence in a perfectly competitive equilibrium prices are determined without reference to any particular social or institutional context, representing merely a summation of individual evaluations. Money is no more a social institution in this sense, for money too arises spontaneously out of the individual attempt to maximise utility. The inconveniences of direct barter originally led some enterprising individual to attempt to achieve exchange through the mediation of a third good that was highly exchangeable. As others imitated the innovator that good came to take on the character of money. Thus money too had a rational origin as a technical instrument invented by individuals in order to perfect the process of utility-maximisation.

Consideration of production did not fundamentally alter this model of society. Production was considered to be simply a technical means of transforming higher into lower order goods. The extension of the division of labour and the selection of technically and economically efficient methods of production emerged spontaneously out of the rational economic activity of individuals and brought both individual and social advance. With increasingly advanced methods of production the division of labour affected the internal organisation of production, as well as the relation between different branches of production. The rational allocation of productive resources depends on the mobility of factors of production between alternative uses, and on their being the objects of independent evaluation, so that they can always be allocated to the most productive form of their employment. This depends on the existence of a free market for the factors of production, which depends in turn on the factors of production being independent from their owners, as exchangeable commodities. In particular, the rational development of exchange and the division of labour leads to, and depends on, the separation of ownership of labour from ownership of the means of production. It is a matter of indifference *who* owns the different factors of production, and it may be that the same individuals own both labour and means of production, although the growing scale of production makes this increasingly unlikely. What matters is only that labour and the means of production are traded as commodities, so that their alternative uses can be subjected to rational evaluation. Thus the separation of the labourer from the means of production was not the social foundation of capitalist exploitation, it was a necessary result of the development of economic rationality, and a condition of its further advance.

The completion of the development of economic rationality arrives with the emergence of credit, through which the ownership of the means of production is separated from their control. The efficient employment of the means of production requires scarce entrepreneurial skills, and so the ownership of the means of production will soon be concentrated in the hands of those who have such skills. However the concentration of ownership would be a barrier to the further development of economic rationality, if it were not in turn subjected to the discipline of the market, since past success is no guarantee of future achievement, particularly if capital is transferred to other hands by, for example, inheritance. The institution of credit provides the mechanism by means of which this barrier is overcome, separating the employment of the means of production from the ownership of capital, so that capital can flow freely to its most profitable outlets.

The system of money and exchange, of the division of labour, of private property, of wages, rent and profit, the exchange values of goods and of productive factors to which they gave rise, were all rational and, ultimately, natural phenomena in the sense that they expressed nothing but human wants and technical constraints that could not be modified by any social intervention. Thus, for Walras, exchange value 'once established, partakes of the character of a natural phenomenon, natural in its origins, natural in its manifestations and natural in essence' (Walras, 1954, p. 69). Wieser termed the values derived by pure theory 'natural values', for the value of a good depended only on its scarcity relative to human desires. In the same way the theoretical values of wages, rent and profit depended only on the scarcity and technical productivity of the factors of production to which they corresponded in relation to the desirability of the goods they produce. Thus for Jevons, profits and wages were determined by 'natural laws'.

However much marginalism defined itself in opposition to classical political economy, it represented much more a reformulation than a rejection of the latter doctrine. On the one hand, marginalism altered the basis on which capitalist society was evaluated. Where classical political economy sought to establish the rationality of capitalist society on the basis of a theory of distribution and growth, marginalism sought to do so on the basis of capitalism's allocative efficiency, viewing problems of growth simply as problems of allocation of resources over time. To this extent classical political economy became merely a special case within the marginalist framework. On the other hand, marginalism made it possible to dispense with the classical theory of class by introducing techniques that made it possible to analyse factor prices independently of the ownership of those factors. Thus marginalism was able to proclaim itself more scientific than classical political economy in attaining a higher degree of generality.

Marginalism followed classical political economy in attributing revenues to the owners of factors of production according to the 'trinity formula'. However, for classical political economy the revenues that accrued to the owners of the different factors of production were each determined according to different principles, and this introduced a necessary differentiation of class interest into the heart of the model, thus giving rise to a class-based model of society.

The marginalists found the asymmetry of treatment of the different factors of production one of the most unsatisfactory aspects of the classical theory. Formally, they argued that if economics was to make convincing claims to be a generalising science then it must be able to establish general principles that would govern the pricing of all goods, including the factors of production, without admitting of exceptions or introducing extra-economic factors. Thus, for example, the distribution of ownership of the factors of production was of no more relevance to the determination of their value than it was in the case of finished goods. It was only the inadequacy of the classical theory of value that led the classical political economists to espouse exceptional theories for the value of the factors of production. The great merit of the marginal utility theory of value was that it could be applied with complete generality.

The significance of the marginalist criticism of the classical theory of distribution was not simply methodological. Revenues, according to the marginalist theory, did not accrue to social classes, they accrued to factors of production, and they accrued to factors of production according to the same general principles. Each factor, whether it was labour, capital or land, received a reward corresponding to its individual contribution to production and so to final utility. In this

The marginalist theory of society

respect there was no more qualitative difference between capital and labour than there was between different varieties of labour. Neither labour nor capital received their rewards as labour or as capital, but only as individual factors each making its distinctive contribution. Hence there was no need for any concept of class mediating between the individual and her revenue. In particular the doctrine of the wages-fund, according to which wages were determined by sharing out a fixed sum amongst the entire working class, had to be rejected (although Böhm-Bawerk resurrected it in a revised form). On the one hand, there was no such fixed magnitude. On the other hand, labour was not homogeneous, so the wages of different categories of labour had to be determined independently of one another, according to their contribution to production. In the same way the idea of profits as a residual had to be rejected, for profits corresponded to the marginal productivity of capital and were equalised as capital was distributed among branches of production in order to equalise that marginal productivity. 'I conceive that the returns to capital and labour are independent of each other', wrote Jevons in criticising the classical concept of the falling rate of profit (Jevons, 1970, p. 246).

In eliminating the classical theory of class, marginalism finally completed the 'naturalisation' of capitalist society, that classical political economy had begun, by purging political economy of its residual historical content. The distributive shares of different members of society were no longer related to one another, but only to the contribution of each individual to production and of the product to final utility. Profit, rent and wages accrued to capital, land and labour whoever happened to own those factors of production, for they corresponded simply to the marginal productivity of the appropriate factor of production. The theory said nothing about the original distribution of goods, and so said nothing about the person to whom the revenue would ultimately accrue, for this was clearly a matter that concerned the particular social and institutional arrangements of a particular society. In separating the analysis of the pricing of productive factors from consideration of distribution, economics could separate the analysis of capitalist economic relations from consideration of the distribution of wealth and power historically associated with those economic relations. For classical political economy, and later for Marx, the two aspects of capitalist society were inseparably connected with one another. For marginalism the relation between the two was a purely contingent historical relationship. Wages, rent and profit were natural categories that simply expressed the scarcity of productive resources: 'The distribution of income and the apportioning of yields (to factors of production) are two entirely distinct problems' (Wieser, 1927, p. 113).

The radical separation of distribution from production and exchange removed the concept of class from the domain of economics, to set economics on an uncompromisingly individualistic foundation. However, the removal of its social content from the field of economics simultaneously defined a space in which sociology could emerge as a complementary discipline. We have seen in the last chapter that the classical sociology of the nineteenth century arose out of a critique of the economic liberalism of classical political economy, whose laws defined the proper economic, social and political relations between the classes. However, in rejecting the 'dogma of self-interest' on which the classical economic laws were based, in favour of higher moral or political values, sociology simultaneously cut itself off from the liberal foundations of political economy in individual reason, and so could not provide any rigorous liberal alternative to the political economists' analysis of class relations.

The separation of distribution from production and exchange redefined the boundaries between economics and sociology, making it possible for sociology to accept the marginalists' theory of production and exchange as an account of the 'economic' relationship between the individual and nature, without thereby having to accept a particular theory of class and distribution, and associated theories of the proper constitutional and moral order of society. Thus the marginalist revolution, in seeking to define the possibility and limits of social reform, simultaneously defined both the possibility and the limits of the complementary discipline of sociology, as the science which explored the comparative and historical variability of the moral and institutional framework of economic life.

Facts and values in economic science

Marginalism claimed to offer a natural science of the economic dimension of society, analysing economic phenomena in abstraction from particular social or institutional arrangements and so abstaining from making any judgements about the propriety of such arrangements. The laws that economics develops are natural, or 'positive', laws that neither imply nor impose any moral or political judgements.

This claim to value-neutrality on the part of marginalism would appear to be belied at once by the observation that the capitalist system as presented by marginalism was not simply a fact, but was also an ideal. The free market system was claimed to represent the perfect self-realisation of individual rationality in achieving the optimal allocation of resources on the basis of a given distribution of tastes, skills and resources. The apparent paradox is resolved when we realise that the society the marginalists described was ideal not because it corresponded to the evaluations of the theorist, but because it offered the most perfect expression of the preferences of the members of the society. The exchange economy was simply a rational instrument, a means through which individuals could seek to achieve their economic ends. It was the most perfect such instrument in the sense that anything that could be achieved outside the market economy could be achieved more economically within it, while it remained purely an instrument, so that it imposed no constraints on the ends that could be achieved through it.

The marginalist model was formulated at a very high level of abstraction. It did not describe capitalist society as it was, it described an idealised version of capitalism. On the one hand, it was based on the ideal concepts of the rational economic actor, perfect competition, etc. On the other hand, it was an abstraction from the historical reality of capitalist society, which idealised reality in abstracting from all those features that disfigured the reality of capitalism and that offended liberal sensibilities. It was therefore not a theory that could be applied directly to the reality of capitalism, although its vulgarisers did so apply it for their apologetic purposes.

The marginalists were well aware that their abstractions did not correspond directly with reality and they did not seek to defend them as such. Thus Menger stressed that the pure theory rested on certain assumptions, including assumptions about perfect knowledge, perfect foresight and an absence of constraint, that did not necessarily apply in reality. In the real world 'real prices deviate more or less from *economic* ones', while the laws of economics were those 'holding for an analytically or abstractly conceived economic world' (Menger, 1963, pp. 71–3). The pure theory offered an abstraction that represented an ideal world against which reality could be measured and against which proposed reforms could be evaluated. It is therefore no criticism of the marginalist analysis to note that reality does not correspond to its abstractions: insofar as the real world does not accord with the abstractions of marginalism it is not the economic theory that is in error, but the real world that is in need of reform.

The marginalist model provided a standard against which reality could be measured. As such it provided a model that could theorise the possibilities of reform. Menger, Pareto and J. B. Clark were conservatives, who stressed the virtues of capitalism and used marginalism primarily to berate and restrain over-enthusiastic reformers. Others, such as Walras, Jevons, Wicksell, Wicksteed, Wieser and Marshall, were reformists to some degree, recognising the extent to which the reality of capitalism departed from the marginalist model. For these thinkers marginalism provided a means not simply to defend capitalism, but also to evaluate objectively the possibilities of reform. Thus they recognised the harmful effect of monopoly in the real world and made proposals for the regulation or abolition of monopolies. They saw a need to improve the moral and material conditions of labour, proposing educational reforms to increase the productivity of labour and to give it a more civilised character. Some were even ready to contemplate the redistribution of wealth, especially through death duties and the taxation of landed wealth. However, the fundamental assumptions of the marginalist model set limits to even the most radical reforms which could be contemplated within its framework. Reform could only seek, by one means or another, to realise the ideal defined by the marginalist model. The rationality of the fundamental institutions and social relations of capitalist society could not be questioned, so that even the Fabians' 'Socialism', which drew on the new economics, could only conceive of socialism as a perfected capitalism. The marginalist model thus served to define clearly and precisely the limits of reform as well as its possibilities.

The marginalist model is well able to accommodate the fact that reality diverges from the model. However, such divergences are considered to be contingent social and historical phenomena and are not to be explained as inseparable aspects of the operation of the capitalist economic system. They are, therefore, not the concern of the economist. Nevertheless, in recognising the reality of the blemishes on the face of capitalism, marginalism recognises the need for complementary disciplines to study the source of these divergences. For some economists these complementary disciplines were considered to be empirical and historical disciplines that simply studied the specific institutional environments of different economies, particularly the specific patterns of distribution of property. In this respect the work of the German Historical School and the related schools of 'Sociology' had already shown their worth. However other economists were more perceptive and saw that the divergences between the marginalist model and capitalist reality could themselves have a systematic character, and so could be the subject matter of a rigorous sociology that did not simply attribute social evils to moral deficiencies, or to the demon drink, or to problems of adjustment, or to cultural survivals from an earlier evolutionary stage.

Modern sociology retained the idea, developed by its nineteenth century predecessors, that the defects of capitalism are specifically capitalist phenomena, arising out of the economic relations of capitalist society, but, unlike its predecessors, it rejected the idea that such defects were inherent in capitalist economic relations. This modern sociology expressed a liberal conception of reform, according to which the task of social reform was not to create a new kind of society, in which economic relations were subordinate to the moral and political order, but to perfect capitalism by ensuring that its reality corresponded to the marginalist ideal. The possibility of such a sociology was opened up by the self-conscious abstraction of marginalist economics, which abandoned the totalising ambition of classical political economy, to mark out a space for the complementary discipline of sociology, the central subject matter of which would be the foundations, exercise and abuse of *power* in society. Such a sociology would, like its predecessors, be *critical* of the economists' model of liberal capitalism, in the sense that it would draw attention to the limits of the applicability of that model as an account of actually existing societies. But at the same time, unlike its predecessors, it would recognise the validity of that model within those limits.

Economics established the 'formal rationality' of capitalism as a system of provision for human need, but it did so in abstraction from the 'substantive irrationality' which arose primarily from the abuse of inequalities of wealth and power. The central issue which confronted sociology was therefore that of the relationship between the 'formal rationality' of capitalism and its 'substantive irrationality'. On the one hand, if the substantive irrationality was a contingent feature of the institutional forms within which capitalism had developed historically, then institutional reform could remedy the defects of capitalism in order to realise its inherent rationality. In this sense sociology would be a subordinate discipline to economics. On the other hand, if the substantive irrationality of capitalism was inherent in the institutional forms of capitalist economic relations (such as money, competition, the division of labour, wage-labour, the capitalist enterprise), then capitalism could not be reformed, and the distinction between the 'formal rationality' and the 'substantive irrationality' of capitalism, based on the radical separation of form and content, became untenable, which in turn threw into question the status of the distinction between 'economics' and 'sociology' as autonomous disciplines.

At first sight this separation of the formal rationality of capitalism from its substantive irrationality appears perfectly legitimate. The two aspects may have been inextricably linked in the past, but they can be distinguished analytically from one another, the rational model of the 'social economy' describing not so much the imperfect past of capitalism as its realisable future. However, what is at issue is not the possibility of constructing an abstract model of a rational society, but the explanatory value of such an analytical construct. If the historical development and present operation of capitalist society has been inseparable from its 'substantively irrational' consequences, is it really plausible to argue that such consequences are contingent? Can the market, as a formally rational allocative mechanism, be legitimately detached from the social relations of class inequality and class exploitation with which it has always been associated? Or is inequality and exploitation inherent in the generalised rule of the market? Can the formal analysis of exchange be detached from consideration of the substantive content of exchange? Before turning to the rise of modern sociology we clearly need to explore rather more closely the relationship between the rational and the irrational in marginalist economics.

7

The Irrationality of Marginalist Economics

The foundation of the marginalist abstraction of the 'economy' from 'society', of the ideal rationality of capitalism from its contingent social forms, is its demonstration of the 'formal rationality' of the fundamental institutions of capitalist production, distribution and exchange. The rationality of these institutions is formal in the sense that they have a purely instrumental significance in relation to human action, providing only a technical means through which individuals can most efficiently achieve their ends, and so impose no substantive constraints on the ends pursued. It is only on this basis that social values can ultimately be reduced to the subjective evaluations of individuals. On the other hand, if the fundamental institutions of the capitalist economy could be shown to have a *necessary* substantive significance in subjecting individuals to social constraint, the marginalist abstraction of form from content, formal from substantive rationality, economy from society, would be deprived of any coherent foundation, and its ideal model would cease to have any explanatory validity.

For marginalism the constraints imposed on the individual by competition are not imposed by particular social relations, but express only the relative scarcity of goods in relation to human wants. The resources with which the individual is initially endowed define the material limits to which the individual can satisfy those wants. Production and exchange provide the means by which the individual can expand subjective utility within those material limits by transforming less into more desirable goods. The institutions of capitalism then provide the means by which the necessary conflicts of interest between individuals in the face of natural scarcity can be optimally reconciled on the basis of subjective assessments of individual utility. In particular, the freedom of the market ensures that every individual has the maximum opportunity to increase the subjective utility of the goods in her possession, while ensuring that no such increase is achieved at the expense of any other individual.

I have already looked in some detail at Marx's critique of the rationalistic naturalism of classical political economy in his youthful critique of alienated labour, which he developed more systematically in his analysis of the fetishism of commodities and the 'trinity formula'. Marx showed that the individual is only constituted as a *private* individual, and property as *private* property, on the basis of a mode of social production in which the co-ordination of social labour is achieved through the alienated form of the exchange of the products of labour as values. The apparent form of exchange as the exchange of things between private individual property owners is accordingly only the fetishised form of appearance of social relations between people. The exchange relation is therefore inexplicable in abstraction from the particular social relations it articulates: the form of exchange cannot be detached from its social content, a content which political economy only conceals by attributing social powers to things. Similarly, the technologistic conception of production is only the fetishised form of appearance of capitalist social relations of production, in which the production of things is subordinated to the production, appropriation and accumulation of surplus value, as the alienated form of surplus labour.

To the extent that marginalist economics took over the liberal foundations of classical political economy, in its concepts of the abstract individual, private property, the division of labour, exchange, money, capital and wage-labour, Marx's critique applies to marginalist economics with as much force as it applied to classical political economy and does not need repeating here. From this perspective marginalism retreats from the Ricardian attempt to connect labour to its social forms, which defined the scientific ambition of classical political economy, to provide no more than a systematic formalisation of the fetishised forms of appearance of capitalist social relations of production.

On the other hand, in abandoning the project of providing a comprehensive theory of society marginalism restricted its ambition. It is not in itself a criticism of marginalist economics to argue that it abstracts the analysis of exchange from the historically specific social relations which are articulated in the exchange relation, because this is precisely what the marginalists present as their scientific achievement. They did not deny the specific socio-historical character of capitalist

The Irrationality of Marginalist Economics

social relations, but assigned their study to the subordinate disciplines of social economics and sociology. In order to show the relevance of Marx's critique of political economy to the critique of marginalist economics we have to show that this abstraction is illegitimate by establishing the incoherence of marginalist economics in its own terms. The central argument of this chapter is that the *formal rationality* of the fetishised forms of appearance of capitalist social relations cannot be abstracted from the *substantive irrationality* which derives from the irrationality of the social relations of capitalist production which they articulate. I will develop different aspects of this argument in the following sections.

I will start off by showing that the marginalist analysis of systematic exchange depends on its abstraction from the 'ignorance' and 'uncertainty' which is not merely a subjective deformation of an objective rationality, but which *necessarily* characterises a system of commodity production. As soon as we recognise ignorance and uncertainty we find that exchange can no longer be reduced to a formal mechanism which relates subjective evaluation to natural scarcity, but is a social institution which has substantive, and irrational, results.

These results are not purely accidental, but are determined by the character of the social relations of production whose reproduction is mediated through the exchange of commodities, and which determine that the 'substantively irrational' results of exchange are systematic. In particular, the market regulation of the social division of labour in a hypothetical society of petty producers tends to lead not to the advance in the wealth of the nation, but to the cumulative growth of inequality, and subsequent economic and social breakdown. This explains why it is individually and socially rational to regulate the social division of labour within such a society directly, and why subordination to the market has historically had to be imposed on petty producers by force.

The forcible imposition of the rule of the market does have a certain rationality, but this is not the 'formal rationality' of a system of provision for human need, but the substantive class rationality of a system of exploitation which is based on relations of economic dependence, culminating in the forcible separation of the direct producers from their means of production and subsistence.

Marginalism treats the separation of the direct producers from their means of production as a rational development of the division of labour as the 'factors of production' come within the sphere of the formal rationality of exchange. The rationality of the competitive determination of wages, rents and profits rests on the assimilation of wages, rent and profits to the general theory of price, as the revenues which accrue to the owners of particular commodities. However this assimilation faces insuperable difficulties, above all in the case of profit. The failure to explain profit as the 'price' of capital has fundamental implications, for it means that it is impossible to assimilate the theory of distribution to the theory of exchange, and so to reduce the rationality of capitalist class relations to the 'formal rationality' of exchange.

Finally, I turn to the dynamic relation between production, consumption and exchange in a capitalist society, from which marginalism abstracts in considering only a static equilibrium. In abstraction from the dynamics of the market the starting point of analysis is arbitrary: there is no more and no less reason to follow Marx in regarding the social relations of production as primary, or to follow political economy in seeing the social form of distribution as primary, or to follow marginalism in seeing individual consumption as primary. However, once we turn to the dynamic relationship between these different moments of the system of social production as a whole we find that the starting point is no longer arbitrary, but is determined by the social form of production. Moreover, we find that the market cannot be reduced to a rational means of regulation of social production, whether in accordance with the development of the forces of production, the accumulation of surplus value, or the needs of consumers, but is a contradictory means of regulation, expressing the contradictions inherent in the social form of production.

The irrationality of exchange and the problem of money

The marginalist theory of capitalist society starts with the elementary exchange between two isolated individuals, possessing different sets of goods, and then seeks to show that the results achieved in the analysis of this elementary exchange relation continue to hold for increasingly complex systems of production, distribution and exchange. However, as soon as we have regard to the social form of exchange, we find that such a generalisation is illegitimate. The limits to the rationality of exchange becomes apparent as soon as we move beyond the immediate exchange of use-values to a *system* of exchange, in which the rationality of the individual exchange is conditional on the

The irrationality of exchange and the problem of money 211

rationality of the system as a whole.

The rationality of the elementary exchange relation is intuitively obvious. Each party to the exchange has full knowledge of the opportunities available to her, which comprise the goods in her possession and those offered by the other party to the exchange. Each party can then offer to trade, on the basis of their subjective evaluations of the relative utilities of the goods in play, and can choose to exchange to the extent, and only to the extent, that such exchanges increase utility. Thus the rationality of exchange is constrained only by the physical resources in the possession of the individual, and the subjective judgements of the parties to exchange, so that prices express nothing but individual assessments of the relative utility of things. The generalisation of this result from the elementary exchange to a system of exchange, composed of a multiplicity of elementary exchanges, would seem to be a formality. The generalisation of the commodity form, as more and more things become the objects of exchange, merely expands the opportunities for increasing utility through exchange, without imposing any additional constraints on the individual, so long as that individual is always free to choose not to exchange.

This generalisation is illegitimate, for as I have argued in Chapter Four, it conceals a change in the *form* of the exchange relation which is of fundamental significance. In the immediate exchange relation things were exchanged as objects of direct utility. However, a system of exchange does not consist in a multiplicity of such immediate and symmetrical exchanges, but comprises *mediated* exchange relations, in which each exchange is *asymmetrical*, no longer involving the direct exchange of use-values for one another, but the exchange of use-values for values. As a use-value a commodity is a mere thing, but as a value the commodity is necessarily a socially determined thing, so that exchange can only be analysed as a socially determined relation, the rationality of each individual exchange depending on the rationality of the system of which it is necessarily a part.

The implications for the marginalist analysis of exchange become clear as soon as we turn to the explanation of money. For the marginalists money is simply a means of avoiding the inconvenience of barter, which has no substantive implications. However, barter cannot be reduced to the elementary form of immediate exchange, for in barter the individual acquires things through exchange with a view to their subsequent exchange for other things. The 'inconvenience' of barter does not lie in the mediated character of the exchange relation, which requires the individual to enter two exchange relations instead of only one, for this is as much the case when money serves as the mediating term in the exchange as it is when any other commodity plays that role. The 'inconvenience' of barter lies in the fact that the first exchange is conditional on the outcome of the second, the results of which cannot be known with certainty. I may wish to exchange corn for meat, but the butcher may want not corn but cloth. The butcher may be willing to accept my corn in exchange for her meat, with a view to subsequently exchanging the corn for cloth with somebody else. In this event neither of us wants the corn in itself, but only as the means of exchange for something else: corn serves in this exchange not as a use-value, but as a value. However, in exchanging meat for corn the butcher runs the risk of not being able to make the subsequent exchange on the anticipated terms, and this is where the 'inconvenience' of barter lies.

The use of durable, infinitely divisible commodities, with a high value in relation to their volume, as means of exchange certainly removes some of the physical inconvenience attached to less suitable commodities, but it does not solve the fundamental problem of barter, that exchanges are made conditional on an uncertain outcome. If corn is not in general demand the butcher will be unwilling to accept corn in exchange for meat, but the introduction of money does not solve this problem, for if corn is not in general demand I will no more be able to exchange my corn for money than I was able to exchange it for meat. On the other hand, if I am able to sell my corn for money, the rationality of this exchange is not determined by the conditions of this exchange alone, but also by my uncertain expectation of the future price of meat. It is the uncertainty of the outcome of particular exchanges that disqualifies particular commodities from serving as the means of exchange, and gives rise to money as the universal equivalent. However money does not remove the uncertainty attached to particular exchanges, it merely expresses that uncertainty in a universal form. Money does not *resolve* the inconvenience of barter, it *generalises* it. Far from expressing the rationality of exchange, money expresses the irrationality of a system of social production in which provision for human need is achieved only through the alienated form of commodity exchange.

The explanation of money presents problems of a different order from those raised by recognition of inequalities of wealth and power, because the existence of money cannot be explained without abandoning the most fundamental assumptions of the marginalist model. In the elementary act of exchange the agents of exchange knew with certainty the range of opportunities available to them, expressed in the reciprocal offers of each party to the exchange. If the exchange-ratios of all commodities, in the present and the future, are generally known, the results achieved in the analysis of the elementary act of exchange can be generalised to a system of indirect exchange. However, in the absence of uncertainty as to future exchange-ratios, every commodity can serve indifferently as means of exchange, and there is no need for one commodity to serve as a universal equivalent. On the other hand, if we recognise the existence of ignorance and uncertainty we can explain the emergence of money, but it is no longer legitimate to generalise the results achieved in the analysis of the elementary act of exchange.

The irrationality of exchange and the problem of competition

The marginalist results can only be generalised to a system of indirect exchange if all the parties to exchange have certain knowledge of both the direct and indirect present and future opportunities that confront them. This knowledge is presented to them in the form of a set of market prices. However, to the extent that this set of prices does not define a market-clearing general equilibrium, these prices will change as soon as exchanges take place, leading to unanticipated, and possibly undesirable, outcomes. Thus the rationality of the outcome of individual exchanges presupposes that the system of exchange will always and instantaneously achieve a market-clearing general equilibrium.

This is an illegitimate abstraction from the ignorance and uncertainty which characterises judgements in the real world, not only because its relaxation undermines the marginalist results, and not only because it makes it impossible explain the emergence of money, but also because it makes it impossible to explain the social form of exchange as *competition*. Marginalism itself recognises that ignorance and uncertainty is of the essence of the system of competitive exchange, for this is the basis of its defence of the market against its socialist critics: it is only competition which can regulate social production on the basis of individual needs because it is only through the social processes of competition that individual subjective judgements are expressed in an objective form. However, the proof of the rationality of the outcome of the competitive process presupposes that every individual can anticipate that outcome, in which case competition would be unnecessary.

The more acute economists recognised the unreality of their fundamental assumptions, and sought various devices to get around it. Thus Walras recognised the conditionality of the rationality of each individual exchange on the rationality of the system as a whole in his device of *tâtonnement*, according to which an auctioneer takes conditional bids until he reaches a market-clearing set of prices (which must include prices for all anticipated future transactions), at which point all bargains are struck. Such a device would be perfectly sound as a methodological abstraction, if the results obtained could be sustained at lower levels of abstraction. However the introduction of ignorance and uncertainty immediately makes the model indeterminate, so that the results can only be sustained at lower levels of abstraction by making arbitrary and gratuitous assumptions. Walras's device is not only unrealistic, it is also ideologically extremely subversive: while it makes it abundantly clear how far removed is the marginalist model from the reality of capitalist society, it provides a basis on which to develop a quite different application of the model, in which the auctioneer is replaced by the central planning agency of a socialist society. This was the main reason why the second generation Austrians, Hayek and von Mises, were so strongly opposed to Walrasian general equilibrium theory.

The neo-Austrians reinterpreted the market as a dynamic information system, in which individuals convey information about their preferences through the prices they pay. For the neo-Austrian model it is no longer necessary to assume that every individual has perfect knowledge and perfect foresight, because knowledge is no longer an attribute of the individual, but is conveyed by market prices. The freedom of the market is not defended on the grounds of a necessary tendency to equilibrium, but on the grounds of its efficiency as an information system: the freer and more pervasive are market transactions, the greater the quality and quantity of information which the market can convey.

Market disequilibrium creates the opportunity for profit by exploiting price differentials between markets. Entrepreneurs make their

The irrationality of exchange and the problem of competition 215

profits by acquiring and acting on the knowledge of such market opportunities, and in so doing act as arbitrageurs, moving the system as a whole towards equilibrium. Failure in the market may be the result of circumstances which could not possibly have been anticipated, but the market has the advantage of rapidly identifying and correcting such unavoidable errors. However, failure in the market is more often the result of a failure to acquire and act on the requisite knowledge of market opportunities, for which the individual alone must bear the blame and suffer the cost. This differential success and failure leads to economic inequality, but such inequality by no means supports the socialist belief in the deficiencies of the market. First, only the market can provide the information about consumer preferences on which a desirable allocation of resources depends. Second, however unequal might be the outcome, the perfect market offers the most perfect equality of opportunity. Third, the rewards of success and the penalties of failure provide the incentives to enterprise on which the dynamic efficiency of the market depends.

The neo-Austrian model is vastly superior to the Walrasian model, in regarding the operation of the market as a dynamic process, and in taking seriously the problem of disequilibrium. However, in attempting to make the model more realistic, the neo-Austrians have to abandon the rigour of the Walrasian system, with the result that they have no rational way of establishing their fundamental proposition of the beneficence of the market, which rests on nothing more than faith. In recognising that the market can never achieve equilibrium, the neo-Austrians abandon the possibility of demonstrating the rationality of a market solution since, even if the market process is an *expression* of the interaction of individual preferences, there is no way of showing that the market outcome is in any sense a *realisation* of those preferences. In particular, because the neo-Austrians have no way of conceptualising the formal properties of their model, they have no way of establishing the supposedly stabilising character of entrepreneurial activity, and so the socially beneficial character of entrepreneurial freedom. In short, the neo-Austrians offer a more realistic model of exchange, but the conclusions they draw from it have no rational foundation. This is why in practice the neo-Austrian defence of the market rests primarily on their critique of the bureaucratic irrationality of the state, and above all of state socialism, and on the associated claim that the freedom of the market is the necessary and sufficient condition for political freedom and democratic participation.

Alfred Marshall sought a realistic, but no more satisfactory, solution by considering the system of exchange as the sum of a large number of separate markets, and by distinguishing the short-run from the long-run. His assumption of *ceteris paribus* let him explore the interaction of supply and demand in each market separately, first in the short-run and then in the long-run, the latter seen as the outcome of a series of short-run equilibria. This approach required less restrictive assumptions, and made it possible to consider the 'micro-economic' implications of market 'imperfections' arising from the existence of monopoly powers, ignorance and uncertainty, but Marshall had no way of systematically exploring the interaction of the various markets, merely assuming that the system as a whole was no more than the sum of its parts.

The significance of the interaction between markets for the demonstration of the rationality of exchange was considerably underestimated, until the work of Keynes, because the validity of Say's 'law of markets' was almost universally assumed. Within the framework of Say's law the imperfect operation of the market might lead to a sub-optimal allocation of resources, which implied that some incomes were lower than they might otherwise have been, while others might be higher, which may be undesirable, but is hardly a disastrous result. The significance of Keynes's *General Theory* was that it showed that, as soon as the necessary ignorance of economic actors is recognised, the outcome of market processes depends on expectations, which are necessarily non-rational, and which can easily prove de-stabilising not only in particular markets, but in the system as a whole. Thus Keynes showed that the outcome of the necessarily imperfect operation of the market was, in general, not simply the misallocation of resources, but the instability of the system of social production, leading to cyclical fluctuations, mass unemployment and possibly even persistent depression.

Keynes restricted his attention to labour and financial markets, within the Marshallian framework, without realising that his critique had more general application: the sources of instability could not be confined to the level of the 'macro-economic' adjustment of financial markets, but had a 'micro-economic' origin, in the interaction of markets and of economic actors, and so were pervasive and systemic. This led Keynes considerably to over-estimate the ability of the state to stabilise the market by 'macro-economic' intervention, not realising that the state was an economic actor like any other. As the neo-

Austrians forcefully argued, despite the greater range of its powers, and the greater resources at its disposal, the knowledge and foresight of the state was necessarily as limited as that of other actors, and so its interventions as likely to prove destabilising as to stabilise the system as a whole.

Keynes's results threatened to bring the whole marginalist apparatus tumbling down. The only way in which economics could handle those results was to neutralise them, reducing them to the effect of Keynes's particular assumptions about the formation of expectations in the face of ignorance and uncertainty, which could be eliminated simply by changing those assumptions. However the significance of Keynes's arguments was more than merely showing the possibility of general unemployment, a phenomenon very familiar to all but economists. Much more fundamentally, Keynes recognised that once the ignorance and uncertainty necessarily facing economic actors was admitted, there could be no presumption that the 'rational' decisions of economic actors would have rational results. Keynes did not fully appreciate the significance of this insight, because he had no understanding of the systematic character of the irrationality of the capitalist system of exchange.

For Keynes, irrational outcomes were merely the 'unanticipated consequences' of rational action which, because they were unforeseeable, did not compromise the rationality of the judgements of which they were the result. However, if the irrationality of those outcomes is systematic, then the irrational consequences of 'rational' individual judgements cease to be unforeseeable, and the rationality of those judgements is thrown into question. Keynes could not see the systematic irrationality of capitalist exchange because he had no conception of the *social form* of exchange as the contradictory form of reproduction of capitalist social relations of production.

The marginalist failure to conceptualise the irrationality of exchange derives from its attempt to conceive of the outcome of exchange in abstraction from the social processes of competition which regulate exchange relations. The starting point of Marx's critique of political economy was precisely his and Engels's critique of the classical abstraction from the economic instability and social conflict which were the inseparable complements of the tendency to equilibrium. Engels, in his *Outlines of a Critique of Political Economy*, argued that the economists' law of competition depends on the consistent *failure* of the market to achieve equilibrium:

demand and supply always strive to complement each other, and therefore never do so ... The economist comes along with his lovely theory of demand and supply, proves to you that "one can never produce too much", and practice replies with trade crises, which reappear as regularly as the comets ... Of course these commercial upheavals confirm the law, confirm it exhaustively — but in a manner different from that which the economist would have us believe to be the case. What are we to think of a law which can only assert itself through periodic upheavals? It is certainly a natural law based on the unconsciousness of the participants. If the producers knew how much the consumers required ... then the fluctuations of competition and its tendency to crisis would be impossible (CW, 3, pp. 433–4).

Marx took up the same argument in his *Comments on James Mill*, noting that

Mill commits the mistake — like the school of Ricardo in general — of stating the *abstract law* without the change or continual supersession of this law through which alone it comes into being ... The true law of political economy is *chance*, from whose movement we, the scientific men, isolate certain factors arbitrarily in the form of laws (CW, 3, p. 211).

With just as much right one could regard the fluctuations as the law and the determination by the cost of production as chance ... it is solely these fluctuations, which, looked at more closely, bring with them the most fearful devastations and, like earthquakes, cause bourgeois society to tremble to its foundations — it is solely in the course of these fluctuations that prices are determined by the cost of production. The total movement of this disorder is its order ('Wage Labour and Capital', *SW*, pp. 77–8).

When we look at the reality of competition we find that we are far away from the perfect rationality of the marginalist world of general equilibrium. In their early works Marx and Engels tended to regard the instability of the market as the accidental result of its 'anarchic' processes. However, in his later work Marx came to see that the crisis-tendencies inherent in capitalist exchange had systematic foundations in the contradictory form of capitalist production, so that the 'formal rationality' of capitalist exchange is inseparable from the 'substantive irrationality' of capitalist production.

The irrationality of exchange and the division of labour

As a purely formal relationship, exchange is a relation of freedom and equality, a symmetrical relationship between individuals defined only by their difference from one another. However the real foundation of exchange, that gives the relationship its content, is the differentiation of the parties to exchange on the basis of their differentiated roles within a system of social production. Thus the content of the exchange relation cannot be reduced to its form, its content is to be found outside itself in the systematic social differentiation that is expressed through the exchange relation. Moreover the exchange relation is not simply the *expression* of the social form of production, but is the relation that *mediates* the material and social reproduction of the system of production. The rationality of exchange cannot, therefore, be detached from consideration of the rationality of the social form of production which it articulates. For marginalism the social form of production is reduced to the technical division of labour, of which capitalism is only a rational development.

The starting point of the marginalist analysis is the isolated individual confronting an external natural world in a relation of *scarcity*, which is a natural relation imposed by the need to labour in order to meet the individual's needs. The arrival of another individual immediately transforms the relation of scarcity into a social relation by providing a new object of need, and a new means of meeting that need by exchanging products as commodities. Even this elementary and accidental social relation presupposes a social differentiation, for if the parties to exchange were identical there would be no desire to exchange.

If exchange is to be regular and systematic, it can only be on the basis of regular and systematic social differences, and in particular, an extended division of labour within which the productive activity of the members of society is oriented to, and co-ordinated through, the system of exchange.

The division of labour imposes constraints as well as offering opportunities. The resources with which the individual sets out are not indifferent things. The particular characteristics of those things define the possible mode of participation of the individual in society: the skills and tools of the carpenter define the role of the individual in society as that of a carpenter. Similarly the needs of the individual are no longer private needs, a matter of individual preference. To reproduce her material and social existence as a carpenter the individual has to acquire not only her means of subsistence, but also the requisite tools and raw materials. Thus both the needs and the resources of the individual are socially constrained.

With the development of a division of labour regulated through the market the individual can only secure her own physical and social reproduction through the sale and purchase of commodities. Subjection to the rule of the market may provide opportunities for material gain, but it also carries the risk of physical and social extinction if the individual is not able to secure her social reproduction through market exchange. The rationality of the individual act of exchange therefore presupposes the rationality of the system of exchange as the mediating term in the material and social reproduction of the system of social production.

The irrationality of the social regulation of petty commodity production by competitive exchange appears as the emergence of social inequalities compromises the reproduction of the system. The origins of such inequalities may be contingent: wealthier households may owe their favoured position to their skill and frugality, to a favourable demographic balance between productive and unproductive household members, to favourable market conditions, or to good fortune. But once such inequalities emerge they tend to become cumulative: the better off are better able to weather crises, to improve the methods and expand the scale of their production, while the less fortunate may have to consume or sell their raw materials and means of production. Thus the unrestricted development of the 'propensity to truck, barter and exchange' in such a society would lead not to growing prosperity, but ultimately to the economic and social breakdown of the society.

For marginalist economics the polarisation of wealth, and the consequent breakdown of social production, is attribute to chance misfortune or misjudgement as the 'unanticipated consequence' of individual action. Thus the 'formal rationality' of the original act is not compromised by the 'substantive irrationality' of the outcome. However, the fact that this specific outcome may have been *unanticipated* by no means implies that such an outcome was *unforeseen*. The knowledge that the future is uncertain is sufficient to alert the individual to the risk of committing her very existence to the vagaries of the market, and to establish the rationality of the self-conscious organisation of social production, through which the advantages of the division of labour can be secured without running any of its risks.

It is because of the social irrationality of exchange, rather than because of any irrational commitment to custom and tradition, that societies based on petty production normally seek to regulate social production directly, and strongly resist the commodification of production, or confine it within very strict limits. Far from being a spontaneous development of individual rationality, the 'freedom' of the market is profoundly irrational for its victims, which is why it has had to be imposed on society by force, from within or without, however much such force might be concealed behind legal forms as the enforcement of contract or foreclosure on loans and mortgages.

The cumulative growth of inequality in the wake of the commodification of petty production may give rise to the emergence of new social forms, in which inequality becomes the systematic foundation of social production, based on the separation of the direct producers from their means of production and subsistence. This separation is no more the outcome of the rational evaluation of new opportunities, nor the 'unintended consequence' of rational action, than is the commodification of the means of production and subsistence. The forcible separation of the direct producers from the means of production has only been the historical outcome of an intense, diffuse, violent and long-drawn-out class struggle.

The dispossession of the direct producers does not simply introduce one more commodity, labour-power, to the market. More fundamentally, it transforms the social form of production, and in so doing it transforms the dynamics of the market. Before turning to the dynamic role of the market in the reproduction of capitalist social relations, however, we need to examine more closely the marginalist demonstration of the rationality of capitalist production.

The irrationality of capitalism: the marginalist theory of profit

For marginalism the development of capitalist social relations of production is only a rational development of the technical division of labour. The separation of the labourer from the means of production makes it possible to achieve the technological advantages of large scale mechanised production, while the commodity form of labour-power provides the labourer with the opportunity to seek the most favourable outlet for her talents, and enables the entrepreneur to direct labour to the most productive uses. The process of production itself was seen merely as a technical process through which material inputs were transformed into material outputs, the subordination of the labourer to capital being imposed not by the social form of production, but by the technical requirements of co-ordination and control.

This analysis implies that wages, rent and profits are prices like any others, in this case the 'prices' of the co-operating 'factors' of production, based only on subjective judgements of utility in the face of a naturally imposed relation of scarcity. The difference between wages and profit is qualitatively no greater and no less than, for example, that between the wages of different categories of labour, or between the prices of cabbages and peas. Profit could as well be seen as the 'wages' of capital, or wages as the 'profit' on the labourer's 'investment' in the production and reproduction of her labour-power.

We have already considered Marx's critique of the 'irrationality' of the 'trinity formula' on which this theory is based. This irrationality becomes apparent as soon as we ask what are wages, rent and profits the price of? What is the commodity that is bought and sold to realise this price? In the case of wages and rent marginalism can provide some coherent answer to this question, for wages and rent appear as the price paid by capitalists for the 'productive services' of land and labour. But what commodity is bought and sold to realise profit? This is a problem to which marginalism and its successors have devoted a considerable proportion of their intellectual energies. The versions of the theory of profit proposed are many and varied, and here we can only outline the issues at stake.

The basic approach is to identify the source of profit in the 'marginal productivity' of capital, and to determine its magnitude in association with the subjective 'time-preference' of individual economic actors. Although it can be shown to be the case, under appropriate assumptions and within the marginalist framework, that the equilibrium rate of profit will equal the 'marginal productivity of capital' and the 'marginal rate of substitution' of present for future goods, the issue is the explanatory value of such an equation.

Wieser sought to establish the foundations of profit in the physical productivity of capital in the 'simple economy', in abstraction from all social institutions. To define capital in the simple economy it is necessary to 'eliminate from the current, practical concept every reference to the pecuniary form of capital and to private property. Every suggestion of capitalistic power and exploitation of workers

The irrationality of capitalism: the marginalist theory of profit 223

must be banished.' Thus capital must be defined in physical terms as *natural economic capital*, that is, as produced means of production acting within the process of economic reproduction. Profit is then explained by the contribution made to production by natural economic capital. Thus 'the productivity of economic capital is primarily physical' and 'the rate of interest is nothing more or less than an expression of the marginal productivity of capital ... It indicates the utility cost which might be obtained by other uses of cost-capital' (Wieser, 1927, pp. 62, 133, 138).

The argument has a certain intuitive plausibility, for we are accustomed to thinking of the means of production as 'productive'. However, intuition here rests on ideological familiarity and not on reason, for the idea of the physical productivity of the means of production, independent and distinct from that of labour or land, is not something that has any meaning. Jevons was well aware of this, and of its implications:

> we must regard labour, land, knowledge and capital as conjoint conditions of the whole produce, not as causes of a certain portion of the produce. Thus in an elementary state of society, when each labourer owns all three or four requisites of production, there would really be no such thing as wages, rent or interest at all. Distribution does not arise even in idea, and the produce is simply the aggregate effect of the aggregate conditions. It is only when separate owners of the elements of production join their properties, and traffic with each other, that distribution begins, and then it is entirely subject to the principles of value and the laws of supply and demand. Each labourer must be regarded, like each landowner and each capitalist, as bringing into the common stock one part of the component elements, bargaining for the best share of the product which the conditions of the market allow him to claim successfully (Jevons, 1970, Preface to Second Edition, pp. 68–9).

Thus it is impossible to define profit independently of the existence of exchange and of capitalist social relations.

Although profit only exists within capitalist social relations, it may be possible to abstract from those social relations in the determination of profit if profit can be given a naturalistic, if not a universal, foundation. Although wages, profit and rent only arise in a capitalist society, it may be possible to show that they nevertheless only express individual evaluations of utility, so that their rationality can be established independently of the social form of production. Jevons believed that he could achieve this on a different foundation from that of the physical productivity of the means of production. His theory was developed by Böhm-Bawerk.

Böhm-Bawerk argued that profit cannot be attributed to the means of production, for the means of production are simply commodities that are used in production and there is no reason why their use should in itself yield a surplus. Moreover, the means of production form only one component part of capital: the sum of money which attracts a profit comprises the money laid out to purchase all the requisite conditions of production: land, labour-power, raw materials, stocks, machinery, etc., and profit depends not only on the magnitude of the capital, but also on its turnover time. For Böhm-Bawerk, capital is used to buy labour and commodities that have been produced by previous applications of labour. According to the marginalist model, labour has already been paid for its contribution to production, while commodities have likewise been bought at their value. Hence there is no reason to believe that the mere consumption of these commodities will yield a surplus, while the consumption of other commodities does not. Moreover capital is not a physical magnitude, but a sum of value and its magnitude is determined, among other things, by the rate of profit. The magnitude of capital cannot therefore be specified independently of the formation of the rate of profit. The overall conclusion is that theories based on the marginal productivity of the means of production cannot give profit a naturalistic foundation.

Böhm-Bawerk tried to get around this problem by arguing that capital was not an independent factor of production, but could be reduced to the past contributions of the original factors of production, land and labour. Profit arose not on the basis of the supposed physical productivity of the means of production, but on the basis of the time taken for a process of production to be completed. The essential form of capital was not the means of production, but the fund of means of subsistence that was required to sustain the labour force for the duration of the process of production. It was this wages-fund that was advanced as capital. The time for which a given capital would have to be advanced would depend on the 'roundaboutness' of the method of production.

Roundabout methods of production are adopted because they are more productive. For example, productivity may be increased by spending time initially on making more sophisticated means of production instead of producing immediately with direct labour. The existence of a subsistence fund, as the natural form of capital, makes it possible to engage in more roundabout, and so more productive, methods of production. The owner of the subsistence fund makes it available to the workers in return for a profit which corresponds to the productivity of more roundabout methods of production. The workers, on the other hand, offer the owner of the subsistence fund a profit because their produce is increased by more roundabout methods of production.

The Jevons-Böhm-Bawerk approach to the productivity of capital is certainly superior to that of Wieser, but it does not avoid the fundamental problem of all such approaches. The problem is that the definition of the 'period of production' necessarily involves the cumulation of labour-inputs over time, and this cumulation has to be carried out on the basis of given wages and a given rate of profit. Production periods can therefore only be specified for given wage rates and a given rate of profit, and so the relative productivity of different methods of production depends not only on the physical relation between inputs and outputs, but also on the distribution between wages and profits. Thus this theory falls on the same grounds as did the theory that attributed profit to the physical productivity of the means of production. Accordingly the 'efficiency' of capitalist production cannot be reduced to the efficient allocation of physical resources in relation to individual judgements of utility, and the separation of allocation and distribution, of the 'formal' and 'substantive' rationality of capitalism, cannot be sustained.

It is certainly the case that some methods of production are more productive than others, and, under certain conditions, it may be possible to specify the relative productivities of different methods of production. However, in general it is necessary to reduce outputs and inputs to a common standard to measure productivity, and this standard can only be a value-standard. This means that the 'productivity' of different methods of production cannot be specified in physical terms but only in terms of value. This is, of course, appropriate since the aim of capitalist production is the maximisation of profit, not physical productivity. Thus the concept of the physical productivity of the means of production or of more roundabout methods of production is a concept that has no meaning. It is impossible to specify the productivity of different methods of production in abstraction from capitalist social relations, nor to determine the rate of profit in abstraction from the specific form of distribution. Moreover, it is only under capitalist social relations that this 'productivity' is attributed to capital so as to correspond to a rate of return on capital. There is thus no basis either for the justification or the determination of profit in abstraction from the social relations of capitalist production, nor are there any grounds for identifying the maximisation of profit with the maximisation of utility. Profit is merely a portion of the social product appropriated by capital on the basis of its monopolisation of ownership of the means of production and subsistence.

The theory of capital is only one side of the theory of profit. It supposedly explains the source of profit, but cannot alone explain its magnitude. Why does not investment proceed until the rate of profit falls to zero? To explain the magnitude of profit we have to refer also to the supply of capital. The marginalist answer is that saving is the source of capital and that saving is based on a choice between present and future consumption. If people value present goods more highly than the same goods in the future, they will demand a positive rate of return as the incentive to save. The supply of capital is therefore limited by this 'time-preference', which provides the subjective motive for saving to which interest corresponds as a reward.

Most explanations of this time-preference are based on gratuitous and often implausible psychological explanations. In general there is no reason to expect psychological time-preference to be positive rather than negative; indeed in conditions of uncertainty such *deferred gratification* is a much less plausible, and far less rational, psychological phenomenon than the overvaluation of present satisfactions. If individuals expect to be better-off in the future, present goods will have a higher marginal utility than future goods, so that far from deferring consumption individuals will be prepared to borrow at interest to finance present consumption. In general, the relationship between savings ratios and interest rates is notoriously indeterminate and unstable.

The theory of time-preference is as unrealistic as a theory of the supply of capital as it is inadequate as a justification for profit. Net working class savings may be diverted, through financial institutions, to augment the supply of capital, but the characteristic source of new capital is not workers' savings, but realised profits. The theory of time-preference is quite inappropriate to the consideration of the motivation of the capitalist: the allocation of resources between present and future consumption presupposes a relation of scarcity that is not characteristic

The irrationality of capitalism: the marginalist theory of profit 227

of the relation of the capitalist to the means of consumption. The capitalist's motivation for reinvesting profit is not the provision of future means of consumption, it is the continued production of profit for its own sake, an orientation which is profoundly irrational, but which is imposed on the capitalist by competition, as the condition of his reproduction as a capitalist, for it is only by constantly transforming the methods of production, introducing new technology and new work practices, that the capitalist is able to keep his capital intact. Thus the motivation of capitalists is not an aspect of their irrational subjective orientation, it is imposed on them by the reproduction of the capitalist system.

Keynes rejected the marginalist theory of profit, according to which the rate of interest was determined by the relation between savings and investment, in favour of a theory which related savings and investment through the level of incomes. If savings depend on incomes, a high level of investment will lead to rising incomes which will lead in turn to a high level of net savings to finance the investments. Similarly a low level of investment will lead to stagnating incomes, and correspondingly stagnating savings. Thus the levels of saving and investment are theoretically indeterminate. Even more importantly, if savings are determined primarily by income levels, and not by the rate of interest, the rate of profit and the rate of investment will be determined not by individual preferences, but by the extent of the inequality of income distribution. A high rate of savings and investment will then not express a general preference for future over present goods, but simply a very unequal distribution. This conclusion, developed by Kalecki, has devastating implications for the marginalist attempt to separate consideration of the allocative efficiency of capitalism from 'political' judgements of the equity of the underlying distribution, for it means that the most fundamental allocative judgement, that concerning the allocation of resources between consumption and investment, is primarily determined by the distributive judgement.

Keynes was well aware that his rejection of the marginalist theory of interest undermined the marginalist justification for profit, so that he returned to the classical justification of capitalism in terms of its dynamic efficiency, although with less confidence than did his classical predecessors. This justification was based on the presumption that the growth in the wealth of the nation depends on a high rate of productive investment, and that the primary source of productive investment was profit, so that any redistribution of profit, in favour of wages, rent or unproductive expenditure, would diminish investment to the detriment of the growth of the wealth of the nation. This justification cannot be sustained within the individualistic framework of marginalist economics because the close interconnection between productive investment and technological advance means that those whose actions determine the dynamic efficiency of capitalism are not necessarily those who benefit from it. This was precisely the dilemma that Adam Smith captured acutely: for Smith the growth of the wealth of the nation depended on the capitalists' maintaining a high level of productive investment. However the beneficiaries of this growth were the workers, the landowners and the state, while the capitalists faced the prospect of a falling rate of profit, and so sought to restrict investment. For Keynes too the declining 'marginal efficiency of capital' and the 'liquidity trap' threatened to lead to falling investment, stagnation, and even chronic depression.

For both Smith and Keynes the justification of profit lay in its role as the source of productive investment, and it was only justified to the extent that it was in fact employed productively. The implication, tentatively drawn out by Keynes, is that expenditure out of profits cannot not be left to the whim of the capitalist, who should be subjected to moral and fiscal pressure to employ his capital productively, and the regulation of the rate of investment could not be left to the market, but had to be undertaken by the state on behalf of society as a whole.

The theory of profit is undoubtedly the weakest internal link in the marginalist attempt to demonstrate the rationality of capitalism, because it proves impossible to reduce the social relations of capitalist production to any natural or technological foundation. This not only means that capitalist social relations cannot be attributed any independent rationality, but it also means that, within those social relations, the rate of profit has no substantive significance, corresponding neither to any 'productive contribution' of capital, nor to any subjective assessment of utility, but only to the appropriation of a portion of the social product without equivalent.

The contradictory social form of capitalist production

In the previous two sections I have criticised the marginalist attempt to establish the rationality of capitalist exchange and of capitalist production. We now have to put production and exchange together, to

The contradictory social form of capitalist production 229

locate the source of the fundamental irrationality of exchange, which is to be found in the contradictory social form of capitalist reproduction.

The forcible separation of the direct producer from the means of production defines the historical origins of the capitalist mode of production. However this separation is not sufficient to secure the reproduction of the social relations of capitalist production. This reproduction is problematic because in the course of its reproduction the capitalist mode of production suspends its own foundations. The capitalist begins with a sum of capital in the form of money, with which he buys labour-power and the requisite means of production. The worker begins with nothing but her labour-power, which she sells to the capitalist. Once this exchange has been completed, the worker is no longer propertyless, but has the means to buy the requisite means of subsistence. The capitalist, meanwhile, has transformed his capital into a mass of commodities and labour-power which are, in themselves, worthless. The social reproduction of the capitalist mode of production now depends on the particular use made of the commodities in the hands of the worker and the capitalist: the worker must use the money in her possession to reconstitute herself, physically and socially, as a wage labourer. The capitalist must use the means of production and labour-power in his possession to reconstitute himself as a capitalist.

The reproduction of labour-power (or the 'productive services' of labour) depends on the worker spending the money received in wages on the commodities required to secure her physical reproduction as a labourer. According to the economists wages are determined by the supply of and demand for labour-power. The demand is determined by the productivity of labour as a factor of production, the supply by the subjective preference of the worker for income as opposed to leisure. However the limits within which wages are determined are not set by the interaction of personal preference and technical constraint. The income needs of the worker are not matters of taste; they are socially constrained. The worker has a need for a certain level of income to sustain a socially conditioned level of subsistence. Moreover, the worker has not merely to reproduce herself physically, but has to ensure that she has the qualities required to fulfil her particular role in production, defined socially by the conditions of labour. The worker's needs for income and leisure are not defined exogenously, as in the marginalist model, they are constrained by the need socially imposed on the worker, and mediated through the labour market, to reproduce herself as a particular kind of worker.

The physical reproduction of the worker is not a sufficient condition for the social reproduction of the worker as a wage-labourer. If wages rise significantly above the socially determined subsistence level there will be no compulsion on the worker to return to work for the next period. The form of the wage-relation therefore not only determines the needs of the worker as a consumer, it also determines that the relation between those needs and the worker's resources will be a relation of scarcity — not the natural scarcity depicted by the economists, but the socially constructed scarcity imposed by the dynamics of capitalism. It is this relation of scarcity that forces the vast majority of workers to assume a 'rational' orientation to work and to consumption, working to maximise their incomes, and carefully allocating their scarce resources to ensure that they can meet their subsistence needs, rather than assuming the 'hedonistic' orientation of the bourgeoisie, for whom work can be a means of self-realisation and consumption a source of pleasure. The capitalist system of production, far from representing the most rational means of resolving the problem of scarcity, depends on the reproduction of scarcity, whether by the restriction of wages or the inflation of needs.

The demand for labour-power is no more determined by technical considerations than is the supply determined by subjective preference. Labour-power will be purchased by the capitalist so long as tne marginal productivity of labour exceeds the wage. However the marginal productivity of labour is not a technical but a value-magnitude, measuring the extent to which the capitalist can compel the labourers, individually and collectively, to work beyond the labour-time necessary to produce the value equivalent of the wage. Thus the determination of the demand for labour-power by the marginal productivity of labour simply expresses the fact that labour-power will only be employed to the extent that the worker is willing to subject herself to the domination of capital, to alienate her creative powers and employ them not to realise her own talents, nor to enrich herself, but to produce under the capitalist imperative to maximise the intensity and duration of labour in order to enrich the capitalist.

Capitalist exploitation and domination is not the contingent result of the abuse of capitalist power, it is the alienated social form to which the worker is forced to submit as the necessary condition under which she can secure her own physical and social reproduction. The labour-market, far from being the means by which individuals freely make

The contradictory social form of capitalist production 231

choices between income and leisure subject to the technical constraints of labour productivity transmitted through the market, is the means by which the subordination of the worker to capital is reproduced. Thus the reproduction of labour-power is ultimately subordinate to the reproduction of capital.

The subordination of labour to capital is not a matter of the subjective will of the capitalist, nor of the capitalist's abuse of his economic power. The capitalist has no choice but to seek constantly to intensify labour, to extend the working day, and to transform methods of production in order to realise to the full the possibilities of reducing the necessary labour-time. Under capitalism this compulsion is imposed neither by technology, nor by the will of the capitalist, but by competition.[1]

Capitalist competition is not the rational instrument through which social production is subordinated to human needs, depicted by the marginalists. Competition is the form in which capital presents itself as a barrier to its own reproduction. The pressure of competition is the result of a constant tendency to the *overproduction* of commodities, which threatens the less successful producers with liquidation. However this tendency to overproduction is not merely an accidental dislocation of the market, but is the expression of the inherent tendency for capitalism to develop the forces of production *without regard to the limits of the market*. This tendency is profoundly irrational, but this irrationality is again not the result of any subjective irrationality on the part of capitalists, but of the objective irrationality of capitalism, determined primarily by the *uneven development of the forces of production* as capitalists struggle for a competitive advantage by developing new methods of production.

In the first instance the development of new methods of production is the means by which an individual capitalist can realise a surplus profit, by producing at lower cost than his competitors. This opportunity defines the subjective incentive to develop the forces of production, and to exploit the opportunity to the full by expanding production without regard to the limits of the market. But when

---

[1] The fate of socialism in the twentieth-century should remind us of Engels's warning that state ownership of the means of production is not a sufficient basis for overcoming the alienation of labour. Such alienation persists so long as the human activity of workers as producers is subordinated to a need imposed on the workers to reduce their labour-time to a minimum, instead of being subordinated to the human needs and abilities of the workers themselves.

the innovating capitalist throws the greater mass of commodities onto the market the immediate result is an intensification of competitive pressure.

In the face of competitive pressure the less advanced capitalist can only respond by intensifying labour and extending the working day, unless or until he can amass sufficient capital to introduce the more advanced methods of production in his turn. However, the more advanced capitalist has an equally strong incentive to intensify labour and extend the working day, to capitalise on his immediate advantages. Moreover, as the new methods of production are generalised, and as backward producers increase their output to meet the competitive challenge, the pressure of competition increases, so that even the most advanced producers may be compelled to lengthen the working day and to intensify labour in the face of the growing overproduction of commodities. The degradation and exploitation of labour is not the result of the abuse of power by cynical capitalists, it is inherent in the objective dynamics of the capitalist mode of production. It is capitalist 'rationality' which determines that the development of the forces of production, far from being the means of harnessing the creative powers of labour, compels capitalists to crush such creative powers, far from being the means of realising human skills, compels capitalists to destroy such skills, far from reducing the burden of labour, compels capitalists progressively to intensify labour. It is hardly surprising that the contradictory tendencies of capitalist development necessarily give rise to a class struggle in which the workers, individually and collectively, resist the imposition of the 'irrational rationality' of capitalist production (Clarke, 1988, 1990).

The pace of development of the productive forces in a particular branch of production is not determined by the desire to satisfy human wants or by the emergence of new human needs, but by such factors as the pace of technological advance, the gestation period of new investment, and the size and age of the existing stock of fixed capital, which serve to encourage and sustain the overaccumulation of capital. However, even if productive capacity is expanded without regard to the limits of the market, the expanded product has to be sold if the enlarged capital is to be realised and the reproduction of capital achieved. This determines the tendency of capitalism to develop the market on a global scale. Thus the expansion of the market and the creation of new needs is not the cause of the dynamism of the capitalist mode of production, but the consequence of capital's

The contradictory social form of capitalist production

attempts to overcome the barriers to its reproduction presented by the tendency to the overaccumulation and uneven development of capital. However the growth of the market, far from liquidating the tendency to the overaccumulation of capital and the overproduction of commodities, only serves to give that tendency a renewed stimulus by sustaining the opportunity for surplus profit.

Sooner or later the overaccumulation of capital is bound to appear in the form of a growing overproduction of commodities, leading to falling prices, and backward capitalists will eventually no longer be able to sustain their losses. However, production will not be brought back within the limits of the market through the smooth transfer of capital and labour to new branches of production, for the capital employed is tied up in stocks and means of production which have been devalued by the fall in prices, while the workers may not have the skills required for alternative occupations, and may be geographically remote from new employment opportunities. Thus production is only brought back within the limits of the market by the devaluation of capital, the destruction of productive capacity, and the redundancy of labour. This adjustment may take place piecemeal and gradually, or it may occur more dramatically, in the face of a generalised crisis.

The tendency for capitalist accumulation to take the form of overaccumulation and crisis is characteristic of all branches of production at all times, but it is developed unevenly, so that its characteristic form of appearance is the uneven development of the various branches of production, which gives rise to growing disproportionalities between the various branches of production, which can only be rectified by the mechanism of restructuring through crisis. The accumulation of capital can be sustained in the face of such disproportionalities by the expansion of credit, which stimulates the growth of the market, accommodates disproportionalities, smooths the liquidation of less profitable capitals, and absorbs bankruptcies, but at the same time risks stimulating the further overaccumulation of capital, accompanied by inflation and speculation, carrying the risk of a general crisis of overaccumulation. Such a general crisis is not confined to a few capitalists in a few branches of production, but reverberates through the system as a whole, as bankruptcies precipitate a chain of defaults and as cuts in production lead to a contraction of the market in a cumulative spiral of decline. The general crisis is not a pathological eruption in the normally placid course of capitalist development, the result of the subjective ignorance or misjudgements of capitalists or politicians, but is only the most dramatic expression of the permanently crisis-ridden character of accumulation.

Enough has been said to make it clear that as soon as we have regard to the social form of capitalist production we find that it is only on the basis of the laws of capitalist production that we can understand the laws of capitalist exchange. The tendency for capitalists to expand the forces of production without regard to the limits of the market is not a result of their subjective irrationality, but of the objective irrationality of a system of production geared not to production for social need, but to production for profit, and in which the primary source of surplus profit is not the exploitation of market opportunities, but the development of new methods of production, the cultivation of new needs, the intensification of labour, and the extension of the working day.

The 'substantive irrationality' of capitalism is not the contingent result of ignorance, uncertainty and the abuse of power, but is the necessary outcome of the contradictions inherent in the social form of capitalist production, the substantive content that subverts the 'formal rationality' of exchange.

8

From Marginalism to Modern Sociology

Economic theory, social economics and the tasks of sociology

The 'marginalist revolution' emerged in response to the problem of conceptualising both the possibilities and limits of social reform, so overcoming the apparently unbridgeable gap between the dogmatic liberalism of political economy and the opportunistic reformism of sociology and historicism. Many of the marginalists came to economics specifically in order to give a rigorous foundation to sociology and to historicism. Menger and Walras saw their work as bringing rigour to the tradition of 'vulgar economy' associated with the German Historical School. Jevons formulated his economics within a Spencerian framework, while Wieser was also inspired to turn to economics by reading Spencer. Walras formulated his economics within a reformist framework that owed much to Comte and St Simon, while Wicksteed came to marginalism from Comte and Henry George. Alfred Marshall had studied moral sciences and saw economics as a continuation of those studies. Thus marginalism developed not in opposition to the sociological and historicist traditions, but as an essential complement to them, providing the rigorous foundation that they had hitherto lacked.

The complementarity of marginalism, on the one hand, and sociology and history, on the other, was not immediately apparent, not least because some of the pioneers of the marginalist revolution used the new theory to assert the virtues of a regime of *laissez-faire* against the claims of social reform. Thus Jevons was engaged in constant polemic with sociologists and social reformers, while Menger was involved in an acrimonious methodological debate with Schmoller, the *Methodenstreit*. While the debate between economics, on the one hand, and sociology and history, on the other, remained a debate between economic liberalism and social reform, the two schools of thought found themselves implacably opposed to one another, each asserting its own exclusive claims.

By the 1890s it was clear that social and political reform in Britain, Austria and Germany had succeeded in establishing a constitutional and political framework within which the working class could be persuaded, at least for the moment, to pursue its political aims peacefully and constitutionally. The reformers were triumphantly vindicated. However, once the success of reform was generally accepted the terrain of debate shifted. The most pressing issue was not that of whether or not to introduce social reform, legalise trade unionism and admit sections of the working class to the suffrage. The issue was now how far should such reform go?

While liberals had to concede exceptions to the *laissez-faire* principle, particularly in the determination of the terms and conditions of labour, social reformers had to concede that the discipline of the market must continue to have a major role to play if the advance of the working class was not to compromise the continued existence of capitalism. It was at this point that it became essential to work out a more rigorous relationship between economics and sociology, and to establish a stable intellectual division of labour between the complementary disciplines. The development of modern sociology involved both recognising and setting limits to the claims of the economists as the basis on which to reinterpret established sociological traditions.

The first important stage in this process was the development of 'social economics', which introduced the concept of 'economic power'. The theoretical importance of this was that it reintroduced the concept of class that had been expelled from the pure theory of the capitalist economy by the marginalist revolution. However the concept of class employed here is quite different from the concept developed by classical political economy and by Marx. In the latter theories the social relations of capitalist society were necessarily class-relations, the concept of social class defining the objective basis on which the individual participates in society by defining the point of insertion of the individual into the social relations of production, distribution and exchange.

The marginalist revolution abolished the classical theory of distribution, and so expelled the concept of class from economics in favour of a purely individualistic theory of economic relations. The concept of class now appears at a lower level of abstraction, becoming a purely sociological concept in the sense that it now characterises particular social groups that arise out of the free association of individuals on the basis of their perception of a common economic interest. It is now economic interest that underlies the formation of classes, not the existence of classes that underlies the conflict of interest. Common economic interest can in principle be found in any situation in which the fate of a number of individuals depends on the terms of the purchase or sale of a given commodity, so there is no reason to limit the application of the concept to capitalists and workers as a whole.

From this standpoint, physicians and officials, e.g., would also constitute two classes, for they belong to two distinct social groups, the members of each of these groups receiving their revenue from one and the same source. The same would also be true of the infinite fragmentation of interest and rank into which the division of social labour splits labourers as well as capitalists and landlords — the latter, e.g., into owners of vineyards, farm-owners, owners of forests, mine-owners and owners of fisheries (*Capital*, III, p. 863).

Within the framework of marginalism classes arise not on the basis of the relations of production, as in Marxism, nor on the basis of the relations of distribution, as in classical political economy, but on the basis of exchange relations. A class arises out of the appreciation of a common interest in the purchase or sale of a particular commodity, as a means of seeking to improve the terms on which that commodity is traded to the advantage of that class. A class conflict is the socially organised manifestation of the conflict of interest that is inherent in any exchange as each party seeks to achieve exchange on the most favourable terms.

The ideological and political implications of this displacement of the concept of class should be clear. The immediate implication is that class conflict is no longer fundamental to capitalist economic relations, but rather is a superficial disturbance that arises as special interests seek to subvert the competitive process to their own ends. For the economic liberal the formation of classes, and the consequent class conflict, is entirely illegitimate, and the state is required to legislate to prevent the formation of agreements in restraint of trade by means of which classes seek to pursue their ends. For the reformist the imbalance of resources between labour and capital requires some correction, which may justify the association of workers in properly regulated trade unions in order to achieve a countervailing power.

The Fabians went further still in believing that it was impossible to prevent the abuse of economic power so long as capital remained in private hands. This did not lead the Fabians to reject marginalist economics. For the Fabians Wicksteed's marginalism showed the possibility of a rational economic system and countered the Marxist theory of class exploitation. Thus the Fabians proposed that the state should peacefully assume the functions of capital in order to achieve in reality the marginalist ideal. The Fabian's state capitalism did not involve any fundamental transformation of social and political relations, but simply a transfer of given functions from capitalists to managers and administrators.

In France and Germany considerable importance was attached to the preservation of the middle-class and particularly of small rural producers, in the face of capitalist competition, by the provision of credit, the formation of rural co-operatives, the reform of tenancy laws and by protective legislation. In all these cases, however, the theoretical framework is the same. Social classes and class conflict only arise to the extent that the operation of the market is imperfect. They are not expressions of the fundamental character of capitalist economic relations, but merely imperfections hindering its smooth operation.

The theory of the social economy

The study of the social framework of capitalist economic activity first emerged as the complementary discipline of *social economics*. In many cases social economics was essentially an empirical discipline, investigating the distribution of income, conditions of employment and unemployment, provision for the poor and the sick, etc.. However, attempts were also made to develop a more systematic approach to the social framework of capitalism, developing social economics as a theoretical, and not simply as an empirical, discipline, on the basis of the marginalist analysis of the economy. In Britain, the Fabians played a pioneering role in this respect, and Pigou led the development of social economics as a rigorous branch of the discipline. Elsewhere one of the most important contributions was that of Wieser, most notably in his *Social Economics* [1914], which is significant both for

The theory of the social economy

the clarity of its exposition and for the influence it had on Max Weber.

Wieser originally took up the study of economics inspired by a reading of Herbert Spencer, and was attracted by Menger's attempt to get beyond the conception of society as an organism by tracing the origins of organic institutions in individual behaviour. Although a follower of Menger, he recognised more clearly than did Menger the need for reform and for an adequate understanding of the social context of the capitalist economy. This was the theme of his books *Law and Power* [1910] and *The Law of Power* [1926], but was developed most systematically in *Social Economics*, which brought clearly into view the connection between Wieser's economics and his programme for sociology. *Social Economics* was published in 1914 as part of the *Grundriss der Socialökonomik* edited by Max Weber, a series of which Weber's *Economy and Society* and an early version of Schumpeter's *History of Economic Analysis* appeared as subsequent volumes. Weber is reported to have made it a condition of his participation in the project that Wieser should write the economic theory section of the series, but the volume that resulted is more than an exercise in pure economic theory (Translator's Introduction to Wieser, 1927, p. xi).

In the Preface to the Second (1924) Edition Wieser made explicit the concerns that motivated him in writing the book. The problem that he confronted was that the capitalist economy was based on the pursuit of personal interests, but this made it possible for individuals to use their power to override the general interest. The 'highest task of theory' was thus to show 'in what relations this consciousness and power were in harmony and in opposition to the creation of the social, state and world economy' and so to what extent it was necessary to curb such power. Theory would thus define the tasks of 'enlightened statesmanship . . . in particular it will point the way to needed reforms' and would serve the state in showing 'those most general elements of management and value which have always existed and will always exist'. The context of this need for reform was the rise of the proletariat. 'Almost everywhere in Europe the proletariat has come forward with such strength that it must be considered and a counter-reform of the economic order proposed' (Wieser, 1927, p. xvii). This is something that classical economics could not accommodate because it was formulated at such a high level of abstraction that it neglected questions of power, conflict and economic evil.

The classical theory does not go to the root of the economic interconnections sufficiently to explain the meaning of a developed national economy. It does not enable us to refute the socialistic criticism of the prevailing order; it has, on the contrary, supplied the most important arguments of that criticism. The classical theory of freedom, above all, results in a vindication of capitalistic domination (Wieser, 1927, p. 411).

Wieser starts with the *theory of the simple economy* which abstracts from all social institutions, providing a general explanation that is 'not dependent on the form of exchange'. Essentially it is the model of an ideal organic society directed by a single individual who adopts a 'rationalistically utilitarian point of view' (Wieser, 1927, p. 11). This abstraction made it possible to theorise a society in which individual and social rationality were identical, in which the good of one was the good of all. The elements of this economy were individuals with given needs and preferences, producing scarce goods with scarce land, labour and means of production. The result attained was the familiar marginalist equalisation of relative marginal utilities.

In the *theory of the social economy* exchange and private property were introduced. The results derived from the theory of the simple economy still held for the exchange economy, which was simply a sum of simple economies, so long as we abstract from the abuse of power. 'Whenever we disregard the stress of economic power we shall find that the utility value of the simple economy is precisely the same economic value which functions in the transactions of economic exchange'. However, such an abstraction is no longer legitimate: 'An economic theory that should suffice for our times is inconceivable without a social theory that is consistent with the fact of power' (Wieser, 1927, pp. 144, 154).

Social power is the basis on which social classes are formed. However, social superiority is not based entirely on property, but on any factor that bestows a favourable market position on its holder. Thus such factors as education also play a role, and it is important to take account of horizontal divisions based on the division of labour. Thus power in our society is multidimensional, based on the possession of a favourable market situation. In the social economy we are no longer dealing with the abstract individual of utilitarianism. In economic conduct, argued Wieser, the individual was determined by social forces: 'needs, impulses and egoism itself are dominated by social powers'. Hence economic rationality was embodied in the norms of society. In accepting the norms of society the 'socially educated individual' transformed her egoism into 'social egoism' (Wieser, 1927, p. 160). Thus the implications of the existence of social stratification and of differences of power were moderated as normative restraints limited the abuse of power and position.

The normative regulation of egoism means that, if we abstract from crises and panics and assume a voluntary subordination to law and morality, the exchange economy still has the result that 'production values ... are unified and concentrated, and their apportionment to the individual branches of production take place as by a social plan. The spirit of a social economy is complied with, although there is not a unitary social management'. Thus 'where the general conditions are considered socially satisfactory and morally and legally correct the general price is found also to be the just, or equitable, price' (Wieser, 1927, pp. 206, 184).

Wieser was not so naive as to believe that these ideal conditions pertain in our society, for he argued that the polarisation of wealth and power is too great for normative restraint to be effective. Overcompetition of the poor in labour markets forces down wages, while overcompetition of the rich in product markets leads to overproduction, so to have a well-ordered market controls on competition are required. Moreover victory in competition goes not to the most efficient but to the largest capitals, which are best able to survive 'revolutions of trade'. The effect is the increasing polarisation of society as the industrial middle classes are displaced into the proletariat and the proletariat is deskilled. The rich are satiated, the poor overworked and underpaid, morally and culturally debased. Under the 'capitalistic relations of employment' workers lack the will to work. Thus the 'contrasts of capitalistic affluence and proletarian misery become too glaring' and if this polarisation becomes extreme 'it would then be obvious ... that social economy had wholly lost its significance' (Wieser, 1927, pp. 210, 383, 381, 405).

This description of the tendencies of developed capitalism is hardly that of an apologist for the existing order. Indeed the symptoms that Wieser identified are precisely those contradictions that Marx saw as inherent in the capitalist system: extremes of wealth and poverty, class polarisation, overwork and unemployment, satiation and cultural debilitation, centralisation of capital and overproduction. However Wieser was insistent that these deficiencies are not inherent in capitalism, nor do they counterbalance the positive features of the capitalist system. The capitalist economy alone is able to allocate resources efficiently so that production is maximised. Thus 'it may well be that a system of rules, which distributes very unequally the enormous gains to which it is instrumental, is after all more beneficial to the mass of the citizens than another, doling out its much smaller proceeds according to "principles of right and reason"' (Wieser, 1927, p. 398). The task was not to abolish capitalism, but to perfect it by eliminating the abuse of power.

Two different directions of reform opened up from this analysis. One was to seek to curb the abuse of power by removing the restrictions to competition that arose from monopolisation, state intervention and ignorance. It was in this direction that most of the second-generation Austrians, including von Mises and Hayek, developed the marginalist analysis. Wieser, however, was more realistic, realising that capitalism's defects were the results of competition in an unequal society, not the results of curbing competition. He therefore favoured reformist solutions that extended the legal and administrative regulation of economic relations through the encouragement of trade unionism, protective legislation, factory legislation, compulsory insurance, housing policy, control of speculation, land reform and state and municipal enterprises. There was no reason to believe that these measures could not resolve the problem of power within the exchange economy, for there was no evidence that exploitation is inherent in exchange. The urgent need was to 'lay down for modern policy full theoretical foundations' that would make it possible to delimit the 'boundaries and instruments permitted to State policy' (Wieser, 1927, p. 410).

Wieser recognised the defects of actually existing capitalism, which he saw as the result of the inevitable emergence of inequalities of wealth and power, and the associated breakdown of normative regulation, to which capitalism gave rise. But at the same time he insisted that such defects were not inherent in capitalism, but only in the abuse of inequalities of wealth and power, which could be checked by a rationally informed state policy. Thus the 'substantive irrationality' of capitalism could be separated from its 'formal rationality', a proper programme of reform checking the former in order to realise the latter.

Social economics went beyond the abstractions of the pure theory of the exchange economy by introducing the concept of economic power. However this concept alone, important as it is, was hardly a sufficient foundation on which to build a sociology. Social economics continued to be a branch of economics, rather than of sociology, in resting on the assumption that social action can be explained as an expression of the rational self-interest of the individual, and in reducing social power to economic power.

This left two gaps to be filled by a renewed sociology. On the one hand, an 'economic sociology' was required that could explain the normative regulation of rational economic action by exploring the formation of Wieser's 'social egoism', Comte's 'social love' or Smith's 'moral sentiments'. Such an economic sociology would also have to explore the character and determinants of economic power and the formation of social classes. On the other hand, social economics provided no means of understanding the consequences of social action not oriented solely to economic ends, or of social power that rested on other than purely economic foundations.

In particular, social economics had no means of dealing with the state and political power. The state was called on to implement a programme of social reform and to regulate the class struggle as though it were a neutral benevolent institution standing above society. However the state was itself an object of class struggle, and of intense political debate as to its proper role. Socialists on the one side threatened either to destroy the state or to use it to abolish capitalism. On the other side, monopoly capital threatened to subordinate the state to its own ends, backing its resistance to the demands of the working class, furthering its advance at the expense of smaller capitalists and petty producers, pursuing its imperialist aims in the colonies, and threatening to drag the nation into inter-imperialist wars. Social economics helped to clear the space for modern sociology, but that space had still to be filled.

Max Weber and the German Historical School

It was Max Weber, more than anyone else, who defined the relationship between marginalist economics, on the one hand, and historical and sociological investigation, on the other. It is in this sense that we can see Weber as the true founder of modern sociology in that it was he who defined their respective fields for both economics and sociology, establishing the limits of economics and defining the space to be filled by sociology. Max Weber was born in 1864 and was trained in law and economics within the tradition of the German Historical School.

He was a member of the *Verein für Sozialpolitik* from 1888 until his death in 1920.[1]

The older generation of the *Verein*, led by Schmoller and Adolph Wagner, favoured the Bismarckian approach to social reform, believing that class conflict was a pathological phenomenon that could be suppressed by the state, while the condition of the working class could be ameliorated within a paternalistic and bureaucratic framework of social reform and political regulation of the economy. Such an approach proved to have severe limitations. While bureaucratic regulation stifled economic initiative and so restricted the expansion of the German economy, the Social Democratic Party, although illegal, was advancing from strength to strength. Junker domination of the Prussian State meant that the expansion of capitalist agriculture, and the consequent proletarianisation of the rural population, was advancing with little restraint, with potentially disastrous political consequences. While the older generation of the *Verein* placed their faith in the neutrality and rationality of the Prussian bureaucracy, the younger generation, of which Weber was a part, along with Sombart, Tönnies and Brentano, saw the bureaucracy as self-interested and as morally and politically stultifying, and so looked for more liberal solutions.

The younger generation believed that the rise of social democracy could not be attributed to exceptional causes, but had to be explained on the basis of the existence of a fundamental opposition of class interests within capitalist society and of the tendency for classes to organise in order to further their interests. Marxism had an obvious theoretical appeal to some of the younger generation, although they rejected Marxist political conclusions on the basis of neo-Kantian arguments about the separation of fact and value: Marx was right to draw attention to class conflict as a central feature of capitalist society, but his theory could not dictate how that conflict ought to be resolved.

The younger generation rejected socialist solutions, which they saw as suffering from the same defects of bureaucratism as did conservatism, and sought instead to establish the political conditions

---

[1] Most interpretations of Weber see his work as deriving from the philosophical traditions of German Idealism, and specifically the neo-Kantian revival. While this tradition is crucial in defining the terms of his argument, I think its impact on its substance, and on its wider significance, has been considerably over-emphasised, while that of marginalism has been largely neglected. The discussion in this chapter aims to redress the balance, not to give a complete account of Weber's work.

under which the class struggle could be regulated and subordinated to national ethical and political goals. They favoured the liberalisation of state policy, freeing capital from the more restrictive burdens imposed on it, while looking to properly regulated trade unionism and, to some extent, constitutional reform, as the means of assimilating the working class. Thus the recognition of the existence of class struggle did not compromise their adherence to a fundamentally liberal theory of capitalist society or to liberal solutions to the social problems to which capitalism gave rise.

In their concern for social reform as the alternative to revolution the younger generation of the *Verein* found much in common with the revisionist wing of social democracy, which sought to divorce the reformist activity of social democracy from its revolutionary political rhetoric, a position that looked to Fabianism and to marginalist economics for theoretical support. For the younger generation of the *Verein* trade unionism and co-operation had lost their menacing appearance and could offer a basis on which the working class could acquire the most *petit-bourgeois* of moral qualities and through which the working class could be incorporated into a national ethical and political framework. The younger generation therefore sought to reconcile the existence of economic conflict between the classes with the ethical and political consensus on which a liberal state had to rest. It was clear that neither the free market nor a corporatist or socialist bureaucracy could provide a satisfactory framework within which conflicts of economic interest could be resolved. Thus the younger generation of the *Verein* was preoccupied with the complementary issues of the nature and limits of the free market, on the one hand, and the nature and limits of the liberal state, on the other, their solutions ultimately resting on profoundly moralistic foundations. This generation saw in Max Weber their most outstanding spokesman.

Weber's early work was very much within the mainstream of the Historical School. His first published works were two theses on medieval trading companies and on the agrarian history of Rome. Although Weber was hailed by the great classical scholar Theodor Mommsen as his true heir, he came to believe that contemporary ethical and political problems could not really be solved by drawing lessons from the fate of Rome, so he turned his attention to the direct study of contemporary society and began to look in different directions for his comparative material.

The most interesting of Weber's early works, at least for the light it throws on his own orientation, is the research that he conducted under the aegis of the *Verein* on 'The conditions of rural labour in Germany beyond the Elbe', published in 1892. This research was ostensibly a study of the impact of capitalist development on the rural social structure of Eastern Prussia and showed how the expansion of capitalist agriculture had eroded patriarchal relations in agriculture, reducing the labour force to a rural proletariat. Under the impact of such a development the Prussian rural workers were emigrating to the towns and were being replaced by Polish peasants, who were prepared to work for lower wages and under conditions of abject subordination to their employers. Such a development was hardly unique to Prussia, nor was Weber by any means the first to observe it. The importance of Weber's contribution lies not in its substantive content so much as in the lessons Weber drew from his study, which indeed motivated it in the first place.

For Weber the development of capitalism in rural Prussia was undoubtedly progressive if evaluated in purely economic terms. However, economic criteria alone were not sufficient to evaluate social developments or policies to modify such developments. Thus the development of capitalism was increasing the productivity of agriculture, fostering the accumulation of capital and enriching the ruling Junkers, but it was doing so at the expense of the ethical and political foundations of the nation. The sturdy independent Prussian peasant, whose moral qualities had contributed in no small way to the virtues of the Prussian State, was being eliminated, replaced by a dependent workforce of much inferior cultural quality which was prepared to work under the most exploitative and degrading conditions. Moreover this new workforce was not only culturally inferior, it was also culturally alien and so a potential fifth column in the event of political or military threats from the East. Finally, the development of capitalism, in undermining patriarchal relations in agriculture, was establishing the conditions for the growth of class conflict in the countryside. The development of capitalism in rural Prussia was therefore strengthening the Junkers economically, while turning the Junkers into a section of the capitalist class, but it was eroding the ethical and political foundations of national security in the most sensitive eastern border regions.

The conclusion was that, on the one hand, the degeneration of the Junkers to a section of the capitalist class meant that their political rule was now that of a self-interested clique, the consequences of which would prove catastrophic to the national interest. On the other hand, Weber found it difficult to see in the *bourgeoisie* a class that could provide the political leadership for a truly national policy, putting the political interests of the 'power state' above sectional interests. Such leadership would have to regulate capitalist development in accordance with national political and ethical ideals, and in particular to regulate the capitalisation of agriculture by closing the eastern border and by resettling Germans as protected agrarian petty producers.

Weber's study of the Prussian peasant closely links Weber's own political and theoretical concerns with the traditions of the *Verein*. His study not only anticipates his own later work; it also embodies all the central themes of the political and academic orientations of the *Verein* — the subordination of academic research to pressing political concerns; the insistence on the primacy of ethical and political criteria in the evaluation of economic policy; the emphasis on the priority of national over sectional interests; the focus on the state as the embodiment of the nation; the nostalgic evocation of patriarchal relations; the insistence on the positive ethical virtues of *petit-bourgeois* morality and the political necessity of sustaining a strong and independent *petit-bourgeoisie* as the basis of a powerful national state. Despite this Weber was never entirely at home in the *Verein*, although his differences did not really emerge into the open until after his recovery from a serious nervous breakdown at the turn of the century.

Weber's critique of the *Verein*, and more generally of the German Historical School, was made explicit in a series of methodological essays largely written as he emerged from his breakdown. Weber's arguments in these essays are often close to those of Menger which precipitated the *Methodenstreit*. However, Weber did not simply abandon the methodological prescriptions of the Historical School for the scientific methodology of marginalist economics. On the one hand, the positions Weber developed in his methodological writings were at least to some extent already implicit in his historical works. On the other hand, Weber achieved what many have seen as a methodological synthesis of the positions of the contending parties. However, if there is a synthesis, its basis is definitely on the Austrian side of the divide. Thus on the two essential and fundamental points of difference Weber aligns himself unequivocally with Menger. On the one hand, Weber endorsed Menger's insistence that economics is not an ethical science, in the sense that it cannot give rise to ethical prescriptions but must be conducted on a strictly objective basis. On the other hand, he endorsed Menger's insistence that historical interpretation presupposes that the social sciences have an analytical core in the form of a pure theory of typical relationships.

Weber had never been happy about the subordination of the work of the *Verein* to particular political ends. While he endorsed the emphasis of the *Verein* on conducting research that was 'value-relevant', that would inform contemporary ethical and political debate, he insisted that the research itself had to be conducted with a scrupulous regard for objectivity and that the results of the research could not impose particular ethical or political conclusions. Research could provide only the facts that could inform debate. To reach ethical conclusions it was necessary to judge those facts in accordance with chosen ethical criteria. The argument was extremely disingenuous, however well-intentioned, for while the facts might never be able to impose a particular judgement, they could certainly be formulated in such a way as to leave little room for serious choice, an excellent example of which would be Weber's own study of the Prussian peasantry.

Problems of methodology: Menger and Weber

The most important methodological contribution made by Weber concerns the role of theory within the social sciences, and here again his position is much closer to that of Menger than it is to the Historical School. To bring out the relationship I shall present Weber's views in relation to those of Menger.

Menger wrote his *Problems of Economics and Sociology* as a counterblast to the Historical School's rejection of the abstraction of classical political economy. Menger agreed that classical political economy was too abstract to provide a sufficient 'basis for the practical sciences of national economy, and thus also of practice in this field' (Menger, 1963, p. 27). However the failings of classical political economy should not lead to a condemnation of all abstraction in the name of a purely pragmatic approach to the facts. Such pragmatism could for Menger lead only to socialism as the Historical School's enthusiasm for reform sponsored by the state was untempered by any adequate theory of the limits of reform or of the nature of the state. Without such a theory state intervention is proposed as the solution to every social problem until the whole of society is engulfed by the state.

Menger argues that the proper response to the failures of classical political economy is not to reject theory, but to construct a more adequate theory on the basis of a clear recognition of the abstract character of such a theory and of the distance that separates theoretical abstraction from concrete historical understanding. Thus Menger distinguishes the theoretical from the historical and practical sciences. Historical understanding is related to an individual process of development, whereas theoretical understanding subsumes the event under a law of succession or of coexistence that is derived from a theory, in this case of the economy. The two are distinct because the theory is necessarily abstract, concerned with 'the *general nature* and the *general connection* of economic phenomena' (Menger, 1950, p. 37).

The distinction between the historical and the theoretical orientations for Menger corresponds to a distinction between the methods of the inductive elaboration of empirical laws and the deductive elaboration of theoretical statements. The theoretical orientation establishes exact laws that 'simply bear within themselves the guarantee of absoluteness', being based on the deductive elaboration of the '*simplest elements* of everything real, elements that must be thought of as strictly typical just because they are the simplest'. The exact theory of economics, therefore, comprises what would nowadays be called a hypothetico-deductive elaboration of 'an analytically or abstractly conceived economic world' (Menger, 1950, pp. 59–60, 73). The exact laws formulated in this theory are to be distinguished from empirical laws, and they do not depend on empirical laws for their confirmation. Indeed they cannot be confirmed empirically because they are abstract idealisations that rest on certain presuppositions that may never apply in reality.

The typical forms on which theory is based can never give rise to a full understanding of reality since the 'types' represent an idealisation of reality, their 'phenomenal forms' not necessarily corresponding to the infinite complexity of the corresponding 'empirical forms'. Thus in reality different examples of the same phenomenon are never identical, so that an historical orientation that seeks to grasp the individual process of development can never rest content with theoretical knowledge of ideal typical relations, but must seek the empirical relations between 'real types'. For this reason Menger strongly opposed the mathematical formulation of economic theories, since this gave to economic relations an exactness that they never enjoyed in reality. Thus Menger, like Marx and for similar reasons, proliferated concrete arithmetical examples rather than attempting to achieve a spurious generality through algebraic formulation. On the other hand, Menger argued that the historical orientation could never get beyond empirical relations and so could never achieve more than the knowledge of contingent empirical laws.

Since theoretical argument is based on abstraction from, and idealisation of, reality, it always seeks to understand reality from a particular point of view. Thus economics seeks to understand reality from the point of view of the 'precautionary activity of humans directed towards covering their material needs' (Menger, 1950, p. 63). Theoretically the economic aspect of phenomena can be studied in abstraction from all other aspects, although historically the economy can only be understood in connection with the total life of a nation. Thus historical understanding rests on the contributions of the totality of the social sciences 'no one of which teaches us to understand full empirical reality' (Menger, 1950, p. 62). The abstraction of economics is legitimate and fruitful not because the economist believes the 'dogma of self-interest' (Schmoller), but because economic provision in accordance with the individual's own well-being is among the most common and most important human efforts and impulses.

Theoretical knowledge is the necessary foundation of the historical orientation. Although the historical orientation aspires to knowledge of the singular sequence of events, the basis of such knowledge can only be the typical forms elaborated in theory. Although the simple types, and the laws by which complicated phenomena are built up from the simplest forms, are abstract and universal, historical investigation constantly reveals new empirical variants of these types and more complex elaborations of the simple types. Thus the absolute character of theoretical understanding by no means makes it inapplicable to historical understanding. However, these types and typical relationships are not derived from the study of history, nor do they develop historically; they are based on '*experience* in general' (Menger, 1950, p. 116), that is to say, on the universality of the economic problem of the rational provision for material needs.

Weber's methodological position was in many respects very similar to that of Menger, although the similarity does not necessarily reflect a direct influence, but could as well express a common substantive ambition within a common neo-Kantian framework. Weber's specific methodological departures from Menger very closely parallel his substantive critique of Menger's approach to economic theory.

Problems of methodology: Menger and Weber

Weber, like Menger although for somewhat different reasons, was dissatisfied with the pragmatism of the Historical School both politically, in its readiness to see the solution of all social problems in the benign intervention of the state, and methodologically, in its subordination of theoretical investigations to political concerns, that led to a purely pragmatic empiricism. Thus Weber, like Menger, sought to define and defend a specific role for theory within the social sciences, without falling back on the absolutism of classical political economy which claimed an exclusive legitimacy for theoretical understanding. Theory for Weber, as for Menger, was necessarily abstract, concerned with typical relationships and the construction and elaboration of ideal-types to which no reality would exactly correspond. Historical understanding was only possible on the basis of such typical constructs, but could not be exhausted by such typifications. Finally, Weber, like Menger, argued that the recognition of the legal, political and ethical dimensions of social life did not invalidate the scientific autonomy of economics since any science sought only a partial understanding of reality, a full historical understanding requiring the participation of all the social sciences.

Where Weber departed from Menger most fundamentally was in his characterisation of the typical foundations of social theory. For Menger economics is concerned with the universal economic problem of the rational provision for human material needs. The types on which economic theory is based are therefore elaborations of the principles of rational choice, and for the Austrian School economics is a branch of *praxiology*, the general theory of rational choice. Praxiology was originally seen as a branch of a universal psychology, so that the laws of economics had a psychological foundation and a universal validity.

For Menger, economic theory elaborated on the general categories of human experience, its universal and absolute character being verified by the introspective examination of the 'practical consciousness of economic relations' (Wieser), its certainty expressing the certainty of intuitive knowledge. The universality of economic theory rested ultimately on the supposed universality of economic rationality. In this respect the institutions of capitalist society are the products of the progressive realisation of this rationality.

For Weber, as for his colleagues in the Historical School, economic rationality is not such a self-evident universal truth. On the one hand, the single-minded pursuit of economic goals could be at the expense of ethical and political goals which were valued more highly. Thus, for example, the Junkers' pursuit of profit on their eastern estates was at the expense of the political security of the nation. On the other hand, the rational adaptation of means to ends is only one possible value-orientation that is characteristic of a particular society, but that does not have universal validity. Thus economic theory is not based on an ideal-type that expresses the certain intuitive knowledge of a naturalistic psychological orientation; it is based on an ideal-type that expresses a particular value-orientation that has its own historical origin. The institutions of capitalist society cannot be seen as the products of a universal rationality, for the historical origins of this form of rationality have themselves to be explained. Previous forms of society are not to be dismissed as less developed versions of our own, for they are based on different value-orientations to be captured by distinct ideal-types. 'Economic "laws" are schemata of rational action. They cannot be deduced from a psychological analysis of the individual' (Weber, 1975, p. 202).

Menger's belief in the realistic psychological foundations of economic theory led him to contradict the distinction on which he had initially insisted between historical and theoretical knowledge in going on to claim 'empirical *validity*, in the sense of the *deducibility* of reality from "laws", for the propositions of abstract theory' (Weber, 1949, p. 87). For Weber, by contrast, the ideal-type had no reality of its own; it was strictly a 'Utopia', an heuristic device facilitating the formulation of hypotheses and the exploration of historical connections. For Weber, therefore, the validity of the ideal-type could not transcend those historical circumstances in which its reality as a meaning-principle could be attested and those historical examples to whose understanding it contributes. Thus Weber insisted that theory could never give rise to a distinctive form of knowledge. It was merely a tool that could be used in achieving the only valid form of knowledge, knowledge of specific historical events (Weber, 1949, p. 44).

Weber's ideal-type was a hypothetical construct that was based not on the introspective understanding of the universal principles of experience, but on the historical understanding of the typical complexes of values that motivate actors in different societies at different times. The elaboration of such ideal-types depended for Weber, by contrast to Menger, on detailed and extensive comparative and historical investigation that can assist the analyst in the construction of the complexes that make up the ideal-type. Thus Weber retained the essential features of Menger's methodology, while reversing the relation of priority between historical and theoretical understanding, with the ideal-types of theory depending for their elaboration and for their validity on historical research.

Weber's emphasis on the character of ideal-types as value-constructs reflected the concern that he inherited from the Historical School to emphasise the extent to which capitalist rationality was itself a particular ethical ideal contrasting sharply with the ethical ideals of a feudal paternalism. Capitalist rationality had particular ethical implications; for example, in opening up economic conflicts that had previously been subordinated to the sense of community through the subordination of self-interest to duty. However this does not mean that Weber has to be seen in this respect as a follower of Schmoller as against Menger, for even here at the essential point Weber sided with Menger.

For the German Historical School the ethical orientation of political economy implied not only that capitalist rationality was an ethical ideal. Much more importantly it implied, firstly, that economic ideals could not be considered in abstraction from ethical and political ideals, so that economics could not be abstracted from an all embracing history. From this point of view capitalist rationality could be criticised from the standpoint of higher ethical ideals, for example the ideals of community or of self-sufficiency and independence, that capitalism undermined. This position Weber rejected as clearly and as emphatically as did Menger:

> The belief that it is the task of scientific work to cure the 'onesidedness' of the economic approach by broadening it into a *general* social science suffers primarily from the weakness that the 'social' criterion (i.e. the relationships among persons) acquires the specificity necessary for the delimitation of scientific problems only when it is accompanied by some substantive predicate.

There cannot be a 'general' science of the social, for the 'generality' of the term 'social' 'rests on nothing but its ambiguity. It provides, when taken in its "general" meaning, no specific *point of view*, from which the *significance* of given elements of culture can be analysed' (Weber, 1949, pp. 67–8). Thus Weber was unhappy about the use of the term 'sociology' that had strong connotations of just such a spurious generality.

The second implication of the ethical orientation for the Historical

School was that the rejection of the 'dogma of self-interest' was a rejection not only of a social theory based on egoism, but more fundamentally of a social theory based on the individual, in favour of an approach that gave full weight to the importance of historically specific institutions such as the state, the community and the family as the transcendent source of ethical ideals and object of ethical obligations.

Menger recognised the necessary role that such institutions played in historical understanding. Thus history

> cannot solve its problems by investigating and cataloguing the vast quantity of *singular phenomena* of human life. Rather, it can do justice to it only by bringing together what is individual in the real world from the point of view of *collective phenomena* and making us aware of the nature and the connection of the above phenomena to those large *collective phenomena* which we call nation, State, society. The fates of single individuals, their acts *per se*, are not the subject matter of history, but only the fates and acts of nations (Menger, 1950, p. 117).

However, Menger was at his most insistent in rejecting the organicism of the German Historical School that led it to postulate such collective phenomena as *sui generis* realities. At the level of historical understanding an organic perspective may be necessary and it may even serve to orient theoretical research. But it must always be recognised as provisional. The most fundamental task of theoretical understanding was precisely to undermine the dangerous illusions to which organicism gave rise by discovering the individual foundations of collective institutions.

Once collective institutions were attributed their own rationality there was no limit to their elaboration, and State Socialism was the inevitable result. Thus it was politically as well as theoretically essential that rationality should be attributed to such institutions only to the extent that they could be shown to express in their functioning the rationality of individual actors.

Theory was essential to defend the ideals of liberalism against collectivist over-enthusiasm. Thus Menger posed 'perhaps the most noteworthy problem of the social sciences: How can it be that institutions which serve the common welfare and are extremely significant for its development come into being without a *common will* directed toward establishing them?' (Menger, 1950, p. 146.)

Menger answered by arguing that where such institutions did not have a pragmatic origin in a common intention they could arise only as unintended results of individual action. The fundamental task of the social sciences in this respect, therefore, was to trace the origin of organic social phenomena as the unintended consequences of the individual actions that gave rise to them in order to evaluate them in relation to individual rationality. Menger accordingly turned to do just this for such institutions as money, prices, exchange, private property and the division of labour, which were explained as the results of the collective emulation of individual initiatives and so as the social crystallisation of individual rationality.

In his liberalism Weber again aligned himself firmly with Menger against the organicism of the Historical School. Although Weber followed the Historical School in emphasising the importance of ethical ideals, he insisted that those ideals were not transcendent, but could only be individual ideals, ideals that were chosen not imposed. Thus, although it is true that Weber reconciled, however uneasily, the 'positivism' of marginalism with the 'idealism' of the Historical School, the reconciliation was on the basis of the marginalist conception of society and the marginalist conception of the social sciences. Weber differed from Menger in two essential respects. On the one hand, he rejected Menger's belief in the universality of economic rationality, considering the latter to represent a specific ethical ideal and not a psychological universal. On the other hand, he rejected Menger's over-enthusiastic confidence in the virtues of a regime of economic liberalism. It was on the basis of these two essential differences that Weber built his systematic sociology, but this sociology was built as a complement to, and not a substitute for, the marginalist conception of the economy.

The problem of rationality

The methodological convergence between Weber's sociology and marginalist economics is only a symptom of their substantive affinity. The two shared a common liberal individualist starting point. Weber fully accepted that marginalism provided an adequate account of economic action in a capitalist society and, at least at the economic level, of the origins of the specifically economic institutions of capitalist society. Thus Weber accepted Menger's account of the rational origins of money and of market exchange, and the marginalist conception of the economic institutions of capitalism as embodiments of economic rationality, as technical means adapted to the achievement of economic ends, and so as 'facts', at least in relation to the ethical ideal of economic rationality.

What Weber rejected about marginalist economics was its 'naturalism', and its implicit subordination of ethical and political ends to the single ideal of economic rationality. For Weber, by contrast, economic rationality could only be a subordinate ethical ideal, evaluated positively not for its own sake but only for its contribution to national prosperity, social stability and the cultural and political strength of the nation. Thus Weber sought to locate marginalist economics within a broader framework. In doing so, however, Weber was in no way distancing himself from the theoretical achievements of marginalism, but only from the exaggerated faith of some of the marginalists, most notably Menger and Böhm-Bawerk, in the virtues of economic liberalism. Thus Wieser, for example, saw economics in very similar terms to those of Weber and sought to develop his own approach to the subject along essentially Weberian lines, though his achievements were limited. Elsewhere in Europe the most notable developments were those made in sometimes idiosyncratic ways by the Fabians, building on the economics of Wicksteed. Thus Weber was by no means alone in seeing in marginalist economic analysis the foundations on which a liberal, reformist, but non-Marxist theory of society could be built.

The starting point of Weber's sociology was his insistence on the historical specificity of capitalist rationality. Marginalism offered an economic theory that was appropriate to a society within which this was indeed the characteristic value-orientation, but in taking economic rationality as a psychological absolute it ignored the question of the limits of its validity. The first task of sociology was to mark out those limits by establishing a typology of value-orientations, within which capitalist rationality would be only one possible orientation to action. This would make it possible to view the institutions and modes of economic action characteristic of a capitalist society within their historical context. The basis of this investigation, for Weber, could only be the comparative and historical study of different societies.

Weber's comparative and historical writings are well-known. In them he sought to locate the specific defining characteristics of capitalist rationality and the historical source of that rationality in the

The problem of rationality

development of Christianity, and on this basis to contrast Christianity with the other great world religions and to trace the development of the institutional framework of modern capitalism, including its legal, political and cultural institutions, as aspects of the development of the particular ethical orientation of capitalist rationality.

These studies are of value in their own right, but we are concerned with them only in their role in the development of Weber's systematic sociology. From this point of view the purpose of the studies was to permit the elaboration of a series of ideal-types that would provide the conceptual framework of that sociology. Weber elaborated these ideal-typical concepts systematically in *Economy and Society*, a work that is fragmentary and incomplete but within which the general thrust of Weber's sociology is clear.

The fundamental concept of sociology for Weber is the concept of social action.

> Sociology ... is a science concerning itself with the interpretive understanding of social action and thereby with a causal explanation of its course and consequences. We shall speak of 'action' in so far as the acting individual attaches a subjective meaning to his behaviour — be it overt or covert, omission or acquiescence. Action is 'social' in so far as its subjective meaning takes account of the behaviour of others and is thereby oriented in its course (Weber, 1968, I, p. 4).

Sociological explanation therefore aims to discover the source of social relations and social institutions in the meaningful orientation of individual social action. The primitive terms of sociology are not social relations, as they are for Marx, but the abstract individual of liberal social theory, with given material interests and a given set of values.

Since action is meaningful it always involves the selection of means to an end on the basis of a particular value-orientation. This provides one criterion according to which different types of action can be classified. Thus Weber distinguishes four types of action according to their value-orientation. The most fundamental type of action, which is the point of reference for the understanding of all types of action, is defined as *'instrumentally rational (zweckrational)*, that is determined by expectations as to the behaviour of objects in the environment and of other human beings; these expectations are used as 'conditions' or 'means' for the attainment of the actor's own rationally pursued and calculated ends'. The other three types of action are all in some sense irrational. Value-rational action is defined by the pursuit of a value for its own sake; affectual action 'determined by the actor's special affects and feeling states' and traditional action 'determined by ingrained habituation' (Weber, 1968, I, pp. 24–5).

The difference between these four types of action seems at first sight to be fairly clear. However, this clarity is illusory and disappears as soon as any attempt is made to apply the classification. Nor are any of the alternative formulations offered by Weber any clearer. Although the typology defines distinctive value-orientations of action, any attempt to apply the typology to the meanings that actions have for particular individuals runs into familiar problems connected with the attribution of motives. A consumer buying a packet of cornflakes in a supermarket may explain the action in terms of either the instrumental rationality of consumer choice, the value-rationality of a belief in the unique nutritive powers of cornflakes, the affectual impact of the packaging, or tradition ingrained by habit. Weber was well aware of these problems, which is why he insisted that his ideal-types related not to the actual meanings that actions have for particular individuals, but to the typical value-orientations of hypothetical actors. Thus in the formulation of typical explanations, the problem of attribution of motives does not arise. However this does not dispel the problem, since Weber insists that his ideal-types have validity only to the extent that they are amenable to empirical evaluation. Weber used his fourfold typology particularly with reference to the motives underlying recognition of the legitimacy of domination, but its practical usefulness is undermined here precisely by the problem of attribution of motives.

Even at the typical level, it is by no means clear that the latter three motives can be distinguished from one another. Thus Weber's fourfold typology effectively broke down into a dualistic typology of rational and irrational action, most of Weber's systematic sociology involving the application of the contrast between rational and traditional or customary action (the concept of 'charisma' has a special role to play, but I shall leave it aside here). In its fullest development instrumental rationality is characteristic only of a capitalist society, so the concept of 'traditional', or, more generally, irrational action is a residual category that covers the typical orientation of action in all non-capitalist societies. Hence, although Weber included very extensive discussion of types of traditional action in his work, the analytical value of the typology was simply to demarcate capitalist

The problem of rationality

from non-capitalist societies. Thus the pivot of Weber's comparative, historical and theoretical sociology is the distinctiveness of 'formal' or 'instrumental' rationality.

Weber recognised that the concept of rationality enjoyed a special privilege in his sociology, but insisted that this privilege was only a methodological one. The ideal-type of rational action

> has the merit of clear understandability and lack of ambiguity. By comparison with this it is possible to understand the ways in which actual action is influenced by irrational factors of all sorts, such as affects and errors, in that they account for the deviation from the line of conduct which would be expected on the hypothesis that the action was purely rational (Weber, 1968, I, p. 6).

The implication is that if it is possible to propose a rational interpretation of a particular course of action that course of action will fall under the ideal-type of instrumentally rational action. If it is not possible to construct such a rational interpretation the action will fall under the ideal-type of irrational action.

Clearly a great deal depends on the meaning of rationality. As a formal concept rationality implies no substantive judgements and refers essentially only to the consistency with which somebody acts. In this sense beliefs are rational if they are non-contradictory and action is rational if it is consistent with beliefs. However in this sense the rationality of actors is a necessary condition for the intelligibility of action and so a necessary presupposition of any attempt at interpretation or explanation. Thus if rationality referred to formal rationality in this sense then all meaningful behaviour, in other words all action, would be rational.

If the specific characteristics of 'rational' social action cannot be characterised by a formally rational value-orientation in the sense just discussed, it must have some substantive content.

Instrumental rationality is supposedly distinctive in that it is a form of rationality which is indifferent to the substantive content of the values pursued, whereas in the other forms of action the substantive content of those values dictates a particular course of action. The archetypal form of instrumentally rational action is rational economic action, in which the market provides a means by which individuals may satisfy their wants, whatever may be the content of those wants. In this sense the market imposes no substantive constraints on the wants which may be satisfied by its means. Similarly, bureaucracy defines a rational form of administration, whatever may be the ends which those in command of the bureaucracy may choose to pursue. Thus Weber's characterisation of the 'formal' or 'instrumental' rationality of the typical forms of action in a capitalist society seems to be based on an extension of the marginalists' concept of economic rationality, according to which the fundamental economic institutions of capitalist society have a purely instrumental significance, in providing a means of achieving human ends which is indifferent to the ends pursued in imposing no substantive constraints on the individuals who enter those institutions.

On the other hand, Weber also recognises that from an alternative evaluative standpoint the consequences of such instrumental rationality are to be judged substantively irrational. Thus the rule of the competitive market is fundamentally inconsistent with the attempt to order life in accordance with the values of equality, fraternity and brotherly love, while bureaucratic domination is inconsistent with the values of freedom and personal autonomy. The implication is that the rationality of the market, or of bureaucratic domination, is *not* purely formal, but also involves substantive evaluative judgements: in particular, the judgement that 'the end justifies the means'. The rationality of the market or of bureaucracy is defined in relation to the single-minded pursuit of monetary gain or of political and administrative domination, and so, far from being 'instrumentally rational', is archetypally 'value-rational'. This issue is absolutely fundamental, because, as we have seen in the last chapter, the validity of the abstraction of marginalist economics, and of the definition of sociology as a complementary but autonomous discipline, hinges on the validity of the economists' abstraction of the 'formal rationality' of economic action, and of the institutions typically derived therefrom, from any substantive considerations. If economics is concerned not with the rational allocation of resources, but with fundamental value conflicts, expressing fundamental conflicts of material and ethical class interest, then there is no basis on which the 'economic' can be abstracted from the 'social'.

Weber only conceals the substantive implications of instrumental rationality from himself by regarding such implications as the 'unintended consequences' of instrumentally rational action. However this argument cannot be sustained, for one of the defining features of instrumental rationality is the anticipation of the results of such action, and it can hardly be claimed that the substantively irrational results of such action cannot be anticipated. Not only can such results be anticipated, but they also determine the resistance to such action on the part of those who are the object of its substantively irrational effects, a resistance which Weber recognises as being inherent in such action in recognising that economic, political and legal rationality are not indifferent modes of action, but are modes of *domination*. Before developing the implications of this criticism we need to explore more closely the connection between marginalist economics and Weber's sociology.

The marginalist foundations of Weber's sociology

Although Weber takes the marginalist characterisation of the formal rationality of economic action as his model, he regards economic action as only one manifestation of a formally rational orientation to action. Actions may be classified not only on the basis of their typical value-orientations, but also according to the types of end to which they are directed. Thus economic action is distinguished from political or religious action according to the goals that are pursued in each case. It is on the basis of the distinctive goals of economic action that Weber argued that the abstraction of economic theory is legitimate.

Marginalist economics provided an adequate theory of the economic consequences of the pure type of rational economic action. Although Weber rejected the tendency of economic liberalism to make economic rationality an absolute ethical ideal, at the expense of cultural, moral, religious and political ideals, he defended the autonomy of economic theory, and correspondingly of economic sociology, on the basis of the distinctiveness of the mode of orientation of economic action that makes it legitimate to abstract from consideration of action oriented to non-economic ends. Political or religious actions are not oriented to economic gain, even though they may have economic implications. They are therefore considered as 'economically oriented actions', and not as 'economic actions'. Thus, although economic action depends on the existence of a legal and political order, it is legitimate to analyse economic action in abstraction from that order. Any particular economic action will, of course, be undertaken in the light of the existence of such an order, but from the point of view of theoretical investigation such an order must be taken as given. Correspondingly the legal, political and religious orders must be the subject of independent investigation, however much they might be influenced in practice by economic factors, in accordance with the distinctive modes of orientation of their typical forms of action.

Weber had no objections to the marginalist theory of the economy, provided only that it knew its own limits. Thus Weber constantly stressed that he was not offering an alternative economic theory and that he did not wish to become involved in economists' disputes. He insisted that the 'theoretical insights' of economic theory 'provide the basis for the sociology of economic action' which did not in any way call them into question. Weber's task was merely to elaborate the sociological concepts implicit in such an economic theory. His scheme 'is intentionally limited to sociological *concepts* ... restricts itself to working out a sociological typology ... to supply a scaffolding ... to develop a systematic scheme of classification' (Weber, 1968, I, pp. 68, 116).

The fundamental concept implicit in economic theory is the concept of 'rational economic action'. The first task of Weber's economic sociology was therefore to elaborate this concept and to establish the connections between it and the fundamental institutions of capitalist society. This elaboration involved Weber in elucidating the social theory implicit in marginalist economics. Weber began his discussion of the 'sociological categories of economic action' with a series of fundamental definitions:

> Action will be said to be 'economically oriented' so far as, according to its subjective meaning, it is concerned with the satisfaction of a desire for 'utilities'. 'Economic action' is any peaceful exercise of an actor's control over resources which is in its main impulse oriented towards economic ends. 'Rational economic action' requires instrumental rationality in this orientation, that is, deliberate planning (Weber, 1968, I, p. 63).

Rational economic action therefore involved, primarily, the systematic orientation of production and exchange to the acquisition of utilities through the allocation of resources in conditions of scarcity.

The definition of rational economic action made no reference to the conditions under which such action was carried out, but referred only to the subjective orientation of action. However such action necessarily involved the quantification of alternative courses of action in order that the alternatives could be rationally evaluated. Hence rational economic action presupposed the possibility of economic calculation.

The marginalist foundations of Weber's sociology

In principle rational action was possible 'where calculation is carried out in terms of physical units', however such calculation could only be based on the subjective evaluation of utilities and disutilities which Weber claimed raised serious difficulties so that

> the actual solution is usually found partly by the application of purely traditional standards, partly by making very rough estimates ... As accounting in kind becomes completely rational and is emancipated from tradition, the estimation of marginal utilities in terms of the relative urgency of wants encounters grave complications; whereas if it were carried out in terms of monetary wealth and income, it would be relatively simple.

Consequently

> from a purely technical point of view, money is the most 'perfect' means of economic calculation. That is, it is formally the most rational means of orienting economic activity. Calculation in terms of money ... is thus the specific means of rational, economic provision (Weber, 1968, I, pp. 87–8, 86).

The possibility of properly rational economic action depended on the possibility of monetary calculation. Thus the development of rational economic action was identified with the development of the 'formal rationality of economic action', which was defined as 'the extent of quantitative calculation or accounting which is technically possible and which is actually applied' (Weber, 1968, I, p. 85), and this possibility was identified in turn with the development of monetary accounting.

Economic action was initially defined in terms of an orientation of action to the satisfaction of a desire for utilities. Such action would take place within the context of a *budgetary unit*, such as the household. Budgetary accounting sought to relate anticipated needs to anticipated resources. 'The possibility of complete monetary budgeting for the budgetary unit is dependent on the possibility that its income and wealth consist either in money or in goods which are at any time subject to exchange for money; that is, which are in the highest degree marketable' (Weber, 1968, I, p. 87). The formal rationality of economic action in the budgetary unit therefore depended on the generalisation of commodity production. Fully rational economic action is possible for a budgetary unit only within a developed capitalist society.

Exchange in a developed market economy takes place on the

basis of the equalisation of relative prices and relative marginal utilities. This equalisation takes place not only contemporaneously, but also over time. According to some versions of marginal utility theory, to which Weber adhered, economic actors have an (irrational) preference for present as against equivalent future goods. According to this theory this time-preference is the basis of profit, since the prices of goods which take time to produce must be marked up in order to compensate those who have provided capital for the loss of utility involved in waiting for its return. Although time-preference is a universal phenomenon, it only becomes the basis of profit within a developed market-economy within which resources can be allocated in accordance with relative marginal utilities. Thus within such an economy we find the emergence of the profit-making enterprise, oriented to the acquisition of profit and differentiated from the budgetary unit. The emergence of such an enterprise expresses the orientation of economic actors to the rational allocation of resources over time.

Because of their different orientations to action it is essential to rational economic action that the budgetary unit and the profit-making enterprise should be separate from one another. Thus

> from the point of view of business interest, the interest in maintaining the private wealth of the owner is often irrational, as is his interest in income receipts at any given time from the point of view of the profitability of the enterprise ... This fact implies the separation as a matter of principle of the budgetary unit and the enterprise, even where both, with respect to powers of control and objects controlled, are identical (Weber, 1968, I, pp. 97–8).

The formal rationality of economic action in the profit-making enterprise depends on the commodity character and free disposal of the resources under its control. Thus the 'principal conditions necessary for obtaining a maximum of formal rationality of capital accounting in production enterprises' are defined as the 'complete appropriation of all material means of production by owners'. This involves the freedom of markets, subordination of management to ownership, free labour and free labour-markets, freedom of contract, a 'mechanically rational technology', 'formally rational administration and law', 'the most complete separation possible of the enterprise ... from the household or budgetary unit' and 'a monetary system with the highest possible degree of formal rationality' (Weber, 1968,

I, pp. 161–2) — in short the competitive capitalist economy of marginalist economics.

The generalisation of the market economy was not only the condition of rational accounting and so the formal rationality of economic action, but also the condition of the 'technically rational organisation of the work process'. This was firstly because of the 'sheer superiority and actual indispensability of a type of management oriented to the particular market situations' where 'management has extensive control over the selection and modes of use of workers' and where 'free labour and the complete appropriation of the means of production create the most favourable conditions for discipline'. Secondly, it was because the fear of starvation gave those without substantial property an incentive to work while it provided incentives to enterprise for those with property (Weber, 1968, I, pp. 137–8, 110).

For all his insistence on the culturally specific character of economic rationality, it turns out that Weber's account of the conditions of rational economic action reformulates in more rigorous terms the explanation of the fundamental institutions of capitalist society already presented by marginalist economics, and most notably by Menger, on the basis of a universalistic conception of rationality. The institutions of private property in the means of production, exchange, the division of labour, money, wages, prices and profits were all conditions for and expressions of the formal rationality of economic action. It was this account, which I criticised in the last chapter, that was the foundation of Weber's sociology. The distinctiveness of Weber's contribution lay not in his 'economic sociology', but in his situating the formal abstraction of marginalist economics within a broader analytical framework, thereby creating the possibility of developing sociology not in opposition to economics, but as an autonomous and complementary discipline. To see the basis of this contribution we need to turn to Weber's methodology.

Economy and society

The analysis of marginalist economics is conducted at a very high level of abstraction. It presents itself as a formal analysis of the ideal conditions and consequences of rational economic action in abstraction from any particular society. Economics thus studies the eternal and ahistorical forms of reason and so is a deductive *a priori* enterprise.

Throughout the nineteenth-century, as we have seen, various schools of 'sociology' emerged to complement or contest the abstraction of economics, sociology studying the contingent institutional and moral framework within which the economic forms appear. This is in essence the opposition between marginalism and the German Historical School. The relationship between economics and sociology was always one of tension, as neither was able to accommodate the other. Thus, in the *Methodenstreit*, Menger and Schmoller each claimed to have discovered the only appropriate form of knowledge of society. Menger criticised historicism on the grounds that knowledge necessarily involved the formulation of general laws, while Schmoller criticised marginalism for trying to apply its abstract laws to reality.

In his methodological writings Weber sought to achieve a reconciliation of the two positions in arguing that theory is necessary to historical explanation, while denying that theory in the social sciences could be a distinctive form of knowledge with its own independent validity. The deductive method of economics produced only hypotheses, in the form of ideal-types, which were necessary to historical understanding, but whose explanatory power lay only in the historical relationships they illuminated. Sociologists have pored over Weber's methodological writings to find the key to the sociological method, but Weber's 'ideal-types' hang uneasily between descriptive categories and explanatory concepts without ever resolving the tension between the two. The ambiguity of the concept of the ideal-type focuses the methodological dilemma without resolving it. However Weber's real achievement lay not in formulating a prescriptive methodology for the social sciences, but in achieving a substantive reconciliation of economics and sociology so as to make possible a unified, though differentiated, liberal social theory.

Weber's typology of action ascribed a particular place within the social sciences to economic theory. Economic theory was concerned to elaborate the economic conditions for, and implications of, the pure type of rational economic action. Foremost amongst the economic conditions for rational economic action were the fundamental institutions of capitalist society: private property, the market, money, the division of labour, wages, and profits. These institutions were therefore explained, at the level of abstraction of economic theory, as instrumental expressions of economic rationality. Although these institutions were the manifestations of historically specific social relations that have developed in the course of the production and reproduction of human social existence, they were not conceptualised at this level of abstraction as specific historical developments but as the embodiment of an abstract and ahistorical rational principle.

Sociology cannot rest content with such an abstract deductive account of the structure of capitalist society. Society is not made by metaphysical principles, but by real people interacting with one another on the basis of their particular needs and aspirations. If sociology were to be reconciled with economic theory it needed to situate the abstractions of economic theory within the concrete framework of everyday social life. Weber's typology of action made this possible, locating economic theory as one among several branches of social science, concerned with the abstract investigation of one dimension of social life. Economics alone could not give knowledge of concrete societies; such knowledge could only be achieved by the totality of the social sciences. Economic sociology was concerned to locate the abstractions of economic theory within the concrete reality of social action, while other branches of sociology concerned themselves with the conditions for, and implications of, action oriented to non-economic ends.

Although economic theory was only one branch of the social sciences, it nevertheless enjoyed an especially privileged position. However much the institutions abstractly theorised by economics were located historically, however much the historian and sociologist explored the specific socio-historical circumstances within which they came into being, they remained also the supra-historical manifestations of reason and so the universal foundations of a society characterised by its formal rationality, capitalism.

Weber recognised the crudity of Menger's account of the origins of the fundamental institutions of capitalist society, according to which one individual rationally appreciated the advantage of, for example, money and was then imitated by others. Thus Weber recognised that the origins of capitalism lay in the struggles for power and material gain of an earlier age, so that money, credit, exchange, the separation of labour from the means of production, were all developed by particular interests seeking their own advantage. But this particularity of origin did not undermine the identification of these institutions with formal rationality; it merely meant that the progressive rationalisation of economic action was an uneven and discontinuous process that was often compromised by particular interests. The universal significance of all these institutions remained their formal rationality, and not the particularity of their origin.

Economic theory had this special status because the rationality on which it was based, and which was expressed in monetary calculation, was supposedly a purely formal rationality. The institutions to which it gave rise were therefore the instruments of reason, the institutional forms of a universal principle, and so the presuppositions and foundation of rational social action, and not the products of specific actions. Hence the theoretical status of an explanation of market exchange as 'the archetype of all rational social action' (Weber, 1968, I, p. 635) was quite different from that of an explanation of a particular exchange relation in terms of the needs, aspirations and circumstances of particular individuals who meet in the market. The market provided a formal framework within which rational social action takes place, without dictating the terms of exchange and so the content of that action. A particular exchange may even involve an attempt to subvert the rationality of the market by violating its principles, but in that case the exchange eschewed not only the principles of the market but also the principles of rationality. Economic theory, and its concept of rational economic action, was therefore the foundation of any sociological investigation of capitalist society in providing the formal framework that was the condition of possibility of rational action. It was for sociology to fill this framework with social content.

Sociology should not be concerned with singular acts but with 'courses of action that are repeated by the actor or (simultaneously) occur among numerous actors since the subjective meaning is meant to be the same' (Weber, 1968, I, p. 29). Such repetition may be simply the manifestation of usage, custom or habit, sustained by inertia and convenience. Alternatively it may, as in economic theory, be a manifestation of the repeated rational appreciation of identical situations and so be explicable in terms of rational self-interest. However, it may also be the result of an orientation of action to a *legitimate order* of normative regulation, whether in the form of convention or of law. Convention is a spontaneous form of normative regulation emerging out of social relations; law is a compulsory form of regulation imposed by an organisation. An adequate account of social action, including economic action, had to consider not only the rational orientation to self-interest, but also the formation of, and orientation to, the legitimate orders of social organisations. Where the economic institutions of the market, money etc., provided the necessary formal framework for rational social action, the social institutions of organisations with their legitimate orders provided its contingent historical framework. It was on this basis that Weber differentiated 'economy' and 'society', 'economics' and 'sociology'. Economics remained a deductive discipline, establishing the formal instrumental rationality of the fundamental institutions of capitalist society. These institutions provided the framework within which actors, through their meaningful interaction with others, engaged in social action and created concrete social relations and concrete social institutions.

Weber's sociology was primarily concerned with establishing a typology of organisations according to the ends which motivate their formation and inform their direction, the means available to those ends, the value-orientation of action typical to them and their internal dynamics. It was quite possible, and indeed very likely, that the formation of these organisations would subvert the formal rationality of the competitive market system, for they were established precisely to achieve ends that could not be achieved directly through rational economic action. The existence of organisations could not simply be taken as given. Their origins had to be sought in the individual actions that gave rise to them and sustain them. Such 'collectivities must be treated *solely* as the resultants and modes of organisation of the particular acts of individual persons, since these alone can be treated as agents in the course of subjectively understandable action' (Weber, 1968, I, p. 13).

Although they are singular products, organisations may be classified according to the typical orientation of action that gives rise to them. Thus economic organisations are established and administered with a view to achieving economic ends: the budgetary unit as an economic organisation is oriented to the satisfaction of a desire for utilities and the profit-making enterprise is oriented to making profits. Other economic organisations will arise on the basis of economic interests, as individuals with a common interest associate in order to advance that interest, usually by monopolising advantages and so regulating exchange in their own interests. The most notable such organisations are trade unions and cartels.

Organisations will also be formed to further the pursuit of non-economic ends. A political organisation is one in which the membership is subject to domination by an established order which is maintained within a certain territorial order by the threat of force. A political organisation is therefore directed to the attainment and imposition of coercive power. In contemporary society the only strictly political organisation, in this sense, is the state, which claims a monopoly of the means of physical violence. However the state determines the existence of a *political community*, within which politically oriented action, that is to say action oriented to affecting the direction of the state, is channelled through political parties.

A 'hierocratic organisation' is one 'which enforces its order through psychic coercion by distributing or denying religious benefits' (Weber, 1968, I, p. 54). Religious action is the action of such an organisation; religiously oriented action is action oriented to influencing the direction of the organisation. Hierocratic organisations were particularly important for Weber because they were defined by their orientation to, and imposition of, ideal ends, and as such could influence the value-orientation of action in all spheres of social life.

Organisations may also be classified according to the means adopted by those in authority to achieve their ends. Any organisation that is more than a spontaneous voluntary association will be characterised by a system of domination which will typically involve an administrative staff and a system of legal regulation. According to the value-orientation of action typical of the leadership of the organisation there will be typically different forms of law and of domination. Thus Weber developed an elaborate typology of such forms as the core of his sociology of law and his sociology of domination.

Weber insisted on the autonomy of political and religious ends in relation to economic ends. Political action is directed to the achievement of political power for its own sake, not as a means to material gain. Religious action is oriented to ideas for their own sake, and not to provide a moral gloss for material interest. Thus the ideal-types of action and corresponding organisation must be formulated in abstraction from one another. However in reality it is true that the autonomy of economic, political and religious action is not maintained. Thus churches, states, political parties have to engage in economic action to sustain themselves as corporate entities, and may intervene in economic life to achieve their political and religious ends. Economic actors and economic organisations may orient their activity to political and religious organisations to achieve their economic ends. Thus a cartel may seek political favour, a trade union legal protection and a party religious sanction. Financiers may encourage the state to increase its indebtedness; industrialists may encourage it to protect them from competition; imperialists may encourage its expansionism;

and capitalists may seek to use the state to oppress the working class. None of these practical relationships, however, undermine the fact that for Weber the state and the church were in essence autonomous and directed to other than economic ends. If that autonomy was destroyed, they would cease to be political or religious organisations.

It is this typology of action that defines the place of the concept of 'class' in Weber's sociology. Classes arise as associations of individuals pursuing a common economic interest. Weber defined a class as 'all persons in the same class situation', a 'class situation' being defined in turn as 'the typical probability of (1) procuring goods, (2) gaining a position in life and (3) finding inner satisfactions, a probability which derives from the relative control over goods and skills and from their income producing uses within a given economic order'. The concept of class situation therefore refers to a common economic interest that derives from a common economic situation, defined in terms either of the possession or absence of property ('property class') or of the type of economic activity, for example, the branch of production of an entrepreneur or the occupation of a worker ('commercial class'). A *social class* is then defined as 'the totality of those class situations within which individual and generational mobility is easy and typical'. Thus social classes are defined as the working class, the *petit-bourgeoisie*, the propertyless intelligentsia and specialists, and the 'classes privileged through property and education' (Weber, 1968, I, pp. 302, 305).

Although the concept of social class defines a common interest among, for example, workers in different occupations or entrepreneurs in different branches of production because of the possibilities of social mobility between them, there is no reason why individuals should necessarily be aware of their common class situation and still less why they should necessarily establish class organisations on that basis. 'A *uniform* class situation prevails only when completely unskilled and propertyless persons are dependent on irregular employment. Mobility among, and stability of, class positions differs greatly; hence the unity of a social class is highly variable' (Weber, 1968, I, p. 302). Class situation is only one basis of economic organisation and one that does not easily succeed because of class divisions. It goes without saying that the concept of class is not appropriate to the conceptualisation of action directed to non-economic ends, however much class factors may contingently intrude on the activity of such organisations as parties or status groups. Thus there is no more justification for reducing the uniformities of social action to the single concept of class, than there is for reducing them to rational self-interest. Conflicts of economic interest are inevitable, so there is an inherent tendency to class-formation in capitalist societies, but classes may be more or less significant groupings at different historical periods. Correspondingly, there will be a greater or lesser tendency for class factors to play a role in the formation of parties and status groups. However, such interdependencies have to be investigated empirically as they arise, and cannot prejudice the essential autonomy of ends on the basis of which different forms of action, organisation and social relation arise.

Weber's sociology offered a pluralistic conception of society that he contrasted with the 'reductionism' of both Marxism and vulgar economic liberalism. Although economic theory defined the formal framework of a rational economic system, it did not specify its concrete historical content. In pursuing their economic, political and religious or ethical interests individuals create a range of social relationships and social organisations that provide the institutional environment within which social life takes place. The variety and complexity of social existence cannot be reduced to uniform expressions of the rational pursuit of self-interest. Such a reduction ignores the importance of ethical and political goals in social life, and ignores the prevalence of custom and tradition and of affectual orientations to action even in a capitalist society. Hence an adequate theory of society has to complement economic theory with sociology.

Weber's pluralistic conception of society bases its differentiation of types of action and of social institution on the differentiation of the substantive ends typical of each kind of action. For Weber the differentiation of social institutions, according to the typical ends to which they are adapted, is not a universal feature of society, but is itself the historical result of the progressive rationalisation of society, on the model of the rationality of the economic division of labour: the functional differentiation of institutions is 'efficient' in the sense that each specialised institution can select appropriate means to achieve its distinctive ends. However this does not mean that each type of action, and each type of institution, defines an independent sphere, for each has implications for the others. As we have seen, the economic reproduction of the state and the church has to be secured, while the reproduction of typically economic institutions presupposes certain political and ethical conditions.

Moreover these different ends are not necessarily consistent with one another. The attempt of the church to realise religious ends may be compromised if it has to preoccupy itself with economic concerns, just as the economic reproduction of the business enterprise is compromised if its operation is subordinate to other than purely economic ends. The rationality of the functional differentiation of social institutions, according to the typical ends pursued, derives precisely from the potential conflict between the requirements of those distinct ends. The differentiation of institutions does not eliminate this conflict, but only externalises it, so that the problem now arises in the relationship between institutions.

Recognition of this conflict between competing ends was precisely the problem from which Weber embarked on his sociological enterprise. In his work on the Prussian peasants Weber showed that the unrestrained pursuit of economic goals undermined the economic and political reproduction of the state. Thus the objective tendency was for economic rationality to subvert political rationality. On the other hand, for Weber political ends were superior to economic ends, from which he drew the conclusion that the exercise of economic rationality had to be morally and politically restrained.

Although Weber rejected the reductionism of both Marxism and economic liberalism in espousing a pluralist conception of society, he believed that capitalist society had a coherence and a unity that was given by the typically rational orientation of action in capitalist society. However this rational value-orientation is not a specifically economic phenomenon. The rationalisation of the capitalist economy is simply one aspect of a process that can also be observed in religion, in law and in the characteristic forms of domination of Western European society. According to Weber this process cannot be reduced to the requirements of economic rationality; on the contrary, the development of economic rationality is only one manifestation of the development of an instrumentally rational value-orientation. The time has come to explore more closely just what this rationality involves.

The typology of action and the theory of society

The basis of Weber's sociology was his typology of social action, which was the conceptual foundation of his entire scheme of ideal-types. Marginalist economics took as its starting point the abstract individual, whose actions were determined according to the rational pursuit of economic ends, and developed the pure theory of rational economic action. However Weber's typology of action established that rational economic action was only one among a variety of forms of social action, defined according to the value-orientation of action and the ends to which that action was directed. Thus economics is only one branch of the social sciences, building a theory of the institutions and social relations that can be regarded ideal-typically as the consequences of rational economic action. Sociology has to put economics in its place within the field of the social sciences, and has to complement economic theory with a comparable ideal-typical investigation of those forms of action that cannot be characterised by a rational orientation to economic ends, and the institutions and social relations that arise on the basis of such action. This ideal-typical investigation could not, for Weber, produce theoretical truths, as a distinctive form of knowledge, but it did generate the fundamental concepts which provided the basis for comparative and historical investigation and so for particular sociological explanations.

The primitive concepts of Weber's sociology were, on the one hand, the abstract individual and, on the other hand, the value-orientation of action and the ends to which that action was directed. A sociological explanation had been achieved once social action, social relations and social institutions had been related back to the orientation to ends and values of the individuals whose actions gave rise to those social relations and social institutions. It was therefore fundamental to Weber's aim of establishing a conceptual foundation for the social sciences that the typology of ends and of value-orientations be established prior to, and independently of, the social relations and social institutions to which they give rise. If this were not the case the ends and value-orientations of action would in turn be amenable to sociological explanation and they would cease to be the primitive concepts of sociology. The typology of ends can be used to exemplify the argument, before we turn to the typology of value-orientations.

The typology of ends was the basis on which Weber established the autonomy of economic, political and ethical or religious action, and so of economics and the other branches of the social sciences. Although Weber stressed that the ideal-types could only be established by thorough comparative and historical investigation, the autonomy of these different forms of action, and of the institutions and social relations to which they gave rise, was not established empirically.

The typology of action and the theory of society 275

Weber observed, for example, that political and religious means were frequently used to economic ends and that success in achieving political and religious ends was frequently dependent on the availability of economic means. The basis of this differentiation is therefore not empirical but conceptual. However if we ask what is the conceptual basis of the differentiation of ends we find ourselves caught at once in a vicious circle.

Economic action is action oriented to the provision of the material means of human existence. Defined in this stark way the definition could be considered to be prior to the social institutions to which it gives rise, so that an instrumental explanation of these institutions is not incoherent, although as soon as we look at a particular society we might doubt the adequacy of this characterisation: provision for material needs is only secured through *social* production, so that action oriented to such provision has to be oriented to the *social reproduction* of the actor as an economic agent. If the substantive content of both the ends of economic action and the means at the disposal of the individual are necessarily socially defined, economic action cannot be categorised in abstraction from the particular institutional form of the social relations of production.

Political and religious action are defined in terms of ends that have no meaning outside the institutions to which they supposedly give rise. Thus political action is defined by an orientation to the exercise of political power; politically oriented action to the acquisition of such power. Political action therefore presupposes the existence of a political organisation, without which political power does not exist. In the same way religious action presupposes the existence of an hierocratic organisation. Hence the definition of the ends of social action presupposes the existence of precisely those social institutions which the typology of ends was set up to explain.

The only way out of this vicious circle is to postulate an inherent irrational quest for power and metaphysical sustenance as a defining characteristic of the human psyche. This, however, is just the kind of psychologistic irrationalism from which Weber sought to rescue the social sciences. The only conclusion must be that the explanation of the specific characteristics of economic, political and religious action must itself be sociological and cannot be referred to the typology of ends, since that typology presupposes the phenomena it seeks to explain. However Weber did not draw this conclusion, characteristically falling back at this crucial point on his historicist empiricism, which insisted that historical interpretation is ultimately the only valid form of knowledge. The result was that the explanatory power of his sociology was limited to a potential ability to interpret the reproduction of those social phenomena, on the basis of the subjective interpretation of socially determined and socially effective human needs and aspirations.

While the typology of ends established the autonomy of the different forms of action, and so of the different branches of the social sciences, the typology of value-orientations was the basis on which the coherence and unity of society was established. The cultural unity of a capitalist society was defined by the typically rational value-orientation of action in such a society. I have already noted that the typology effectively reduces to the contrast between rational and irrational action, the distinctions between different types of irrational action referring to typical motivation rather than to typical value-orientation. The typology therefore depends on the definition of the 'formal rationality' characteristic of a capitalist society. I have also noted that the definition of this 'formal rationality' derives from the marginalists' characterisation of rational economic action. However Weber insisted that the economy is only one sphere of application of the broader principles of 'instrumental rationality'. Clearly Weber's interpretation hinges on the characterisation of the 'rationality' of 'instrumentally rational' action independently of its economic form.

It is fundamental to Weber's sociology that the formally rational value-orientation can be defined abstractly, and not reduced to the specific economic rationality of capitalist society. If this were not the case his sociology would be threatened by a reductionism for which the characteristic value-orientation of capitalist society would be the expression of capitalist economic rationality, so that the rationality of political and religious action would not be inherent in those forms of action, but would be an expression of their relation to economic action, and the rationality of economic action would in turn be the consequence and not the cause of capitalist economic institutions.

We have seen that Weber insisted that economic rationality was only one form of rationality and that the development of the capitalist economy was only one aspect of the rationalisation of western society. The Protestant ethic and the bureaucratic State are not expressions of the development of capitalist rationality; all three are, in principle, autonomous expressions of the development of a rational value-orientation in all spheres of social life. However, we have already seen

The typology of action and the theory of society

that formal rationality, in the sense of consistency and determinateness of relations between motives and actions, is a necessary condition for the intelligibility of action, and so a necessary condition for any interpretative sociology, without in any sense being sufficient for the definition of an instrumentally rational value-orientation to action in Weber's sense. Weber's 'formal rationality' therefore necessarily involves substantive considerations.

In practice Weber's explorations of 'irrational' forms of action were conducted on the basis of the presupposition of the formal rationality (in the logical sense) of all action. Thus he analysed, for example, patrimonialism in terms of the rational requirements of administration appropriate to a particular society and of the rational responses of different actors to the situations in which they found themselves. Patrimonialism, or calculation in kind, did not persist because of an irrational failure to adapt means to ends, but because the means for a more 'rational' adaptation were not available. The 'rationality' of the forms of action typical of a particular society lay not so much in the subjective orientation of the actors, as in the extent to which the social institutions in which their actions were embedded had been subordinated to the principles of a particular form of rationality, 'instrumental' or 'formal' rationality. Thus the 'irrationality' of patrimonialism and calculation in kind was measured against the 'rationality' of bureaucratic administration and monetary calculation as less against more adequate means of achieving the given end. Measured against other ends, however, patrimonialism and calculation in kind might appear rational, while bureaucratic administration and monetary calculation would be irrational. Thus the privileged status of 'formal rationality' in Weber's sociology does not lie simply in its expressing the rational adaptation of means to ends. So what is peculiarly 'rational' about 'formal rationality'?

Weber's definition of formal rationality differed according to the sphere of activity with which he was concerned. Thus economic rationality referred to economic action and was defined in terms of the extent of money calculation. However such a definition was obviously not appropriate to the characterisation of rational forms of law, domination or religion. Each of these was characterised in turn in its own way. Thus rationality was expressed in formal law, bureaucratic domination and a secularised religion. The common feature of all these cases was the determination of a course of action in accordance with a set of general rules rather than a particular prescription or a capricious whim. Very broadly, the degree of rationality was identified with the degree of generality of the rules applied to the determination of a particular course of action, and so with the relative absence of particularistic regulation.

On what basis is the degree of abstraction of regulations identified with the degree of rationality? Weber suggests that the rationality of such a system lies in the degree to which the consequences of action are *predictable*. It is certainly the case that the existence of a set of rules makes it possible to predict with some degree of accuracy the decisions of a legal, bureaucratic or hierocratic authority, and so to anticipate the consequences of a particular course of action. The peculiar 'rationality' of such a set of institutions is not defined by the subjective orientation of the actor calculating the consequences of action, but by the objective 'rationality' provided by the degree of predictability of those consequences which is made possible by the existence of a set of rules. Although the decisions of a despotic ruler might not be governed by a legal system, this does not imply that those living under a despotic administration will have to abandon rationality; it merely means that they will have to base their calculations on their knowledge of the considerations the despot will be likely to bring to bear on their case. To the extent that despotic rule is capricious such calculation will involve considerable indeterminacy.

The predictability of the imperative judgements of others certainly makes it easier to anticipate the consequences of a particular course of action, so making it more likely that the end achieved will be the end intended. However the predictability of the consequences of action is by no means the exclusive prerogative of of an abstract system of regulation. The rule of custom and tradition, or even the decisions of a despot, may attain at least as high a degree of predictability. Thus the peculiar rationality of an abstract system of regulation cannot lie simply in the predictability of its decisions.

The other feature of such a system that Weber emphasised is its 'impersonality'. An abstract system of regulation not only makes it possible to anticipate with some degree of accuracy the consequences of a particular action, but it also applies to every individual without regard to their personal characteristics or social status. However, there is nothing inherently rational about such a system. Indeed Weber recognised that the abstract character of the system implied that it would be 'substantively irrational', for the fact that the same set of rules applied regardless of personal circumstances meant that the substantive consequences of those rules would differ from person to person: freedom of contract was the freedom of the capitalist to appropriate surplus value and the freedom of the worker to submit to the direction of the capitalist; the same freedom is the freedom for the enrichment of the one and the enslavement of the other. The application of the abstract principle of equality before the law in an unequal society is a means and a condition for the reproduction of that inequality. This may be rational for the rich, but its rationality for the poor is by no means obvious!

Weber was undoubtedly correct to argue that monetary calculation, formal law and bureaucratic domination could not be identified completely with capitalism, so that instrumental rationality could not be referred to the interests of a particular class. Monetary calculation, formal legal systems and bureaucratic domination long preceded the development of modern capitalism, and arise in societies and in areas of social life that apparently have little or no connection with capitalist economic forms. However, they do seem to be closely associated with the development of commercial and money capital, on the basis of the growth of commodity production, which are phenomena that are historically very much older, and geographically far more widespread, than capitalist forms of production.

More importantly, it is their association with the competitive regulation of economic activity, which only comes to fruition with the development of modern capitalism, that marks these impersonal forms of regulation as 'rational' in comparison with any alternative forms. This is quite simply because the competitive regulation of economic activity requires the freedom of action from particularistic legal, political and religious constraints. The decisions of legal, political and religious authorities will have economic implications. Competitive regulation requires that these implications should be not only predictable, but that they do not favour one branch of economic activity or one actor against another. However this immediately implies that the 'rationality' of abstract forms of legal, political and hierocratic regulation is not derived from the subjective rationality of individual actors, since each individual would prefer to secure preferential treatment, while all others are subject to anonymous regulation. Nor is this rationality inherent in the characteristic legal, political and religious ends pursued, for it is often antithetical to such substantive legal, political and religious considerations as 'justice', 'power' or 'salvation'. The rationality of these abstract and impersonal forms of regulation can only be derived from the objective rationality of competitive forms of economic regulation. Abstract forms of regulation are 'rational', and their rationality is 'formal', because they do not have substantive implications for the outcome of the competitive process, and so do not undermine the rationality inherent in the latter. Thus we find ourselves back with the marginalists' characterisation of the abstract rationality of capitalism as the foundation of the general principle of rationality, not merely as one of its manifestations. Weber's 'formal rationality', as the subjective orientation to action typical of modern society, reduces to the marginalists' 'economic rationality', as the objective characteristic of capitalist economic institutions.

The same might be argued of religious belief. Weber recognised that it is not possible to characterise any system of belief as inherently more rational than any other. Thus the this-worldly asceticism of Calvinism, that is the defining characteristic of the Protestant ethic, is not in itself any more rational than alternative systems of religious belief. What gives particular sorts of religious belief a privileged rationality within Weber's scheme is not their inherent qualities, but the fact that they do not impede, or that they actually promote, the development of economic, legal and bureaucratic rationality, in short the development of capitalism. Thus the Protestant ethic may be very rational in a capitalist society, since hard work and frugality are the necessary qualities of a good wage-labourer, while savings and the reinvestment of profits are the key to survival as a capitalist. But it is only within an emerging capitalist society, in which the accumulation of the products of labour becomes the basis of social production and the means to the accumulation of wealth, that the 'this-wordly asceticism' of the Protestant ethic furthers the development of the social relations of capitalist production. In a different kind of society hard work and frugality would lead merely to the accumulation of useless things, which may be devoted to the glorification of God or the relief of the poor, but which would have no other social significance. In themselves the Protestant ethic, formal law and bureaucratic domination are no more rational than any other forms. It is only their privileged relationship to capitalist economic rationality that makes their designation as 'rational' an appropriate one.

We have to conclude that bureaucratic, legal, religious and economic rationality are not independent manifestations of a purely formal principle of rationality. The rationality of the first three is conditional on the rationality of the last one. Thus the characterisation of the institutions and social relations of capitalist society as being rational depends on the characterisation of the rationality of economic action in a capitalist society.

Weber identified the 'formal rationality' of rational economic action with the possibility and extent of money calculation. From this he derived the rationality of the fundamental institutions of capitalist society: the generalisation of commodity production and exchange, the separation of the labourer from the means of production, the separation of the household from the productive enterprise, the separation of ownership from control of the means of production, the development of the joint-stock company, the credit system, etc., are all rational developments because they extend the scope of money calculation. The question we have to ask is in what sense is money calculation especially rational? Can its rationality be defined in purely formal terms, or does it depend on the presupposition of the substantive rationality of capitalist social relations? Is capitalism the expression of the rationality of economic action, or is money calculation simply the form of economic rationality appropriate to capitalism? Does capitalism express the development of economic rationality, or does economic rationality express the development of capitalism?

Economic action is rational when it involves an instrumentally rational orientation to the satisfaction of a desire for utilities. To what extent is monetary calculation a condition of such rationality? Weber asserted that monetary calculation on the part of the budgetary unit was more rational than calculation in kind because of the reliance of the latter on the subjective evaluation of advantages which made it impossible to quantify alternatives objectively. This fundamental argument is fallacious, and almost trivially so in view of Weber's conception of sociology.

Calculations in kind undoubtedly involve the subjective evaluation of the benefits that flow from alternative dispositions of resources, but this is no less true of monetary calculations. In the latter case the budgetary unit has to decide how much of each available good to sell and how much of each good offered on the market to buy at prevailing market prices. Money is the means of comparison, but what is being compared is the subjective evaluation of alternative courses of action on the basis of anticipated marginal contributions to utility in each case. Since subjective evaluation is the defining characteristic of action for Weber, calculation in money is a no more rational means of allocating resources in accordance with considerations of utility than is calculation in kind.

Money calculation cannot be characterised as peculiarly rational on the basis of the value-orientation of individual action, but only on the basis of the supposedly superior rationality of monetary prices over subjective evaluations of utility. In other words the supposed rationality of monetary calculation has nothing to do with its *subjective* rationality, but derives from the supposed *objective* rationality of the market through which monetary prices are determined. Thus the supposed 'formal rationality' of monetary accounting presupposes the substantive rationality of capitalism as a means of satisfying human wants and meeting human needs.

When we turn to the profit-making enterprise the situation is different, but this is definitionally the case since the profit-making enterprise is defined by an orientation not to utilities but to profit, an objective quantitative difference between income and expenditure. In this case monetary calculation is the appropriate form of rational economic action not because of the particular rationality of money calculation, but because of the substantive orientation of action to profit. The rationality of monetary calculation in this case is simply an expression of the rationality of the profit-making enterprise, and so again presupposes the substantive rationality of capitalist economic institutions.

In neither of these cases can the rationality of monetary calculation be characterised in terms of a peculiarly rational value-orientation of action. The rationality of monetary calculation cannot be reduced to the subjectively rational orientation of action, but can only be established as an expression of the objective rationality of the market and of the profit-making enterprise as means for the provision of human needs: monetary calculation can only be *subjectively* rational to the extent that it provides an *objectively* more rational means of achieving given economic ends.

The coherence of Weber's sociology rests on the validity of the economists' demonstration of the *objective* economic rationality of the capitalist economic system, a demonstration whose validity Weber took for granted, but one which accords neither with reason nor with experience. Weber only avoids the inevitable conclusions by adopting the economists' designation of this objective rationality as purely *formal*, with no substantive implications and so with no evaluative significance. However, as I have argued at length above, this designation rests on the illegitimate abstraction of the economic institutions

The typology of action and the theory of society 283

of capitalist society from the social relations within which they are necessarily inscribed: on the abstraction of exchange relations from the social relations of production and distribution; on the abstraction of the life of the commodity from the life of the commodity owner; on the abstraction of the state of perfect equilibrium from the conditions of ignorance and uncertainty in which economic decisions are made; on the abstraction of economic relations from consideration of the social power inherent in such relations; in short, the abstraction of an ideal world of the 'economy' from the reality of 'society', and in this sense on the 'naturalisation' of economic relationships. It is only on this basis, which forcibly abstracts consideration of formal economic relationships from consideration of their substantive material and social implications, that the rationality of the capitalist economy can be designated as a purely 'formal' rationality. Correspondingly the distinction between the 'formal rationality' of capitalism and its 'substantive irrationality' does not express a dilemma inherent in capitalism, between its supposed economic efficiency and its undoubted social injustice, but a dilemma constructed by the liberal social theorist, between her ideal justification of capitalist society and everyday reality.

Weber's sociology, like marginalist economics, rested on the abstraction of the social actor from the social relations within which she was inserted in taking the ends and value-orientations of action as the given starting point of sociology. We saw in the last chapter that the marginalist characterisation of the abstract individual presupposed the social relations of production within which the individual was inserted, which appeared in a fetishised form in the needs and resources attributed to the individual economic actor. In the same way we have now seen that Weber's characterisation of both the ends and the value-orientations of action presupposes the social relations within which the individual is inserted, and to which action is oriented, a presupposition which is concealed by Weber's implicit reference to the 'naturalisation' of social relations of marginalist economics, so that the mutable social constraints, which define the limits of the subjective rationality of 'formally rational' economic action, are fetishised as immutable natural and technological constraints, and the contradictions of capitalism appear as the unavoidable fate of humanity.

The immediate implication is that the rationalisation of European society, of which the development of capitalism is for Weber only one aspect, cannot be seen as a generalised change in the value-orientation of action in the direction of a purely formal rationality, even if, as in Weber's sociology, this rationality is not given an absolute value. The 'rationality' of capitalism is not merely historically specific, it is bounded by the social forms of production and reproduction characteristic of a particular form of society, outside of which such a value-orientation would be profoundly irrational.[2] If it is to be seen as a rational process it can only be seen as the process through which the particularistic and traditionalistic barriers to the development of the social relations of capitalist production are swept away. Weber's attempt to conceptualise the coherence of capitalist society, to explain how law, the state and religious belief just happen to take on forms appropriate to rational economic action, leads back to the economic reductionism that Weber sought to avoid.

As I have already noted in relation to the 'rationality' of political legal, and religious action, where Weber simply took the existence of a state, a church, and an intellectual and cultural environment as historically given, Weber only avoids confronting the dilemma with which he had presented sociology by falling back on an historicist empiricism at this critical point. Weber recognised that the 'formal rationality' of capitalism was compromised by its 'substantive irrationality'. He recognised that the institutional domination of this formal rationality corresponded to the interests of a particular class. He recognised that the peculiar rationality of 'formally rational' forms of legal and political domination lay in their relationship to the capitalist economy. He recognised that the historical birth of capitalism was marked not so much by the advance of reason as by pervasive class violence. All these considerations would appear to undermine his typology of ends and value-orientations, which attributes primacy to the principles of 'formal rationality' over its particular expressions, and which purports to establish the autonomy of distinctive value-spheres. However Weber does not draw this conclusion, because his

---

[2] This is as true of the orientation of the capitalist as of anybody else: capitalist enterprise is only rational on the basis of an appropriate development of the forces and social relations of production. Thus it is not sufficient to replace the term 'instrumental rationality' by the term 'capitalist rationality' to salvage Weber's sociology as, for example, Marcuse (1965) tends to do, since the rationality of such a value-orientation cannot be referred to a class interest without referring also to the social relations which such an interest expresses. Thus the development of capitalism cannot be explained as the consequence of the development of any kind of rationality, whether it be 'formal' or 'capitalist', but only in terms of the historical development of the social relations of production.

methodological insistence that his 'ideal-types' are purely hypothetical constructs, which do not make any knowledge-claims, renders these ideal-types immune from rational criticism.

For Weber sociological understanding had to take actually existing society as its given starting point, and could only achieve an interpretative understanding of action within that given framework. Thus Weber severely limited the explanatory power of sociology (and of economics) in making it into a discipline that merely elaborated a typology that could provide the basis for the only valid form of knowledge, that of the historical interpretation of meaningful action. Sociology cannot explain either the ends that actors set for themselves, the values that orient those ends or the social relations within which action takes place. All that it can do is to elaborate the hypothetical consequences of action on the basis of those ends, values and social relations, achieving an interpretative account of the subjective aspect of the reproduction and transformation of economic, social and cultural relations.

Weber's empiricism, which confines sociology to the interpretative understanding of the superficial forms of appearance of social relations, explains the strong streak of irrationalism running through his sociology, for the ultimate foundations of social action are not amenable to rational explanation. The subjective orientation of action is ultimately arbitrary and the choice of particular ends and value-orientations irrational. Whereas for Menger organic social institutions developed through the collective emulation of individual initiatives based on a recognition of the rationality of the innovation, for Weber rationality was itself not an ultimate value, and so could not provide the ultimate basis of sociological explanation. The development of the economy and society was not the development of a universal reason, for capitalism was rational only from one point of view, that of formal rationality.

This irrationalism explains the pivotal role of the concept of *charisma* in Weber's sociology. The ultimate basis of social change is changes in the system of values underlying social action. The need for such changes arises to the extent that existing values do not provide a completely coherent image of the world as a meaningful whole. However, changes in values cannot be explained in terms of the subjective rational evaluation of alternative sets of values, on the basis, for example, of class interests, since interests are not defined independently of the view of the world in which they are embedded.

Thus, while there may be an 'elective affinity' between the values ultimately adopted and the interests of those adopting them, there are no rational grounds for adopting or modifying a particular set of values in the first place. The conclusion is that the adoption of new values can only be explained in terms of their irrational appeal. It is this irrational appeal, often attached to the personality of the proponent of the new values, which is captured in Weber's concept of charisma. New values are constantly emerging, but the generalisation of normative innovations cannot be a process of rational emulation, but only of the irrational substitution of one set of beliefs for another. Thus new values only become a significant social force when they are proposed by a personality who attracts a following on the basis of her charismatic appeal. When this following acquires a critical mass it is given an institutional form. It is through this 'routinisation of charisma' that the new values acquire an institutional permanence and authority which facilitates the generalisation of their appeal.

Capitalist rationality and the dilemmas of modernity

For Weber, the rationality of capitalism consists in the increasing subordination of economic activity to the single-minded pursuit of economic ends, but this development is profoundly irrational from other than a narrowly materialistic point of view. The substantive irrationality of capitalism is not simply a matter of Weber's own personal judgement, but of the values embedded in other spheres of social life, and in particular in politics and religion. Weber's diagnosis of the substantive irrationality of modern society is complex, and notoriously ambiguous. In this section I can do no more than outline what appear to be its fundamental principles before indicating the problem which it defines for sociology.

Weber recognised that the substantive irrationality of capitalism is the necessary and inevitable accompaniment to the generalisation of the 'formal rationality' that characterises the capitalist economy. However for Weber such irrationality is not the result of *capitalism*, but of the wider process of rationalisation, as the defining feature of modernity, of which capitalist economic rationality is only one aspect. This rationalisation, following the logic of the division of labour, involves the radical separation of different spheres of social life, according to the typical ends pursued, and the rational adaptation of means to ends in each of those spheres. Thus the economic, political and religious spheres, as well as art, music, literature, science, the erotic, etc., each acquire a relative autonomy from one another, as the condition for the single-minded pursuit of their characteristic ends. Within each of these spheres taken separately means are rationally adapted to ends.

This fragmentation of social life comes into conflict with the essential unity of society, both objectively and subjectively. Objectively, as we have seen, economic action has political and religious implications, so that the single-minded pursuit of economic ends comes into conflict with the pursuit of political and religious ends, while the dominance of economic and bureaucratic rationality is a barrier to the attempt to achieve substantive ethical ends, particularly on the part of the poor and the powerless. Subjectively, the fragmentation of experience leads to a fundamental incoherence at the heart of the modern personality, which comes into conflict with the need to develop a coherent view of the world. The substantive irrationality of modern society has its foundations in this fragmentation and incoherence of the system of values.

The original impetus towards the rationalisation of modern society lay in the emergence of a coherently rationalist world-view. However, the rationalisation of society soon acquires its own momentum. The fragmentation of modern society, and the rationalisation of its separate spheres, constitutes an 'iron cage' which imposes a formally rational orientation to action on its participants in each relatively autonomous sphere. Thus market competition imposes rational behaviour on every participant in economic life: the capitalist can only remain a capitalist if he subordinates his activity to the goal of profit maximisation. If he runs his firm on the basis of principles of brotherly love he will soon go bust. Similarly the worker has to subordinate herself to the work ethic, and rationally calculate her household budget in order to make the most of her scarce resources. The bureaucrat is similarly constrained by bureaucratic rules and procedures to conduct her business in accordance with the canons of bureaucratic rationality, and those subject to the rules have to calculate their consequences.

Within a capitalist society the anonymous rule of the market and inequalities of wealth tend to secure the dominance of the economic sphere, so that value conflicts tend to be resolved in favour of economic rationality. Political and hierocratic organisations, writers, artists and intellectuals, have to have as much regard to their economic viability as does the capitalist enterprise, while the power and patronage of the rich helps them to secure the dominance of their interests in all social spheres. However socialism, far from resolving the contradiction between the formal rationality and the substantive irrationality of modern society, threatens to develop this contradiction to its ultimate limits in supplanting the dominance of economic rationality by the dominance of bureaucratic rationality, sacrificing the economic rationality and relative political freedom of capitalism for the ultimate nightmare of a totalitarian bureaucratic tyranny.

The contradiction between the formal rationality and the substantive irrationality of modern society cannot be overcome through the dominance of one form of rationality, embedded in one sphere of social life, over all others, but only by developing some means of resolving value conflicts on the basis of a coherent system of overarching values. The dilemma is that for Weber the fragmentation of social life makes it increasingly difficult to sustain any coherent view of the social world as a whole, let alone to reshape the world in accordance with such a view, and equally makes it very difficult to develop a shared view of the world, which can unite significant social groupings. Weber tended to follow the logic of his argument to take a pessimistic view of humanity's tragic fate, leaving the individual to scrabble in the ruins to construct a personal meaning as best she may. The only possibility of salvation lay in the emergence of a charismatic figure, who could provide moral and political leadership on the basis of a coherent world view. The ultimate tragedy is that this diagnosis led Weber to promote the inclusion of the clause in the Weimar constitution which permitted Hitler to come to power as just such a figure a decade after Weber's death.

Weber offered an acute, and extremely influential diagnosis of the contradictions of modernity, the only such diagnosis which stands comparison with that of Marx in recognising that the 'substantive irrationality' of modern society is not simply a pathological deformation of a rational normality, but is inherent in the process of 'rationalisation'. Weber recognised that the contradiction between the 'formal rationality' of modern society and its 'substantive irrationality' is not simply a matter of an arbitrary subjective evaluation, but is an objective feature of modern society, expressed in the conflict between systems of values, and within the individual personality, which has objective historical consequences. But unlike Marx, Weber could not get to the roots of this contradiction in the alienated forms of social

Capitalist rationality and the dilemmas of modernity

labour because he saw such forms of labour as rational. Thus he remained trapped within a dualistic theory of capitalist society in which the individual subject confronts an objective social world which is indifferent to meaning and impervious to action, whose objectivity is defined *functionally*, in relation to ends which have become detached from their individual foundations and embedded in the social structure.

Weber's diagnosis of the contradictions of modernity is a mystification of the fundamental contradictions of the capitalist mode of production, but it remains a very powerful diagnosis because it is a very acute expression of the forms in which those contradictions appear to experience. Weber's misanthropic and pessimistic fatalism reflected the circumstances of time and place, and of the cultural and intellectual milieu in which he wrote, so that his own solution was hardly supportive of the liberal project. Nevertheless he defined the dilemmas confronting liberalism in the wake of the marginalist revolution in economics, dilemmas which any rigorous liberal sociology would have to resolve.

The central problem was a simple one: how to define sociology as a discipline which is both critical of marginalist economics, in establishing the socio-historical limits of economic rationality, while at the same time recognising the limits to sociology embodied in the liberal principles of individual rationality expressed in the economic theories of marginalism. This theoretical problem expressed the fundamental dilemma of modern liberalism: is it possible to formulate a critique of the inhumanity of modern capitalism on the basis of precisely those liberal principles of which modern capitalism is the expression and the result? It is because Weber was acutely aware that there were no simple solutions to this simple problem that he could define the dilemmas confronting sociology so acutely.

9

Marx, Marginalism and Modern Sociology

The antinomies of sociology and the dilemma of liberalism

We are now in a position to return to the question posed in the first chapter of the character and scientific status of the reorientation of social thought that took place at the end of the nineteenth-century. There is little doubt that such a reorientation did in fact take place, and that this reorientation did not simply involve a change in a number of elements of a given system. It involved a fundamental change in the 'structure of the theoretical system' (Parsons, 1949, p. 7). According to Parsons this change was marked by the substantive advance represented by the emergence of a voluntaristic theory of action out of the convergence of the earlier positivistic and idealistic theories of action. However, I hope to have shown in the course of this book that the development of marginalism and of Weberian sociology was not marked by such a substantive scientific revolution. The substantive foundation of marginalism and of Weber's sociology continues to be the naturalistic conception of the social relations of production of capitalist society that characterised nineteenth-century classical political economy, vulgar economy, sociology and historicism. The end of the nineteenth-century saw a reorientation of social thought, not a scientific revolution. In Parsonian terms this reorientation was marked by a reformulation of the relationship between the theory of action and the theory of social structure.

Classical political economy, Comtean sociology and German historicism developed their theories as theories of social structure. Political economy was particularly concerned with the economic structure of capitalist society, while sociology and historicism superimposed on this economic structure a concern with capitalist moral and political institutions. The economy, morality and the state were treated for theoretical purposes as *sui generis* realities, whose development was ideally regulated by the structural laws of economic, moral and political evolution.

Although formulated as theories of social structure, political economy, sociology and historicism shared a liberal social and political orientation, seeing capitalist society as an expression of the needs and aspirations of rational individuals, and evaluated the institutions of capitalist society in relation to individual rationality. This did not mean that these theories were formulated on the basis of a rationalistic theory of action, whether positivistic or idealistic, for the theories were not formulated at the level of the theory of action. The rational individual who underpinned and legitimated the social structure characterised by the theory was not a real but an ideal individual. The conformity of the social structure with individual needs and aspirations was not conceptualised directly, by revealing the origins of social institutions in the actions of real individuals, and establishing the adequacy of those institutions to the individuals' needs and aspirations. Rather the rationality of the social structure in question was explained in terms of its results, by showing that those results conformed objectively to the abstractly defined needs and aspirations of the ideal rational individual.

The achievement of the ideal society could not be entrusted to the spontaneous advance of individual reason, for the existence of ignorance, vanity, prejudice, superstition and the abuse of power were barriers to its realisation. Thus the progressive development of society depended on the subordination of the action of individuals to the reproduction of the social structure within which they were inserted. For classical political economy this implied the subordination of the individual, the state and civil society to the market through which the classical economic laws would spontaneously impose a harmonious social order. For sociology and historicism the market alone was not an adequate basis for the realisation of a rational and harmonious social order, and the operation of the market had to be confined within limits set by morality and by the state. In each case, however, the social structure to whose reproduction individuals were subordinated was defined by the social relations of capitalist production, and the ideal rationality of society was an expression of the naturalistic rationality of capitalist relations of production as the necessary expression of the division of labour. It is this common naturalisation of the social constraints imposed by capitalist social relations that defines the common ideological foundations of all these theories of capitalist society.

It is important to stress the liberalism of these nineteenth century theories, despite the fact that this liberalism was abstract. Thus the subordination of the individual to the reproduction of the social structure was not seen as the imposition of an alien authority on the individual, but as the imposition of an authority adequate to the true needs and aspirations of the individual. Thus, to the extent that individuals were enlightened by the appropriate doctrines, and so appreciated the rationality of the ideal social order, they would submit themselves voluntarily to the authority of the market, the enlightened legislator and the moral reformer.

The viability of this abstract liberalism, and correspondingly the viability of its abstract social theories, rested on the viability of the constitutional arrangements through which the beneficent rule of capital could be enforced for the benefit of all. It was the growing reluctance of the organised working class to submit to such rule, and its insistence on being admitted to the constitution on its own terms, that undermined not only the paternalistic rule of capital, but also the social theories that expressed this rule in the form of an abstract liberalism that subordinated real individuals to an ideal rationality. As the rationality of capitalism faced a growing intellectual, moral and political challenge, the rationalist critique of capitalism passed from the hands of liberalism into those of socialism. If liberal reformism was to distinguish itself from socialism it had to re-evaluate its own foundations.

The reorientation of social thought at the turn of the century revolved around the marginalist revolution in economics. Marginalism was based on a rejection of the classical theory of distribution, associated with the theory of class, on the basis of which classical political economy had developed its economic laws, in favour of a rigorously individualistic theory of the capitalist economy, based on the classical theories of production and exchange, but reformulated within the framework of the theory of action. Classical political economy had centred its analysis on production, and established the ideal rationality of capitalist relations of distribution and exchange in terms of their conformity with the requirements of the expanded reproduction of the system of production. Marginalist economics centred its analysis on the individual allocating scarce resources to alternative uses. For classical political economy the individual actor was passive, playing a mediating role in the expanded reproduction of the system, subordinated by relations of distribution and exchange to the requirements

The antinomies of sociology and the dilemma of liberalism

of that reproduction. Thus the theory of action was subordinate to the theory of social structure. For marginalism, by contrast, the economic actor was the subject of the capitalist system of production, distribution and exchange, which was analysed as the means by which the allocation of resources could be optimally achieved on the basis of given preferences and a given initial distribution. Thus for marginalism the theory of social structure was developed on the basis of the theory of action. This made it possible to reconstitute social theory on a rigorously individualistic foundation, which sought to provide a coherent foundation for a critique of all forms of utopianism on the basis of a pragmatic liberal reformism.

The development of marginalism introduced significant changes of emphasis in the understanding of capitalist society. Where classical political economy centred its analysis on questions of growth and distribution, marginalism centred its analysis on questions of allocation and exchange. Where classical political economy justified capitalism on the basis of its development of the forces of production, marginalism justified it on the basis of its allocative efficiency. Where classical political economy developed its laws of distribution on the basis of the natural laws of population and agricultural productivity, marginalism justified distribution relations in terms of the productive contributions of the appropriate factors of production. However marginalism remained on essentially the same ideological foundations as its predecessors, those foundations being defined by the naturalisation of capitalist relations of production.

Indeed marginalism, in rejecting the classical theory of class, abandoned precisely that element of classical political economy that contained within it the possibility of recognising that capitalism rests not on the rational adaptation of society to its natural foundations, but arises on the basis of historically specific social relations of production. Thus marginalism completed the naturalisation of capitalist social relations by narrowing the scope of economics, in assigning the analysis of distribution to complementary sociological and historical disciplines, whilst broadening its ambition, in seeking to analyse the conditions for the optimal allocation of resources appropriate to any society. The development of marginalist economics, far from representing a scientific revolution, removed from political economy its most promising elements to achieve an ideological reformulation of political economy appropriate to the economic and political maturation of capitalist society.

Nineteenth century sociology and historicism developed in opposition to classical political economy, but I have argued that they rested on common ideological foundations. We find the same relation of complementarity between marginalist economics and modern sociology. However, whereas nineteenth-century sociology and historicism had to oppose the absolutist claims of political economy, marginalism created a space within which economics and sociology could coexist as complementary disciplines. Economic theory is an abstract deductive science that establishes the ideal rationality of the fundamental economic institutions and social relations of capitalist society. *Social economics* was the complementary discipline that would study the contingent institutional barriers that impeded the realisation of the ideal rationality of capitalist economic relations. The practical and theoretical task of social economics was to make capitalism adequate to its own rhetoric. Its ideological function was to locate the irrationality of actually existing capitalism at a lower level of abstraction than its rationality, as defined by economic theory.

Social economics was essentially an empirical discipline, deriving its concepts from economic theory and measuring reality against the ideal established by the marginalist theory. However the marginalist theory also created the space within which sociology could develop a broader critique. The framework within which such a sociology could develop was that of the theory of action. The concepts of economic theory, and the concept of *economic power* that was the single theoretical contribution of social economics, were elaborated on the basis of the abstract model of the rational economic actor. Consideration of other ends and of other value-orientations of action provided a basis on which other forms of social action could be conceptualised. Moreover the economists' rational economic actor was an abstract concept, whose appropriateness depended on the dominance of a rational orientation to economic ends in actually existing society. Thus sociology had also to explore the socio-historical circumstances under which such an orientation was in fact predominant. On the basis of the *voluntaristic theory of action* sociology could locate both itself and economics as complementary social sciences.

It was Weber who most rigorously articulated a systematic foundation on which sociology could develop as an autonomous branch of the social sciences. Weber was able to do this because he rejected the primacy accorded by the economists to economic rationality as an ethical ideal, insisting that political, religious, moral or aesthetic criteria provided just as valid a basis for evaluation, and correspondingly provided just as valid an orientation of social action.

Sociology could become an autonomous discipline because it would study forms of social action that could not be comprehended by economics: it could embrace all those phenomena that could not be reduced by the *dogma of self-interest*. In this sense it was Weber who developed the conceptual foundations for both modern economics and modern sociology. These foundations were classically elaborated in the 1930s for modern economics by Lionel Robbins in *An Essay on the Nature and Significance of Economic Science* and for modern sociology by Talcott Parsons in *The Structure of Social Action*. However, it was only with the economic, social, political and *intellectual* reconstruction of the capitalist world after the Second World War, a reconstruction motivated above all by the concern to find a place for the working class within a liberal economic and political world system, that the older traditions were finally swept away, the social sciences constituted on unequivocally liberal foundations, and the intellectual division of labour between 'economics' and 'sociology' rigorously institutionalised.

Despite the fact that modern sociology has developed in opposition to the naturalistic rationalism of marginalist economics, it nevertheless rests on the same ideological foundations. These ideological foundations are not necessarily formulated explicitly, for the intellectual division of labour that separates sociology from economics and assigns the task of analysis of the social relations of capitalist production to economics, establishes the ideological foundations of sociology outside its own domain. Thus Weber, although consistently critical of the naturalism of marginalist economics, nevertheless presupposed the marginalist naturalisation of capitalist social relations in taking the abstract individual as his starting point and in identifying the defining characteristic of capitalist society as the rational value-orientation of that individual. The ideological foundation of modern sociology, in the naturalistic conception of the economy developed by marginalist economics, is necessarily implicit in the definition of the object of sociology, 'society', as distinct from the object of economics, the 'economy', which establishes both the character and the limits of sociological explanation.

It is important to stress that the distinction between 'economy' and 'society', and the corresponding division of labour between economics and sociology, so taken for granted today, is a modern invention, whose general acceptance and academic institutionalisation, in its modern form, only dates back to the 1940s. It is a distinction that was forged by the marginalists in opposition to the overweening ambition of the sociological and historicist critics of political economy, for whom economics would merely be 'a congeries of miscellaneous disconnected facts, or else it must fall in as one branch of Mr Spencer's sociology'. Against this the marginalists insisted that *'there must arise a science of the development of economic forms and relations'* (Jevons, 1970, p. 49) . It was on the basis of the development of this abstract science, and of the recognition that such a science 'must be interpreted as the formulation of the relations of a limited group of analytical elements in the broader concrete system of action' (Parsons, 1949, p. 757), that the intellectual division of labour between economics and sociology was worked out.

The distinction between economy and society is not an empirical distinction, but a conceptual one, resting on the conceptual distinction between the essential rationality of capitalism and its social reality, a distinction that in turn rests on the definition of economic relations as essentially asocial, concerning not relations between people, but relations of subjective evaluation of things by abstract individuals, mediated by the technical relations of production and the formal relations of exchange. The definition of the nature and significance not only of modern economics, but also of modern sociology, depends on the legitimacy of the economists' abstraction of social actors from their social and historical context, an abstraction that is based on the definition of economics not as the science of a particular set of social relations, but of a particular orientation of action, 'the science which studies the processes of rational acquisition of scarce means to the actor's ends by production and economic exchange, and of their rational allocation as between alternative uses' (Parsons, 1949, p. 266).

Sociology is not necessarily content to occupy the space allocated to it by marginalist economics. However, as we have seen in the case of Weber's sociology, the sociological critique of the narrow economic rationalism of marginalist economics cuts the ground from under its own feet. This presents any critical sociology with an acute dilemma, which appears in the irreconcilability of the voluntarism of the theory of action, that defines the autonomy of sociology, with the implicit naturalism of the theory of social structure on which it ultimately rests.

The antinomies of sociology and the dilemma of liberalism

Although sociology can define its object and formulate its methodology within the framework of the theory of action, the theory of action cannot provide the ultimate foundation of sociological explanation. The theory of action abstracts the individual from the social relations within which alone she exists as a social individual. Thus a formal sociology, like that of Simmel, which seeks to explain social relations as the product of the subjective orientation of action, can never achieve such an explanation, since any such explanation presupposes a substantive context for social action which is defined by the very social relations that the reference to action purports to explain. On the other hand, the theory equally abstracts these social relations from the action of individuals, through which alone they are reproduced and transformed. The result is that a 'structural' sociology ends up referring the explanation of the social relations of capitalist production to the functional requirements of their own reproduction, a circularity which is only broken by the marginalist 'naturalisation' of capitalist social relations, as the rational expression of the natural and technological conditions of social existence.

This dilemma pervaded Weber's sociology, but it was not of Weber's making: it is the constitutive and irresoluble liberal dilemma on which modern sociology is based. Weber evaded rather than resolved it by limiting the scope of sociology to the interpretative understanding of concrete social situations, and representing the dilemma as the inescapable fate of humanity.

Weber's liberal empiricism provides an attractive way out of the liberal dilemma. Weber's methodology of the ideal type even provides a means by which sociology can aspire to a degree of generality, giving a semblance of intellectual rigour to sociological empiricism. However the methodology of the ideal-type is unable to provide any rational foundation for the generalisations which it produces, because it provides no other grounds for the abstraction on which it is based than the empathic understanding of the motivation of the hypothetical actor. While most sociologists may be content to tell plausible stories, and to give such stories a spurious scientific authority by backing them up with statistical investigations, sociology cannot be content to take its object — social relations and social institutions — as given. These social relations and social institutions have a systematic social significance that it is the task of sociology to elucidate by elaborating the systematic connections between norms, values, social relations and social institutions. To evade the liberal dilemma is not to resolve it.

The liberal dilemma lies in the contradiction between the voluntaristic theory of action, which is the necessary basis of any liberal democratic theory that believes that a legitimate social order is compatible with the freedom of the individual property owner, and the naturalistic theory of social structure which defines the objective constraints which characterise such action as social. This dilemma defines the terms within which modern sociology has developed. However, the two poles of the contrast are not independent of one another. Rather they are constituted as complementary, but mutually exclusive, perspectives on society by the ideological abstraction of the individual, on the one hand, and nature, on the other, from the historically developed social relations of capitalist production which alone mediate the relation between the individual and nature and within which alone nature and the individual exist socially. Thus modern sociology is condemned to exist within a world defined by a series of abstract dualisms which reflect the inadequacy of its foundations but which nevertheless structure sociological debate: structure–action; object–subject; positivism–humanism; holism–individualism; society–individual; explanation–understanding; order–conflict; authority–consent. Through all the twists and turns of sophisticated theoretical debate the same themes constantly recur. It would be tedious to go through every 'original' thinker in detail. In the next sections I can only indicate the Achilles heel of modern sociology in the broadest outlines (c.f. Clarke, 1981).

The marginalist foundations of Parsonian functionalism

Weber fell back on a liberal empiricism because he was unable to resolve the dilemma with which he had confronted sociology. On the one hand, Weber explained the social relations and social institutions of capitalist society in terms of the generalised process of 'rationalisation', which was only the subjective expression of the naturalistic theory of capitalist social relations developed by marginalist economies. From this point of view a 'rational' value-orientation was imposed on society as the means of achieving economic and administrative efficiency. On the other hand, Weber insisted that such a 'rational' value-orientation was culturally and historically specific to Western civilisation, and undermined the 'substantive rationality' embodied in alternative value-orientations, which appealed to higher values, but which had no

The marginalist foundations of Parsonian functionalism

rational foundation. Thus Weber's sociology was caught between the naturalistic rationalism of marginalist economics and the romantic irrationalism of German idealist philosophy. To the extent that modern sociology has not simply evaded the Weberian dilemma by relapsing into a complacent empiricism, it has remained strung between these two poles. The rationalistic elements in Weber's sociology provided the basis of the Parsonian tradition, while the Frankfurt School of Critical Theory developed out of Weber's irrationalist critique of capitalism.

Paradoxically it was Parsons, who had acclaimed the voluntaristic theory of action as the basis of modern sociology, who assimilated sociology back into the naturalistic ideology of modern economics, drawing heavily on the organic evolutionism of nineteenth-century sociology, and in particular on the functionalism of Durkheim and, increasingly, of Spencer. In *The Structure of Social Action* Parsons had identified the roots of the crisis of contemporary liberalism, in the face of the threat of the authoritarian collectivisms of the left and the right, as lying in the restricted conception of the individual inherited from the liberal social theories of the nineteenth century. Parsons defined the task of sociology as nothing less than the salvation of liberalism, which was to be achieved on the basis of the sociological critique of marginalist economics pioneered, above all, by Weber, a critique which brought cultural values to the centre of the stage as the mediating link between individual and society. However Parsons argued that Weber's radical individualism prevented him from resolving the dilemma with which he had confronted sociology, of reconciling the constitutive role of the subject with the constraining character of social structures.

Parsons criticised Weber for failing to address the problem of order in failing to give any account of the processes by which the subjectivity of the social actor is reconciled with the objective constraints of social reproduction. From this point of view the central weakness of Weber's sociology lay in his belief that ends and values are historically contingent, and purely a matter of individual choice. For Parsons, by contrast, values are constituted socially, and articulated in cultural value-systems. It is the cultural value-system which mediates between the subjectivity of the individual and the objectivity of social structure. The adoption of values cannot be a matter of individual choice, because social individuals only exist through their incorporation into such value-systems. This incorporation is achieved through the socialisation of the child, and reproduced through mechanisms of social control.

Parsons developed his 'structural-functionalism' in response to the problem of explaining how the ends and value-orientations of action are so defined as to make possible the reproduction of the social relations within which actors exist and that structure the subjective orientation of action. Parsons distinguished between the universal generic properties of 'action systems' and the contingent forms of such systems in particular societies. On this basis he sought to establish a *generic* connection between the functional requirements of social reproduction and the characteristics of the system of norms and values which oriented social action, without postulating a necessary *genetic* connection between the two. This involved a cybernetic conception of the individual, society and nature, according to which each sub-system sought to secure its own harmonious integration and, through the hierarchical organisation of such systems, the integration of the system as whole. Thus the norms and values of society change as sources of strain, emerging particularly from developments in the economy which mediates the relation between humanity and nature, are transmitted, through the dislocation of the system of cultural values, to the individual personality, whose efforts to resolve the psychological tensions which arise leads to changes in norms and values which secure the re-integration of the system as a whole. In this way Parsons believed that he had resolved the 'problem of order' on a reconstituted liberal foundation. Social integration was maintained by a cultural system which was not enforced by an authoritarian state or church, but by the self-regulation of the individual personality within the social community. Values are neither imposed on the individual by society, nor are they freely adopted by the atomic individual, they develop within society as an inter-subjective realm of cultural communication. From the Parsonian viewpoint Weber's pessimism expressed his lack of faith in the possibility that a pluralistic liberal democratic society could provide the institutional framework within which a normative consensus could reconcile social reproduction with individual aspirations.

Parsons's elaborate schemata only resolved the problem of order by shifting it to the cultural level, and turning it into a tautology. His postulated universals transposed the objective 'problem of order' into a subjective problem, in defining the generic properties of action systems in terms of the normative requirements imposed by the need to resolve the problem of order. An orderly and well-integrated society was therefore one in which social institutions were adapted to both the objective and subjective conditions of social order, the reconcilability of which was guaranteed by the supposedly universal properties of action.

Within Parsons's action frame of reference economics was attributed its place as the theory appropriate to a particular sub-system of the social system, defined in relation to the 'adaptive' function of the system of action, while sociology, political science and psychology provide theories appropriate to the other functions of 'goal-attainment', 'integration' and 'latent pattern-maintenance'. However the apparent subordination of economics to sociology, in the form of the general theory of action, is only superficial, for the general theory of action is itself based on the generalisation of the theory and methods of marginalist economics. Thus the universals of the general theory of action are defined in relation to the universal constraints of nature and technology, which are the only objective constraints on social action and the only non-arbitrary source of social and cultural change. These constraints ultimately express the functional imperatives defined by the marginalists' naturalistic conception of the social relations of capitalist production, while the possibility of normative consensus is defined by the economists' characterisation of the rationality of the economic institutions of a capitalist society. In this way Parsons extended the marginalist naturalisation of capitalist social relations from the sphere of the economy to that of society, treating the state, religion, the family and the personality as rational expressions of the natural and technological conditions of existence of industrial society. In so doing Parsons undermined the hard-won autonomy of sociology by subordinating the interpretation of social action to the supposedly objective requirements of social reproduction.

Structure and action in 'Post-Parsonian' Sociology

Parsons sought to resolve the Weberian dilemma by adopting Durkheim's conception of society as a transcendental moral order which mediates between the subjectivity of the individual personality and the objectivity of nature and of technology. Within the Parsonian framework the conflict between the aspirations of the individual and the normative expectations of society is only an index of a failure of integration of the sub-systems which comprise society as a cultural order. However the source of this failure may lie on the side of the normative expectations of society, or it may lie on the side of the aspirations of the individual. How is Parsons to decide whether social conflict is the result of a lack of integration between particular cultural sub-systems, or whether it is the result of a failure of socialisation and social control? Is socialism a personality disorder, or does it express a conflict between the values of equality, justice and freedom, embedded in civil society and expressed through the political system, and the reality of economic exploitation? And how is this conflict to be resolved? Is it to be left to the spontaneous development of society, with the risk that psycho-pathological disorders will infect the system as a whole, leading to further disintegration? Or is it to be resolved by the state, with the risk that necessary social reforms will be blocked by escalating repression?

At its most abstract level Parsons's schema offers no answer to such questions, precisely because there is no principled means of establishing the boundary between the voluntarism of action and the constraint of structure. In Parsons' own elaboration of his system the answer is clear: the instrumental rationality of the economic institutions of capitalist society give them an absolute status to which all the other sub-systems of society have ultimately to adjust. To the extent that the other sub-systems are not functionally adapted to the reproduction of the economic sub-system, the appropriate response to social conflict is social reform. To the extent that such an adjustment has been achieved, the appropriate response to social conflict is psycho-therapy and socio-therapy. The agency which determines and implements the appropriate response is the democratic state, but this only raises the question of the character and limits of the legitimacy of the state. For Parsons the legitimacy of the state derives from the formation of a normative consensus within a formally democratic and pluralistic political system. However this makes the state the foundation of its own legitimacy, which violates the most fundamental principles of liberalism.

Parsons's sociological enterprise provided a powerful ideological underpinning for the project of restoring a liberal democratic capitalism on a world scale in the wake of World War II, and a celebration of the liberal democratic optimism of the Eisenhower era. However, the persistence of social, political and cultural conflict cast a growing shadow over Parsons's complacent optimism, and in particular brought the limits of his liberalism to the fore. Within Parsons's system the role of subjectivity was strictly circumscribed by the functional need to resolve the problem of order, and the resources available to the subject to resolve that problem were limited to those provided by the cultural system. Parsons had only resolved the problem of order by abolishing the integrity of the subject.

Despite the inadequacy of Parsons's solution of the liberal dilemma, his system nevertheless defined the framework within and against which sociology has developed in the second half of the twentieth century. Sociology has sought to build on Parsons's formulation of the dilemma by 'bringing the subject back in', explaining the articulation and development of cultural systems not in terms of the functional imperatives imposed by the problem of order, but as the negotiated product of inter-subjective communication. During the 1960s and 1970s the dominant critiques of Parsons came from the phenomenological and symbolic interactionist traditions, which drew particularly on the work of Alfred Schutz, George Herbert Mead and Harold Garfinkel, to see society as a symbolic order. However these solutions merely shifted from one pole of the dilemma to the other, restoring the constitutive role of the subject, but evading the problem of order by denying the objectivity of the sources of conflict which threatened such order. The rejection of Parsonian explanation merely led back to the superficiality of a relativistic interpretative sociology.

Neo-Weberianism provided a more radical critique of the 'culturalism' of both Parsonian and phenomenological sociology in insisting on the irreducibility of conflicts of material interests, political aspirations and cultural values, as articulated by classes, parties and status groups within a pluralistic economic, political and cultural system. However neo-Weberianism only resurrected the dilemma in its Weberian form, for it could not define any coherent basis on which to reconstitute the unity of a society riven by conflict and fragmentation, nor could it reconcile its analysis of the objective foundations of conflict with a subjective approach to meaning. Thus neo-Weberianism merely led back to an empiricist approach to issues of power and social conflict.

The fragmentation of sociology in the 1970s led to a proliferation of schools of thought, each of which offered a partial solution to the Weberian dilemma, but none of which was able to resolve it. The 1980s saw a swing of the pendulum back towards a synthetic reconstruction which would solve the problem by reconstituting a systematic sociology. This 'Post-Parsonian' sociology, developed with different emphases by Habermas, Giddens and Alexander, sought to reinsert a

Weberian concern with meaning into the Parsonian framework. On the one hand, Post-Parsonian sociology replaced Parsons's functionally defined universals of action with universals which were supposedly inherent in the constitutive activity of the subject in the development of inter-subjective systems of meaning. On the other hand, it followed Lockwood in distinguishing between 'social integration' and 'system integration' to distinguish between the normative consensus, which defined the rules of the game, and the diversity of norms and material interests, which defined the conflicting aspirations of the various players. Social integration does not require system integration, but only a general agreement to abide by the rules of the game, and to respect the outcome of the resolution of conflict according to those rules. The problem remains, however, of drawing the line between the two. Where does the boundary between social integration and system integration, between structure and action, between 'materialist' and 'idealist' explanation, between 'practical' and 'communicative' interests lie?

Although Post-Parsonian sociology avoids Parsons' reification of society, it does not resolve the problem of subject and object, action and structure, which Parsons defined as the problem of order, but simply reformulates it as a dualistic conception of society. On the one hand, society exists as an objective structure, defining the normative and material context of action, while on the other hand society is constituted as an inter-subjective realm of meaning by the intentions of social subjects.[1] Actually existing society is a battleground between these two aspects of society, in which it is impossible to determine *a priori* which will prevail.

Post-Parsonian sociology certainly offers a more critical solution to the problem of order than did Parsons, but it is not clear that it is any more satisfactory. The possibility of order presupposes that there is a rational basis for consensus, which for Parsons lies in the instrumental rationality of the capitalist economy. Post-Parsonian sociology retains the radical separation of the 'instrumental rationality' of the fundamental institutions of capitalism as a means of provision for human material need from the 'substantive irrationality' of capitalism as a

---

[1] Habermas founds this dualistic view of society in the duality of reason. Instrumental reason constitutes society as an objective structure, impenetrable to subjective evaluation, while communicative reason constitutes society as an inter-subjective realm, unconstrained by the purposively rational pursuit of 'practical interests'. Although the terms of the argument are different in the work of Giddens and Alexander, the form is the same.

means of realising human cultural aspirations. The realisation of these latter aspirations depends not on transforming the social relations of production, but on confining the application of instrumental rationality to its proper sphere, the economy, building a substantively rational society by strengthening the sphere of 'culture' or 'civil society', in which the interaction of free and equal individuals can lead to the formation of a rational normative consensus.

The possibility of a reconciliation of the instrumental rationality of the capitalist economy and the substantive rationality of civil society clearly rests on the radical separation of 'labour' and 'social interaction', of 'instrumental' and 'communicative' reason, of 'objectivity' and 'subjectivity', of 'structure' and 'action', which was the basis of the marginalist revolution in economics. The Post-Parsonian solution, no less than those of Parsons and Weber, clearly implies that the productive and allocative efficiency of capitalism as a form of social production, as theorised by marginalist economics, can be radically distinguished from the substantive irrationality of capitalism as a form of domination.

Post-Parsonian sociology is caught between the irreconcilable poles of structure and action. Like Parsons's theory, it can explain both structure and action, but it cannot explain both at the same time. If the structure is given, the scope of action is defined, but its limits are already arbitrarily pre-determined. If the structure is not given, then the scope of action is unconstrained and there is no space for the structure to occupy. Explanation can only be based on teleological determinations external to either structure or action, located in the transcendental realm of 'culture', the 'life world' or 'structuration', which only serves to reconstitute the problem at another level. In practice the Post-Parsonians evade the issue, like Weber before them, oscillating arbitrarily between the point of view of structure and the point of view of action, and so reducing their sociology to an evaluative framework in which to achieve an interpretative understanding of social action which has no explanatory power. The dilemma remains because it is inherent in the radical separation of structure and action, economy and society, instrumental and communicative reason, which defines the analytical foundations of marginalist economics and modern sociology. Post-Parsonian sociology does not advance beyond Hegelian philosophy and classical political economy because it can only see the individual alternatively as a cultural construct, leading to a romantic organicism, or as a biological individual, leading to a naturalistic liberalism. It cannot identify the *social* foundations on which individuality is constructed as a form of sociability, because those foundations are naturalised by the hidden presupposition of private property which, as Marx showed, is the foundation of liberal social thought. This prevents it from addressing the fundamental question which was the starting point of Marx's critique of liberal social theory: *how* do relations between people take the alienated form of relations between things?

The limits of Marxism and the legacy of Marx

I have argued through this book that Marx's early theory of alienated labour, later developed in his theory of the form of value and the associated theory of commodity fetishism, offers a devastating critique of the conceptual foundations of liberal social theory, and defines an alternative basis on which to conceptualise the forms of capitalist social relations in which human sociability appears in the form of objective constraint. However, orthodox Marxism, far from building on Marx's critique of political economy, has neutralised its critical power by assimilating Marxism to the political economy and the materialist conception of history from which Marx had sought to disengage himself. This assimilation has equally defined the basis for the dominant critiques of Marxism, which have drawn on the Weberian critique of the naturalistic economism of marginalist economics. Thus Habermas has presented his sociology as one which derives its inspiration from the humanism of the young Marx, although its foundations are unequivocally Weberian, and categorically rejects the 'anthropology of labour' which supposedly underpins Marx's early theory of alienated labour and his subsequent adoption of the labour theory of value. However the power and originality of Marx's work is as much lost by its assimilation to liberal sociology as it is by its assimilation to liberal economics.

The dominant interpretations of Marx derive from the ways in which Marx's work has been appropriated ideologically within the context of the political polarisation of the socialist movement provoked by the Bolshevik Revolution. It is a marked feature of this polarisation that both sides share a common ground in distinguishing between Marx's early writings, in which he supposedly developed his philosophical world view ('dialectical materialism'), and his mature works, in which he developed his 'economics'. Differences of

The limits of Marxism and the legacy of Marx 307

interpretation concern not Marx's 'economics', but the status of this 'economics' within his theory as a whole, which is defined by the philosophy within which it is supposedly inserted. Thus the struggle within twentieth century Marxism to claim the legacy of Marx has been primarily a philosophical struggle.

The orthodox interpretations of Marx's mature works have been overwhelmingly 'economistic', in assimilating Marx to the conceptual framework of classical political economy, seeing the foundation of his 'economics' in the classical labour theory of value, reinterpreted as a theory of exploitation according to which the appropriation of surplus labour in the form of profit was based on the ownership of the means of production by the capitalist class, so that the class character of capitalist society is constituted by the *property* relations which determine the form of distribution, while socialism was reduced to a change in property relations, from private to state property. Marx's critique of political economy was seen as an historicist critique, which noted the historical specificity of the capitalist mode of distribution, which political economy supposedly ignored, to point beyond capitalism to a new form of society. Thus political economy was adequate to the early stages of capitalist development, in which the private appropriation of the product fostered the development of the forces of production. But in a mature capitalist society such a mode of *distribution* acts as a fetter on the development of increasingly socialised *production*, calling for new forms of property. The subjective expression of this objective contradiction lies in the conflict between the rationality of the capitalist, representing an outdated mode of distribution, and that of the working class, representing socialised forms of production.

According to this interpretation, the fundamental contradiction of capitalist society derives from the contradiction between the laws of production, which determine the progressive development of the forces of production, and the laws of distribution, defined by the private appropriation of the product. This contradiction is in turn only a particular manifestation of the fundamental laws of 'historical materialism', according to which the driving force of history is the development of the forces of production. Particular forms of property are appropriate to the development of the forces of production at particular stages in history. However, the development of the forms of property lags behind the development of the forces of production, as the class whose interests are served by that form of property seeks to hold onto its economic and political power, until such time as the contradiction between the two provokes a revolution in the form of property. Thus Marx's 'historical materialism' is identified with that of the Enlightenment, in seeing the historical development of society as the adaptation of social institutions to the unfolding of quasi-natural historical laws, with the link between the two being constituted by the class interests defined by ownership of the means of production, the difference being that Marx carries the historical process one stage further (Clarke, 1980b).

It is hardly surprising that this critique of political economy 'on the basis of political economy' should be vulnerable to the critique of classical political economy developed by marginalist economics, which focussed precisely on the labour theory of value, and by sociology, which focussed on the narrow economism shared by orthodox Marxism and liberal economic theories. It is hardly surprising that orthodox Marxism has equally been unable to formulate a coherent theoretical critique of marginalism and modern sociology, since it rests ultimately on the same abstract foundations. Orthodox Marxist critiques of liberal social and economic theories have tended to be ideological critiques, insisting that all theories express a particular class perspective, the difference between Marxism and liberal social theories being reduced to the class perspectives they express, without addressing the question of the theoretical coherence of the claims either of Marxism or of liberal social theory at all.

The gap between the orthodox interpretations and Marx's own work stands out in the extent to which the former abolished the constitutive role of labour, which was the basis of Marx's theories of alienated labour and commodity fetishism. The theory of commodity fetishism played a central role in the orthodox interpretation of Marx, but it was not seen as the culmination of Marx's early analysis of the alienated forms of social labour and his mature analysis of the value-form, but was reduced to an ideological illusion which *reflected* the social relations arising in the sphere of exchange, expressing the competitive relations between fragmented groups of workers, which are exploited politically and ideologically by the bourgeoisie. Within the Second International it was believed that this illusion was contradicted by the workers' experience of the *unmediated* relation of exploitation in production, and so would be overcome by the growing unity of the organised working class, expressing the socialisation of the forces of production (Kautsky, 1925; Bogdanov, [1897] 1979). This confidence underpinned the socialist faith in the compatibility, indeed the identity, of socialism and democracy.

As the expected revolution failed to arrive, and the spontaneous development of the working class movement appeared to lead in the direction of reform, rather than of revolution, the idea that the illusions of commodity fetishism would be dissipated by the spontaneous development of the class struggle was one increasingly confined to the radical left, represented above all by Rosa Luxemburg and the Council Communists. The majority of Marxists came to see the illusions of commodity fetishism, which underlay the rise of reformism, as a veil drawn over the immediate experience of the working class which could only be penetrated by a scientific understanding of capitalism. This led to a radical separation between the 'reality' and 'appearance' of capitalist social relations, between 'economics' and 'politics', and to a growing emphasis on the relative autonomy of politics and on the role of the subjective element in the class struggle, embodied in the revolutionary Party.

The pervasiveness of the illusions of commodity fetishism implied that truth could not be gained from experience, but only through scientific knowledge of the 'economic' laws of motion of the capitalist mode of production, and the historical laws of development of society. Similarly politics could not be based on experience, but only on the scientific knowledge of the possible. The foundations of Marxism no longer lay in the everyday reality of the class struggle, but in the philosophy of science which determined the scientific status of the Marxist laws. This posed serious problems at a time when the continued validity of those laws was being thrown into question. Thus the fate of Marxism appeared increasingly to depend not on the historical development of the class struggle, but on the outcome of philosophical battles within the working class movement.

The philosophical debates within Marxism developed in parallel with, and drew heavily on, contemporary debates within bourgeois philosophy which were addressing essentially the same issues, allbeit from a different perspective, of the methods of social science, of the character of historical laws, and of the relation between fact and value, between economics and politics.

The most fundamental division which emerged within Marxism was that between those who drew on neo-Kantianism and those who developed a specifically Marxist version of neo-Hegelianism. The former adopted Engels's characterisation of the 'materialist dialectic' as no more than the method of modern science, and were increasingly willing to revise Marxist orthodoxies in the light of the subsequent development of capitalism and of a return to Marx's texts. Such revisions did not necessarily lead to a weakening of Marxism — the period produced some of the most original and creative thinking in the bleak history of orthodox Marxism. However, the defeat of the revolutionary upsurge in Western Europe after the First World War, and the polarisation of the socialist movement in the wake of the Bolshevik Revolution, left little space for a revolutionary Marxism independent of the Bolshevik and reformist orthodoxies.

The triumph of right-wing revisionism was the triumph of the neo-Kantian critique of Marxism pioneered by Bernstein and Fabianism. This interpretation of Marx accepted the marginalist critique of the labour theory of value, rejected the theory of commodity fetishism as metaphysical, and distinguished the immediate tasks of social democracy, which were to express the economic interests of the working class within capitalism, from the achievement of socialism, which was seen as an ethical goal. This critique of orthodox Marxism, and of the character of the socialist project, closely paralleled that of Weber. Thus there has been a cross-fertilisation and interweaving of social democratic reformism and Weberian sociology throughout the twentieth century, producing a 'synthesis' of Marx and Weber, which has nevertheless rested on unambiguously Weberian foundations.

Lenin sought to found the scientific status of Marxism in the philosophy of dialectical materialism. Dialectical materialism was invented by Plekhanov, deriving from Feuerbach more than Hegel, and in his hands was a rigidly monistic materialism, seeing history as the expression of the dialectic of Matter, rather than of the Idea. The role of dialectical materialism was to underpin the scientific status of the Marxist philosophy of history, and of 'Marxist political economy', insulating the eternal truths of Marxism from empirical evaluation. Marxist-Leninist orthodoxy was canonised in Stalin's *Dialectical and Historical Materialism*, which was merely an expansion of Lenin's short essay *Karl Marx*, which introduces the Moscow edition of Lenin's *Selected Works*. In Stalin's hands dialectical materialism fossilised the economistic Marxism of the Second International, reducing it to a set of formulae to be ritually incanted and indiscriminately applied, with the Party as the arbiter of truth.

Marx's own work provides as powerful a critique of orthodox Marxism as it does of liberalism. However the revitalisation of 'Western Marxism' was not based on a return to the texts of Marx, but drew primarily on the neo-Hegelian critique of the sociology of Simmel and Weber pioneered by Gyorgy Lukács.

Lukács and and the foundations of 'Western Marxism'

Social democratic revisionism not only abandoned the revolutionary aspirations of Marxism, it also diluted Weber's critique of capitalism in the priority which it gave to the immediate economic interests of the working class over the ethical goals of socialism. Although Weber was a harsh critic of Marxism, his critique of capitalism was in many ways truer to the spirit of Marx than was that of the economistic Marxism of his day, for Weber addressed not only the undoubted exploitative features of capitalism, but also the dehumanisation and cultural degeneration inherent in capitalist 'rationalisation'. We have seen that Weber's pessimism derived from his radical Kantian individualism, but Hegel had already shown the way beyond Kant's individualism. It was on this basis that Gyorgy Lukács developed his critique of economistic positivism in his seminal work *History and Class Consciousness*, first published in 1923, which laid the foundations of 'Western Marxism'. The focus of Lukács interpretation of Marx was the theory of commodity fetishism.

In *History and Class Consciousness* Lukács presented a radical Hegelian interpretation of Marx, which drew heavily on the neo-Kantianism of Simmel and Weber. Although Lukács's book has been acclaimed as a remarkable anticipation of Marx's theory of alienation, the term is hardly used by Lukács, who places the concept of 'reification' at the heart of the analysis, a concept which Lukács was the first person to employ in any systematic way. Lukács's work provided a grid through which many commentators read Marx's *Manuscripts* when they were eventually published, as we have already seen, but Lukács's theory of reification has very little in common with Marx's theory of alienated labour.

Lukács took his central idea of a social form as the reified product of human action from Simmel, drawing particularly on his *Philosophy of Money*, in which Simmel argued that money was a social form which had originally developed as the rational means to a human end, namely to facilitate exchange, but which then became reified and transformed into an end in itself, so that human values and human relationships were correspondingly transformed into the means to that end. Simmel's argument has echoes of Marx's theory of commodity fetishism, which is not surprising because it was designed as a critique of Marx's theory, based on the marginalist critique of the labour theory of value. Thus Simmel took up Marx's theory of social form, but detached it from the analysis of alienated labour to set it on liberal foundations. This led to a view of commodity fetishism as an essentially ideological phenomenon, a particular manifestation of a universal process of reification through which social forms acquire an autonomous existence, detached from the subjectivity which gave rise to them.[2]

For Simmel the irrational inversion of subject and object, means and ends, could not be explained as an ideological reflection of capitalist social relations, since the generalisation of capitalist social relations already presupposed the subordination of human values and human relationships to the single end of monetary gain. Thus the fetishism of commodities was the condition for the development of capitalism, not a reflection of an underlying economic process. To explain this development Simmel replaced Marx's theory of 'commodity fetishism' with a philosophical account of the development of money from a means to an end in terms of a more general phenomenological process of inversion of means and ends. For Lukács this meant that Simmel could 'not go further than a description' of 'the most external and vacuous forms' of reification, making them 'independent and permanent by regarding them as the timeless model of human relations in general', divorcing these 'empty manifestations from their real capitalist foundation' so that he could not relate them to 'the basic phenomenon of reification itself' (*HCC*, pp. 94–5).

This did not lead Lukács directly back to Marx's theory of commodity fetishism to locate Simmel's analysis historically. Indeed he proclaimed a Marxist intellectual *tabula rasa* in his bizarre declaration that 'orthodoxy refers exclusively to *method*', so that an orthodox Marxist could accept the disproof of 'all of Marx's theses *in toto* — without having to renounce his orthodoxy for a single moment'

---

[2] Simmel himself drew attention to Marx's account of alienated labour in *Capital*: '[the object] isolates and alienates itself from the working subject through the division of labour ... The finished effort contains emphases relationships, values which the worker did not intend' (Simmel, 1968, pp. 40–1, quoted in Rose, 1978, p. 33), but Simmel insisted that the alienation of labour was only part of a wider process. Simmel's philosophical critique of Marx's theory of commodity fetishism was closely related to Böhm-Bawerk's critique of Marx's theory of value.

(*HCC*, p. 1). Lukács turned for his re-evaluation of Marxism to Weber, who had brought Simmel's analysis some of the way down to earth. Against Simmel, Weber saw reification not as a universal phenomenological process, but as the expression of a particular system of values, characterised by 'instrumental rationality', which gives rise to particular forms of social relation as an 'unintended consequence'. However Weber could show no way out of the 'iron cage' created by instrumental rationality, because he regarded such a form of rationality as the necessary condition for economic and political progress, whatever the human cost. Thus for Weber, as for Simmel, a truly human viewpoint could only be expressed by an alternative set of values, which for Lukács represented no more than a subjective and romantic evaluation of an increasingly alien world. Lukács believed that he could break out of this melancholic moralising by drawing on Hegel to break Weber's identification of instrumental rationality with the Reason of History.

For Lukács, as for Weber, what appears rational to the individual in a capitalist society becomes irrational as soon as it is regarded from the point of view of the whole. However, for Weber the fragmentation of modern society means that the point of view of the totality is increasingly inaccessible to the participants in that society, so that Weber's critique of the substantive irrationality of capitalism tended to be that of a marginalised commentator. For Hegel the point of view of the totality is that of Reason, which reaches its fruition in Hegel's own philosophy. However for Lukács such a perspective is not available to the individual, however great a philosopher that individual might be. 'The totality of an object can only be posited if the positing subject is itself a totality ... In modern society only the *classes* can represent this total point of view' (*HCC*, p. 28).

The class perspective of the bourgeoisie remains a limited perspective because it regards its own rule as absolute, and so remains bound to its class viewpoint.[3] 'It was necessary for the proletariat to be born for social reality to become fully conscious. The reason for this is that the discovery of the class-outlook of the proletariat provided a vantage point from which to survey the whole of society' (*HCC*, pp. 19–20). If Hegel provided the methodological key in adopting the point of view of the totality, Marx brought this totality down to

---
[3] This implies that bourgeois ideology is *true* within its own limits, so that, for example, political economy offers a true account of the workings of the capitalist economy, while remaining '*in ignorance of the objective economic limitations of its own system*' (*HCC*, p. 64).

earth by locating it in the emerging self-consciousness of the universal class.

The point of view of the totality is not a mechanical reflection of the experience of the working class: 'the class consciousness of the proletariat, the truth of the process "as subject" is itself far from stable and constant; it does not advance according to mechanical "laws". It is the consciousness of the dialectical process itself: it is likewise a dialectical concept' (*HCC*, p. 40). Thus the point of view of the totality only emerges through the unremitting theoretical criticism of more restricted viewpoints, each of which contains a partial truth. The partiality of this truth is not measured by its distance from some eternal truth, but by the internal contradictions to which the universalistic aspirations of each particular ideology give rise, contradictions which appear externally in the contradiction between contending, and apparently mutually exclusive, ideologies. In particular, the point of view of the totality implies the re-unification of subject and object, and so the dialectical synthesis of the one-sided Hegelian focus on 'ideology' and the one-sided Marxist focus on the 'economy'.

Although this synthesis is achieved through the Hegelian process of theoretical critique, and so remains on the side of ideology, Lukács claims that it transcends Hegelian idealism in adopting the standpoint of the universal class, so it represents not merely a speculative unification of subject and object, but the self-realisation of their unity. Moreover this is not merely a speculative commitment, it is a practical one, for, as Lenin has shown, the 'form taken by the class consciousness of the working class is the *Party*' which, as Rosa Luxemburg perceived, is the '*bearer of the class consciousness of the proletariat and the conscience of its historical vocation*' (*HCC*, p. 41).

The achievement of proletarian self-consciousness confronts formidable barriers, the most serious of which is the 'separation of the economic struggle from the political one', which derives from the 'contradiction between its immediate interests and its long-term objectives'. Its immediate objectives are tied to its concrete situation which is 'by its very nature an integral part of the existing capitalist society' (*HCC*, p. 7!), while its achievement of its long-term objectives depends on its overcoming the particularity of concrete demands by integrating immediate interests into a 'total view'. This means that it is important not to follow opportunism in mistaking '*the actual, psychological state of consciousness of proletarians for the class*

Lukács and and the foundations of 'Western Marxism' 315

consciousness of the proletariat' (*HCC*, p. 74). 'The objective theory of class consciousness is the theory of its objective possibility' (*HCC*, p. 79), behind which lies the proletariat's necessary aspiration towards the truth (*HCC*, p. 72). The true essence of class consciousness 'can only become visible in its authentic form when the historical process imperiously requires it to come into force, i.e. when an acute crisis in the economy drives it to action' (*HCC*, p. 40).

The integration of immediate interests into a 'total view' can only be achieved '*in the consciousness of the proletariat itself*' (*HCC*, p. 71). But the development of this consciousness is impeded by the fact that 'in a world where the reified relations of capitalism have the appearance of a natural environment it looks as if there is not a unity but a diversity of mutually independent objects and forces' (*HCC*, p. 70). Thus 'reification' is the primary ideological barrier to the development of proletarian self-consciousness.

Lukács located the source of reification in the 'fetishism of commodities', in which 'a relation between people takes on the character of a thing and thus acquires a "phantom objectivity", an autonomy that seems so strictly rational and all-embracing as to conceal every trace of its fundamental nature: the relation between people' (*HCC*, p. 83). However Lukács did not derive the ideological form of the fetishism of commodities from the alienation of labour, but if anything the other way around: 'the universality of the commodity form is responsible both objectively and subjectively for the abstraction of the human labour incorporated in commodities', although he adds that 'this universality becomes historically possible because this process of abstraction has been completed' (*HCC*, p. 87).

The alienation of labour and the fetishism of commodities are both explained in Weberian terms, as the result of 'the principle of rationalisation based on what is and *can be calculated*' (*HCC*, p. 88). This rationalisation is synonymous with 'the progressive elimination of the qualitative, human and individual attributes of the worker' as the 'process of labour is progressively broken down into abstract, rational, specialised operations', while, with Taylorist methods, this 'rational mechanisation extends right into the worker's "soul"'(*HCC*, p. 88). This rationalisation 'must declare war on the organic manufacture of whole products based on the *traditional amalgam of empirical experiences of work*' (*HCC*, p. 88). The resulting 'fragmentation of the object of production necessarily entails the fragmentation of its subject' (*HCC*, p. 89).

'Just as the capitalist system continuously produces and reproduces itself economically on higher levels, the structure of reification progressively sinks more deeply, more fatefully and more definitively into the consciousness of man' (*HCC*, p. 93). Moreover this reification affects not only economic relations, but also legal and political institutions. Lukács substantiates this claim not by quoting Marx's account of the alienated form of the state, which has nothing to do with the principle of rationalisation, but with a long quote from Weber (*HCC*, pp. 95–6). As for Weber, the process of rationalisation is an all-embracing process, so that the process of reification weaves an all-embracing cage as 'it stamps its imprint upon the whole consciousness of man' (*HCC*, p. 100). Nevertheless, while this reason secures 'the rationalisation of isolated aspects of life', the total process is relatively irrational (*HCC*, pp. 101–2). The explanation of this irrationality is again Weberian, it is the result of the unintended consequences of rational individual action, which arise because the individual cannot possibly be aware of the societal consequence of her atomistic actions. Thus arises the contradiction between form and content, between Weber's 'formal rationality' of capitalism and its 'substantive irrationality', a contradiction which, like the 'alienation' of labour, is a consequence of the division of labour.

Unlike Weber, Lukács finds a chink of light, which contains the potential for a new dawn. The manual worker, it turns out, is not really alienated, 'for his work as he experiences it directly possesses the naked and abstract form of the commodity' (*HCC*, p. 172) — the exploitative relation is transparent since the manual worker has no human interest in her work. Unlike the intellectual or the bureaucrat, the manual worker has not sold 'his humanity and his soul' (*HCC*, p. 172), so retains her human aspirations which conflict with the dehumanisation of 'rationalised' labour. These aspirations do not immediately lead to the formation of class consciousness, because they do not immediately penetrate the systematic illusions of commodity fetishism, so that 'as long as he does not consciously rebel against it' reification 'cripples and atrophies his "soul"' (*HCC*, p. 172), but they do represent 'an *aspiration towards society in its totality*, regardless of whether this aspiration remains conscious or whether it remains unconscious for the moment'(*HCC*, p. 174), and it is this aspiration that gives a necessary direction to the development of proletarian class consciousness, a direction which leads it to penetrate the illusions of reification.

This is necessarily a brief summary of Lukács's theory. However an immediate observation is that the one thing missing from Lukács's account is any coherent theory of the *alienation* of labour. As Lukács noted almost fifty years later: 'labour as the mediator of the metabolic interaction between society and nature, is missing', so that 'the most important real pillars of the Marxist view of the world disappear ... this means the disappearance of the ontological objectivity of nature ... But it also means the disappearance of the interaction between labour ... and the evolution of the men who labour' (*HCC*, p. xvii). The 'fetishism of commodities' is not the result of the alienation of labour, but of the reification engendered by the progressive rationalisation of society which accompanies the development of the division of labour, which fragments the experience of labour, both subjectively and objectively. The dehumanisation of labour is the subjective result of the subordination of labour to the anonymous forces of rationalisation and the division of labour. This leads to an inverted interpretation of Marx's theory of alienation, according to which the alienation of labour is not the source of mystified and estranged social relationships, but describes the unself-conscious reflection of the experience of reification. Thus the alienation of labour is a *reflection* of other social processes, just one manifestation of the wider societal phenomenon of reification.

Lukács's theory rests on a view of reification as a reflection of the pervasive rationalisation of society, a process through which all human powers become incorporated in things, in which social relations become properties of things, and in which '*all* relationships between men in the world of capitalism appear as relations between things' (Marcuse, 1955, p. 112, my emphasis). This alienated world may be a distortion of a properly human reality, but it is the world in which modern men and women are condemned to live, a world in which human beings are stripped of their human powers, in which they are subordinated as atomistic individuals to a world of objects, subject to the constraining power of immutable laws.

This theory of reification contrasts sharply with Marx's theory of alienated labour, within which alienation is hardly a passive experience, it is an *active* process in which labour is the subject, a process of 'labour's self-alienation'. Since Lukács separates alienation from its origins in the activity of labour, and sees it only as the passive reflection of a totalising process of reification which defines the ideological framework of human experience, Lukács is no better able than

Simmel to explain the socio-historical foundations of alienation, nor to locate the possibility of overcoming it.

For Lukács the basis on which reification can be overcome is the worker's 'humanity and his soul' which alone remains unmarked by reification. However it is not at all clear how the human aspirations of workers, which are necessarily fragmented and repressed by the rationalisation of labour, can make themselves socially effective. In *History and Class Consciousness* Lukács oscillates between an 'ultra-leftist' view of true consciousness as emerging spontaneously from the struggle of the proletariat 'when an acute crisis in the economy drives it to action' and a 'Leninist' view of truth as the product of a totalising science,[4] the two being reconciled by his assertion that the proletariat adopts the viewpoint of the totality. Lukács was soon persuaded to renounce his 'ultra-leftism' and to adhere unequivocally to the Leninist position. However his work had already acquired a life of its own.

The Dialectic of the Enlightenment

Lukács's theory of reification was taken up as the basis of a reinterpretation of Marxism by the Frankfurt School of Critical Theory, and particularly by Max Horkheimer and Theodor Adorno (1972), which eventually rejected the Marxist elements in Lukács's account, to set the theory of reification back on its Weberian foundations. This process was completed by Habermas's assimilation of Critical Theory back into the mainstream of modern sociology. However Habermas's critique of Marxism expresses not so much the inadequacy of Marx's own work as the inadequacy of Lukács's original interpretation.

For Lukács reification was the product of the Weberian process of rationalisation. However in Lukács's own account it is not clear whether reification is the product of the subordination of reason to the power of capital, or whether it is the product of 'instrumental reason' in itself. The former interpretation would take us back towards Marx, locating the source of reification in alienated labour and the

---

[4]Lenin insisted, in *What is to be Done*, that 'the consciousness of the working masses cannot be genuine class-consciousness, unless the workers learn ... to apply in practice the materialist analysis and the materialist estimate of *all* aspects of the life and activity of *all* classes, strata and groups of the population' (*SW*, 1, pp. 181–2).

The Dialectic of the Enlightenment

fetishism of commodities.[5] The latter interpretation, which was that of the Frankfurt School, would seem to take us back to the Weberian dilemma, for if rationality is an essential achievement of humanity, and reification a necessary result of the advance of Reason, alienation would appear to be the inevitable price of progress. The critique of alienation could then be no more than a contemplative moralistic critique, whether in the form of Weber's moralising critique of humanity's tragic fate, or the equally impotent irrationalist critique of bourgeois reason developed by Nietzsche and Heidegger, or Husserl's contemplative transcendental project of overcoming alienation through the rediscovery of the meaning imposed on the world by human intentionality, all of which have served, as noted in Chapter 3, as grids through which to read Marx's early works. The Frankfurt School sought a way around this dilemma by distinguishing between the 'instrumental reason' which leads to reification, and some more fundamental form of reason, drawing particularly on Weber's distinction between 'instrumental rationality' and 'value rationality'.

We have seen that Lukács derived his theory of reification from Simmel's phenomenological analysis of the inversion of means and ends and from Weber's account of rationalisation, which Lukács identified with the limited class perspective of the bourgeoisie. Adorno and Horkheimer replaced Lukács's 'reductionist' theory of the class origins of rational domination by looking for its origins within the rationalist project itself, going back to Nietzsche's instrumental view of truth as the expression of the 'will to power'. The central concern of the Frankfurt School, raised by the tyrannies of Hitler and Stalin, was that of the relationship between reason and domination, which they saw as lying at the heart of Weber's sociology. Adorno and Horkheimer traced the link between reason and domination back to its roots in the Enlightenment. They saw the limitations of the Reason of the Enlightenment in its totalitarian ambition, based on the belief that

---

[5] This was the direction in which Lucien Goldmann, Lukács's most faithful and creative follower, developed the theory of reification, although he still saw the theory of commodity fetishism only as a theory of ideology, linking the base to the superstructure, not as a theory of the *social forms* of capitalist production and reproduction. Thus he characterises commodity fetishism as 'a social process' through which 'value appears to *man's consciousness* as an objective quality of the commodity' (Goldmann, 1958, p. 1439). Alfred Sohn-Rethel, in a book written in the 1930s but only published in the 1960s (1978), inverted the relation between commodity fetishism and rationality proposed by the Critical Theorists of the Frankfurt School to develop a penetrating analysis of the social foundations of bourgeois reason. Mészáros (1970) and Arthur (1986), as we have seen, similarly refer the theory of commodity fetishism back to an Hegelian interpretation of the dialectic of labour.

human liberation is to be achieved by the intellectual and practical domination of nature. However the boundary between the natural and the human worlds was not fixed, but was a construct of Reason. The ambition to subordinate the external world to reason soon confronts human aspirations as a barrier to its project, which it overcomes by assimilating humanity to nature in reducing men and women to means to its transcendental ends. Thus reification is a result of the totalitarian ambition of instrumental reason, and Lukács's critique of capitalism is replaced by the critique of the Reason of the Enlightenment.

Although the Enlightenment promised human liberation through the rule of Reason, the Reason of the Enlightenment turned out to be not the key to human liberation, but the means of domination of nature and of humanity. The exercise of reason supposedly depends on the ability to capture the world in a net of fixed analytical concepts, predictably related by rigid mechanical laws. Thus the rationalist project implies the reduction of nature and humanity to the role of means and the status of things. However these concepts and laws can never be adequate to a human world in a state of permanent change. This inadequacy appears not simply from a subjective point of view, but also objectively, within the realm of ideas, in the form of the necessary emergence of contradictions which arise in any system of totalitarian thought when it confronts a world in change. In particular, within the thought of the Enlightenment, the contradiction appears between the values espoused by the Enlightenment and the impoverished means it adopted to realise those values, between its 'instrumental rationality' and its 'value rationality'. Thus the critique of reification comes not from outside, whether from the privileged experience of labour, or from a privileged insight into some human essence, but from within.

The limits of bourgeois thought, for the Critical Theorists as for Lukács (following Weber), are revealed through a theoretical critique which draws out the contradictions to which its limited viewpoint gives rise. Where the Critical Theorists broke with Lukács was in rejecting his belief that Marxism offered a system of thought which could overcome the limitations of the Enlightenment project by subordinating reason to the aspirations of a universal class. For Adorno and Horkheimer Lukács's interpretation of Marxism abandoned the critical power of Marx's dialectic to assimilate it to the Enlightenment project, Lukács's 'proletariat' being a purely metaphysical construct which serves not to undermine but to legitimate the totalitarian ambitions of reason. They saw the roots of this degeneration in Marx's own work, criticising what they saw as Marx's anthropology of labour, his fetishising of the working class, his reification of nature, and his positivist conception of science. For Adorno and Horkheimer no system of thought can ever be adequate to the world, so that the task of critical reason is always negative. The result was that their critique remained essentially sceptical, unable to define any positive political project because they had no existential basis on which to define such a project.

Although Marcuse shared much of Adorno's and Horkheimer's critique of instrumental reason, his work drew more on Heidegger than on Nietzsche, as we have seen. This gave his critique an existential foundation, which that of Adorno and Horkheimer lacked, on which to base his political commitment. For Marcuse reification derived not from the Enlightenment project as such, but from the subordination of reason to capitalist domination (Marcuse, 1971). Thus Marcuse sought to locate the power of critical reason in the human needs and potentialities which capitalism could not fulfill. However his anthropological approach led him to seek these human aspirations not within capitalism, but in spheres uncontaminated by capitalist rationality, and this led him to reject the working class as the social base of the critique of instrumental rationality. His search for the source of this critical power led Marcuse first to Freud and later to those 'marginalised' social strata whose needs and potentialities had not been subordinated to capitalist rationality. Moreover, although Marcuse saw capitalism as lying behind the domination of 'instrumental reason', it was not the capitalist *deformation* of instrumental reason, but instrumental reason itself which was the source of the evils of modern society. Thus Marcuse directed his critique as much against modern science and technology as against capitalist exploitation.

The starting point of Habermas's thought was the attempt to recover the liberating power of the reason of the Enlightenment from the irrationalism of the project of the Critical Theorists, without falling back on a 'foundationalism' which gave that power a transcendental foundation. Habermas's system of thought is based on the distinction between the activity of labour, in which human beings transform nature through the instrumentally rational application of technical rules and procedures, and the activity of 'communication', in which human interaction is based on the communication of mutual needs and interests, which presupposes a system of institutionalised rules which make communication possible. The rational foundation of society as a collective order then lies in the necessary presuppositions of human communication.

Communication presupposes a commitment to truth, and the only rational basis of truth is a consensus freely reached between the parties to communication. Thus a rational society is one in which the legitimacy of social institutions is underpinned by such a 'rational consensus'. The sphere in which such a consensus is formed is the sphere of civil society, and the rationality of a consensus formed in civil society is determined by the degree to which communication in civil society is marked by the freedom and equality of the interacting parties. Thus Habermas does not see the degeneration of reason as inherent in the Enlightenment project, but as deriving from the displacement of communicative reason by instrumental reason as the rich and powerful subordinate reason to their own practical interests.

Habermas's project brings Critical Theory full circle, returning first to a reformulation of the Weberian dilemma and then, in his later work, to the normative functionalism of Talcott Parsons. Habermas certainly provides normative functionalism with a critical edge that it lacked in Parsons's hands, but his theory still rests on the dualism of structure and action, of the 'positivist' and the 'idealist' theories of action, which derives, as I have argued, from the abstraction of the economy from society. Thus, in taking as his starting point the marginalist characterisation of the economy as the sphere of labour, in which human beings transform nature through the rational application of technical rules and procedures, Habermas presupposes the instrumental rationality of capitalist relations of production and exchange supposedly demonstrated by marginalist economics, leaving only the initial allocation of resources, which determines the distribution of the product, as a matter for substantive evaluative judgement. Thus Habermas does not question the rationality of alienated labour, but looks beyond the sphere of labour both for the 'practical interests', which derive from the inequality of distribution, and which lie behind the subordination of society to instrumentally rational forms of domination, and for the 'communicative interests' which underlie the possibility of human liberation. By denying that the sphere of labour is a sphere of communication in which the communicative interests of the working class are suppressed, Habermas denies the possibility of restoring the human qualities of labour to the activity of labour itself. However Marx's theory of alienated labour shows that the contrast between communicative reason and instrumental reason is not a contrast between two forms of reason, corresponding to distinct interests, but is a contrast between the inherently social character of human existence and the alienated forms in which human sociability is expressed.

For Critical Theory instrumental reason, which supposedly implies the reduction of human beings and of nature to the status of means to the attainment of given ends, is necessarily a reason of domination. But if this is the case, the question immediately arises of what is 'rational' about this form of rationality. Is domination the price that must inevitably be paid, for good or ill, for the benefits of economic and technological progress and administrative efficiency, as Weber and the economists implied? Or is this domination a culturally specific and ultimately irrational feature of Western Modernity, implicit in the contradictory character of the Dialectic of the Enlightenment, which proclaimed the liberating power of a stunted instrumental reason, as Horkheimer and Adorno argued? Or is it capitalism which has imposed this restricted 'capitalist' rationality on humanity, in the guise of a neutral 'technical reason' as the means of securing and reproducing its 'specific dominative interests', as Marcuse argued (1965, p. 16)? Or does the dialogic 'communicative reason' of civil society provide the antidote to the monologic 'instrumental reason' of economic and political domination, as Habermas argues? Or does the deformation of reason lie elsewhere, in the alienated form of labour, which underlies the inversion of means and ends, as Marx had argued?

The irrationality of capitalism and the alienation of labour

Lukács and the Critical Theorists offered a variety of means of resolving Weber's dilemma, but their solutions all remained within the framework of Weber's diagnosis of the contradictions of modernity because they retained Weber's conception of the development of modern capitalism as a progressive *rationalisation* of society, a conception whose coherence, I have argued, derives implicitly from marginalist economics. The result was that, like Weber, they sought the possibilities of human liberation in *another form of reason*, whose source they variously identified in the proletariat and its Party, in the sphere of art and high culture, in the unconscious, in marginalised social strata, or of civil society, which had managed to avoid incorporation into the instrumental reason of modernity.

The reason for this assimilation of Critical Theory to the Weberian perspective was the failure to look behind orthodox Marxism to the work of Marx. For orthodox Marxism dominative reason was reduced to the interests of a dominant class. The Critical Theorists shared Weber's critique of this reductionist concept of 'instrumental reason', on the grounds that rationalisation and the associated process of reification pervades the whole of modern culture. Workers are as ready as capitalists to treat others as things in pursuit of their own interests. Workers as much as capitalists seek to satisfy their human needs by the acquisition of things. Thus rationality is not so much the instrument of domination, as the ideology which conceals domination by 'naturalising' the human objects of domination, and so assimilating social relations to the world of nature. For the Critical Theorists this assimilation is the result of the 'fetishism of commodities', in which social qualities appear in the form of things, but the fetishism of commodities is itself seen as a construct of instrumental reason, and so as an ideological phenomenon. Their critique of capitalism is therefore reduced to a cultural critique.

Marx's theory of alienated labour provides a way beyond the antinomies of modern sociology, which seek to reconcile the subjective rationality of capitalism with its objective irrationality on the basis of an abstract concept of the individual and an abstract concept of reason. The world of alienated labour is not a world under the rule of instrumental reason, but a profoundly irrational and contradictory world in which any form of rationality is subverted by the systematic dissociation of the intentions of human actors from the outcome of social action. This dissociation is not the result of the arbitrary intervention of unforeseen circumstances, but is the systematic result of the alienated forms of social labour through which human sociability is imposed by the subordination of the individual to a thing. Thus 'alienation' is not the result of a subjective attitude to labour, the expression of a 'reified consciousness', but is an objective characteristic of the social forms of capitalist production and reproduction, of which 'reification' is the subjective expression. Similarly the reified consciousness cannot be seen as an expression of the deformed Reason of the Enlightenment, since it is the alienated forms of social labour which define the limits of the rationality of that Reason. Competition imposes the 'rationality' of capitalism on individuals as an objective force, submitting capitalists no less than the working class to its contradictory logic, but in abstraction from the fragmentation of social relations imposed by the rule of competition, which is only another expression of the alienated forms of social labour, the 'rationality' of capitalism is profoundly irrational. Finally, if capitalism is profoundly irrational, domination cannot be seen as immanent in the rationalist project of the Enlightenment, but on the contrary, that project leads to the radical critique of the stunted reason of capitalism.[6]

The contradictions of capitalism do not derive from the contradiction between one form of reason and another, whether between formal and substantive rationality, or between capitalist and proletarian reason, but from the contradictions inherent in the irrationality of alienated forms of social production. The irrationality of capitalism is an 'unintended consequence' of subjectively rational action, but it is a consequence which is systematically embedded in, and determined by, forms of social relation whose social character is not given immediately, arising from social interaction between people engaged in co-operative activity, but is imposed on people by the *mediated* form of social relations, in which the social character of their labour confronts them in the form of a thing. It is Marx's demystification of the 'fetishism of commodities' through his analysis of the value-form that makes it possible to penetrate the apparently objective character of this social determination to re-establish its human origins.

For Marx the fetishism of commodities is not simply an ideological mystification, to be referred back to a constitutive subject, whether that subject be a class interest or the dominative interest of reason itself. The fetishism of commodities is only the reflection of a real social process, constituted by the social relations of alienated labour. It really is the case that social labour only appears in the form of a thing, and it really is the case that the products of labour confront the labourer as an objective power. However, alienation is not the expression of an ideological process of 'reification' in which subjectivity is eradicated. Alienation is a process which starts from labour as the subjective element which is never effaced. It is not that human powers become incorporated in things, but that human qualities *appear in the form of* the properties of things. It is not that social relations *appear as* relations between things, but that social relations *appear in the form of* relations between things. These forms of appearance arise not because relations between things *replace* or *conceal* relations between persons,

---

[6] In this respect Horkheimer and Adorno were right to assimilate Marx to the Enlightenment project, and Habermas was right to rescue the rationalism of the Enlightenment from their critique.

but because relations between persons are *mediated* by things. Thus reification does not constitute a self-sufficient world which is imposed on human beings, but rather a world which is only constituted and reproduced through human activity, and so a world which can always be reclaimed by that activity.

The theory of commodity fetishism does not provide a *solution* to the sociological 'problem' of the relation between subject and object, individual and society, structure and action, because it denies the legitimacy of the sociological formulation of the problem. The formal opposition and the formal reconciliation of individual and society is a problem which can neither be posed nor resolved in the abstract. Individuals only exist within social relationships, whose particular forms are constituted historically, while social relationships only exist between individuals, and are reproduced and transformed by the practical activity of individuals. The radical opposition of individual and society is not constitutive of the human condition, but is the historical result of the development of the particular alienated forms of human sociability characteristic of capitalist society. Unlike Durkheim, who explained the constraining character of social facts by their quality as things, Marx insisted that the fact that commodities are things implies that they 'therefore lack the power to resist man' (*Capital*, I, p. 78).

In a capitalist society it really is the case that the subject confronts society as an objective and constraining world beyond human control. Thus the antinomies of modern sociology are not simply intellectual fabrications, but are the intellectual expression of real oppositions. This is why, for all their faults, Weber and the Frankfurt School of Critical Theory could offer a penetrating diagnosis of the human condition, without being able to explain it, or to see any way of overcoming it.

The antinomies of modern sociology can be understood theoretically as an expression of the alienated forms of capitalist social relations. However they cannot be overcome by theory, but only by overcoming the alienated forms of social relations in practice. This is what Marx meant when he wrote in his Eleventh Thesis on Feuerbach: 'The philosophers have only *interpreted* the world, in various ways; the point, however, is to change it'. Commodity fetishism cannot be overcome in consciousness, through the subjective recovery of the human meaning of alienated social forms, without overcoming it in practice, by developing new social forms in which the social character

The irrationality of capitalism and the alienation of labour 327

of human activity is expressed directly. For Marx this practice could only be that of the working class.

The opposition of individual and society is not an immutable structural characteristic of modern society, but is only reproduced through the reproduction of the alienated forms of social labour. This reproduction is not automatic, but is the outcome of a pervasive and permanent class struggle in which the working class resists its subordination to the alienated forms of capitalist domination. The working class is not simply the object of domination of the 'instrumental rationality' of capitalism. However alienated may be the forms of social labour under capitalism, the fact nevertheless remains that the creative powers of co-operative labour remain the only source of social wealth, and of the surplus value appropriated by the capitalist class.

For Marx the contradiction inherent in the social form of capitalist domination is that the production and appropriation of surplus value depends on capital developing the creative powers of social labour, and so developing the working class as a collective social power, while the reproduction of capitalist domination depends on capital restricting the development of this social power within the limits of the social relations of capitalist production by securing the fragmentation of the working class and the restriction of its subjective aspirations. The subjective expression of this contradiction is to be found in the development of the class struggle, which cannot be reduced to the opposition of consciously articulated class interests, expressing conflicting and mutually exclusive forms of 'class reason', but more fundamentally expresses the contradictions of capitalist 'rationality', which simultaneously develops and represses the aspirations of the working class. The objective expression of this contradiction lies in the necessarily crisis-ridden character of capitalist accumulation, which again does not derive from the imperfect subordination of society to capitalist rationality, which can potentially be overcome by the perfected rationality of 'organised capitalism', but is inherent in the contradictory form of that 'rationality', in the contradiction between the tendency for capital to develop the productive forces without limit and the need to confine their development within the limits of the social relations of capitalist production. Thus the source of the critical opposition to the dehumanisation imposed by capitalist society does not lie outside the sphere of capitalist 'rationality', but within it, as the expression of its inherent contradictions. As Marx argued, the limit to capital is capital itself.

Marx was naively optimistic in his belief that socialism would inevitably arise out of the spontaneous development of the contradictions of the capitalist mode of production, but the tragedy of Marxism, in both its Leninist and its Western variants, was that it abandoned Marx's faith in the ability of the working class to achieve its own emancipation. This led Marxism to detach the liberating potential of Marx's critique of capitalism from its concrete foundations in the socialisation of the working class, to locate it not in the collective organisation of the working class, but in the alienated forms in which the socialisation of labour developed under capitalism, as the concentration and centralisation of capital. Socialism was then identified not with the transformation of social relations of production, but only with the nationalisation of the means of production, so that human social powers confronted the individual in the equally alienated form of the state. The Critical Theorists, on the other hand, detached Marx's critique of capitalism from any social or historical foundation, to reduce it to a philosophical critique whose tragedy was that it found itself increasingly in the interstices of culture and on the margins of society.

The collapse of state socialism, in both its Communist and Social Democratic forms, heralds the death of Marxism in the forms in which it has dominated the twentieth century. It would be naively optimistic to expect that the collapse of old orthodoxies will necessarily create the conditions for a rebirth of Marxism. Nevertheless the collapse of state socialism does nothing to overcome the contradictions of capitalism, nor to resolve the antinomies of liberalism. Indeed the polarisation of wealth and power, the tendencies to the overaccumulation and uneven development of capital, the dehumanisation of culture and society, the removal of human destiny from any form of human control, have developed to an unprecedented degree and on a global scale. As the twin threats of economic and ecological crisis become ever more menacing the need to develop new social forms becomes ever more urgent. In such circumstances it may be that Marxism can recover its heritage, to resume the project which Marx initiated of linking an emancipatory social theory to an emancipatory social practice.

Bibliography

Adorno, T. and Horkheimer, M. (1972) *Dialectic of the Enlightenment*, Herder and Herder, NY.
Alexander, J. (1982–4) *Theoretical Logic in Sociology*, RKP, London.
Althusser, L. (1969) *For Marx*, Penguin, Harmondsworth.
Arthur, C. (1986) *Dialectics of Labour*, Blackwell, Oxford.
Arthur, C. (1988) 'Hegel's Theory of Value' in M. Williams, ed., *Value, Social Form and the State*, Macmillan, London, pp. 21–41.
Backhaus, H.-G. (1969) 'Zur Dialektik der Wertform', in A. Schmidt, ed., *Beiträge zur marxistischen Erkenntnistheorie*, Suhrkamp, Frankfurt.
Backhaus, H.-G. (1974–8) 'Materielen zur Rekonstruktion der Marxschen Werttheorie', *Gesellschaft*, Frankfurt, 1, 2, 11.
Bell, D. (1959) 'The Rediscovery of Alienation', *Journal of Philosophy*, LVI, 24, pp. 933–952.
Blauner, R. (1964) *Alienation and Freedom*, Chicago UP, Chicago.
Bogdanov, A. (1979) *A Short Course of Economic Science* [1897], Hyperion Reprints, Westport, Conn.
Booth, C. (1887) *Conditions and Occupations of the People of Tower Hamlets, 1886–7*, Edward Stanford, London.
Bottomore, T. and Goode, P. (1978) *Austro-Marxism*, Clarendon, Oxford.
Bottomore, T. and Rubel, M. (1956) *Karl Marx: Selected Writings in Sociology and Social Philosophy*, Watts, London.
Burke, E. (1907) 'Thoughts and Details on Scarcity', in *The Works of Burke*, OUP, London, Vol VI.
Claes, G. (1984) 'Engels' Outlines of a Critique of Political Economy (1843) and the Origins of the Marxist Critique of Capitalism', *History of Political Economy*, 16, 2, pp. 207–232.
Clarke, S. (1980a) 'The Value of Value', *Capital and Class*, 10, pp. 1–17.
Clarke, S. (1980b) 'Althusserian Marxism', in S. Clarke et al., *One-Dimensional Marxism*, Allison and Busby, London and Schocken, New York, pp. 7–102.
Clarke, S. (1981) *The Foundations of Structuralism*, Harvester, Brighton and Barnes and Noble, NJ.
Clarke, S. (1988) *Keynesianism, Monetarism and the Crisis of the State*, Edward Elgar, Aldershot, and Gower, Vermont.
Clarke, S. (1990) 'The Marxist Theory of Crisis', *Science and Society*, 54, 4, pp. 442–67.

Cohen, G.A. (1970) 'On Some Criticisms of Historical Materialism' *Aristotelian Society Supplement*, 44, pp. 212–42.
Cohen, G.A. (1978) *A Defence of Historical Materialism*, OUP, Oxford.
Colletti, L. (1972) *From Rousseau to Lenin*, NLB, London.
Colletti, L. (1975) 'Introduction' to Marx, K. *Early Writings*, Penguin, Harmondsworth.
Comte, A. (n.d.) *A System of Positive Polity*, 2 Vols, Franklin, New York.
Cornu, A. (1934) *Karl Marx, L'Homme et L'Oeuvre*, Alcan, Paris.
Dobb, M. (1940) *Political Economy and Capitalism*, Routledge and Kegan Paul, London.
Dobb, M. (1973) *Theories of Value and Distribution*, Cambridge UP, Cambridge.
Draper, H. (1977–8) *Karl Marx's Theory of Revolution*, 2 Vols, Monthly Review, New York.
Elliott, J. (1979) 'Continuity and Change in Marx's Theory of Alienation', *History of Political Economy*, 11, 3, pp. 317–62.
Elson, D., ed., (1979) *Value*, CSE Books, London; Humanities, NJ.
Elster, J. (1985) *Making Sense of Marx*, CUP, Cambridge.
Engels, F. (1962) *Anti-Dühring*, FLPH, Moscow.
Evans, M. (1984) 'Karl Marx's First Confrontation with Political Economy', *Economy and Society*, 13, pp. 115– 152.
Ferguson, A. (1966) *Essay on the History of Civil Society*, Edinburgh UP, Edinburgh.
Feuer, L. (1962) 'What is Alienation? The Career of a Concept', *New Politics*, I, 3, pp. 116–134.
Feuerlicht, I. (1978) *Alienation*, Greenwood, Westport, Conn.
Fine, B. and Harris, L. (1979) *Rereading Capital*, Macmillan, London.
Gide, C. and Rist, C. (1948) *A History of Economic Doctrines*, Second Edition, Harrap, London.
Goldmann, L. (1958) 'Réification', *Temps Modernes*, 156–7, pp. 1433–1474.
Grossmann, H. (1977) 'Marx, Classical Political Economy and the Problem of Dynamics', *Capital and Class*, 2, pp. 32–55, and 3, pp. 67–99.
Hennings, K.H. (1985) 'A Note on Marx's Reading List in his *Economic and Philosophical Manuscripts* of 1844', *Economy and Society*, 14, 1, pp. 128–137.
Hilferding, R. (1975) *Böhm Bawerk's Criticism of Marx*, Merlin, London.
Howard, D. (1972) *The Development of the Marxian Dialectic*, Southern Illinois UP.
Howard, M.C. and King, J. E. (1985) *The Political Economy of Marx*, 2nd edition, Longman, London.
Hyppolite, J. (1969) *Studies on Marx and Hegel*, Heinemann, London.
Jahn, W. (1957) 'Der ökonomische Inhalt des Begriffs der Entfremdung der Arbeit in den Frühschriften von Karl Marx', *Wirtschaftswissenschaft*, 6.
Jevons, S. (1883) *Methods of Social Reform*, Macmillan, London.
Jevons, S. (1970) *The Theory of Political Economy*, Penguin, Harmondsworth.
Kautsky, K. (1925) *The Economic Doctrines of Karl Marx*, A. and C. Black, London.

Korsch, K. (1970) *Marxism and Philosophy*, NLB, London.
Kozlov, G.A., ed., (1977) *Political Economy: Capitalism*, Progress, Moscow.
Kühne, K. (1979) *Economics and Marxism*, 2 Vols, Macmillan, London.

Lenin, V. (1913) 'The Three Sources and Three Component Parts of Marxism', in *Selected Works*, Volume 1.
Lenin, V. (1961) *Collected Works*, Vol. 38, FLPH, Moscow.
Lenin, V. (n.d.) *Materialism and Empirio-Criticism*, FLPH, Moscow.
Lenin, V. (SW) *Selected Works*, 3 Vols, FLPH, Moscow, n.d.
Lukács, G. (1971) *History and Class Consciousness*, Merlin, London.
Lukács, G. (1975) *The Young Hegel*, Merlin, London.
Maguire, J. (1972) *Marx's Paris Writings*, Gill, Dublin and Macmillan, London.
Mandel, E. (1962) *Marxist Economic Theory*, Merlin, London.
Mandel, E. (1971) *The Formation of the Economic Thought of Karl Marx*, Monthly Review Press, New York.
Marcuse, H. (1932) 'Neue Quellen zur Grundlegung des Historischen Materialismus', *Die Gesellschaft*, IX, 8, pp. 136–74, translated in *Studies in Critical Philosophy*, Beacon Press, Boston, 1973.
Marcuse, H. (1955) *Reason and Revolution*, Humanities, New York.
Marcuse, H. (1965) 'Industrialisation and Capitalism', *New Left Review*, 30, pp. 3–17, and in O. Stammler, ed., *Max Weber and Sociology Today*, Harper and Row, New York, 1971, pp. 133–51.
Marcuse, H. (1973) 'On the Philosophical Foundation of the Concept of Labour in Economics' [1933], *Telos*, 16, pp. 9–37.
Marx, K. (1956) *The Holy Family*, FLPH, Moscow.
Marx, K. (1968) *Selected Works*, FLPH, Moscow.
Marx, K. (1971) *Contribution to the Critique of Political Economy*, Lawrence and Wishart, London.
Marx, K. (1973) *Grundrisse*, Penguin, Harmondsworth.
Marx, K. (1975) *Early Writings*, Penguin, Harmondsworth.
Marx, K. (1976) *Value Studies*, New Park, London.
Marx, K. (1983) *Letters on 'Capital'*, New Park, London.
Marx, K. (GI) *The German Ideology*, Progress, Moscow, 1964.
Marx. K. (PP) *The Poverty of Philosophy*, FLPH, Moscow, n.d.
Marx, K. (TSV) *Theories of Surplus Value*, 3 Vols, FLPH, Moscow, n.d., 1968, 1972.
Marx, K. and Engels, F. (CW) *Collected Works*, Lawrence and Wishart, London, 1975–.
Mattick, P. (1978) *Anti-Bolshevik Communism*, Merlin, London.
Mattick, P. (1983) *Marxism: Last Refuge of the Bourgeoisie*, Merlin, London; Sharpe, New York.
McLellan, D. (1970) *Marx Before Marxism*, Macmillan, London.
Meek, R. (1963) *The Economics of Physiocracy*, Harvard UP, Cambridge, Mass.
Meek, R. (1973) *Studies in the Labour Theory of Value*, Lawrence and Wishart, London.

Meek, R. (1976) *Social Science and the Ignoble Savage*, CUP, Cambridge.
Menger, C. (1950) *Principles of Economics*, Free Press, Glencoe.
Menger, C. (1963) *Problems of Economics and Sociology*, University of Illinois Press, Urbana.
Mészáros, I. (1970) *Marx's Theory of Alienation*, Merlin, London.
Mill, J.S. (1965–77) *Collected Works*, 19 Vols, RKP, London.
Morishima, M. (1973) *Marx's Economics*, CUP, Cambridge.
Naville, P. (1957) *De l'aliénation à la jouissance*, Rivière, Paris.
Negri, A. (1984) *Marx Beyond Marx*, Bergin and Garvey, Mass.
O'Neill, J. (1982) *For Marx Against Althusser*, UP of America, Washington.
Oakley, A. (1984) *Marx's Critique of Political Economy*, Routledge and Kegan Paul, London.
Oakley, A. (1983) *The Making of Marx's Critical Theory*, RKP, London.
Ollman, B. (1971) *Alienation*, CUP, Cambridge.
Pannekoek, A. (1975) *Lenin as Philosopher*, Merlin, London.
Parsons, T. (1949) *The Structure of Social Action*, Free Press, Glencoe.
Pashukanis, E. (1978) *General Theory of Law and Marxism*, London.
Petty, Sir Wm, (1963) *Political Arithmetick*, in *Economic Writings*, Vol. I, Reprints of Economic Classics, New York.
Plamenatz, J. (1954) *German Marxism and Russian Communism*, Longman, London.
Ricardo, D. (1951) *Works and Correspondence*, Vol. IV, CUP, Cambridge.
Ricardo, D. (1971) *Principles of Political Economy and Taxation*, Penguin, Harmondsworth.
Roemer, J. (1982) *A General Theory of Exploitation and Class*, Harvard UP, Cambridge, Mass.
Rosdolsky, R. (1977) *The Making of Marx's Capital*, Pluto, London.
Rose, G. (1978) *The Melancholy Science*, Macmillan, London.
Rubin, I.I. (1972) *Essays on Marx's Theory of Value*, Black and Red, Detroit.
Rubin, I.I. (1978) 'Abstract Labour and Value in Marx's System'[1927], *Capital and Class*, 5, pp. 107–139.
Schacht, R. (1971) *Alienation*, George Allen and Unwin, London.
Schumpeter, J. A. (1987) *Capitalism, Socialism and Democracy* [1942], Unwin, London.
Seligman, E. (1903) 'On Some Neglected English Economists', *Economic Journal*, XIII.
Simmel, G. (1968) 'On the Concept and Tragedy of Culture', in *Conflict in Modern Culture and Other essays*, Teachers College, NY.
Smart, D. (1978) *Pannekoek and Gorter's Marxism*, Pluto, London.
Smith, A. (1976) *Theory of Moral Sentiments*, Clarendon, Oxford.
Smith, A. (WN) *The Wealth of Nations*, 2 Vols, Dent, London, 1910.
Smith, G. (1866) *Morning Star*, 24 July.
Sohn-Rethel, A. (1978) *Intellectual and Manual Labour*, Macmillan, London.
Spencer, H. (1896) *Principles of Sociology*, 3 Vols, Williams and Norgate, London.

Spencer, H. (1904) *An Autobiography*, 2 Vols, Williams and Norgate, London.
Steedman, I. (1977) *Marx after Sraffa*, NLB, London.
Sweezy, P. (1942) *The Theory of Capitalist Development*, Dobson, London.

Toynbee, A. (1969) 'Ricardo and the Old Political Economy' in *Toynbee's Industrial Revolution*, David and Charles, Newton Abbot.
Uchida, H. (1988) *Marx's Grundrisse and Hegel's Logic*, Routledge, London.
Walras, L. (1954) *Elements of Pure Economics*, Allen and Unwin, London.
Weber, M. (1949) *The Methodology of the Social Sciences*, Free Press, New York.
Weber, M. (1968) *Economy and Society*, 3 Vols, University of California Press, Berkeley.
Weber, M. (1975) *Roscher and Knies*, Free Press, Glencoe.
Weisskopf, W. (1971) *Alienation and Economics*, Dutton, New York.
Wieser, F. von (1927) *Social Economics*, Allen and Unwin, London.

Index

action, theory of, 1–4, 10–11, 167, 290–4, 297, 299, 301
Adorno, Th., 318–21, 323, 325
Alexander, J., 3, 303–4
alienation, 6–7, 50–1, 59, 63–82, 85–7, 89, 91–2, 96–9, 101–3, 105, 107, 110, 116, 118, 128, 132, 134, 142, 144, 165, 208, 212, 230–1, 288, 306, 308, 311–2, 315–9, 322–8
Althusser, L., 65
Anderson, J., 41
Arthur, C., ix, 50, 56, 69–70, 72, 76, 89, 319

Backhaus, H.-G., 97
Bailey, S., 144, 146
Bastiat, F, 147, 150
Bell, D., 67
Bentham, J., 22, 110
Bernstein, E., 310
Blauner, R., 65
Bogdanov, A., 93, 308
Booth, C., 174
Bottomore, T., ix, 52
Brentano,L., 244
Bukharin, N., 182
Burke, E., 186, 189, 196

Cairnes, J. E., 144, 173
capital, 8, 12, 21, 25, 30, 41–9, 62–3, 68–69, 75, 79, 83–4, 86–8, 92–3, 95, 98, 100–3, 108, 110, 113–46, 150–71, 174, 176, 181, 188, 191, 197, 199–201, 208, 210, 218, 222–33, 237–8, 241, 243, 245–6, 264, 279, 292, 312, 318, 326–8

capitalism, 6, 7, 9–11, 38, 43, 45–7, 64, 66, 71, 74, 76–7, 84, 92–6, 98, 113, 119–120, 129, 135, 142, 153–7, 159–61, 163, 165–6, 168–9, 178, 182–4, 186–187, 194, 200, 203–7, 219, 225, 227–8, 230–2, 234, 236, 238, 241–3, 245–6, 253, 256–7, 267, 279–89, 292–4, 296, 299, 302, 304–5, 307, 309–17, 320–8
Carey, H., 147, 150
Cazenove, J., 146
charisma, 258, 285–6
church, 154, 156, 271–3, 284, 300
Claes, G., 63
Clark, J. B., 204
Clarke, S., 39, 97, 232, 298, 308
class, theory of, 12–13, 19–21, 25–9, 32–5, 39–45, 83–4, 117–8, 121–34, 157–9, 167–8, 186, 199–202, 236–8, 244–5, 271–2, 293, 307
Cohen, G. A., 67, 95
Colletti, L., 52, 56, 76, 94
commodity fetishism, 6, 51, 84–5, 97, 103–4, 110, 112, 114, 126, 129, 132, 134, 208, 306–26
competition, 10, 28, 30, 31–2, 61–3, 119, 130, 133, 136, 138–9, 142–3, 149, 154–4, 160, 161, 163, 173–4, 187–8, 193–4, 203, 206–7, 213–4, 217–8, 227, 231–2, 238, 241–2, 270, 287, 324–5
Comte, A., 3, 5, 155, 157–61, 165–6, 175–6, 179, 235, 243
Corn Laws, 40, 43, 44, 152, 186

Index 335

Cornu, A., 50
Cournot, A. A., 184

distribution, theory of, 5, 9, 25, 37–42, 84, 126–40, 144–50, 156, 160, 165–6, 174, 177, 184–5, 199–202, 210, 236, 292, 307
division of labour, 4, 17, 21–4, 27–8, 31–2, 37–9, 62, 68, 69, 71–6, 79, 83, 87–90, 101–2, 109, 111–2, 123, 126, 129, 142, 157, 159, 161, 165, 168–70, 195, 198–9, 206, 208–9, 219–21, 236–7, 240, 255, 265–6, 272, 286, 291, 295–6, 309, 312, 316–7
Dobb, M., 68. 93, 95, 141, 182
Draper, H., 52
Dunoyer, C. B., 158
Durkheim, E., 1, 161, 175, 179, 299, 326

economic theory, 3, 9, 10, 95, 100, 109, 148, 156, 166, 187, 195, 197, 204, 239–40, 250–1, 256, 261–2, 266–8, 272, 274, 294
economics, viii–ix, 8–10, 31, 35, 48, 50–1, 61, 91–3, 95, 129, 144, 148, 155, 182–3, 186–91, 194–5, 200–9, 217, 220, 228, 235–6, 238–9, 242–3, 245, 247–51, 253, 255–6, 260–2, 265–7, 269, 273–4, 283, 285, 289, 292–6, 299, 301, 305–9, 322, 323
Elliott, J., 68, 72
Elson, D., 97
Elster, J., 95
ends, 1, 2, 5, 10, 23–4, 34, 39, 52, 148, 151, 164, 167, 179–80, 193, 203, 207, 237, 243, 248, 252, 256, 258, 260–2, 267–79, 282–9, 294, 296–7, 299–300, 312, 319–20, 323
Engels, F., 44, 57, 59, 61–3, 67, 73–4, 77, 80, 90, 94, 98, 102, 217–8, 231, 309

Enlightenment, 5, 13–18, 35–9, 57–8, 95, 308, 318–25
Evans, M., 63, 76
exchange, theory of, 4, 9, 37, 61–3, 73–4, 104–9, 120–6, 148–9, 166, 189–99, 202–3, 206–23, 228–9, 234, 236–7, 240–2, 255–6, 262–3, 265, 267–9, 281, 283, 292–3, 296, 308, 311, 322

Fabians, 178, 204, 238, 256, 310
Ferguson, A., 16, 34
Feuer, L., 65
Feuerbach, L., 51, 57, 64–7, 72, 310, 326
Feuerlicht, I., 67, 72
Fine, R., ix
Fine, B., 95
freedom, 4, 6, 24, 34, 11, 110, 122, 125, 129, 143, 148–9, 167, 174, 179, 181, 189, 193, 207, 214–5, 219, 221, 240, 260, 264, 279, 288, 298, 302, 322
Freud, S., 321

Garfinkel, H., 303
Garnier, Marquis G., 156, 161
George, H., 235
German Historical School, 5, 34, 83, 155, 161–6, 175–6, 179, 186, 188–9, 196, 205, 235, 243, 245, 247–55, 266, 310
Giddens, A., 303–4
Gide, C., 148
Godwin, W., 94
Goldmann, L., 319
Gossen, H. H., 184
Gray, J., 146
Grossmann, H., 97

Harris, L., 95
Hayek, F., 214, 242
Hegel, G., 1, 6, 36, 51–60, 63, 70–1, 78–81, 86–7, 91, 310–3
Heidegger, M., 65, 319, 321
Hennings, K., 63, 76
Hess, M., 64

Hildebrand, B., 163, 164
Hilferding, R., 52, 97
Hobbes, T., 56
Horkheimer, M., 65, 318–21, 323, 325
Howard, D., 68
Howard, M., 71
Hume, D., 21, 22, 31, 39, 73
Husserl, E., 65, 319
Hyppolite, J., 56

ideal-type, 252, 259, 266, 297
individualism, 11, 32, 34, 59, 65, 161, 166, 168, 170, 176, 298, 299, 311
Ingram, J., 175
irrationality, 3, 11, 78, 128, 179, 205–6, 209, 212, 215, 217–8, 220–2, 229, 231, 234, 242, 277, 283–8, 294, 304–5, 313, 316, 324–5

Jahn, W., 68
Jenkins, F., 173
Jevons, S., 183–4, 187, 189, 194, 199, 201, 204, 223–5, 296
Jones, R., 177

Kantianism, 1, 244, 250, 310–1
Kautsky, K., 50, 93, 308
Keynes, J. M., 216–7, 227–8
Kierkegaard, S., 65
King, J., 71
Knies, K., 147, 163–4
Korsch, K., 52
Kozlov, G., 94

labour theory of value, 26–7, 40–3, 47–8, 51, 77–8, 94–118, 132–48, 164
labour-power, 72, 75, 79, 94, 99, 101, 108, 115–7, 122–31, 136–9, 221–2, 224, 229–31
laissez-faire, 20, 148, 155, 161, 166, 168, 179, 189, 235–6
Lenin, V. I., 50–1, 57, 310, 314, 318
LePlay, P.-G.-F., 175
Leslie, C., 173
List, F., 162–4

Locke, J., 59, 79, 137
Lockwood, D., 304
Longfield, M., 146
Luxemburg, R., 309, 314

Maguire, J., 71
Maine, H., 177
Malthus, T., 41, 44, 46, 94, 144, 146, 150,
Mandel, E., 68, 72, 93
Marcuse, H., 65–6, 284, 317, 321, 323
marginalism, ix, 8–9, 95, 183, 185–8, 192–4, 196–7, 199–204, 207–10, 213, 219, 221–2, 235, 237–8, 244, 255–6, 266, 289–90, 292–4, 308
Marshall, A., 1, 77, 192, 204, 216, 235
Marx, K., viii, ix, 1, 5–7, 9, 11, 13, 38, 43–4, 47, 49–99, 100–4, 106, 110, 113–7, 126, 132, 134, 136–42, 147, 155, 165, 177, 183, 201, 208–10, 217–8, 222, 236, 241, 244, 249, 257, 288, 306–8, 310–3, 316–28
Mattick, P., 52
McCulloch, J., 44, 48, 144–5, 147
McLellan, D., 50, 68
Mead, G.H., 303
Meek, R., 17–8, 22, 93, 182
Menger, C., 183–4, 188–9, 195–8, 203–4, 235, 239, 247–56, 265–7, 285
mercantilism, 19, 39, 73, 78, 94, 106
Mill, James, 48, 72–3, 75–7, 108, 144–5, 147
Mill, J. S., 12, 144–5, 147, 152, 155, 161, 170, 171, 173, 177, 187, 218
Millar, J., 34
Mises, L. von, 214, 242
Mommsen, T., 245
money, 19, 26, 39–40, 45, 60, 69, 72–6, 78, 90–91, 100, 101, 103–8, 113–4, 122–3, 126–8, 130, 149, 164, 173, 189, 195–9, 206, 208,

Index 337

211–3, 224, 229, 255–6, 263, 265–8, 277, 279, 281–2, 311–2
Morishima, M., 97

natural law, 15–17, 20–1, 23, 31, 35, 37–8, 112, 152, 199, 218, 293
naturalism, 57–8, 92, 100, 126, 208, 256, 295–6
nature, 3–4, 14, 16–8, 20, 23–4, 34–8, 44, 50, 54, 56–9, 64, 66, 68, 74, 76–7, 82, 91–2, 100–1, 103, 109–10, 130, 142, 159, 165, 173, 186, 197, 202, 245, 248–9, 254, 295–6, 298, 300–1, 314–5, 317, 320–4
Naville, P., 65
needs, 9, 11, 17–8, 53–5, 57–8, 60, 64, 66, 72, 74, 76–7, 82, 85, 102, 104–5, 107, 111, 119, 121, 123, 127, 146, 167, 175–6, 195–8, 210, 214, 219–20, 229–32, 234, 240, 250–1, 263, 267–8, 275–6, 282–3, 291–2, 321, 324
Negri, A., 91
Nietzsche, F., 65, 319, 321

O'Neill, J., 65
Oakley, A., 67, 76
Ollman, B., 71
Owen, R., 146, 151
Oxford Movement, 179

Pannekoek, A., 52
Pareto, V., 1, 204
Parsons, T., 1–4, 6, 167, 290, 295–6, 299–305, 322
Pashukanis, E., 52
petty commodity production, 107, 112–3, 138, 163–4, 168, 176–7, 209, 220–1, 243, 247
Petty, Sir Wm., 12–13
Physiocrats, 19–21, 29, 31, 132, 156
Pigou, A., 238
Plamenatz, J., 67
political economy, 1, 4, 6–9, 11–13, 34, 39–40, 43–4, 47, 49–52, 56, 58–64, 67, 70–1, 73–4, 76–111, 116–7, 119, 121, 126, 128, 132, 134, 139–40, 142, 144, 147–87, 196, 199–202, 205, 208–10, 218, 235–7, 248–51, 290–6, 305–8
political theory, 12, 16, 24, 34, 79, 154
Poor Laws, 40, 42–4, 151
power, 6, 8, 10, 18, 20, 30, 37–8, 49, 51–2, 59, 63–4, 66, 72–5, 78–9, 81, 84–5, 103, 106, 114, 118, 124, 129, 140, 143, 149, 151, 153–5, 158–60, 162–3, 171, 178–9, 181, 201, 205, 212, 222, 230–2, 234, 236, 238–43, 247, 266–7, 270, 275–6, 279, 283, 285, 288, 291, 294, 303, 305–7, 317–21, 323, 325–8
praxiology, 195, 251
production, social relations of, 7, 9, 38, 58, 75, 81–2, 89, 93–4, 96–7, 102–3, 107–12, 114, 123, 128, 135, 153, 158, 166, 177, 208–10, 217, 237, 275, 283–4, 290, 291, 293, 297, 305, 322, 328
production, theory of, 4, 37, 83, 109, 118–20, 147–8, 157, 159, 165–6, 177, 185, 191–2, 198–9, 202, 221–8
profit, 25–29, 31, 35, 38, 40–9, 83, 90, 94, 98–9, 117, 126–7, 129–33, 135, 137–9, 145–7, 150, 154, 167, 174, 185, 191–3, 199, 201, 210, 214, 222–8, 231, 233–4, 252, 264, 269, 282, 287, 307
property, 5, 7, 9, 11–16, 19–20, 22–5, 30, 33, 38–9, 44, 46–7, 49, 51, 53, 56, 59–63, 67–91, 94, 96–7, 101–2, 109–12, 115, 121–2, 124–5, 140, 142, 148, 152, 154–5, 159, 171–2, 177–8, 186, 193–4, 197, 199, 205, 208, 222, 240, 255, 265–6, 271, 298, 306–8,
Proudhon, P.-J., 50, 60–1, 63, 67, 70, 76, 78, 87, 89, 91

psychology, 195, 251, 301

rational economic action, 10, 195, 243, 250–2, 257–65, 273–84, 294, 307

rationality, 6–7, 9, 10–11, 37–8, 56, 60, 84, 109–10, 112–3, 142, 170, 187, 193–7, 199, 200, 204–7, 209– 21, 223, 225, 228, 232, 234, 240, 242, 244, 251–69, 272–3, 276–89, 291–2, 294, 296, 298, 301–2, 304–5, 307, 313, 316, 319–5, 327

Rau, K., 161

Read, S., 146

reform, 8, 18, 45, 56, 87, 91, 142, 146, 152–3, 159, 161, 166, 169–73, 175, 177, 178, 180–1, 183, 186, 189, 202, 204–5, 235–6, 238–9, 242–5, 302, 309

reification, 311–28

religion, 5, 14, 51, 77, 82, 158–9, 161, 164, 179, 273, 277, 286, 301

rent, 20–1, 25–9, 31, 35, 38, 40–6, 61, 83–4, 87, 90, 98–9, 126–33, 137, 140, 147–50, 167, 185, 192–3, 199, 201, 210, 222–3, 228

Ricardo, D., 13, 40–9, 58, 77–9, 84, 86–7, 93–8, 100–1, 103, 108, 116–7, 133–5, 140, 144–5, 147, 149–50, 153–4, 218

Rist, C., 148

Robbins, L., 295

Roemer, J., 95, 97

Rogers, Th., 175

Roscher, W., 147, 163–6

Rosdolsky, R., 91

Rose, G., ix, 312

Rubel, M., 52

Rubin, I. I., 51–2, 97

Sartre, J.-P., 65

Savigny, F. K. von, 189, 196

Say, J.-B., 44, 77, 100, 132–4, 140, 144–6, 149, 156–7, 159–61,, 177, 184, 216

Sayer, D., 141

scarcity, 17, 127, 187, 189, 190–1, 194–5, 197, 199, 202, 207, 209, 219, 222, 226, 230, 262

Schacht, R., 67

Schmoller, G., 175, 177, 196, 235, 244, 250, 253, 266

Schumpeter, J., 95, 239

Schutz, A., 303

Scrope, G., 146

self-interest, 3, 6, 10, 22–4, 61, 109–10, 121, 148–9, 155, 157–60, 164, 166, 174–5, 179, 189, 202, 243, 250, 254, 268, 272, 295

Seligman, E., 147

Senior, N., 144, 146

Simmel, G., 297, 311–3, 318–9

St. Simon, 155, 157, 235

Sismondi, J., 44–5, 154

Smart, D., 52

Smith, A., 3, 5, 13, 16, 19, 21–35, 37–49, 56–9, 61, 63, 75, 77–9, 84, 87–8, 93–5, 101, 103, 132–4, 144–6, 153, 156–7, 159–62, 165, 168, 184, 228, 243

Smith, G., 172

social economics, 10, 209, 235–43, 294

socialism, viii, 8, 10, 46–7, 49, 51, 94, 97, 152, 154–5, 157–8, 164, 166, 181, 189, 196, 204, 215, 231, 248, 254, 288, 292, 302, 307, 309–11, 328

sociology, viii, ix, 1, 2–3, 8, 10–2, 51, 93, 155, 160, 165–7, 175, 177, 179–81, 202, 205–6, 209, 235–6, 239, 242–3, 248, 253, 255–62, 265–74, 276–7, 281–6, 289–91, 294–9, 301, 303–6, 308, 310–11, 318–9, 324, 326

Sohn-Rethel, A., 97, 319

Sombart, W., 244

Spencer, H., 1, 161, 168–70, 175–6, 179–80, 235, 239, 296, 299

Stalin, J., 310

Index

state, viii, 5, 10, 14–6, 18–24, 27, 30–2, 45, 49, 52–6, 60, 69, 71, 77–9, 133, 142, 154, 156, 161–4, 166–7, 169, 171, 174–5, 178–9, 181–2, 188, 215–7, 223, 228, 231, 237–9, 242–8, 251, 254, 270–3, 276, 283–4, 290–1, 300–2, 307, 314, 316, 320, 328
Steedman, I., 95
surplus-value, 50, 108, 114–9, 123–4, 130–1, 135–9
Sweezy, P., 93

Thornton, W., 173
time-preference, 222, 226, 264
Toynbee, A., 174–5
trade unions, 8, 42, 151–2, 171–3, 181, 238, 244–5, 269–70
trinity formula, 126–9, 131–3, 148, 156, 165, 200, 208, 222

Uchida, H., 91

value, theory of, 8, 26–7, 35, 40, 42–3, 45, 47–8, 51, 77, 87, 91, 94–102, 117, 132–7, 139, 144–8, 150, 164, 185, 199–200, 306–8, 310, 312
value-form, 6, 97–9, 100–103, 108, 113, 137, 306, 308, 325
value-orientation, 10, 252, 256–7, 259, 269–70, 273–4, 276–72, 282, 284, 295, 298
Verein für Sozialpolitik, 175, 244–8

wage-form, 129, 137
wages-fund, 41, 45, 100, 150–1, 173–4, 201, 224
wages, 8, 25–9, 31, 33, 35, 38, 40–3, 45, 83–4, 87, 90, 98–100, 117, 126–7, 129–31, 133–4, 147, 149–51, 154, 158, 173–4, 181, 185, 192–3, 199, 201, 210, 222–5, 228–30, 241, 246, 265–6
Wagner, A., 244

Walras, L., 183–4, 188, 194, 199, 204, 214, 235
Weber, M., viii, 1, 10–1, 65, 239, 243–90, 294–300, 305, 310–11, 313, 316, 319–20, 323–4, 326
Weisskopf, W., 71
West, Sir E., 41
Wicksell, K., 204–5, 235, 238, 256
Wieser, F. von, 194–5, 199, 202, 204, 222–5, 235, 238–43, 251, 256
working class, 6–8, 40, 42, 45–7, 50, 60, 92–3, 97–8, 122, 143–144, 146, 149–52, 157–8, 167–74, 176, 181, 186, 201, 226, 236, 243–5, 271, 292, 295, 307–9, 311, 313–6, 321–2, 324, 327–8